Gathering the Meanings

Gathering the Meanings

The Compendium of Categories

The Arthaviniścaya Sūtra and its Commentary Nibandhana

Translated from the Sanskrit
with an introduction and notes
by N. H. Samtani

Dharma Publishing

TIBETAN TRANSLATION SERIES

Dharma Publishing gratefully acknowledges the generous support of Michael Gray in sponsoring the publication of this book.

Library of Congress Cataloging-in-Publication Data

Tripiṭaka. Sūtrapiṭaka. Arthaviniścayasūtra. English
Gathering the meanings : the compendium of categories : the Arthaviniścaya sūtra and its commentary, nibandhana / translated from the Sanskrit with an introduction and notes by N.H. Samtani.
p. cm. -- (Tibetan translation series)
Includes the translation of Arthaviniścayasūtranibandhana by Vīryaśrīdatta.
Includes bibliographical references and index.
ISBN 0-89800-268-0 (cloth : alk. paper) -- ISBN 0-89800-267-2 (paper : alk. paper)

[DNLM: 1. Vīryaśrīdatta. Arthaviniścayasūtranibandhana--Early works to 1800.] I. Samtani, N. H. (Narayan Hemandas), 1924- II. Vīryaśrīdatta. Arthaviniścayasūtranibandhana. English. III. Title. IV. Series.
BQ2240.A775 E5 2002
294.3'85--dc21

2002067693

Frontispiece: Site of Śrī Nālandā Mahāvihāra, the great Buddhist monastic university.

Produced under the auspices of the Yeshe De Project.

Typeset in Adobe New Aster
Printed and bound in the USA by Dharma Press

10 9 8 7 6 5 4 3 2 1

To

My Affectionate Teachers

VENERABLE BHIKKHU J. KASHYAP

and

PROFESSOR V.V. GOKHALE

with profound esteem and

intense gratitude

Contents

Publisher's Note

For more than thirty years, Dharma Publishing has supported the growing interest in Buddhism in the English-speaking world by publishing authentic teachings of the Buddhist tradition. Translations of canonical texts are especially important in furthering this aim, for when students focus their efforts on teachings presented by the Buddha or the great commentators of later centuries, they can be confident that their study will bear rich fruit.

This new volume presents a Sūtra in which the Buddha sets forth the principal topics of the Abhidharma. These essential teachings convey in a comprehensive and rigorous manner the topics that Dharma students should master in order to travel the path to liberation from suffering. The commentary, by an eighth century master from the famed Buddhist university of Nālandā, is detailed and precise. For those who understand the significance of these teachings, it can also be inspiring.

Works from the Northern tradition of Abhidharma are not readily available in English, and those few that have been published can be difficult for non-specialists to comprehend. The present work, while challenging in its own right, is accessible to anyone willing to invest effort. For experienced Dharma students, it provides a wealth of indispensable information, as well as hidden treasures that manifest on repeated readings. Its publication fills an important gap, and the staff of Dharma Publishing and Dharma Press are privileged to present it.

The care with which Professor Samtani has worked on this translation could serve as an inspiration for scholars in any field. The scholarly apparatus he provides adds immeasurably to the value and importance of the work. At the same time, he has been very cooperative in helping us shape the text to be of benefit to Dharma practitioners as well as scholars. Toward this end, we have made numerous editorial decisions, two of which we note here. First, the Sūtra itself is presented twice: once in its entirety in the first part of the book, where it appears without notes or Sanskrit equivalents, and again embedded (in italics) in the commentary, with full scholarly apparatus. Second, footnotes have been divided into two categories. The first, consisting of numbered notes, contains material that supplements or clarifies the text. The second, designated in the text with the symbol '°', presents notes on terminology and variant readings. These 'term notes' are keyed to the 'folio numbers' given in the margin, which refer to pages in Professor Samtani's published edition.

To make the text more accessible, we have worked with Professor Samtani to reduce the number of Sanskrit terms given parenthetically. For students interested in Sanskrit terminology, the following highly simplified rules for pronunciation may be helpful: 'ś' and 'ṣ' are both pronounced 'sh', 'c' is pronounced 'ch', 'ñ' is pronounced 'ny', and vowels are pronounced as in the Romance languages. All other diacriticals may be disregarded.

Finally, the title for this book, *Gathering the Meanings*, was chosen by the Dharma Publishing editorial staff because it evokes with some degree of elegance the significance of the Sūtra and its commentary. It should not be considered a translation of the Sanskrit title, which Professor Samtani has rendered "Compendium of Categories."

Introduction

I am happy that the English translation of the Arthaviniścaya-sūtra (AVS) along with its Commentary, the Nibandhana (AVSN), is finally being published. This is the second translation of the Sūtra in a Western language,[1] but the Commentary has never previously been translated in any language.

After I published the Sanskrit edition of the Arthaviniścaya-sūtra and its Commentary (Nibandhana), Edward Conze, made the following remarks:

> For the teaching of Buddhism in universities, this is a very important and in fact indispensable book. Exact English equivalents can be found only rarely for Sanskrit Abhidharma terms and a thorough training in their traditional definitions is therefore a necessary foundation for any real understanding of Buddhist theory. It would be useful to cyclostyle the more significant parts of the book and issue them to our students together with a literal, accurate, and idiomatic English translation.[2]

After that, Prof. Etienne Lamotte, another leading authority on Buddhism, wrote me an encouraging letter dated 18 July 1972 in French from Louvain (Belgium), stating inter alia:

> Your edition, accompanied by a precious commentary, is admirable and based on several manuscripts is faultless from the point of view of textual tradition. The citation from the Canon and its development (commentaries, etc.) make it more useful than the Mahāvyutpatti, published with all its precision. It is an important work and you have done inestimable service to Buddhist Studies.

Prof. J. W. de Jong, another leading Buddhologist, wrote the longest review of AVSN in the Indo-Iranian Journal. Although he pointed out certain minor errors, he made the following positive comments:

> Both the Arthaviniścaya and the Commentary have been carefully edited by Samtani. The annotation contains not only many passages from the Kośabhāṣya and Vyākhyā but also from Pāli commentaries. Very useful are the detailed indices which the editor has provided. Samtani has done everything possible to make the edition as useful as possible.[3]

Such observations and compliments from three leading authorities on Buddhist Studies—and other favorable comments from many scholars, including Professors Hajime Nakamura, Nalinaksha Dutt, G. C. Pande, and L. M. Joshi—were a great source of encouragement to me. Despite being quite conscious of my many lapses and limitations, I was planning to translate not only the Sūtra but also its Commentary, when luckily an offer came from one of the leading publishers of Buddhist works in the West, Dharma Publishing for just such a publication. I set to work with great enthusiasm.

Unfortunately, the translation saw many vicissitudes and was inordinately delayed in the early stages due to reasons that need not be detailed, but for which I consider myself solely responsible. However, I am happy that finally the much awaited translation can at long last be presented to scholars and to students of Buddhism.

The AVS is not only important for the fact that it has been quoted in or referred to in many Buddhist texts, but also because it explains the fundamental Buddhist concepts and categories common to both the Theravāda and Mahāyāna schools. In my view, no student of any school of Buddhism can ignore this important text with its precious commentary, the Nibandhana. It is vital for the study of Buddhism in general and the textual tradition of Buddhism in particular.

After the publication of the critical edition of these two texts by the K.P. Jayaswal Research Institute, Patna, in 1971,[4] the AVS and AVSN gradually began to be referred to or quoted by other authors.[4a] I am sure that with this translation, they will receive more notice, and I am confident that this will provide further impetus to the understanding of Buddhist doctrines. The ever-growing interest in Buddhist Studies, and particularly Buddhist meditation, in the West and in other parts of the world, can only support this development, especially since more than half of the topics dealt with in the texts pertain to meditation. These works present ample materials for understanding meditation practices and their application and even their relevance in the present, troubled age.

The Arthaviniścaya Sūtra is a 'compendium' of important categories frequently mentioned in Buddhist texts. The word Viniścaya (Pāli Vinicchaya), although meaning 'ascertainment', 'examination', or 'analysis', has various other meanings, including that of 'compendium', 'manual', etc. I have discussed these meanings in detail in my introduction to the AVSN.[5]

There are twenty-seven sections in the AVS, each discussing an important category (artha) in Buddhist doctrine. It is difficult to say why only twenty-seven categories were selected and others left out, but there seems to be some importance to the number twenty-seven, as Nāgārjuna's famous Madhyamaka-kārikās also have twenty-seven chapters, as do the Lalitavistara and the Saddharmapuṇḍarīka Sūtra (both important Mahāyāna texts). Should we say that the number twenty-seven has sacred significance, or is this simply accidental?

When it comes to the treatment of the categories, there is no uniform methodology of explanation. Some categories are simply enumerated, some are explained, and yet others are expounded in greater detail—as, for example, the constituents of the Noble Eightfold Path.[6] There is no doubt that the source materials for the AVS can be traced in the vast textual materials scattered in various Buddhist Sanskrit works, and it should be noted that many canonical works in the Pāli tradition contain similar material. However, unconventional interpretations are also added, some of which are not traceable. An example is the explanation of Right Thought, given in Topic XIX. I would be grateful if readers aware of similar explanations in other sources could send me the references.

Whether the AVS belongs to the Hīnayāna or Mahāyāna tradition is difficult to say. The very fact that there are two Chinese versions, smaller and larger (the latter one designating the AVS as belonging to the Mahāyāna school)[7] shows that the Sūtra in its transmission was most likely used by both schools. If we take the shorter recension as being the original, then it would seem that in the course of time, the Mahāyana tradition added more categories. The Tibetan version does not claim that the AVS is a Mahāyāna Sūtra; moreover, this version is not fully based on the Sanskrit manuscript found in Ngor monastery in Tibet, which has formed the basis for the present work.[7a] It is also noteworthy that the explanation of the Noble Eightfold Path in the Tibetan version, (Don rnam par nges pa zhes bya ba'i chos kyi rnam grangs = Arthaviniścaya-nāma-dharmaparyāya)[8] is completely different from the explanation in the Sanskrit version I have relied on, though it does match the Nepalese manuscripts I had consulted. I have given this variation in the appendix of my edition of the AVSN.[9]

The great commentator Yaśomitra stated that the AVS is a Sūtra of the 'Abhidharma' type relied upon by the Sautrāntika school.[10] But there is nothing special in the text of the Sūtra itself that would allow it to be labeled a Sautrāntika or purely Abhidharma text, except that it collects many Buddhist categories, such as the five skandhas (aggregates), the eighteen dhātus (elements), the twelve āyatanas (sense fields) and the twelvefold pratītyasamutpāda (conditioned co-production), etc. All of these, however, are common categories found in many Sūtras as well as in Abhidharma texts. (For relevant citations, see the notes to the translation.)

In form, the Sūtra begins as do almost all Buddhist Sūtras, with the words "evaṁ mayā śrutam" (Thus have I heard). However, in the Commentary,[11] there is an important remark that without being instructed in the Sūtras, one cannot 'investigate into' or 'analyze' (various) dharmas or categories (dharmapravicaya). Vasubandhu, on the other hand, states that instruction in the Abhidharma alone qualifies one for investigation into dharma.[12] Thus the emphasis here is on the importance of the Sūtra as Sūtra. Vasubandhu's comment in the Abhidharmakośa-bhāṣya could be read as a remarkable shift in emphasis. Nevertheless, the classification made by Yaśomitra is certainly accurate in putting this Sūtra in the same category as some of the Pāli Sūtras (Suttas), such as the Dasottara and Saṅgīti-sutta,[13] which also enumerate and explain different categories of classification and definitions, considered as main characteristics of Abhidharma.

From another perspective, the present Sūtra resembles certain manuals, such as the Mahāvyutpatti, the Dharmasaṅgraha, and the Abhidharmasamuccaya, or Pāli canonical works like the Dhammasaṅgaṇi and post-canonical works like Anuruddha's Abhidhammatthasaṅgaha. However, AVS differs from them in that it presents in some sections traditional passages from various other Sūtras, which is not a characteristic of Abhidharma commentaries. This can be observed especially in the sections on rūpa dhyāna (meditations on form), samādhi-bhāvanās (the cultivation of concentration) on form, the four āryasatyas (Noble Truths), the four pratipads (courses for destruction of influxes), the four vaiśāradyas (fearlessnesses or confidences), the ten balas (powers of the Tathāgata), and the thirty-two mahāpuruṣalakṣaṇa (marks of a great personage). The Pāli Abhidharma texts known as the Vibhaṅga[14] does quote Sūtra passages in the explanation of Buddhist terms. But the Vibhaṅga is a 'large text' and contains many Abhidharma technicalities explained in various permutations and combinations, all of which is absent in the AVS. Thus, the compactness of the brief enumerations, together with the explanations and quotations of passages from various Sūtras, place the AVS in a class by itself. It seems to have been used mostly by Buddhist clergy for preaching as well as for citations.

Concerning the date when the AVS first appeared, I have discussed the matter in the Introduction to the AVSN.[15] It is a difficult task to decide the exact date of the original AVS, for the Sūtra has undergone many vicissitudes in the course of its transmission, and categories, quotations, and explanations were added in later manuscripts that were not in the earliest recension. The earliest period for its compilation may be assigned to the first century B.C.E. and the latest to the eighth century C.E., and many alterations and additions seem to have been made to the manuscripts of the Sūtra during this period. As regards its authorship, according to Buddhist tradition, there are no authors of Sūtras except the Buddha himself, who preaches them to an assembly of monks and lay persons etc. at different places. But redactors have always worked on Sūtras, and they have not let us know their names, so that the sanctity of the texts would not be violated. The penchant of Sūtra masters (Sūtradharas) for anonymity can be well contrasted with the craze for name and fame of authors and editors of present times.

Now a few words about the present translation of the texts. There can never be a wholly satisfactory translation, not to speak of a perfect translation. I am quite conscious of the imperfections and faults that can be found here. There are problems galore in translating ancient texts, especially those that have a particular idiom and style and contain technical terminology. Also it is not possible to be uniform in translating technical terms, for the context may affect the rendering of a particular term. In fact, there cannot be an exact English rendering of many of the terms. Even a literal translation may not be so easy. For example, there is no literal translation for terms such as dharma (Pāli dhamma), saṁskāra, vāsanā, bhava, brahma, prajñā, sāsrava, duḥkha (Pāli dukkha), all of which may have very different meanings in different contexts. Then there are the problems of translating adjectival proper names used for the Buddha, such as Tathāgata, Sugata, Bhagavān, and even the name "Buddha" itself. I have mentioned (and sometimes discussed) the different renderings of some words in footnotes and notes on terms and variants. It would be a useful task to collect translations of Buddhist terms from various modern translations of Buddhist texts, in this way creating a Buddhist thesaurus of English renderings. But if one did so, one would see how translators have differed in rendering the same words; indeed, even the same author or translator has sometimes translated the same word differently from one work to the next. I fully expect criticism of my renderings and I shall always welcome suggestions. In general I have endeavored to keep the term near the traditional meaning without being too literal, partly in light of my conviction that this work is suitable for a wide audience, not all of whom will be well informed on Buddhist terminology. I appreciate, however, that some scholars may prefer literalness for better understanding.

The AVS was clearly considered an important text in the Buddhist tradition. It is referenced by Yaśomitra in his Sphuṭārthā as well as in the Abhidharmakośavyākhyā (AKV, Dwarikdas Shastri's edition, p. 15), mentioned in Haribhadra's Abhisamayālaṅkārāloka (P.L.Vaidya ed. p. 433), and included in Nāgārjuna's Sūtrasamuccaya,[16] an anthology of Mahāyāna Sūtras. Its inclusion in the Mahāvyutpatti, its two Chinese versions, and one Tibetan and one Mongolian translation[17] all speak to its honored status, as do the two extant commentaries: the present work by Vīryaśrīdatta and a ṭīkā[18] in the Tibetan Canon.

The Content of the Sūtra

The Arthaviniścaya explains twenty-seven topics or categories of Buddhist teaching: (1) five skandhas (aggregates), (2) five upādānaskandhas (clinging aggregates), (3) eighteen dhātus (elements), (4) twelve āyatanas (sense fields), (5) twelvefold law of conditioned co-production), (6) Four Noble Truths, (7) twenty-two faculties (or controlling principles), (8) four meditations on form, (9) four formless meditational attainments, (10) four sublime states, (11) four courses (of meditation), (12) four cultivations of concentration, (13) four foundations of mindfulness, (14) four right efforts, (15) four bases of psychic powers, (16) five faculties, (17) five powers, (18) seven constituents of enlightenment, (19) Noble Eightfold Path, (20) sixteenfold mindfulness of breathing, (21) four constituents of attaining the stream, (22) ten powers of the Tathāgata, (23) four grounds of the Tathāgata's self-confidence, (24) four kinds of knowledge special to the Tathāgata, (25) eighteen special dharmas of the Buddha, (26) the Tathāgata's thirty-two marks of great personage, (27) eighty minor marks of the Buddha.

The first four sections present traditional lists of terms, found in many extant Pāli and Sanskrit texts. However, the largest portion of the AVS goes to the fifth section on pratītyasamutpāda (conditioned co-production) which could be considered the basic doctrine of Buddhism. The twelve constituents of the formula are enumerated in direct and reverse order.

The largest space in this section is given to avidyā (ignorance), the first of the twelve constituents, which is explained as ignorance of past, present, and future existence, internal and external phenomena (of one's personality), wholesome (kuśala) and unwholesome (akuśala) actions, etc.: a total of thirty items. This is a more extensive list than is found in most Pāli and Sanskrit texts. However, almost the same explanation, with the omission of just a few items, is found in the Pratītyasamutpāda-vibhaṅga-nirdeśa-sūtra (ed. P.L. Vaidya) referred to as the Vibhaṅga by Vasubandhu in the Abhidharmakośabhāṣya.[19] I also find the same explanation in the Nidānasaṁyukta-sūtra, number 14 (edited by Chandrabhal Tripathi with German translation) from the collection of Sanskrit texts found in Turfan.[20]

Then we have an explanation of the remaining eleven constituents of conditioned co-production. The explanation of bhava is given in greater detail under the heading of Kāmabhava (or Kāmaloka = realm of desire). There is mention of the eight hot and cold hells as well as spirits, animals, birds, and human beings. Devas of the kāma-, rūpa-, and ārūpyabhavas (realm of desire and the form and formless realms) are explained as well, and the Commentary amplifies on these explanations. The Sūtra also explains the four form and formless meditations (later called samāpattis) in Sections VIII and IX.

After these two types of meditations, the Sūtra explains the four sublime states (brāhmavihāras). This is one of the major categories of Buddhist teaching. These sublime states (also known as the four immeasurables or the four divine abodes), are loving kindness (maitrī), compassion (karuṇā), sympathetic joy (muditā), and equanimity (upekṣā), all of which a follower of the Buddhist path must practice. The explanation given in this section is the same as that commonly found in many Buddhist texts, and the commentary goes into this category in detail. After this follows an equally important section on the four courses (or paths) for the attainment of intuition (abhijñā) and for extinction of influxes (āsravas). Four aspects or types are explained: painful (or difficult) courses with sluggish or swift intuition and pleasant (or easy) courses with sluggish or swift intuition.

Then we have a section on four kinds of cultivation of concentration (samādhibhāvanā): for the destruction of sensual lust, for the cultivation of happiness in this very life, for acquiring knowledge and insight, and for acquiring wisdom. With regard to the first, the Sūtra speaks of various internal parts of the body on which a monk (or practitioner) must reflect for the extinction of sensual lust. The cultivation of meditation for happiness in this life is born of internal detachment. In the discussion of the samādhi that leads to gaining knowledge and insight, a beautiful simile is given, comparing the mind of the meditator to a cloudless, clear summer sky. The fourth samādhi corresponds to the fourth dhyāna, discussed in Section VIII.

Section XIV deals with right efforts; i.e., four practices for the removal of unwholesome thoughts and the cultivation of wholesome ones. This topic is included as the seventh item in the Eightfold Path (item number seven),[21] where it is called samyagvyāyāma. Then we have a section on psychic powers cultivated through concentration: intention (chanda), energy (vīrya), consciousness (citta), and investigation (mīmāṁsā). This is followed by Sections XVI and XVII on the five faculties and five powers. In Section XVIII the seven constituents of enlightenment (sambodhyaṅga) are enumerated and explained.

Section XIX, on the Noble Eightfold Path, is the second largest section in the Sūtra. Right view is explained as belief in the existence of this and the other world, in charity, in the results of good and bad actions, and so forth. This is not quite the usual explanation, for in early Pāli texts the traditional explanation of right view is knowledge (or comprehension) of the Four Noble Truths. The explanation that follows, regarding right thought, is also unconventional. It is explained as the thought of doing meritorious acts which ripen into Buddhahood.

It may be noted that Sections XIII to XIX present in sequence the thirty-seven bodhipakṣya dharmas (factors or dharmas which aid the gaining of enlightenment); namely, the four foundations of mindfulness, four right efforts, four psychic powers, five (controlling) faculties, five powers, seven constituents of enlightenment, and the noble eightfold path. According to the tradition preserved in the Pāli Canon, the Buddha at the time of his Mahāpārinirvāṇa (the Great Decease) summarized his whole teaching in these thirty-seven essential aspects. Cf. DN II, p. 120; see also DOB II, p. 128 and footnote. It may be further noted that it is categorically stated in the early Pali Nikayas that there is absolutely no dispute regarding these thirty-seven essential dharmas. Cf. MN II, p. 245; MLS III, p. 31.

Section XX explains the sixteenfold mindfulness of breathing. Sixteen practices for awareness of breath are presented, beginning with long and short breaths. This section is followed by Section XXI, on the four constituents of attaining the stream (that flows to nirvāṇa). The explanation is mostly conventional, but certain terms, such as ālayasamudghāta (rooting out attachment) and śūnyatopalambha (realizing voidness) are unusual, and reflect themes taken up in the Yogācāra and Mādhyamika schools of the Mahāyāna. Perhaps they are interpolations. This section is followed by Section XXII on the ten powers (balas) of the Tathāgatas. After this we have Section XXIII, on the four grounds of self-confidence or fearlessness of the Tathāgata, by which his Dharma stands unchallenged by anyone. Due to these four attainments of self-confidence, the Buddha finds the distinguished place in assemblies and utters the lion's roar.

Then we have a section on the four kinds of detailed or special knowledge: knowledge of categories, of dharma, of language, and of ready exposition. By special knowledge of dharma is meant unshakable knowledge of undefiled (anāsrava) dharma and by special knowledge of ready exposition is meant fitting and unhindered speech with clarity of mind, due to mastery of concentration. Section XXV deals with eighteen special dharmas of the Buddha, often mentioned in Mahāyāna texts.

Then follows an important section on the thirty-two marks of a great personage (mahāpuruṣalakṣaṇas). After the enumeration of these marks, the actions done by the Buddha in past lives due to which these marks arose are explained. For instance, the first mark (well-placed feet) was the result of firmly undertaking deeds of merit in the Tathāgata's former existences, as explained in the comment on past action in the Sūtra. The fourth mark (long fingers) arose on the body of the Tathāgata because in previous lives he protected and guarded the Dharma. A thirty-third mark, (Mahā) nārāyaṇa-śarīra-samantaprāsādikatā (having a body that is pleasing (or serene) from all sides, like that of

[Mahā] Nārāyaṇa) has been added. This seems to be interpolation, and I have omitted it in the text and put it in a footnote. Since the Nibandhana comments on this mark, I have put it in the text there. For Nārāyaṇa or Mahānārāyaṇa as a powerful personage of the Hindu pantheon, see note 247 in the present translation. These thirty-two marks along with explanations of their arising from past actions are found in various Pāli and Sanskrit texts, cited in the notes.

The last section (XXVII) mentions the eighty minor (physical) marks of the Buddha. There is no corresponding list of past actions for the arising of these marks in AVS, but some texts do present such accounts.[22]

The Sūtra concludes with the Buddha's instructions to his disciples to follow the dharma and practice meditation in secluded places and not to be indolent, so that there is no remorse later.

The Nibandhana

Now let me briefly review the Commentary on the Arthaviniścaya-sūtra, called the Nibandhana (abbreviated AVSN or Nib.), written by Vīryaśrīdatta of Śrī Nālandā (Mahā)vihāra in the eighth century C.E. It begins with a benedictory verse in praise of the Buddha, which also contains dedicatory words by Vīryaśrīdatta to his teacher (guru). Although the teacher's name is not known to us, the commentator praises him as an expert in the interpretation of terms of the Buddhist Sūtras.

We have then an important introductory exposition on the usual parts of a Sūtra. A Sūtra should have an introduction or beginning, pointing out the place of the Sūtra and the number of monks, etc.; in other words, the circumstances and nature of the assembly of disciples. This beginning should be followed by a preface, a statement of purpose (topic of discourse), and exposition, as well as (logical) connection (anusandhi) between preceding and following statements.

Next the conventional introductory phrase found in Sūtras, "Thus have I heard," is explained. It is said that at the time of the (first) Buddhist council, when five hundred Arhats had eagerly assembled to recite the Sūtras, Venerable Ānanda was specially called upon (lit. requested) to recite what he had heard. Ānanda replied with the words, "Thus have I heard," showing that he was responding to this request. The word "I" therefore refers to Ānanda, confirming his direct hearing. Then the word 'heard' and 'Blessed One' (Bhagavān) are explained, the latter etymologically as well as according to the tradition. The 'Blessed One' (Bhagavān) is the possessor of six virtues; namely, overlordship, beauty, fame, glory, knowledge, and 'effort'. The commentary continues with remarks on 'Śrāvastī', the name of the city where the Buddha taught the Sūtra, and where he often resided. The author indicates that it is named after the great sage Śravasta.

Explaining why monks alone were mentioned as the audience for Sūtras, the commentary quotes Ācārya Rāhulabhadra, who indicated that the assembly was addressed as 'monks' because the monastic community was considered preeminent, superior, proximate, and always in the close company of the Buddha, and because they were more capable of grasping the meaning of the Buddha's teaching. There is also a good explanation of the word Brahmacarya, which is explained as the superior (lit., highest brahma) path (caryā) and the pure or undefiled path that leads to the highest abode (of nirvāṇa).

The first section of the commentary explains the five aggregates; it is worthy of note that unassociated (viprayukta) karma formations are placed under the saṁskāra skandha (aggregate of karma formations).[23] This section is followed by a second one on the clinging aggregates. In justification of the five skandhas, it is said that this form of analysis refutes any false belief in the self (ātman) or anything 'belonging to self'. Often the persons who have not seen reality take the vijñānaskandha (aggregate of consciousness) falsely as self while form (rūpa) and the rest (of the skandhas) are taken as 'belonging to self'. Thus there are only five skandhas, not less and not more.

After this important section come the two sections on the eighteen elements and twelve sense fields (āyatanas), followed by one of the most important sections of all, on pratītyasamutpāda or (the law of) twelvefold conditioned co-production. Vasubandhu in the Abhidharmakośabhāṣya gives two grammatical/etymological explanations of this significant term.[24] The Nibandhana explains one of them as follows:

> Prati indicates repetition in general. The root 'i' means 'to go, 'to disappear'. [The participle] itya signifies 'ought to go', meaning 'perishable' or 'momentary'. Saṁ means 'together', while 'ut' before the root 'pad' means 'arising' or 'producing'. That is to say, the coming [arising] together of causes of perishable things is the law of conditioned co-production.

Pratītya here has not been taken as a gerund (prati + i) but as a derivative noun. This explanation is ascribed to the Sautrāntika teacher Śrīlābha.[25]

The Commentary states that the theory of Conditioned Co-production explains how worldly activity arises, linked to the self and 'what belongs to self'. And this formula is presented for disciples who are confused in regard to the process of (worldly) activity. It also discusses why the Buddha explains the doctrine in two (direct and reverse) ways.

Then there is a long comment on the first constituent of the formula, ignorance (avidyā). This term is explained in the Sūtra through the use of various synonyms, such as adarśana (not seeing), ajñāna (absence of knowledge), sammoha (delusion), and tamas (darkness). The Commentator justifies the use of synonyms by saying that if a disciple misses one of them due to distraction of mind, he can catch the meaning by another synonym, and thus the purpose will be served. He states that the Sūtra explanation of terms is given in view of the particular interests of a trainee, but that Abhidharma texts give a definitive or technical explanation (lākṣaṇika).[26] This is one of several places where the Commentator defends an apparent inconsistency or justifies a difference in the division of categories by saying that the explanation is given in accord with the disposition of trainees (vineya), even quoting a verse in defense of his position (cf. AVSN, p. 112). See also AVSN, pp. 102, 116, 117, 128, 273.

Another very important section in the Nibandhana is the one on the Four Noble Truths (āryasatyas). They are called satyas (truths, facts) and Āryas (noble ones) alone perceive them. Ordinary persons (those who are not Āryas), do not see things in the right way, but in a wrong perspective (viparītadarśanāt). A verse from a Sūtra is quoted on this point: "What the noble ones call happiness, others know as suffering; what others call happiness, the noble ones know as suffering."[27]

In this section the Buddha is compared to a physician who rightly knows the disease (i.e., duḥkha), its origin (or cause = samudaya), which is craving (tṛṣṇā), its removal (nirodha = nirvāṇa), and its remedy, the Noble Eightfold Path. Among the interesting aspects in this section are the explanation of nandī (delight) as 'defiled delight' (kliṣṭa-saumanasya) in the account of the origin of suffering, as well as the explanation of nirodhasatya, the truth of cessation of suffering, as "renunciation, pacification (of desire), absence of attachment (virāga), etc." A famous quotation from a Sūtra is given here to the effect that wise persons should regard even Dharma instruction as a raft (to be left behind when it has served its purpose), and leave even good things behind so that they do not cling to them; all the more so for wrong things.[28]

The sections in the Sūtra on the dhyānas (meditations on form) and samāpattis (formless attainments of concentration) are well explained in the Commentary. With regard to dhyāna it is stated that a person living in this world of desire (kāmadhātu) cannot meditate unless he is devoid of attachment. In the fourth dhyāna physical and mental pleasure are absent, and there remain only equanimity and concentration. The Commentator also refers to the view of some masters that a subtle form persists in formless attainments.[29]

The Nibandhana also contains a detailed explanation of the thirty-two marks of a great personage along with the past actions due to which the different marks appeared on the body of the Buddha. The mention of these marks is frequently made in various Buddhist texts. I hope that their explanation here will throw much light on the theory of a great personage and also its influence on Buddhist art. It also has a moral dimension, demonstrating that innumerable good actions produce good physical features on the body. There are numerous other important comments in the Nibandhana, but considerations of space prevent me from dealing with them.

As stated above, the Nibandhana was written by Bhikṣu Vīryaśrīdatta of Śrī Nālandā Vihāra (the ancient seat of great learning called Nālandā University by some modern scholars) in the eighth century C.E., in the days of King Dharmapāla,[30] as mentioned in the verses of the colophon. By his lucid commentary, Vīryaśrīdatta proves beyond doubt that he is a master exponent of the Buddhist tradition, concepts, and terminology.

The purpose of studying the AVS is dharma-pravicaya (investigation into dharmas) (AVSN, p. 73). This is a constituent of enlightenment (bodhyaṅga) as well as enlightenment (bodhi) itself (ASVN, p. 228). May all beings realize bodhi! With this chanda (wholesome intention), I close this brief introduction. I hope readers will forgive my many lapses and imperfections in translating the words of the Blessed One (Buddhavacana) and the expositions of the great Commentator Bhikṣu Vīryaśrīdatta.

Acknowledgments

It is now my pleasure and privilege to mention a few scholars and friends who helped me prepare the edition of the Arthaviniścaya-sūtra and Nibandhana and its present translation.

First, I would like to pay my homage to Venerable Bhikkhu J. Kashyap, at whose feet I learned my first lessons in Pāli and Abhidharma philosophy. Also, I would like to pay my respects to Professors P. V. Bapat and V. V. Gokhale, but for whose guidance the critical edition as well as the present translation would not have been completed. I am deeply grateful to the great Tibetologists Mahāpaṇḍita Rahul Sankrityayana and Professor Giuseppe Tucci, on whose photocopies of the Arthaviniścaya-sūtra and its Nibandhana I worked. I also cannot forget the encouragement of Professor Prahlad Pradhan, the celebrated editor of the Abhidharmakośa-bhāṣya, who also helped me in checking some important readings.

I am also highly obliged to Professors Edward Conze, J.W. de Jong, Nalinaksha Dutt, K. R. Norman, and K.N. Upadhyaya for reviewing my AVS and AVSN editions. Professor de Jong's long review of my work is still quoted in many reference works. Nor can I forget the celebrated scholar Professor G.P. Malalasekara, who showed a keen interest in my work and mentioned it in the Encyclopedia of Buddhism when the printed edition of the AVS had not yet been published. He regularly encouraged me.

I am ever grateful to Venerable Professor Samdhong Rinpoche, former director of the Central Institute of Higher Tibetan Studies, Sarnath, who was a constant source of inspiration in preparing this translation and discussing with me problems of translation of Buddhist terms. To Lama Tarthang Tulku, I must express my great appreciation, for it was under his insightful direction that Dharma Publishing was established to preserve the prcious legacy of Tibetan Buddhism and to spread the teachings of the Tathāgata through the modern translations of Tibetan and Sanskrit Buddhist texts. Professor Alex Wayman also helped me occasionally by personal discussion and through correspondence. Also, I must thank Professor James Duerlinger of the University of Iowa for going through my draft translation of the Nibandhana and suggesting some changes in translation and style of presentation. I shall remain ever grateful to Professor G.C. Pande for his valuable suggestions for translating some passages. Professor K. Satchidanand Murty also took a keen interest in the publication of my work, and I discussed with him some technical terms, to my great benefit. Timely help received from Professor Lambert Schmithausen, Drs. Chr.

Lindtner, Peter Skilling, and Marek Mejor in sending new information on AVS and AVSN also cannot be forgotten. Professor A.K. Narain's profound interest in Buddhist technical terminology, from which I benefited through discussions with him, was also quite helpful. I must also deeply thank Professor Shoei Ichimura, Director of Zen and Buddhist Studies, Washington, for his sustained interest in my work. Ven. Ngawang Samten is to be deeply thanked for assisting me in surveying the Tibetan version of the Arthaviniścaya-ṭīkā, and for his help in preparing the Tibetan-Sanskrit word lists found at the end of this volume. To Professor A.K. Saran I am obliged for going through my introduction and suggesting a few changes. Professors Vidyanivas Mishra and L.N. Tiwari are also to be greatly thanked for their assistance in the initial stages of this work. Professor C.V. Raghavulu, Vice-Chancellor of Nagarjuna University, deserves special thanks for his abiding interest in publication of this work.

Others who helped are Ven. Doboom Tulku, Professors P.S. Jaini, K.R. Norman, S.S. Bahulkar, Krishna Nath, Ram Shankar Tripathi, Siegfried Lienhard, Heinz Bechert, Richard Gard, Y.C. Simhadri, B.R. Subrahmanyam, Shyam Dev Dwivedi, H.S. Prasad, and Rajagopala Rao. Young scholars who rendered assistance to me include Drs. D.C. Jain, Pradyumna Dube, Lalji Shravak, Dr. (Mrs.) J. Sitaramamma, and Dr. R.K. Ratnam..

I must also thank my brother Gopal Samtani, my wife Kamla Samtani, and Drs. Sujata and Subodh Mahanti for their help in different ways. Mr. J.P. Srivastava (Banaras Hindu University) and Mrs. Sitamma and Mr. S.S. Rao (Nāgārjuna University) are to be deeply thanked for their regular typing assistance. Mr. Chundhary of New World Net Centre of Guntur as well as Mr. Jitendra of CIHTS, Sarnath are also to be thanked for their unfailing assistance in e-mail messages.

Finally, I must thank Mr. Jack Petranker, Senior Editor of Dharma Publishing, and his colleagues for their competent editorial and technical assistance. To Mr. Petranker I am especially grateful for his meticulous approach and sustained interest in the Sūtra and the Nibandhana from the very beginning and his immense patience with me in the publication of this translation.

May all of these individuals earn the merit of their good (kuśala) work done in helping me in various ways in the publication of this sacred Sūtra with its precious Commentary.

Sukhitā vata santu sattvāḥ.
May all beings be happy.
AVSN, p. 196

N.H. SAMTANI

Nagarjuna University
Andhra Pradesh, India
March 2001

APPENDIX

THE ARTHAVINIŚCAYA COMMENTARY (ṬĪKĀ) IN TIBETAN

The sDe-dge edition of the bsTan-'gyur contains a Commentary on the Arthaviniścaya Sūtra in 192 folios (NE 4365). It bears the Sanskrit name Arthaviniścayasūtraṭīkā. A brief survey of this commentary, conducted at my request by Ven. Ngawang Samten of the Central Institute of Higher Tibetan Studies, Sarnath, for whose assistance I am very grateful, shows that this text is not a Tibetan version of the Arthaviniścaya-sūtra-nibandhana (AVSN), the work translated in the present volume. I cannot even call it an extended recension of the present Nibandhana. Instead, it is a version of another Sanskrit commentary on the AVS which to my knowledge has not been found in the original Sanskrit. The colophon to the Tibetan commentary does not name any author or even mention the Tibetan translator.

In the beginning of the Tibetan commentary there is no mention of the introductory verse in praise of the teacher of the commentator, as we find in the Nibandhana. Even the order of the constituents of the body of the Sūtra (nidāna, upodghāta, etc.) is different. Many points discussed in the introductory portion of the Nibandhana are also found in the ṭīkā, often in more extensive form. For example, there is also a long comment on the word 'Śrāvastī', the name of the city where the Buddha delivered many discourses. The term 'Brahmasvara' (sublime voice) is replaced by 'meghasvara' (the sound of cloud).

The sections on the five skandhas, five upādānaskandhas (clinging aggregates), and pratītyasamutpāda (explained by the simile of a tree and its growth), as well as several other sections all contain more material than we find in the Nibandhana. I have not been able to compare the two works in detail, but it can definitely be said that the Sūtra being commented on is the same in both cases, the only difference being that the ṭīkā is based on a copy of the Sūtra which had twenty-six topics (uddeśa), while the present AVS has twenty-seven topics. It may be pointed out that the Alfonsa Ferrari's edition of AVS also has twenty-six sections. It seems that either one section has been omitted or two sections have been combined into one.

Notes to the Introduction

1. A translation of the fragmentary Sanskrit Sūtra into Italian was published in 1944 by Alfonsa Ferrari, along with the text in Roman script and the romanized Tibetan for the missing Sanskrit text. Alfonsa Ferrari, Arthaviniścaya (Testo e Versione), Atti Della Reale Accademia d'Italia Memorie Della Classe Di Scienze Morali e Storiche (Serie Settima, vol. IV-fasc. 13) (Rome, 1944).

2. Journal of the Royal Asiatic Society (London, 1974), Pt. I, Reviews of Books, p. 76.

3. Indo-Iranian Journal, vol. XVII, 1975, Reviews, p. 117.

4. N.H. Samtani (ed.), The Arthaviniścaya-sūtra and its Commentary (Nibandhana), critically edited and annotated with several indices (Patna, 1971).

4a. Some of the most recent works to have come to my notice that quote the AVS and AVSN are Marek Mejor, Vasubandhu's Abhidharmakośa and the Commentaries Preserved in the Tanjur (Stuttgart, 1991) and R.M.L. Gethin, The Buddhist Path of Awakening: A Study of the Bodhipakkhiyā Dhammā (Leiden, 1992).

5. Cf. AVSN, Introduction, pp. 58–59. (References to the AVS and AVSN in the notes to the present work are to the critical edition, cited at note 4 above.)

6. See AVS, pp. 34–42.

7. See the chapter on "Two Chinese Versions," AVSN, Introduction., pp. 31–38.

7a. See "Mss of the Sūtra" in the chapter on "Critical Apparatus," AVSN, Introduction, p. 9.

8. Cf. "Some Remarks on the Tibetan Version," op. cit., Introduction, pp. 39–42. For Tibetan text, see Toh. 317 (NE 317).

9. See AVSN, Appendix I.3, pp. 320–22. The Nepalese copies and Ferrari's edition of AVS also contain this different explanation of the Eightfold Path. See also AVS, p. 34, note 1.

10. Cf. AKV I:4 (Dwa), p. 15

11. Cf. AVSN, p. 72. This shows clearly the Sautrāntika leanings of Vīryaśrīdatta, the author of the Nibandhana. See note 7, ibid. On the problem of the school to which the AVS and AVSN belong, see "The Buddhist School to which the Sūtra and the Commentary May Be Assigned," AVSN, Introduction, pp. 137–149.

12. See AKB I.3, p. 3.

13. See Dīghanikāya (PTS ed.) vol. III, pp. 207 ff.

14. Cf. Vibhaṅga, ed. Mrs. C.A.F. Rhys Davids (London, PTS, 1904); The Book of Analysis, translated by Thittila (London: PTS, 1969).

15. Cf. AVSN, Introduction, pp. 61–66.

16. Cf. Chr. Lindtner, Nāgārjuniana: Studies in the Writings and Philosophy of Nāgārjuna (Copenhagen, 1982), p. 175.

17. See G.P. Malasekera, Encyc. of Buddhism, vol. II, p. 100b.

18. bsTan-'gyur, Toh. no. 4365 (NE 4365) (sDe-dge vol. nyo, fol.1b to 192a).

19. See P.L. Vaidya (ed.), Mahāyāna-sūtra-saṅgraha (Darbhanga, 1961), Introduction, p. 11, AKB III.28, p. 140.

20. See Ch. Tripathi, Funfundzwanzig Sūtras des Nidānasaṁyukta. (Berlin, 1962) (Sanskrittexte aus den Turfanfunden).

21. However, the interpretation is unconventional. It does not speak of the four efforts but of offering salutations (to seniors). See AVS, p. 41. However, the Pāli tradition explains the four efforts almost in the same way as does the samyak prahāṇa section (Section XIV) with some changes in order and phraseology. Cf. DN III, p. 221; MN II, p. 11.

22. Abhi. A., p. 569.

23. On this category of dharmas an important work has been recently published by Collett Cox: Disputed Dharmas: Early Buddhist Theories on Existence (Tokyo, 1995).

24. Cf. AKB III.28, p. 138.

25. Cf. AKV (Dwa), p. 456. See AVSN, p. 98, note 1.

26. Cf. AVSN, p. 111. Which Abhidharma texts Vīryaśrīdatta has in mind here depends on the school to which he belonged. In a fairly recent work entitled Vasubandhu's Abhidharmakośa and the Commentaries Preserved in the Tanjur (Stuttgart, 1991), p. 18, Marek Mejor has addressed this point, saying in reference to de Jong's review of AVS and AVSN: "It has been proved that Vīryaśrīdatta quotes large portions of Vasubandhu's Pratītyasamutpādavyākhyā and Guṇamati's ṭīkā; thanks to the cross-references it is possible to ascertain his adherence to the Kashmirian Vaibhāṣikas." In a footnote Mejor indicates that the results of his research on the Pratītyasamutpādavyākhyā will be published in a separate volume. Despite these comments, my own view is that the school to which Vīryaśrīdatta belonged remains an open question.

27. AVSN, p. 158. Cf. SN IV, p. 127.

28. Cf. MN I, p. 135. Also Cf. Vajracchedikā, Mahāyāna-sūtra-saṁgraha (P.L. Vaidya, ed.), p. 77.

29. Cf. AVSN, p. 189.

30. Cf. AVSN, Introduction, pp. 133–36.

Gathering the Meanings

अर्थविनिश्चयसूत्रम्

ARTHAVINIŚCAYA SŪTRA

Namo Buddhāya 1

Thus have I heard: The Blessed One was once staying in the Eastern Park in the large palace of Mṛgāramātā (the mother of Mṛgāra) at Śrāvastī, together with a large assembly of monks numbering 1,250.

Then the Blessed One addressed the monks, his voice firm, deep, sweet, lofty, and faultless:

"The Dharma, monks, that I shall teach you is virtuous in the 2
beginning, virtuous in the middle, virtuous in the end. It is good in sense and letter, most perfect, pure, and clear, and leads to the highest path. Such is this Dharma discourse on the Compendium of Categories. Listen and fix your mind well and rightly on it, and I shall speak."

"Well said, Lord," the monks answered the Blessed One, giving their assent.

The Blessed One spoke to them thus:

"What, monks, is this Dharma discourse, the Compendium of Categories?

"It contains:

Five Aggregates
Five Aggregates of Clinging
Eighteen Elements
Twelve Sense Fields
Twelvefold Law of Conditioned Co-production
Four Noble Truths
Twenty-two Faculties
Four Meditations
Four Formless Attainments
Four Sublime States
Four Courses (of Meditation)
Four Ways of Cultivating Concentration
Four Foundations of Mindfulness
Four Right Efforts
Four Bases of Psychic Powers
Five Faculties
Five Powers
3 Seven Constituents of Enlightenment
Noble Eightfold Path
Sixteenfold Mindfulness of Breathing In and Breathing Out
Four Constituents of Attaining the Stream
Ten Powers of the Tathāgata
Four Grounds of the Tathāgata's Self-Confidence
Tathāgata's Four Kinds of Special Knowledge
Eighteen Special Dharmas of the Buddha
Tathāgata's Thirty-two Marks of a Great Personage
Eighty Minor Marks of the Buddha

"This, monks, is the list of topics of this discourse on Dharma, the Compendium of Categories.

I

Five Aggregates

"What, monks, are the five aggregates?

"Namely, the aggregate of form, the aggregate of feeling, the aggregate of perception, the aggregate of karma formations, and the aggregate of consciousness.

"These, monks, are the five aggregates.

II

Five Clinging Aggregates

"What, monks, are the five clinging aggregates?

"The clinging aggregate of form, the clinging aggregate of feeling, the clinging aggregate of perception, the clinging aggregate of karma formations, and the clinging aggregate of consciousness.

"These, monks, are the five clinging aggregates.

III

Eighteen Elements

"What, monks, are the eighteen elements? 4

"The eye element, form element, and eye-consciousness element; the ear element, sound element, and ear-consciousness element; the nose element, smell element, and nose-consciousness element; the tongue element, taste element, and tongue--consciousness element; the body element, touch element, and body-consciousness element; the mind element; object of mind element, and mind-consciousness element.

"These, monks, are the eighteen elements.

IV
Twelve Sense Fields

"What, monks, are the twelve sense fields?

"The internal sense field of the eye and external sense field of form; the internal sense field of the ear and external sense field of sound; the internal sense field of the nose and external sense field of smell; the internal sense field of the tongue and external sense field of taste; the internal sense field of the body and external sense field of touch; the internal sense field of mind and external sense field of objects of mind.

"These, monks, are called the twelve sense fields.

V
The Twelvefold Law of Conditioned Co-production

5 "What, monks, is the Twelvefold Law of Conditioned Co-production?

"It holds: 'If this is, that is. If this arises, that arises.' Thus,

through ignorance karma formations are conditioned;
through karma formations consciousness is conditioned;
through consciousness name and form are conditioned;
through name and form the six sense fields are conditioned;
through the six sense fields contact is conditioned;
through contact feeling is conditioned;
through feeling craving is conditioned;
through craving clinging is conditioned;
through clinging the process of coming to be is conditioned;
through the process of coming to be birth is conditioned;
through birth are conditioned decay, death, grief, lamentation, suffering, mental affliction, and unrest.

"Thus arises the entire great mass of suffering.

"[Again,]
through the cessation of ignorance, karma formations cease;
through the cessation of karma formations, consciousness ceases;
through the cessation of consciousness, name and form cease;
through the cessation of name and form, the six sense fields cease;
through the cessation of the six sense fields, contact ceases;
through the cessation of contact, feeling ceases;
through the cessation of feeling, craving ceases;
through the cessation of craving, clinging ceases;
through the cessation of clinging, the process of coming to be ceases;
through the cessation of coming to be, birth ceases;
through the cessation of birth, decay, death, grief, lamentation, suffering, mental affliction, and unrest cease.

"Thus the entire great mass of suffering comes to an end.

Ignorance

"Now, what is ignorance?

"There is ignorance of the past, ignorance of the future, and
ignorance of the present; ignorance of the inner world, the outer 6
world, and both the inner and outer worlds; ignorance of actions, ignorance of the results of actions, and ignorance of both actions and their results; ignorance of good acts, ignorance of bad acts, and ignorance of both good and bad acts; ignorance of cause, ignorance of effect, and ignorance of both cause and effect; ignorance of phenomena produced by causes, ignorance of conditioned co-production, and ignorance of phenomena conditionally co-produced; ignorance of the Buddha, ignorance of the Dharma, and ignorance of the Saṅgha; ignorance of suffering, ignorance of the arising of suffering, ignorance of the cessation of suffering, and ignorance of the path; ignorance of wholesome and unwholesome phenomena; ignorance of the blameworthy and the blameless; ignorance of what should be practiced and what should not be practiced; ignorance of what is inferior and what is superior; ignorance of the dark and the bright.

7 "It is absence of knowledge, lack of insight, absence of realization, darkness, intense delusion, and darkness in the form of ignorance concerning all the six sense fields of contact.

"This is called ignorance.

Karma Formations

"Karma formations are conditioned by ignorance.

"What are the karma formations?

"There are three: karma formations of body, speech, and mind.

"What are the karma formations of the body?

"Breathing in and breathing out. This is a phenomenon of the body; it depends on the body and is linked to the body; it occurs in dependence upon body. Therefore breathing in and breathing out is called karma formations of the body.

8 "What are the karma formations of speech?

"One speaks after applying the mind and investigating, but not otherwise. Therefore initial application of mind and investigation are called karma formations of speech.

"What are mental karma formations?

"The volition of one who is under the influence of passion, of ill-will or of infatuation is a mental phenomenon. It depends upon mind, is fastened to mind and occurs in dependence upon mind. Therefore, volition is called a mental karma formation.

"These, monks, are the three karma formations.

Consciousness

"Consciousness is conditioned by karma formations.

"What is consciousness?

"There are six groups of consciousness. What six? Eye-consciousness, ear-consciousness, nose-consciousness, tongue-consciousness, body-consciousness and mind-consciousness.

"These are the six groups of consciousness called consciousness.

Name and Form

"Name and form are conditioned by consciousness.

"What is 'name'?

"It is the four formless (mental) aggregates. What four? The aggregate of feeling, aggregate of perception, aggregate of karma formations, and aggregate of consciousness.

"This is 'name'. 9

"What is form?

"Whatever is material includes four great elements and all that is derived from the four great elements. What four? The elements of earth, water, fire, and air.

"What is the earth element? That which has heaviness and hardness.

"What is the water element? That which is fluid and drenches.

"What is the fire element? That which is hot and cooks.

"What is the air element? That which is compressible, can spread, and has lightness and motion.

"This, the material, and the former, the mental, are both called collectively 'name and form'.

Six Sense Fields

"The six sense fields are conditioned by name and form.

"What are these six sense fields?

"The six internal sense fields: eye, ear, nose, tongue, body and mind. These are the six sense fields.

Contact

"Contact is conditioned by the six sense fields. 10

"What is contact?

"The six classes of contact. What six? They are eye contact, ear contact, nose contact, tongue contact, body contact and mind contact. This is contact.

Feeling

"Feeling is conditioned by contact.

"What is feeling?

"There are six classes of feeling. Feeling that arises through eye contact is of three kinds: pleasurable, painful, and neutral. Similarly, feeling arising through the contact of ear, nose, tongue, body, and mind is pleasurable, painful, and neutral. This is feeling.

Craving

"Craving is conditioned by feeling.

"What is craving?

"There are six classes of craving: craving for form, craving for sound, craving for smell, craving for taste, craving for touch, and craving for mental objects.

Clinging

"Clinging is conditioned by craving.

"What is clinging?

"There are four kinds of clinging. What four? Clinging to sense desires, clinging to views, clinging to ceremonial practices and observances, and clinging to belief in the existence of the self.

Becoming

11 "Becoming is conditioned by clinging.

"What is the process of becoming? There are three processes of becoming. What three? Coming to be in the realm of sense desires, coming to be in the realm of form, and coming to be in the formless realm.

"What is 'coming to be in the realm of sense desires'?

"[First] there is coming to be in the eight hot hells. What eight? Samjīva, the hell where pain revives; Kālasūtra, the black-string hell; Saṅghāta, the hell of intense oppression; Raurava, the hell that causes screaming and weeping; Mahāraurava, the hell of intense screaming and weeping; Tāpana, the heater hell, Pratāpana, the intense heater hell, and Avīci, the hell of endless torture.

"There is also coming to be in the eight cold hells: Arbuda, where tumors form due to the cold; Nirarbuda, where a multitude of tumors form due to the cold; Aṭaṭa hell; Hahava hell; Huhava hell; Utpala, the hell of blue lotus-like ulcers; Padma, the hell of red lotus-like ulcers; and Mahāpadma, the hell of great lotus-like ulcers.

"Also within the realm of sense desires are ghosts, animals, human beings, and the six classes of gods of the sense-desire realm. What are the six classes of gods? The four great kings, the thirty-three gods, the Yāmas, the gods of Tuṣita paradise, the Nirmāṇaratis, and the Paranirmitavaśavartins.

"And what is 'coming to be in the form realm'? 12

"Among the gods of this realm are the Brahmakāyikā, who belong to the company of Brahmā; the Brahmapurohitā, who serve as priests of Brahmā; the Mahābrahmā gods, who follow Mahābrahmā; the Parīttābhā gods, whose splendor is limited; the Apramāṇābhā gods, whose splendor is immeasurable; the Ābhāsvarā gods, who shine in splendor; the Parīttāśubhā gods, who are limited in auspiciousness, the Apramāṇaśubhā gods, who are unlimited in auspiciousness; the Śubhakṛtsnā gods, who are wholly auspicious; the Anabhrakā, gods of the cloudless heaven; the Puṇyaprasavā; gods of virtuous birth; the Bṛhatphalā, gods of great reward; the Abṛhā gods, whose greatness is limited; the Atapā, gods of serenity; the Sudṛśā, gods of excellent appearance; the Sudarśanā, gods excellent to gaze upon; and the Akaniṣṭhā, highest of the gods.

"And what is 'coming to be in the formless realm'?

"This is as follows: the sphere of infinity of space, the sphere of infinity of consciousness, the sphere of nothingness, and the sphere of neither perception nor non-perception. [For the gods of the formless realm, who take consciousness alone as the object of meditation, there are thus four kinds of existence.] This is called the formless existence.

"These are the three kinds of becoming.

Birth

"Through becoming, birth is conditioned.

"What is birth?

"That which, for various beings and groups of being, progresses through conception, production, coming into existence,
13 descent, rebirth, appearance, obtaining aggregates, obtaining elements, obtaining sense fields, reproduction of aggregates, production of vital organs, and the coming together of similar species. This is birth.

Decay and Death

"Through birth, decay and death are conditioned.

"What is decay [or old age]?

"It is broken teeth, graying hair, a multitude of wrinkles in the skin, decrepitude, a stooped and bent posture, a rattling noise in the throat when breathing, black moles on the limbs, reliance on the support of a staff, the bending over of the body, ripening and disintegration of faculties, decay of karma formations, wreckage, blurring, sluggishness, wasting away, and loss. This is decay.

14 "What is death?

"It is the fall of beings from a group of similar species of being, the passing away, breaking up, disappearance, and demise, the completion of time span and finishing of age, the loss of vital heat, the cessation of vital faculties, the laying down of aggregates. This is death. Together with decay, it is known by the collective name, 'decay and death'.

"This, monks, is Twelvefold Conditioned Co-production.

VI
Four Noble Truths

"What are the Four Noble Truths?

"The Noble Truth of Suffering, the Noble Truth of the Arising of Suffering, the Noble Truth of the Cessation of Suffering, and the Noble Truth of the Path Leading to the Cessation of Suffering.

"What, then, is the Noble Truth of Suffering?

"Birth is suffering, old age is suffering, disease is suffering,
death is suffering, separation from what is pleasant is suffering,
association with what is unpleasant is suffering. What one 15
desires and searches for, if it is not obtained, is also suffering. In
brief, all the aggregates of clinging are suffering. This is the
Noble Truth of Suffering.

"What is the Noble Truth of the Arising of Suffering?

"The craving that leads to rebirth and is accompanied by pleasure and attachment, finding pleasure now here and now there. This is the Noble Truth of the Arising of Suffering.

"What is the Noble Truth of the Cessation of Suffering?

"Complete abandonment and relinquishment, bringing to an end, destruction, removal of attachment, cessation, quietude, disappearance of that very craving which leads to rebirth and is accompanied by pleasure and attachment, finding pleasure now here and now there. This is the Noble Truth of the Cessation of Suffering.

"What is the Noble Truth of the Path Leading to the Cessation of Suffering?

"This is the Noble Eightfold Path beginning with right view; namely, right view, right thought, right speech, right action, right livelihood, right effort, right mindfulness, and right concentration. This is the Path Leading to the Cessation of Suffering. 16

"These, monks, are the Four Noble Truths.

VII
Twenty-Two Faculties

"Now, monks, what are the twenty-two faculties?

"These are as follows: the faculty of sight, the faculty of sound, the faculty of smell, the faculty of taste, the faculty of touch, the faculty of mind, the female faculty, the male faculty, the faculty of vitality, the faculty of physical pain, the faculty of mental pain, the faculty of physical pleasure, the faculty of mental pleasure, the faculty of equanimity, the faculty of faith, the faculty of energy, the faculty of mindfulness, the faculty of concentration, the faculty of wisdom, the faculty of knowing what is unknown, the faculty of perfect knowledge, and the faculty of one whose knowledge has been perfected.

"These, monks, are the twenty-two faculties.

VIII
Four Meditations

17 "And further, monks, what are the four meditations?

"Here, Monks, a monk aloof from sense desires and aloof from evil and unwholesome thoughts attains the first meditation born of aloofness and accompanied by initial thought and sustained thought, and he attains the first meditation with rapture and joy and abides there.

"Putting to rest initial and sustained thought, with mind made inwardly tranquil and absorbed in a single object, he attains the second meditation, devoid of initial and sustained thought, and he abides there.

"Being detached from rapture, he abides in equanimity, mindful and clearly conscious, experiencing in his person that joy of which the Noble Ones say: 'Joyful abides a person who has equanimity and is mindful.' Thus he attains and abides in the third meditation.

"Giving up pleasure as well as pain, with feelings of pleasure and pain disappearing, he attains and abides in the fourth meditation, which is devoid of pleasure and pain and is purified by equanimity and mindfulness.

"These, monks, are the four meditations.

IX
Four Formless Attainments

"What, monks, are the four formless attainments? 18

"Monks, a monk passes wholly beyond the perception of form by eliminating all perception of resistance and paying no attention to different perceptions. [Maintaining the awareness:] 'Space is infinite', he attains and abides in the state of infinity of space.

"Having fully transcended the state of infinity of space, he [maintains the awareness]: 'Consciousness is infinite'. Thus he attains and abides in the state of infinity of consciousness."

"Having fully transcended the state of infinity of consciousness, he [maintains the awareness:] 'There is nothing'. Thus he attains and abides in the state of nothingness.

"Having fully transcended the state of nothingness, he attains to and abides in the state of neither perception nor non-perception.

"These, monks, are the four formless attainments.

X
Four Sublime States

"What, monks, are the four sublime states?

"Monks, a monk with well cultivated, extensive, lofty, non-dual, 19
and immeasurable mind, endowed with loving kindness that is free from enmity, jealousy and harmfulness, applies great zeal in pervading [with loving kindness] a quarter of the world, and attains and abides in that state.

"Likewise, with mind well cultivated, extensive, lofty, non-dual, and immeasurable, endowed with loving kindness that is free from enmity, jealousy and harmfulness, he applies great zeal in pervading [with loving kindness] the second, third, and fourth quarters of the world; and so also above, below and across the whole world, in all regions. And he attains and abides in that state.

"In the same way, a monk with well cultivated, extensive, lofty, non-dual, and immeasurable mind, endowed with compassion that is free from enmity, jealousy and harmfulness, applies great zeal in pervading [with compassion] a quarter of the world, and attains and abides in that state.

"Likewise, with mind well cultivated, extensive, lofty, non-dual, and immeasurable, endowed with compassion that is free from enmity, jealousy and harmfulness, he applies great zeal in pervading [with compassion] the second, third, and fourth quarters of the world; and so also above, below and across the whole world, in all regions. And he attains and abides in that state.

"In the same way, a monk with well cultivated, extensive, lofty, non-dual, and immeasurable mind, endowed with sympathetic joy that is free from enmity, jealousy and harmfulness, applies great zeal in pervading [with sympathetic joy] a quarter of the world, and attains and abides in that state.

"Likewise, with mind well cultivated, extensive, lofty, non-dual, and immeasurable, endowed with sympathetic joy that is free from enmity, jealousy and harmfulness, he applies great zeal in pervading [with sympathetic joy] the second, third, and fourth quarters of the world; and so also above, below and across the whole world, in all regions. And he attains and abides in that state.

"In the same way, a monk with well cultivated, extensive, lofty, non-dual, and immeasurable mind, endowed with equanimity that is free from enmity, jealousy and harmfulness, applies great zeal in pervading [with equanimity] a quarter of the world, and attains and abides in that state.

"Likewise, with mind well cultivated, extensive, lofty, non-dual, and immeasurable, endowed with equanimity that is free from enmity, jealousy and harmfulness, he applies great zeal in pervading [with equanimity] the second, third, and fourth quarters of the world; and so also above, below and across the whole world, in all regions. And he attains and abides in that state.

"These are the four sublime states.

XI
Four Courses (of Meditation)

"And what are the four courses [of meditation]?

"There is a course, monks, that is painful and sluggish in intuition; there is a course that is painful and swift in intuition; there is a course that is pleasant but sluggish in intuition; there is a course that is [both] pleasant and swift in intuition.

"And what is the course that is painful and sluggish in intu- 20
ition? Here a person is by nature extremely lustful, extremely hateful, extremely infatuated. Because of his extremely lustful nature, born of lust, he experiences in every moment pain and dejection. Likewise, because of his extremely hateful nature, born of hatred, and because of his extremely infatuated nature, born of infatuation, he experiences in every moment pain and dejection. Moreover, his five transcendental faculties are weak, not sharp, and slow in accomplishing the destruction of defilements. And what are these five? The faculties of faith, energy, mindfulness, concentration, and wisdom. Because these transcendental faculties are weak and slow, he reaches only slowly the immediate succeeding meditation that destroys the defilements. This is the painful course sluggish in intuition.

"Now, what is the course that is painful but swift in intuition? Here a person is by nature extremely lustful, extremely hateful, extremely infatuated. Because of his extremely lustful nature, born of lust, he experiences in every moment pain and dejection. Likewise because of his extremely hateful nature, born of hatred, and because of his extremely infatuated nature, born of infatuation, he experiences in every moment pain and dejection. His five

transcendental faculties, however, are predominant, sharp, and
21 swift. And what are these five? The faculties of faith, energy, mindfulness, concentration, and wisdom. Because these transcendental faculties predominate and are sharp and swift, he reaches quickly the immediate succeeding meditation that destroys the defilements.

"Now, what is the course that is pleasant but sluggish in intuition? Here a person is almost free from lust, hatred and infatuation. Being free from lust, hatred, and infatuation, he does not experience in every moment pain and dejection born of lust, hatred and infatuation. His transcendental faculties, however, are weak, not sharp, and not swift. And what are these five? The faculties of faith, energy, mindfulness, concentration, and wisdom. Because these transcendental faculties are dull, not sharp, weak, and slow, he reaches only slowly the immediate succeeding meditation that destroys the defilements. This is called the course that is pleasant but with sluggish intuition.

"Now, what is the course that is pleasant and swift in intuition? Here a person is almost free from lust, hatred and infatuation. Being free from lust, hatred, and infatuation, he does not experience in every moment pain and dejection born of lust, hatred and infatuation. Moreover, his five transcendental faculties are dominant, sharp, and swift. And what are these five? The faculties of faith, energy, mindfulness, concentration, and wisdom. Because these transcendental faculties predominate and are sharp and swift, he reaches quickly the immediate succeeding meditation that destroys the defilements. This is called the course that is [both] pleasant and swift in intuition.

22 "These, monks, are the four courses [of meditation].

XII
Four Ways of Cultivating Concentration

"There is, monks, a way of cultivating concentration that when practiced, developed, and repeatedly followed, leads to destroying sensual lust.

"There is, monks, a way of cultivating concentration that when practiced, developed, and repeatedly followed, leads to living happily in this very life.

"There is, monks, a way of cultivating concentration that when practiced, developed, and repeatedly followed, leads to acquiring knowledge and vision.

"There is, monks, a way of cultivating concentration that when practiced, developed, and repeatedly followed, leads to acquiring wisdom.

"Now, monks, what is the way of cultivating concentration 23
that when practiced, developed, and repeatedly followed, leads
to destroying sensual lust?

"Monks, a monk goes into the forest or to the root of a tree or
to an empty uninhabited sheltered place and reflects rightly and
with wisdom on the body as it really is, well placed and situated,
enclosed in skin and full of various impurities from the soles of
the feet upward and from the top of the head downward, [reflect-
ing thus:] 'Here in this body there are the hairs of the head, hairs
of the body, nails, teeth, dirt, filth, skin, flesh, bones, sinews, 24
nerves, kidneys, heart, spleen, pleura, intestines, mesentary,
upper and lower stomach, bladder, liver, excrement, tears,
sweat, saliva, snot, grease, synovic fluid, marrow, fat, bile,
phlegm, pus, blood, head, and brain.'

"Monks, just as a man with keen eyes looking into an open
storehouse full of various grains such as rice, sesame seeds, mus- 25
tard seeds, beans, barley, and māsa recognizes these as the
grains of barley, these as the grains to be plowed, [and so on,] so,
monks, the monk [engaged in reflection] sees his body as it is,
situated and well placed. Thus he reflects on the body as it is,
[full of impurities].

"This, monks, is the way of cultivating concentration that is practiced, developed, and repeatedly followed to destroy sensual lust.

"Now, what, monks, is the way of cultivating concentration that is practiced, developed, and repeatedly followed to live happily in this very life?

"Monks, a monk goes into the forest or to the root of a tree or to an empty, uninhabited, sheltered place, and drenches, saturates, permeates, and suffuses the inner body with rapture and joy, born of aloofness and concentration. There is not a single part of his body that is not suffused and permeated with rapture and joy, born from inner aloofness and concentration.

"Monks, just as in a pond, lotuses of various colors are born
in water, grow up in water, and are sunk in water, all of them
drenched, saturated, permeated, and suffused by cool water, so a
monk goes into the forest or to the root of a tree or to an empty,
26 uninhabited, sheltered place and drenches, saturates, permeates,
and suffuses the inner body with rapture and joy born of aloofness and concentration. There is not a single part of his whole
body that is not suffused with rapture and joy, born of inner
aloofness.

"This is the way of cultivating concentration practiced, developed and repeatedly followed for living happily in this very life.

"What is the way of cultivating concentration that is practiced, developed and repeatedly followed to acquire knowledge and vision?

"Herein, monks, a monk develops well a perception of daylight. He attends to it mentally, sees it and penetrates into it.
Sustaining the perception of daylight, he develops the luminous
mind: as by day, so by night; as by night, so by day; as in front, so
27 behind; as behind, so in front; as below, so above; as above, so
below. Thus with an open and unhampered mind, a monk sustains the perception of daylight and develops a mind that is
evenly luminous, pervading the whole world.

"Monks, as in the last month of summer on a clear, cloudless day, at high noon, when the clouds in the sky have disappeared and light is pure, radiant, and bright, with no darkness, so, monks, a monk develops well the perception of daylight. He attends to it mentally, sees it and penetrates into it. He develops a mind that is evenly luminous: as by day, so by night; as in front, so behind; as behind, so in front; as below, so above; as above, so below. With an open and unhampered mind, a monk sustains the perception of daylight and develops a mind that is evenly luminous.

"This is the way of cultivating concentration that is practiced, developed, and repeatedly followed to acquire knowledge and vision.

"Now what, monks, is the way of cultivating concentration that 28
is practiced, developed, and repeatedly followed to acquire wisdom?

"Monks, a monk goes to a forest or the root of a tree or an empty uninhabited sheltered place, giving up [bodily] pleasure and pain, and with the disappearance of previous feelings of mental pleasure and pain he attains and abides in the fourth dhyāna, which is devoid of pleasure and pain and is purified through equanimity and mindfulness.

"This is the way of cultivating concentration that is practiced, developed, and repeatedly followed to acquire wisdom.

"These are the four ways to cultivate concentration.

XIII
Four Foundations of Mindfulness

"What then, monks, are the four foundations of mindfulness?

"Monks, here a monk abides contemplating the body as body internally: ardent, clearly aware, and mindful, neither covetous nor dejected with the world. Likewise, he abides contemplating the body as body externally: ardent, clearly aware, and mindful, neither covetous nor dejected with the world. Likewise he abides contemplating the body as body both internally and externally: ardent, clearly aware, and mindful, neither covetous nor dejected with the world.

"He abides contemplating feelings as feelings internally: ardent, clearly aware, and mindful, neither covetous nor dejected with the world. He abides contemplating feelings as feelings externally: ardent, clearly aware, and mindful, neither covetous nor dejected with the world. He abides contemplating feelings as feelings both internally and externally: ardent, clearly aware, and mindful, neither covetous nor dejected with the world.

"He abides contemplating the mind as mind internally: ardent, clearly aware, and mindful, neither covetous nor dejected with the world. He abides contemplating the mind as mind externally: ardent, clearly aware, and mindful, neither covetous nor dejected with the world. He abides contemplating the mind as mind both internally and externally: ardent, clearly aware, and mindful, neither covetous nor dejected with the world.

"He abides contemplating mental objects as mental objects internally: ardent, clearly aware, and mindful, neither covetous nor dejected with the world. He abides contemplating mental objects as mental objects externally: ardent, clearly conscious, and mindful, neither covetous nor dejected with the world. He abides contemplating mental objects as mental objects both internally and externally: ardent, clearly conscious, and mindful, neither covetous nor dejected with the world.

"These, monks, are the four foundations of mindfulness.

XIV
Four Right Efforts

29 "Now, monks, what are the four right efforts?

"Monks, a monk generates desire, endeavors, activates energy, exerts his mind, and rightly makes a vow to rid himself of evil and unwholesome thoughts that have arisen.

"He generates desire, endeavors, actvates energy, exerts his mind, and rightly makes a vow not to allow the arising of evil and unwholesome thoughts that have not arisen.

"He generates desire, endeavors, activates energy, exerts his mind, and rightly makes a vow for the arising of wholesome thoughts.

"He generates desire, endeavors, activates energy, exerts his mind, and rightly makes a vow to maintain, preserve, protect, repeatedly enact, increase, and consummate wholesome thoughts that have arisen.

"These, monks, are the four right efforts.

XV
Four Bases of Psychic Power

"Now, monks, what are the four bases of psychic power? 30

"Monks, a monk cultivates the basis of psychic power possessed of concentration born of zeal. Endowed with action involving effort, based on detachment, dispassion, and the cessation [of defilements] that ripens into renunciation, his zeal is neither too sluggish nor too strenuous.

"He cultivates the basis of psychic power possessed of concentration born of energy. Endowed with action involving effort, based on detachment, dispassion, and the cessation [of defilements] that ripens into renunciation, his energy is neither too sluggish nor too strenuous.

"He cultivates the basis of psychic power possessed of concentration born of consciousness. Endowed with action involving effort, based on detachment, dispassion, and the cessation [of defilements] that ripens into renunciation, his consciousness is neither too sluggish nor too strenuous.

"He cultivates the basis of psychic power possessed of con- 31
centration born of investigation. Endowed with action involving effort, based on detachment, dispassion, and the cessation [of defilements] that ripens into renunciation, his investigation is neither too sluggish nor too strenuous.

"These, monks, are the four bases of psychic powers.

XVI

Five Faculties

"Now, monks, what are the five faculties?

"The faculty of faith, the faculty of energy, the faculty of mindfulness, the faculty of concentration, and the faculty of wisdom.

"Now, what is the faculty of faith? It is the faculty by which [a monk] has confidence in four things. What are these four?

"He believes in the right view concerning transmigration in
the world. He takes refuge [in the view] that every karma has
consequences, [thinking]: 'Whatever action I take, whether virtuous or sinful, I shall have to experience the result of that action.'
Therefore, he does not commit sin even for the sake of his life.
32 This is the faculty of faith.

"And what is the faculty of energy? It is the faculty through which he acquires the qualities that he accepts through the faculty of faith. This is the faculty of energy.

"And what is the faculty of mindfulness? It is the faculty through which he guards from loss the qualities that he acquires through the faculty of energy. This is the faculty of mindfulness.

"And what is the faculty of concentration? It is the faculty through which he fixes his mind on the qualities that he guards from loss through the faculty of mindfulness. This is the faculty of concentration.

"And what is the faculty of wisdom? It is the faculty through
which he thoroughly understands and deeply reflects on the
qualities on which he fixes his mind through the faculty of con-
33 centration. And he cultivates the nature of deep reflection on
these qualities. This is called the faculty of wisdom.

"These, monks, are the five faculties.

XVII
Five Powers

"Now, monks, what are the five powers?

"Power of faith, power of energy, power of mindfulness, power of concentration, and power of wisdom.

"These, monks, are the five powers.

XVIII
Seven Constituents of Enlightenment

"What, monks, are the seven constituents of enlightenment?

"Mindfulness, the investigation of dharmas, energy, rapture, tranquility, concentration, and equanimity.

"Monks, a monk cultivates the enlightenment constituent of 34
mindfulness based on detachment, dispassion, and the cessation [of defilements] that ripens into renunciation.

"Likewise, he cultivates the enlightenment constituent of investigation of dharmas based on detachment, dispassion, and the cessation [of defilements] that ripens into renunciation.

"He cultivates the enlightenment constituent of energy based on detachment, dispassion, and the cessation [of defilements] that ripens into renunciation.

"He cultivates the enlightenment constituent of rapture based on detachment, dispassion, and the cessation [of defilements] that ripens into renunciation.

"He cultivates the enlightenment constituent of tranquility based on detachment, dispassion, and the cessation [of defilements] that ripens into renunciation.

"He cultivates the enlightenment constituent of concentration based on detachment, dispassion, and the cessation [of defilements] that ripens into renunciation.

"He cultivates the enlightenment constituent of equanimity based on detachment, dispassion, and the cessation [of defilements] that ripens into renunciation.

"These, monks, are the seven constituents of enlightenment.

XIX
Noble Eightfold Path

"Now, monks, what is the Noble Eightfold Path?

35 "Right view, right thought, right speech, right action, right livelihood, right effort, right mindfulness, and right concentration.

"And monks, what is right view?

" 'There is this world and the next; there are mother and father; there is the giving of alms and the making of sacrifices. There is the ripening fruit of pleasant and unpleasant, good and evil deeds. There are in this world persons who have rightly gone and are well practicing'. This, monks, is the right view, and what is opposed to it is the wrong view.

"What is right thought?

"It is doing virtuous and generous deeds [with the intention that they] ripen into attaining Buddhahood rather than leading to universal sovereignty. This is right thought.

"What is right speech?

"Monks, it is [speech] free from rudeness, falsehood, slander and frivolity. This, monks, is right speech.

36 "What is right action?

"It consists in performing ten wholesome ways of action, through body, speech, and mind. Action of the body is of three kinds: Abstinence from killing a living being, from taking what is not given, and from wrongful conduct in seeking sensual pleasures. Action of speech is of four kinds: Abstinence from falsehood, from slander, from harsh speech, and from frivolous talk.

Action of the mind is of three kinds: Abstinence from covetousness, malice, and wrong views.

"And what is meant by 'killing a living being'?

"A living, sentient being is present, and someone generates the intention to kill, attacks, and takes away its life. This is called killing a living being. It is not 'killing a living being' when the act is done through carelessness or oversight.

"What is stealing? Intending to take to own the wealth of others is called stealing. Taking small portions of the property of mother, father, or brother, or of one's own relations or friends without causing any hindrance is not stealing.

"And what is wrongful conduct in seeking sexual pleasures?
Enjoying the women of others, such as those who are under the
guardianship of master, king, mother, or father. It is also wrongful conduct to seek sexual pleasure in an improper place, where
one should not go, or at the wrong place and time. This is called 37
wrongful sexual conduct.

"These are the three actions of body.

"Now, what is falsehood?

"When one is asked to bear witness and says what is not really so, this is falsehood. [An example:] Claiming to be an Arhat when one is not. To speak in jest is not falsehood.

"What is slander?

"Speech that is not truthful and causes dissension is slander. This is called slander.

"What is harsh speech?

"To address hurtful words to another desiring to cause
anguish is harsh speech. This is called harsh speech. 38

"What is frivolous talk?

"Talk concerning kings, thieves, war, intoxicants, gambling, women, legends, and stories. This is called frivolous talk.

"These are the four actions of speech.

"What is covetousness?

"To desire to own others' wealth is covetousness. [The wish:] 'May whatever wealth he has belong to me': This is called covetousness.

"What is malice?

"The thought of taking away the life of others, of injuring or torturing them, and so forth: This is malice.

"What is wrong view?

"[To maintain views opposed to right view, such as] 'Neither this world nor the next exists', as well as the other views already indicated. [This is wrong view.]

"These are the the three actions of the mind.

"Now, what is right livelihood?

39 "[It is breached when] a monk indulges in hypocrisy, chatter, hinting, extortion, or exhibiting gain to seek gain.

"Now, what is hypocrisy?

"A monk having seen a generous donor coming, immediately sits in the cross-legged position at the side of the road or in an uninhabited place, thinking that the donor will take him to be a meditator and an Arhat and will honor him with gifts. This is called hypocrisy.

"And what is chatter?

"A monk intent on receiving gifts and honor speaks [to donors in this way]: 'O! You are my mother, my father, my sister, my daughter', and other sweet words. This is called chatter.

"And what is hinting?

"A monk having taken a meal repeatedly says: 'The likes of this meal that I have taken is not served in the houses of other laymen.' If said with no intention of seeking gain and honor, this is not a fault; [otherwise] this is called hinting.

"And what is extortion? 40

"A monk does not receive food at a house and wishes to be given it. He says to the householder, 'Those who are not liberal donors go to hell. You are not a liberal donor and you will certainly go to hell.' The donor out of fear of hell makes an offering of food and the monk eats it. This is called extortion.

"And what is exhibiting gain to seek gain?

"A monk purchases beautiful robes with his own money and shows them to laymen, saying 'We received such robes as offerings.' Out of shame, the laymen also give robes, and the monk makes use of them. This is called seeking gain by exhibiting it.

"This, monks, is wrong livelihood. To abstain from such action is right livelihood.

"Now, as to wrong livelihood for laypeople: The sale of poison, weapons, living beings, intoxicants, or flesh, and the crushing of sesame and mustard without first examining them—this is wrong livelihood. To abstain from it, [monks, is known as right livelihood.]

"This, monks, is called right livelihood. 41

"What is right effort?

"Acting rightly through salutation, veneration, rising from a seat to bid welcome, raising the open hands placed side by side in respect. This, monks, is right effort.

"And what, monks, is right mindfulness?

"Monks, a monk sees a woman and passion arises in him. Now he looks at her body externally and internally in its reality and its impure form, [calling to mind:] 'In this body are hairs of the head, hairs of the body, nails, teeth, dirt, filth, skin, flesh, bones, sinews, nerves, kidney, heart, spleen, pleura, upper and lower stomach, intestines, mesentary, bladder, liver, excrement, tears, sweat, saliva, snot, grease, synovic fluid, marrow, fat, bile, phlegm, pus, blood, head, brain, feces, urine and a full array of
impurities.' This, monks, is called right mindfulness. 42

"Now, what is right concentration?

"The four meditations. Here, monks, a monk aloof from sense desires and from evil and unwholesome thoughts attains the first meditation born of aloofness and accompanied by initial thought and sustained thought, and he attains the first meditation with rapture and joy and abides there.

"Putting to rest initial and sustained thought, with mind made tranquil and absorbed in a single object, he attains the second meditation, devoid of initial and sustained thought, and he abides there.

"Being detached from rapture, he abides in equanimity, mindful and clearly aware, experiencing in his person that joy of which the Noble Ones say: "Joyful abides a person who has equanimity and is mindful." Thus he attains and abides in the third meditation.

"Giving up pleasure as well as pain, with previous feelings of mental pleasure and pain having disappeared, he attains and abides in the fourth meditation, which is devoid of pleasure and pain and is purified by equanimity and mindfulness.

"These, monks are the four meditations. This is called right concentration.

"This, monks, is the Noble Eighfold Path.

XX
Sixteenfold Mindfulness of Breathing In and Breathing Out

"Now, what, monks, is the sixteenfold mindfulness of breathing in and breathing out?

43 "Monks, a monk, breathing in mindfully, truly knows: 'I am breathing in.' Breathing out mindfully, he truly knows: 'I am breathing out.'

"Breathing in a long breath, he truly knows: 'I am breathing in a long breath.' And breathing out a long breath, he truly knows: 'I am breathing out a long breath.'

"Breathing in a short breath, he truly knows: 'I am breathing in a short breath.' Breathing out a short breath, he truly knows: 'I am breathing out a short breath.'

"Experiencing all the activities of body he breathes in and truly knows: 'I am breathing in experiencing all the activities of body.' Likewise, he breathes out experiencing all the activities of body and truly knows: 'I am breathing out experiencing all the activities of body.'

"Experiencing rapture he breathes in and truly knows: 'I am breathing in experiencing rapture.' Likewise, he breathes out experiencing rapture and truly knows: 'I am breathing out experiencing rapture.'

"Experiencing happiness he breathes in and truly knows: 'I 44
am breathing in experiencing happiness.' Likewise, he breathes
out and truly knows: 'I am breathing out experiencing happiness.'

"Calming the activities of the body, he breathes in and truly knows: 'I am breathing in calming the activities of the body.' Likewise, he breathes out and truly knows: 'I am breathing out calming the activities of the body.'

"Experiencing the activities of the mind, he breathes in and truly knows: 'I am breathing in experiencing the activities of the mind.' Likewise, he breathes out and truly knows: 'I am breathing out experiencing the activities of the mind.'

"Calming the activities of the mind, he breathes in and truly knows: 'I am breathing in calming the activities of the mind.' Likewise, he breathes out and truly knows: 'I am breathing out calming the activities of the mind.'

"Experiencing the mind, he breathes in and truly knows: 'I am breathing in while experiencing the mind.' Likewise, he breathes out and truly knows: 'I am breathing in while experiencing the mind.'

"With the thought, 'My mind rejoices', he breathes in and truly knows: 'I am breathing in while thinking, "My mind rejoices."'

Likewise, he breathes out and truly knows: 'I am breathing in while thinking, "My mind rejoices."'

"Concentrating the mind, he breathes in and truly knows: 'I am breathing in while concentrating the mind.' Likewise, he breathes out and truly knows: 'I am breathing out while concentrating the mind.'

"With the thought, 'My mind is free,' he breathes in and truly knows: 'I am breathing in while thinking, "My mind is free."' Likewise, he breathes out and truly knows: 'I am breathing out while thinking, "My mind is free."'

45 "Thus, contemplating impermanence, he breathes in and truly knows: 'I am breathing in contemplating impermanence". Likewise, he breathes out and truly knows: 'I am breathing out contemplating impermanence.'

"Contemplating dispassion, he breathes in and truly knows: 'I am breathing in contemplating dispassion.' Likewise, he breathes out and truly knows: 'I am breathing out contemplating dispassion.'

"Contemplating cessation, he breathes in and truly knows: 'I am breathing in contemplating cessation.' Likewise, he breathes out and truly knows: 'I am breathing out contemplating cessation.'

"Contemplating renunciation, he breathes in and truly knows: 'I am breathing in contemplating renunciation.' Likewise, he breathes out and truly knows: 'I am breathing out contemplating renunciation.'

"This, monks, is the sixteenfold mindfulness of breathing in and breathing out.

XXI
Four Constituents of Attaining the Stream

"Now, monks, what are the four constituents of attaining the stream?

"Monks, a noble disciple with faith in the Buddha based on comprehension [reflects]: 'Thus indeed is he the Blessed One, the

Tathāgata, the Perfected One, the Rightly and Fully Awakened One, endowed with knowledge and right conduct, well gone, the Knower of the World, the incomparable charioteer of men to be tamed, the teacher of gods and men, the Buddha, the Blessed One.'

"He has faith in the Dharma based on comprehension [and reflects]: 'The Dharma is well proclaimed by the Blessed One; it is realized [by oneself] in this very life; it is free from the fever [of defilement]; it is timeless, leading onwards [to nirvāṇa]; it is [truly, as the Tathāgata has said,] a thing to "come and see" [for
oneself]. The wise experience it for themselves as the crushing of 46
pride, the removing of thirst, the destruction of attachment, the cutting off of conditioned existence, the realization of the void; as the destruction of craving; as freedom from the passions, as cessation, as nirvāṇa.'

"He has faith in the Saṅgha based on comprehension [and reflects], 'The Blessed One's Saṅgha of disciples is well established in practice; it is on the way to nirvāṇa; it is upright in views; it is on the proper path; it is on the path of Dharma in all
its aspects; it follows the Dharma in all its aspects. Within the 47
Saṅgha are those who are practicing to realize the fruit of attaining the stream and those who have attained this fruit; there are those who are practicing to realize the fruit of the once-returner and those who have attained this fruit; there are those who are practicing to realize the fruit of the never-returner and those who have attained this fruit; there are those who are practicing to realize the fruit of Arhathood and those who are Arhats. Thus the Saṅgha includes the four pairs of persons; the eight classes of individuals.'

"[He reflects,] 'This is the Saṅgha of disciples of the Blessed One, endowed with moral conduct, endowed with concentration, endowed with wisdom, endowed with faith, endowed with learning by oral tradition, endowed with deliverance, endowed with deliverance obtained by knowledge and vision. It is worthy of offerings, worthy of providing hospitality, worthy of obeisance, worthy of paying homage. It is a matchless field of merit, worthy of the offerings made by the world.'

"'This Saṅgha of disciples is endowed with moral conduct dear to the Noble Ones, which is unbroken, flawless, pure, and unblemished; which leads to freedom and cannot be tarnished, which is well finished and well begun, praised by the wise, and not subject to denunciation.'

"These, monks, are the four constituents of attaining the stream.

XXII
Ten Powers of the Tathāgata

48 "Now, what, monks, are the ten powers of the Tathāgata?

"Herein, monks, the Tathāgata knows truly what is possible and what is not possible.

"He knows truly the results of actions and undertakings of the past, future, and present.

"He knows truly the different and diverse dispositions of other beings and of persons.

"He knows truly the world of different and diverse elements.

"He knows truly the higher and lower faculties of other beings.

"He knows truly the way leading to all destinies.

49 "He knows truly the faculties, powers, constituents of enlightenment, meditations, deliverances, concentrations, and attainments of other beings as well as their differences in defilements and purity.

"And also with regard to the former existence of beings, he well remembers their size, their place of birth, and the causes for their birth, [not just] for one, two, three, or four existences, but for myriads of existences, and so on.

"And further, with his heavenly vision, pure and superhuman, he sees beings dying and taking birth in good and bad states in accord with their good and bad deeds of body, speech, and mind, and so on.

"He knows truly and with wisdom the undefiled deliverance of mind through the destruction of defilements.

"These, monks, are the ten powers of the Tathāgata.

XXIII
Four Grounds of the Tathāgata's Self-Confidence

"Now, what, monks, are the four grounds of the Tathāgata's self-confidence?

"The Blessed One, the Tathāgata, the Arhat, the Rightly and Fully Awakened One, firmly maintains as follows:

"If someone charges, 'You have not realized these dharmas,' I
find no ground for such a charge—not in the whole world of 50
devas, Māra, Brahmā, with all its inhabitants, including ascetics, brahmins, gods, men and demons. And finding no ground, the Tathāgata abides calmly and fearlessly. He knows his distinguished place. Having rightly gone to the assembly, he utters the lion's roar and sets rolling the Brahma wheel, not previously set in motion in accord with the Dharma by any śramaṇa or brahmin or by anyone in the world.

"Regarding those things that I have called stumbling blocks, if someone charges, 'For one who practices these things, they are not stumbling blocks,' I find no ground for such a charge—not in the whole world of devas, Māra, Brahmā, with all its inhabitants, including ascetics, brahmins, gods, men and demons. And finding no ground, the Tathāgata abides calmly and fearlessly. He knows his distinguished place. Having rightly gone to the assembly, he utters the lion's roar and sets rolling the Brahma wheel, not previously set in motion in accord with the Dharma by any śramaṇa or brahmin or anyone in the world.

"If some one charges that the noble path leading to deliverance, which I have taught to the disciples, does not, when followed, lead to the right extinction of suffering, I find no ground for such a charge—not in the whole world of devas, Māra,

Brahmā, with all its inhabitants, including ascetics, brahmins, gods, men and demons. And finding no ground, the Tathāgata abides calmly and fearlessly. He knows his distinguished place. Having rightly gone to the assembly, he utters the lion's roar and sets rolling the Brahma wheel, not previously set in motion in accord with the Dharma by any śramaṇa or brahmin or by anyone in the world.

51 "Having myself destroyed the defilements and having firm knowledge that this is so, if someone charges, 'These your defilements are not extinct,' I find no ground for such a charge—not in the whole world of devas, Māra, Brahmā, with all its inhabitants, including ascetics, brahmins, gods, men and demons. And finding no ground, the Tathāgata abides calmly and fearlessly. He knows his distinguished place. Having rightly gone to the assembly, he utters the lion's roar and sets rolling the Brahma wheel, not previously set in motion in accord with the Dharma by any śramaṇa or brahmin or by anyone in the world.

"These are the four grounds of self-confidence.

XXIV
Tathāgata's Four Kinds of Special Knowledge

"Now, what are the four kinds of special knowledge of the Tathāgata?

52 "Special knowledge of categories, special knowledge of Dharma, special knowledge of languages, and special knowledge of ready expositions.

"What is special knowledge of categories?

"Unshakable knowledge of ultimately real categories.

"What is special knowledge of Dharma?

"Unshakable knowledge of undefiled dharmas.

"What is special knowledge of languages?

"Unshakable knowledge of speeches and usages.

"What is special knowledge of ready exposition?

"Unshakable knowledge of speech that is fitting, unhindered, and clear due to mastery in concentration.

XXV
Eighteen Special Dharmas of the Buddha

"What are the eighteen special dharmas of the Buddha?

"The Tathāgata never takes a false step. His speech is neither 53
rash nor noisy. He is never deprived of mindfulness. His mind is never unconcentrated. He has no perception of multiplicity. His equanimity is not due to lack of consideration. His zeal is unflagging. His energy does not diminish. He never loses his mindfulness. He never loses his concentration. His wisdom never fails. His deliverance never fails. He has absolute and infallible knowledge and insight concerning the past. He has absolute and infallible knowledge and insight concerning the future. He has absolute and infallible knowledge and insight concerning the present. All his actions of the body are preceded by knowledge and accord with knowledge. All his actions of speech are preceded by knowledge and accord with knowledge. All his actions of mind are preceded by knowledge and accord with knowledge.

"These are the eighteen special dharmas of the Buddha.

XXVI
Tathāgata's Thirty-Two Marks of a Great Personage

"Now, what are the Tathāgata's thirty-two marks of a Great Personage? Namely:

"Well-placed feet; the soles of the feet marked with a wheel; 54
the heels of the feet large and the ankles prominent; the fingers

long; the hands and feet webbed; the hands and feet soft and tender; seven convex surfaces on the body; legs like those of the
antelope; the private organ concealed in a sheath; the upper part
of the body like that of the lion; the space between the shoulders
well-filled; the shoulders evenly rounded, long arms when standing erect; pure limbs; a neck shaped like a shell; a jaw like that of
the lion; forty even teeth; even teeth that are without spaces;
teeth that are marvelously white; a long tongue; an exquisite
sense of taste; a voice like that of Brahmā and like that of the
Kalaviṅka bird; dark blue eyes; eyelashes like those of a cow;
smooth skin; golden skin; a hair in each pore of the skin; hair
55 that is raised and turns to the right; hair having the color of the
sapphire; brilliant white hair growing on the head between the
eyebrows; a protrusion at the crown of the head; a body of well-
proportioned symmetry, like the banyan tree; (and a body pleasing from all sides, like that of Mahānārayaṇa).

"These are the thirty-two marks of a Great Personage.

[Meritorious Deeds that Account for the Arising of the Marks]

"Having well-placed feet: This mark of a Great Personage arose because in former existences [as a Bodhisattva] the Tathāgata firmly undertook [always to do meritorious deeds].

56 "The soles of the feet marked with a wheel: This mark of a Great Personage arose because in former existences the Tathāgata accumulated merit by giving various kinds of gifts.

"The heels of the feet large and the ankles prominent: This mark of a Great Personage arose because in former existences the Tathāgata did not disappoint other beings.

"The fingers long: This mark of a Great Personage arose because in former existences the Tathāgata protected and guarded the Dharma.

"The hands and feet webbed: This mark of a Great Personage arose because in former existences the Tathāgata brought no dissension to the families of others.

"The hands and feet soft and tender: This mark of a Great Personage arose because in former existences the Tathāgata donated many kinds of robes.

"Seven convex surfaces on the body: This mark of a Great Personage arose because in former existences the Tathāgata gave abundant food and drink. 57

"Legs like those of the antelope: This mark of a Great Personage arose because in former existences the Tathāgata acquired dharmas special to the Buddha.

"The private organ concealed in a sheath: This mark of a Great Personage arose because in former existences the Tathāgata protected the secret mantra and abstained from the sexual act.

"The upper part of the body like that of the lion: This mark of a Great Personage arose because in former existences the Tathāgata practiced good deeds in regular succession.

"The space between the shoulders well-filled: This mark of a Great Personage arose because in former existences the Tathāgata practiced wholesome deeds.

"The shoulders evenly rounded: This mark of a Great Personage arose because in former existences the Tathāgata gave fearlessness and consolation to others.

"Long arms when standing erect: This mark of a Great Personage arose because in former existences the Tathāgata always sought to ascertain how he could help others. 58

"Pure limbs: This mark of a Great Personage arose because in former existences the Tathāgata undertook to practice to his satisfaction the ten wholesome deeds.

"A neck shaped like a shell: This mark of a Great Personage arose because in former existences the Tathāgata donated various medicines to the sick.

"A jaw like that of the lion: This mark of a Great Personage arose because in former existences the Tathāgata practiced to their culmination the wholesome deeds.

"Forty even teeth: This mark of a Great Personage arose because in former existences the Tathāgata practiced consoling all beings.

"Even teeth that are without spaces: This mark of a Great Personage arose because in former existences the Tathāgata united those who were disunited.

59 "Teeth that are marvelously white: This mark of a Great Personage arose because in former existences the Tathāgata guarded well his actions of body, speech, and mind.

"A long tongue: This mark of a Great Personage arose because in former existences the Tathāgata well protected truthful words.

"An exquisite sense of taste: This mark of a Great Personage arose because in former existences the Tathāgata performed inestimable merit and transferred [it] to others.

60 "A voice like that of Brahmā and like that of the kalaviṅka bird: This mark of a Great Personage arose because in former existences the Tathāgata always maintained [the practice of] telling sweet and truthful words and words that caused delight.

"Dark blue eyes: This mark of a Great Personage arose because in former existences the Tathāgata protected other beings as his friends.

"Eyelashes like those of a cow: This mark of a Great Personage arose because in former existences the Tathāgata's intention was never inauthentic.

"Smooth skin: This mark of a Great Personage arose because in former existences the Tathāgata was always inclined to participate in the councils of the Dharma.

"Golden skin: This mark of a Great Personage arose because in former existences the Tathāgata gave beds, rugs, and pleasing garments.

"A hair in each pore of the skin: This mark of a Great Personage arose because in former existences the Tathāgata shunned crowded gatherings.

"Hair that is raised and curls to the right: This mark of a Great Personage arose because in former existences the 61
Tathāgata comprehended with perfect competence the instructions of his teachers, preceptors, and spiritual guides.

"Hair having the color of the sapphire: This mark of a Great Personage arose because in former existences the Tathāgata, with compassion for all beings, laid aside sticks, stones, and other weapons.

"Brilliant white hair on the head between the eyebrows: This mark of a Great Personage arose because in former existences the Tathāgata praised those worthy of praise.

"A protrusion at the crown of the head: This mark of a Great Personage arose because in former existences the Tathāgata respected his teachers and made obeisance to them.

"A body of well-proportioned symmetry, like the banyan tree:
This mark of a Great Personage arose because in former existences 62
the Tathāgata motivated himself and others in concentration.

("A body pleasing from all sides, like that of Mahānārāyaṇa. This mark of a Great Personage arose because in former existences the Tathāgata made images of the Tathāgata, repaired broken stūpas, consoled beings who were fearful, and helped different beings cross [the ocean of saṁsāra].)

"The Tathāgata demonstrated mastery over these innumerable roots of good. This is the reason that the thirty-two marks of a Great Personage were produced in his body.

XXVII
Eighty Minor Marks of the Buddha

"What are the eighty minor marks? 63

"The Buddhas, the Blessed Ones, have copper-colored nails, glossy nails, elevated nails, regular lines in the palm of the hand,

round fingers, large fingers, regular fingers, hidden veins, veins
without knots, hidden ankle bones, level feet, a stride like that of
a lion, a stride like that of an elephant, a stride like that of a
64 swan, a stride like that of a bull, an upright gait, an elegant gait,
straight limbs, round limbs, smooth limbs, regular limbs, a
broad and elegantly rounded body, fully developed sexual
organs, even steps, pure limbs, soft limbs, bright limbs, limbs
that are unimpaired, prominent limbs, firm limbs, and well-proportioned limbs. They cast an aura of pure light that dispels
darkness, and have a round belly, a soft belly, an unbent belly, a
slender belly, a deep navel, and a navel that turns to the right,
They are pleasing to behold from all sides and are pure in conduct. They have limbs free from black moles, hands soft like cotton wool, glossy lines in the palm, deep lines in the palm,
extensive lines in the palm, a face that is not long, looks that produce an original and reflected image, a soft tongue, a slender
65 tongue, a copper-colored tongue, a voice like the roaring of an
elephant or like thunder, a sweet, agreeable, and pleasing sound,
round eye-teeth, sharp eye-teeth, level eye-teeth, regular eye-
teeth, a prominent nose, a clean nose, wide eyes, large eyes,
raised eyelashes, eyes like the petals of a blue lotus, a chest that
is wide and long, elongated eyebrows, soft eyebrows, eyebrows
with level hairs, glossy eyebrows, long and fleshy ears, level ears,
an unimpaired faculty of hearing, a well-shaped forehead, a wide
66 forehead, a full-grown head, hair that is dark like a black bee,
raised hair, soft hair, hair that is not shaggy and hair that is not
rough, fragrant hair. The hands and feet of the Buddhas, the
Blessed Ones, possess auspicious markings such as the śrīvatsa,
svastika, Nandyāvarta, wheel, vajra, lotus, and fish.

"These are the eighty minor marks.

Conclusion

"The Blessed One [previously said], 'The Dharma, monks, that I shall teach you is virtuous in the beginning, virtuous in the middle, virtuous in the end, good in sense and letter, most perfect, pure, clear, leading to the highest path. This is the Dharma discourse that I shall explain, the Compendium of Categories.'

"This has now been said again. 67

["The Blessed One has also said:] 'Monks, there are forest haunts, roots of trees, secluded uninhabited sheltered places, mountain caves, heaps of straw, open spaces, cemeteries, jungles, and remote places. Arrange your lodging there. Meditate monks; do not be indolent. Be not remorseful later.' This is the instruction."

While this Dharma discourse was being presented, the minds of five hundred monks became free from defilements, free from grasping.

Thus the Blessed One spoke. Delighted, those monks and that
whole assembly and the world of gods, men, demons, and gand- 68
harvas rejoiced in what the Blessed One had said.

Here ends the Dharma discourse, the Compendium of Categories.

> Those things which proceed from a cause,
> Of these the Tathāgata has told the cause,
> And that which is their cessation.
> The great ascetic proclaims such a teaching.

Written down in the Saṁvat 319, in the month of Caitra, the ninth date of śukla (pakṣa).

अर्थविनिश्चयसूत्रनिबन्धनम्

Arthaviniścaya-sūtra Nibandhana

The Expository Composition
of the Discourse on the Compendium of (Buddhist) Categories
by Vīryaśrīdatta of Śrī Nālandā Mahāvihāra

Om Namo Buddhāya° 71

Having bowed to the son of Śuddhodana, who humbled the pride of Kandarpa° and whose footstool is worshipped by gods and men, I shall recall the exposition of the Sūtra, having learned it from my guru, an expert in the interpretation of the words of the Sugata.[1]

The framework of a Sūtra

The framework of a Sūtra [contains the following components]:
1. Introduction
2. Preface
3. Purpose
4. List [of topics]°
5. Exposition
6. [Logical] connection°

1. The Introduction here consists of the words beginning 'Thus have I heard' and ending with 'monks numbering 1,250'.

Commentary

2. The Preface consists of introductory words explaining the topics of the Sūtra. It is not auspicious to speak without prefatory words, and so the words are to avoid this fault. Here the Preface begins with 'At that time the Blessed One' and continues to 'The Blessed One spoke to them thus'.

72 3. The Purpose is for getting [the audience] actively involved. One who desires to expound Sūtra should tell [the purpose] in order to command the respectful attention of those who will listen to the Sūtra. Persons of circumspection never do anything anywhere without knowing the purpose. As has been said:

> Having heard the glory [māhātmya] of Sūtra, the hearer cultivates respectful attention. Whatever is heard should be grasped: Therefore, the purpose should be presented at the outset°.

The [aim of] the instruction in the Arthaviniścayasūtra is investigation into dharmas (dharmapravicaya°). Without being instructed in Sūtras, a disciple cannot investigate dharmas. The aim of investigation into dharmas is calming the defilements (lit.
73 sub-defilements) (upakleśas°). And it should be understood that the aim of calming [the defilements] is to reach the highest abode.

The purpose of the Sūtra here is explained in the title, which means "ascertainment of categories" or "investigation (analysis) into dharmas." Thus it is said that analysis of the dharmas is the purpose.

4. The List of Topics is presented for the student's ease of comprehension. When one knows the general topics, one can easily learn the detailed parts. Thus, when a horse has seen the terrain it can proceed without making a false step. Again it may be said that [the list] is for rebutting the superimposition (samāropa°) of [views] and denunciation (apavāda) [of the Dharma]. And here the list (uddeśa) begins with 'What, monks, is this Dharma discourse' and continues to 'This monks, is the list of topics of this discourse on Dharma, the Compendium of Categories'.

5. The Exposition is given to analyze in detail what has been briefly listed. It is like a commentary (vṛtti) on an aphorism (sūtra°); thus, the exposition is like a commentary while the list of topics is like the aphorism. The list, which is a brief, condensed statement, can be readily understood through the explanation, which serves as commentary.

Why not give only the exposition, leaving aside the list of topics? The reply: It is easy to understand the exposition when [it is 74
first] presented in brief. Also, general words require more specific words; thus both the exposition and list of topics are necessary. Again, the general themes are remembered through specific words.

This has also been done to counter in succession two types of faults: non-comprehension (apratipattidoṣa) and the loss of mindfulness. The list of topics and exposition are also given with two kinds of persons in view: those who understand through a brief statement and those who understand through a detailed description.

Here the detailed description starts with 'What monks, are the five aggregates' and continues to the conclusion of the Sūtra: 'Thus spoke the Blessed One'.

6. The Logical Connection (anusandhi) shows the relation between the preceding words and those that follow.

[Conclusion]: The framework of a Sūtra is stated in a verse from an anthology:

> Introductory statement, preface, list of topics with purpose, and exposition with connection. Together these comprise the collection of topics of a Sūtra.

This is the framework of a Sūtra.

The detailed explanation of the opening topics

Now the words of the Sūtra are explained:

THE INTRODUCTION

1 *Namo Buddhāya°*

Thus have I heard: The Blessed One was once staying in the Eastern Park in the large palace of Mṛgāramāta at Śrāvastī, together with a large assembly of monks numbering 1,250.

Then the Blessed One addressed the monks, his voice firm, deep, sweet, lofty, and faultless:

2 *"The Dharma°, monks, that I shall teach you is virtuous in the beginning, virtuous in the middle, virtuous in the end. It is good in sense and letter, most perfect, pure, and clear, and leads to the highest path. Such is this Dharma discourse on the Compendium of Categories. Listen and fix your mind well and rightly on it, and I shall speak."*

"Well said, Lord" the monks answered the Blessed One, giving their assent.

'Thus' (evaṁ) is a particle (nipāta), although used in compar-
75 ison and for many other purposes; here it should be understood in the sense of a reply [to a question]. How? At the time of the [First] Council when 500 Arhats had eagerly assembled to recite [the teachings of the Buddha], Venerable Ānanda was especially requested [with the words]: "Speak as you heard." He replied, "Thus." The meaning is, "As you request, so it is done."

'I' (mayā) excludes anyone else, confirming the direct hearing. The meaning is, "I have heard this from the Blessed One personally and not by hearsay." 'Heard' (śrutaṁ) means acquired through ear-consciousness. This shows the absence of attainment° at that time. Even when there has been attainment, however, since one has not realized the powers, confidences and special dharmas of the Buddha, there is no inconsistency in saying 'heard'.[2]

'Once' [literally, at one time] means 'at one period'. Due to the uninterrupted continuity of the time of hearing, it is one time.
76 This phrase also suggests Ānanda's vast learning (bāhuśrutya),

[for in saying that] this Sūtra was heard at one time, the implication is that other Sūtras were heard at other times. Alternatively, 'once' refers to the phrase that follows: 'The Blessed One was staying'.

Etymologically (nairuktena nyāyena), 'Blessed One' (bhagavān°) means one who has destroyed [literally, broken] the
fourfold Māra: Devaputra, Kleśa, Skandha, and Mṛtyu.[3] Alter- 77
natively the epithet has been interpreted as indicating the possession of [the six] virtues beginning with lordship. As it is said:

"According to tradition (śruti), the Blessed One is blessed with six virtues: [full] lordship, beauty, fame, wealth, knowledge, and effort."[4]

'In Śrāvastī'. Śrāvastī is the city named after the great sage Śravasta, who lived in a hermitage there. It was called Śrāvastī, having been named for that special [association with the] place.

'Staying' (viharati) means that the Buddha was in any of the 78
four postures (īryāpatha): walking, [standing, sitting, or sleeping]; or else that he was abiding in [one of] the four boundless states (apramāṇas): joy, [loving kindness, compassion, and equanimity]. 'Was' indicates the past tense.

Śrāvastī is known to be a very extensive city. Therefore the question arises, 'Where?' The answer: 'In the Eastern Park' (Pūrvārāma). This park is called the Eastern Park because it is in the eastern portion of Śrāvastī, or else because it is to the east of Jetavana.[5] It is known as a park (ārāma) because [people] take delight (āramanti) in it.

Since the Eastern Park also has many locations, the question arises: 'In what place'? The answer: 'In the large palace of Mṛgāramāta [mother of Mṛgāra]'. Mṛgāramātā was a lay woman who had realized the truth (dṛṣṭasatyā), and she had built a palace for [the Buddha].[6] Etymologically, 'palace' (prāsāda) is that the sight of which pleases (prasīdati) the mind of everyone.

Was the Buddha staying alone? The answer: 'with an assembly'. The size of the assembly of monks signifies the immense virtues of the monks as well its large number. The immensity of virtues is indicated by the phrase, 'With an assembly of monks.' A 'monk' (bhikṣu) is one who has destroyed [literally, broken] the defilements such as lust, or who has acquired, according to his capacity, the fruit for attaining the stream (srota-āpatti-phala) and the others or the fruit of the life of the śramana[7] (srāmaṇyaphala). Alternatively, a bhikṣu is so called because enemies who take the form of Māra or other such forms cannot destroy him. The assembly of such persons is called the 'Saṅgha'.

79 'Together with' means 'along with'. The size of number is shown by the words 'together with 1,250'. At the time of the exposition of the Arthaviniścaya, this was possibly the limit of number.

The Introduction has been explained.

The Preface

Then the Blessed One addressed the monks, his voice firm, deep, sweet, lofty, and faultless:

2 *"The Dharma, monks, that I shall teach you is virtuous in the beginning, virtuous in the middle, virtuous in the end. It is good in sense and letter, most perfect, pure, and clear, and leads to the highest path. Such is this Dharma discourse on the Compendium of Categories. Listen and fix your mind well and rightly on it, and I shall speak."*

"Well said, Lord°," the monks answered the Blessed One, giving their assent.

Now comes the Preface, referred to with the words 'Then' [or 'at that time'], and what follows. The word 'then' (tatra) [is used] as an introduction to a sentence. 'Blessed One' has already been explained. 'Firm' (dhīra): The division [of the compound] is 'firm, deep, sweet, lofty.' [Question]: What kind of voice? [Answer]: With such a voice. It is firm because it is fivefold.[8] It is deep because it has brahma sound. It is sweet because it is charged with renunciation (naiṣkramya) and produces happiness. It is not alloyed with [anything whatsoever] that produces vulgar taste. As it is said:

"For those without defilement (araṇa), their voice is too sweet. [For those] with defilements, it is too harsh. Your speech [O Blessed One] is free from the fault of being [too] sweet or harsh."[9]

It is lofty (udāra) because it reaches distant places. As it is said, "It [the voice of the Buddha] pervades all."

'The Dharma, monks, that I shall teach you': Here 'Dharma' means Sūtra in the form of discourse and other [divisions of Buddha vacana] explaining the ultimate truth (nyāya). 'You' means 'for you'; that is, 'concerning you'. 'Monks' (bhikṣavaḥ) is a form of address. This [style] of addressing monks is employed to make the monks attentive when the mind is distracted. Here it may be said that this is done to focus [their] attention on the teaching of the Arthaviniścaya-sūtra.

Question: Why are monks alone mentioned in the address,
and not the other assemblies: nuns, [laymen, and laywomen)? 80
Regarding this Ācārya Rāhulabhadra says:

> "[The Buddha] addressed the monks because they were preeminent, superior, proximate, always in his close company, and able to grasp [the meaning]"[10]

The meaning: Their pre-eminence is because they realize the truth first. It is fit to address them because they are like an elder son. Their superiority is due to their having a higher degree of perfection than others, or again because they are the chief foundation of the whole treasury of virtues. Their proximity is due both to their being pre-eminent and superior and because they sit directly in front [of the Buddha]. They are in his close company because they are recluses of the male type and also because they always closely follow [the Master]. The ability to grasp is due to their well-established awareness, as well as to the supremacy of a male rebirth and to their abundance of wisdom.

[Next,] what is the special characteristic [of the Sūtra]? Answer: It is 'virtuous in the beginning', and so forth. It is virtuous° in the beginning because it explains the precepts concerning morality
81 (adhiśīlaśikṣā). It is 'virtuous in the middle' because it explains
the precepts concerning mind [for the practice of meditation] (adhicitta-śikṣā). It is 'virtuous in the end' because it explains the precepts concerning wisdom (adhiprajñā-śikṣā). Alternatively, this is so because the Sūtra is consistent in the beginning, in the middle, and in the end.

[The Sūtra] is 'good in sense' (svartha) because it is free from perversion in what has been expressed. It is 'good in letters' (suvyañjana°) because it is enriched with vocabulary that can be comprehended.

With this Dharma discourse, [says the Buddha], 'I shall explain the highest path' (brahmacarya°). 'The highest path [or course]' is the pure (anāsrava) path leading to attainment of nirvāṇa. Nirvāṇa is called brahma because it is the highest and the chief (parama-pradhāna) abode. How so? The Sūtra states: 'Thus indeed, he, the Blessed One, is calm; has become cool, is at the highest stage' (brahmībhūta). [Thus, the Buddha says,] 'Now
82 I 'shall explain' [the course] which one follows to reach the 'high-
est course'.

Now, what is the distinctive feature of this highest course? It is said to be the 'sole' course. It is not found among outsiders, but only among followers of Dharma. Because this course is extraordinary [leading to nirvāṇa], it is called the only one. It is further specified as 'perfect'. It is also perfect in being the opponent of the universal defilements. In comparison, the worldly path is no opponent° of the defilements of the highest worldly existence (bhavāgra). Thus it is not perfect.

[This course] is 'pure' because it is free by its own nature. It is completely purified, for it gives birth to a noble lineage, and completely free, for it brings perfect freedom to its noble lineage.

83 'Namely' (yadut) is a particle of explanation: [It points
toward] the Compendium of Categories (Arthaviniścaya). The

name signifies that persons ascertain a category (or term)° by hearing its various divisions [or classifications].

'Dharma-discourse' (dharmaparyāya°) means group or combination of dharmas. 'Listen to it.' 'It' (tat) is a particle meaning 'therefore'. This signifies: Since I shall teach, therefore listen.

This is said to remove° three kinds of faults. 'Listen' removes the first fault of not hearing the words; it enjoins the trainees (vineya) to direct their ears. 'Well' removes the second fault of [wrong] understanding (prajñādoṣa), for one may understand quite the opposite of what the words mean. The phrase 'fix your mind rightly' removes the third fault: not understanding correctly what is meant through a lackadaisical desire to hear. For not grasping the meaning may be due to grasping without respect [or proper appreciation. This is said in order to cultivate respect for the Sūtras.]

In denouncing these three kinds of hearers, they are compared respectively to [three] bowls: one turned upside down; one that is impure; and one with holes. 'I shall speak' means, I shall speak in this way; the idea is that otherwise the rain of Dharma, like rain falling on a bowl that is stored upside down or is impure
or full of holes, will be wasted. I shall 'only speak'; indicating that 84
you yourself must put into practice [my instructions].[11]

"We have been rightly instructed by the Blessed One!" [Thinking] thus, the monks became happy and gave their approbation to the Blessed One. The rest is clear in meaning.

The Preface has been explained.

The List of Topics

The Blessed One spoke to them thus: 2

"What, monks, is the Dharma discourse, the Compendium of Categories?

"It contains:

Five Aggregates

Five Clinging Aggregates

Eighteen Elements

Twelve Sense Fields

Twelvefold Law of Conditioned Co-production

Four Noble Truths

Twenty-two Faculties

Four Meditations

Four Formless Attainments

Four Sublime States

Four Courses (of Meditation)

Four Ways of Cultivating Concentration

Four Foundations of Mindfulness

Four Right Efforts

Four Bases of Psychic Powers

Five Faculties

Five Powers

3 *Seven Constituents of Enlightenment*

Noble Eightfold Path

Sixteenfold Mindfulness of Breathing In and Breathing Out

Four Constituents of Attaining the Stream

Ten Powers of the Tathāgata

Four Grounds of the Tathāgata's Self-Confidence

Tathāgata's Four Kinds of Special Knowledge

Eighteen Special Dharmas of the Buddha

Tathāgata's Thirty-two Marks of a Great Personage

Eighty Minor Marks of the Buddha

"This, monks, is the list of topics of this discourse on Dharma, the Compendium of Categories°."

Next is explained the list of topics (uddeśa), starting with 'What, monks'. This is easy. It should be noted that 'namely' (yadut) is used to explain the list of topics. The list from 'Five Aggregates' through 'Eighty Minor Marks' indicates all the categories (arthas) of the Sūtra. Concluding the list of topics, it is said: 'Such, monks'. Since twenty-seven categories, neither more nor less, provide the framework of the 'Dharma discourse', they are presented as the subject matter° of this Dharma discourse. This is the connection (sambandha).

The list of topics has been explained.

[Next comes the explanation of the topics.]

Topic One

The Five Aggregates

3 *"What, monks, are the five aggregates?*

"Namely, the aggregate of form, the aggregate of feeling, the aggregate of perception, the aggregate of karma formations, and the aggregate of consciousness.

"These, monks, are the five aggregates."

85 Now to explain what requires explanation. 'What, monks' indicates a question. 'Namely' indicates an answer. The word 'namely°' points toward 'the aggregate° of form' and the rest; there is no possibility of any other meaning. Explained here are the [pure] aggregates, those without outflow (anāsrava skandhas). Since the question is later asked, 'What, monks, are the five aggregates of clinging?' it is understood that here the explanation refers to the pure aggregates.

The aggregate of form is that of a meditating yogi (samāpannasya yogino) who has entered into the noble path and is in the state of pure form of unmanifested character (rūpam avijñaptilakṣaṇaṁ°). And whatever feeling (vedanā) is found in aggregate

[literally, group] (kalāpa) is called the aggregate of feeling°. Similarly whatever perception (saṁjñā) is found in a group is the aggregate of perception. Except for feeling and perception, any mental factor (caitta) such as faith, as well the associated and unassociated karma formations (samprayukta and viprayukta
saṁskāras°), such as birth, are called the aggregate of karma for- 86
mations. 'Consciousness' (vijñāna) [as mentioned] in the group is the aggregate of consciousness. The word 'and' (ca) after 'consciousness' denotes conjunction, while the word 'iti°' [a particle used at the end of the sentence] is used in the sense of conclusion. Concluding [the section] it is said, 'These, monks, are the five aggregates'.

Topic Two

The Five Clinging Aggregates

3 *"What herein, monks, are the five clinging aggregates?*

"The clinging aggregate of form, the clinging aggregate of feeling, the clinging aggregate of perception, the clinging aggregate of karma formations, and the clinging aggregate of consciousness.

"These, monks, are the five clinging aggregates."

87 In the explanation of 'clinging aggregate' (upādānaskandha), 'Herein, monks' and the rest presents the question. The word 'herein' (tatrao) is used to introduce a sentence; the word 'monks' is a term of address. The establishing of 'five' [skandhas] is to refute any false belief (graha) in the self (ātmā) or in 'belonging to self' (ātmīya), and also [to clarify] that there are neither more nor fewer. Often persons who have not seen the truth (adṛṣṭa tattva) falsely take the aggregate of consciousness to be the self (ātmagraha) with form and the rest as belonging to However, there are only the five skandhas.

'Five clinging aggregates'.

Clinging (upādāna) means defilement (kleśa). The aggregates

born of defilements are called 'clinging aggregates'. The connecting word ['of'] is missing here, as in the phrase "grass and chaff fire" [i.e., fire of grass and chaff]. There are some who hold that there is no missing middle word, but explain such occurrences as a compound formation, [technically called] ṣaṣṭhi samāsa°. Thus, 'aggregates of clinging' are 'clinging aggregates' in the same way that 'fire of grass' is explained as 'grass fire'.

Now, it is quite proper to include 'beings' (sattvas) within the aggregates of clinging because their actions are drenched (abhiṣyandita) with defilements. However, how can the external states [of existence] come under 'clinging aggregates'? [Reply:] These are also reproduced from defilements. As it is said in the scriptures, the world in all its variety (lokavaicitrayaṁ) arises from actions (karmas).[11a]

Alternatively, these [skandhas] are governed by clinging. For 88
a royal servant, the servant is governed by a king, so here, aggregates are governed by [or subject to] clinging. Hence, they are 'aggregates of clinging'. Being under this control, they give rise to [clinging in] the next existence.

The rest of the meaning is clear.

As for 'aggregate of form' through 'aggregate of consciousness':

Here, 'aggregate of form' means the five faculties starting with the eye, the five objects of these faculties beginning with form, and unmanifested form°.

'Aggregate of feeling' includes pleasure, pain, and neutral feeling. It is further divided into six classes (kāya): feeling arising from eye contact, [feeling arising from ear contact, feeling arising from nose contact, feeling arising from tongue contact, feeling arising from body contact], and feeling arising from mind contact.

'Aggregate of perception' is the distinguishing (pariccheda) of signs (nimitta), such as blue, yellow, long, small, and so on. It is also of six classes, as with 'feeling'.

'Aggregate of karma formations' is all karma formations: wholesome (kuśala), unwholesome (akuśala), and indeterminate (avyākṛta); the associated (saṁyukta) as well as the unassociated (viprayukta), such as the karma formations of possession
89 (prāpti), non-possession (aprāpti), sameness of class (nikāya-sabhāga), faculty of life (jīvitendriya), and the rest.

'Aggregate of consciousness' is apprehension of object of form, etc. It is further divided into six classes of consciousness: eye consciousness, [ear consciousness, nose consciousness, tongue consciousness, body consciousness,] and mind consciousness.

What is the meaning of 'aggregate' (skandha)? It signifies 'heap'. How? This is seen in the Sūtras. For it is said in the Sūtra:

"Whatever form there is, past, future or present, internal or external, gross or subtle, inferior or superior, far or near, all this assembling together is called the aggregate of form."[12]

Since this is from scriptures (vacana), it establishes the
90 meaning of aggregate as 'heap'. Feeling and the other [skandhas] are to be understood in the same way.

Now, why are the skandhas given in this order?

[First Reason]: The ordering principle is grossness. Form is subject to resistance, and so is the most gross. Among the formless skandhas, feeling is the most gross in the way it functions, for people say, "There is feeling in my hand; there is feeling in my foot." Perception is more gross than karma formations, and karma formations are more gross than consciousness. Thus the most gross is mentioned first, and the skandhas are spoken of in order of their diminishing grossness.

[Second Reason]: The ordering principle is the process of defilement. In this beginningless saṁsāra, women and men are mutually infatuated because of form. And this is due to attachment to the feeling of pleasure. And this attachment proceeds from erroneous perception. And this erroneous perception is due to defilement. And consciousness is soiled (saṁkliṣṭa) by defilements. Thus the order accords with the process of defilement.

[Third Reason]: The order accords with [the analogy of a
cooking] pot. Form is the pot and feeling and the rest are the
contents (āśraya). Feeling is food since it is enjoyed; perception
is seasoning, for by grasping the different signs it adds flavor to
the feeling. The karma formations are like the cook, for they 91
assemble past action (vipāka) to hand over to consciousness. And
consciousness is the enjoyer, for it consumes what is presented°.

TOPIC THREE

THE EIGHTEEN ELEMENTS

4 *"What, monks, are the eighteen elements?*

"The eye element, form element,and eye-consciousness element; the ear element, sound element, and ear-consciousness element; the nose element, smell element, and nose-consciousness element; the tongue element, taste element, and tongue-consciousness element; the body element, touch element, and body-consciousness element; the mind element, object of mind element, and mind-consciousness element.

"These, monks, are the eighteen elements."

92 After the five aggregates of clinging, the eighteen elements (dhātus°) are explained, [starting with] the words, 'What are the eighteen elements?' Here the Blessed One has explained the eighteen elements based on the sixfold division into the sets of support (āśraya°), that which is supported (āśrita) and the object [of support] (ālambana).

The supports are the eye element, [ear element, nose element, tongue element, body element,] and mind element. What is supported is eye consciousness, [ear consciousness, nose consciousness, tongue consciousness, body consciousness,] and mind consciousness. The objects of support are the form element, [sound element, smell element, taste element, touch element,] and object-of-mind element (dharmadhātu°).

The order of eye element [and so forth] should be explained.

The order of objects (viṣaya) and elements of consciousness is established [by tradition]. Hence it is said that the five elements beginning with the eye are given first because their object is present [or, because they bear only on the present], while the object of mind is not fixed (aniyata): Sometimes its object is of the present, sometimes of any of three times [present, past, future].

The explanation for why the eye element [and the three others] are presented before the element of body: because the object of the body is derived matter (bhautika viṣaya°) and inconstant (aniyata)—sometimes a primary element (bhūtāni), sometimes derived from primary elements (bhautika rūpa), and sometimes both.

Both eye and ear are given first owing to the objects of eye and ear being farther than [those of] the nose and tongue. For both nose and tongue, the object is close at hand and its activity is not far-reaching. The range of activity of the eye is more extensive than that of the ear, for one can see a river yet not hear the 93
sound. Therefore, the eye is named first. The nose is named before tongue because the activity of the former is more rapid. For example, though the tongue has not yet tasted food, the smell is already perceived.

Again, in the body the eye is placed at the top; below that is the place of ear and below that the place of the nose and then that of the tongue. Still further down is the place of the greater part of the body. And the mind is dependent on them and stands without any place of its own.

[Now] the definition of the eye and the others will be given. The eye, the support of eye consciousness, is a sensitive° material element (rūpa-prasāda) which performs the act of seeing a form.

94 The ear and the others have been similarly explained. It should be specially noted that the sensitive material element is the support of its own consciousness and performs the act of seeing its own object.[13]

What is the meaning of word dhātu? It means 'family' or 'lineage' (gotra). As in one mountain there are many 'families' [mines] of silver, gold, etc., called dhātus, so in one continuous consciousness (santāna°) or basis of personal existence (āśraya°) there are eighteen families, called the eighteen dhātus.

Question: Mines [of ore] (ākara) are called families (gotras). Then what do the eye and so forth extract from these mines? [Reply]: Mind (citta) and mental states (caitta). For the eye and the rest are the cause for the arising of mind and mental states. Thus they are called dhātus.

The elements have been explained.

Topic Four

The Twelve Sense Fields

"What, monks, are the twelve sense fields? 4

"The internal sense field of the eye and external sense field of form; the internal sense field of the ear and external sense field of sound; the internal sense field of the nose and external sense field of smell; the internal sense field of the tongue and external sense field of taste; the internal sense field of the body and external sense field of touch; the internal sense field of mind and external sense field of objects of mind. These, monks, are called the twelve sense fields."

Next the explanation of sense fields (āyatanas°). The question 95
is put, "What are the twelve sense fields?" The answer is: The eye, etc., are the personal (ādhyātmika°) sense fields.

[Objection:] Since there exists no self (ātman), in its absence, how can one speak of the eye as a 'personal' eye? [To illustrate], if there were no morality, how could there be teaching relating to morality?

[Answer:] This is so, but those who maintain the theory of self (ātmavādin) construct that self leaning on the idea of 'self' (ahaṁkāra). Since in reality (tattvataḥ) mind leans on the idea of self, [the name] 'ātman' is applied metaphorically. 'In the self' means 'concerning the self'. Only what concerns the self is 'personal'. When mind, which is metaphorically given the name 'ātman', arises, the sense fields such as the eye, which are its causes, are called 'personal'. They can be considered the support of consiousness.

The eye and the others have been explained.

Now their objects will be explained.

96 Form is twofold, relating to color and shape. Sound is [also] twofold, caused by primary elements that are present (upāttaº-mahābhūtahetuka), as with the sound of the hand or speech; or caused by primary elements [that are not present] (anupāttaº-mahābhūtahetuka), such as the sound of wind, trees, and a river. Smell is threefold: pleasant, unpleasant, and neutral. Taste is of six kinds: sweet, sour, salty, pungent, bitter, and astringent. The tangible (spraṣṭavya) is of eleven kinds: the four [primary] elements of earth, water, fire, and air, and softness, hardness, heaviness, lightness, cold, hunger, and thirst. The element of objects of mind (dharmadhātuº) consists of feeling, perception, karma formations, space (akāśā), cessation through wisdom (pratisaṁkhyānirodhaº), cessation without wisdom (apratisaṁkyānirodhaº), and unmanifested form—seven entities [in all].

97 What is the meaning of āyatana (sense field)? It means 'gate' or 'entryway' for the arising of mind and mental states. Etymologically āyatanas are so called because they extend (tanvanti) an entry (āya) to the arising (utpatti) of mind and mental states.[14] 'Extend' [here] means expand.

The sense fields have been explained.

Topic Five

Twelvefold Law of Conditioned Co-Production

"What, monks, is the Twelvefold Law of Conditioned Co-Production? 5

"It holds: 'If this is, that is. If this arises, that arises.' Thus,
through ignorance karma formations are conditioned;
through karma formations consciousness is conditioned;
through consciousness name and form are conditioned;
through name and form the six sense fields are conditioned;
through the six sense fields contact is conditioned;
through contact feeling is conditioned;
through feeling craving is conditioned;
through craving clinging is conditioned;
through clinging the process of coming to be is conditioned;
through the process of coming to be birth is conditioned;
through birth are conditioned decay, death, grief, lamentation, suffering, mental affliction and unrest.

"Thus arises the entire great mass of suffering.

"[Again,]

through the cessation of ignorance, karma formations cease;
through the cessation of karma formations, consciousness ceases;
through the cessation of consciousness, name and form cease;
through the cessation of name and form the six sense fields cease;
through the cessation of the six sense fields, contact ceases;
through the cessation of contact, feeling ceases;
through the cessation of feeling, craving ceases;
through the cessation of craving, clinging ceases;
through the cessation of clinging, the process of coming to be ceases;
through the cessation of coming to be, birth ceases;
through the cessation of birth, decay, death, grief, lamentation, suffering, mental affliction and unrest cease.

"Thus the entire great mass of suffering comes to an end."[15]

98 Next comes the explanation of conditioned co-production. Concerning this, [the question] is asked: 'What is the law of conditioned co-production?' and so forth.

Now, what is the meaning of 'conditioned co-production' (pratītyasamutpāda°)? The explanation: 'Prati' indicates repetition in general). The root 'i' means 'to go', 'to disappear'. [The participle] 'itya' signifies 'ought to go', meaning [in this case] 'perishable' or 'momentary'. 'Saṁ' means 'together', while 'ut' before the root 'pad' means 'arising' or 'producing'. That is to say, the coming [arising] together of causes of perishable things is the law of conditioned co-production.[16]

[The Sūtra] explains how worldly activity (pravṛtti) linked to the self arises and what belongs to the self (ātman and ātmīya). This is to offer an explanation for disciples who are confused in regard to the process of [worldly] activity.

'Karma formations are conditioned by ignorance'. 'Conditioned by ignorance' means that ignorance (avidyā) is the condition (pratyaya) and cause (hetu) of karma formations (saṁskāra). A similar structure applies to the other constituents (aṅgas) [of twelvefold conditioned co-production].

In this [twelvefold] conditioned co-production, three con- 99
stituents have the nature of defilement (kleśa); namely, ignorance, craving, and clinging. Two constituents have the nature of action (karma); namely, karma formations and the process of becoming (bhava). The seven remaining constituents—owing to being [both] defilement and action—have the nature of being objective entities (vastu°); [they are] consciousness, name and form, the six sense bases, contact, feeling, birth, decay, and death.

Question: If no cause for ignorance can be shown (upadiṣṭa°), saṁsāra must have [an independent] beginning, while if no fruit (phala) of decay and death can be shown, saṁsāra must come to an end. The alternative is that the links [of the chain] would have to be [endlessly] supplemented. That is, there would be no finality.

[Reply]: There is no need to supplement [other constituents as either source or terminus). This is as the Blessed One has explained. From defilement comes defilement; e.g., craving produces clinging. From defilement comes karma; e.g., clinging produces existence and ignorance produces karma formations. From action (karma) come objective entities, e.g., karma formations produce consciousness and existence produces rebirth. [Further], objective entities produce objective entities, e.g., consciousness produces name and form, while birth produces decay and death. [And] objective entities produce defilement; e.g., feeling [leads to] craving.

Since the constituents of existence (bhava) function in this way, it is clear (vijñāpitam) that ignorance, which has defilement as its nature, may arise from objective entities or from defilement. [For example], when they are infused (vāsana) with feeling, the objective entities decay and death give rise to defilement. No other constituent ought to be added, for otherwise the statement in the Sūtra, 'Thus arises the whole great mass of suffering' 100
would be without force.

[Question]: Ignorance is said [in one Sūtra] to be the cause of improper attention (ayoniśo manaskāra°), while another Sūtra says, "Improper attention is caused by ignorance." Still others say that [improper attention] is included under [the constituent] 'clinging'.

[Reply]: Five constituents, being of the nature of karma and defilements, are causal; namely, ignorance, karma formations, craving, clinging and existence. The other seven aṅgas have the nature of fruit.

[Question]: In the Abhidharma,[17] conditioned co-production is explained as pertaining to [both] beings and non-beings (sattvāsattvākhya). [For it is said,] "What is conditioned co-production? All conditioned states (samskṛta dharmas)." [However], here in the Sūtra it is explained as pertaining to beings (sattva) only.

101 [Reply]: There is no inconsistency. The explanation in the Sūtra is intentional, [i.e., given for a specific purpose] (abhiprāyika). The aim is to remove confusion (saṁmoha) caused by an inclination in any trainee toward [accepting] a permanent cause, such as God or the like (Īśvarādi), which imparts movement (saṁsarati) in saṁsāra. The Sūtra teaches conditioned co-production to point out ignorance of the chain of cause and effect (hetuphalaparamparā) as it pertains to living beings. The definitive (lākṣaṇika) explanation is given in the Abhidharma, in the sense that 'definitive' is what defines [literally, produces] the characteristics.

'Grief, lamentation, suffering, mental pain, and despair are produced'. This refers to the domain of both beings and non-beings, objects subject to change in themselves as well as in their personality or frame (ātmabhāva).

'Grief' signifies internal burning caused by the loss of wealth, the loss of dear ones, and so forth. 'Lamentation' is wailing born
102 of grief. 'Suffering and mental pain' will be explained later [see topic seven]. Despair (upāyāsa°) is [mental] strain preceding grief and lamentation.

'Thus arises the entire great mass of suffering'. The word 'thus' points to what immediately follows. 'Entire°' means without any self or what belongs to the self. 'Great' signifies without any beginning or end. 'Mass of suffering' denotes the assemblage of suffering. 'Arising' refers to appearance.

Having explained the functioning [or activity] (pravṛtti) of saṁsāra, its withdrawal (nivṛtti) is now explained: 'Through the cessation (nirodha) of ignorance, karma formations cease', and so on. Thus the doctrine of conditioned co-production is explained in both the direct (anulomataḥ) and the reverse order (pratilomataḥ).

[Question:] Why does the Blessed One begin this teaching in two ways? [Reply]: Due to the different mental dispositions (āśaya) of trainees. As the mental dispositions of trainees differ, each person is suited to a particular instruction. Now, statements in the direct order are for those trainees who wish to know how saṁsāra functions but are confused regarding its sequence. Statements in the reverse order are for those who are confused in deeply understanding (prativedha°) the [whole] sequence of [saṁsāric activity]. Therefore, to teach it both ways benefits [all] trainees.

Subtopic One: Ignorance

"Now, what is ignorance?

"There is ignorance of the past, ignorance of the future, and
ignorance of the present; ignorance of the inner world, the outer 6
world, and both the inner and outer worlds; ignorance of actions, ignorance of the results of actions, and ignorance of both actions and their results; ignorance of good acts, ignorance of bad acts, and ignorance of both good and bad acts; ignorance of cause, ignorance of effect, and ignorance of both cause and effect; ignorance of phenomena produced by causes, ignorance of conditioned co-production°, and ignorance of phenomena co-produced; ignorance of the Buddha, ignorance of the Dharma, and ignorance of the Sangha; ignorance of suffering, ignorance of the arising of suffering, ignorance of the cessation of suffering, and ignorance of the path; ignorance of wholesome and unwholesome phenomena; ignorance of the blameworthy and the blameless; ignorance of what

should be practiced and what should not be practiced; ignorance of what is inferior and what is superior; ignorance of the dark and the
7 *bright. It is the absence of knowledge, lack of insight, absence of realization, darkness, intense delusion, and darkness in the form of ignorance, concerning all the six spheres of contact.*

"This is called ignorance."

103 Is ignorance (avidyā) simply ignorance or is it a state of all previous defilements (kleśa)? [To clarify this issue], the question is put, 'What is ignorance?' The particle 'yaduta°' that follows indicates an explanation.

In 'ignorance of the past', the different aspects of ignorance are [now] explained according to its parts, its base (ālambaṇa) and its synonyms (paryāya). The past is its base, and non-knowledge and similar terms are synonyms.

'The past' here means past births. Non-knowledge (ajñāna°) concerning this means doubting in this manner: "Did I exist in the past?" and so on. 'The future' signifies future births, and is associated with the doubt, "Shall I exist in future?" 'The present' denotes present birth. Non-knowledge concerning this means doubting, "What is this [period of time?]?" "What are we?" and so forth. In this way ignorance associated with doubt (vicikitsā) has been explained. With this, ignorance is explained simply as non-knowledge.

104 Ignorance is the opposite (vipakṣa) of knowledge (vidyā), as a non-friend (or enemy, amitra) [is the opposite of a friend (mitra)]. This is shown by the use of an opposed term.[17a] In some texts the reading is 'ignorance of past as well as future'. It is the ignorance of one who is confused—without any distinction—regarding the functioning of the world (pravṛtti), and who imagines that there is neither past nor future and that a man is as much as the range of his faculties (indriyagocara).

'Ignorance of the inner world' signifies the ignorance through which one maintains that in one's continuity (santāna) of mind there is [permanent] being. This ignorance is said to be associated with the [false] view of the individual [as eternal] (satkāyadṛṣṭi).

'Ignorance of the outer world'. That which is outside is external (bahirdhā): The word 'bahi' should be taken as a participle (nipāta). This is ignorance of what is outside one's continuity [of consciousness].[18] Thus this is special (āveṇikī) ignorance. According to some [schools], this ignorance is also associated with the view that maintains individual eternity. However, this is not correct, because this view is based on one's continuity [of consciousness].[19] It could also be designated 'false knowledge' 105
(mithyājñāna).

With regard to [whether] sense fields [such as] the eye belong to one's own continuity of consciousness or [are] outside it, the eye is considered internal, for it is said in the scriptures that there are twelve internal states.[20] The five objects of one's own and others' continuity of consciousness—form and the rest—are considered external. Alternatively, it is ignorance based on these [twelve] internal and external sense fields that is referred to [literally, stated] here.

'Ignorance of both the inner and outer world.' [All] lack of knowledge of the selflessness of things (nirātmatā), without any distinction between one's own and others' continuity of consciousness, is ignorance of both the inner and outer world. This is also called special ignorance.

'Ignorance of action (karma)'. The ignorance of those who doubt the operation [literally, existence] of merit (puṇya) and non-merit (apuṇya); also the ignorance of those who deny the operation [literally, existence] of merit and non-merit. [Both] are ignorance of action: They differ in that the former is associated with doubt and the latter with false view (mithyādṛṣṭi).

'Ignorance of result (vipāka)'. Just as above, this refers both to those who doubt and those who deny that [actions have] results.

'Ignorance of action and result' means ignorance of both action and its result. This pertains to those who conceive that this world is created by God or by another. This ignorance is associated with adhering to ceremonial practices and observances (śīlavrataparāmarśa). It refers to looking for a cause (hetu) when there is no cause.

106 This [same] ignorance is stated in both cases [i.e., for karma and for its result]. It leads individuals into confusion concerning the result [of karma]. They imagine that there is some other cause, or teach° that the creation of world is without any cause. One who denies the cause does not know the prior cause of a result. In both cases, this ignorance is associated with a false view and is called absence of knowledge.

'Ignorance of good and bad acts'. The characteristics of karma are divided into good [and bad] (sukṛtādi) for the benefit of those with weak faculties. '[Ignorance of] good action' means ignorance of the characteristics of ten wholesome paths of action. [Ignorance of] bad actions means ignorance of unwholesome paths of actions.[21]

'[Ignorance of both] good and bad actions' means ignorance of characteristics of the paths of both good and bad actions that flow either sporadically or continuously in a mixed continuity of consciousness.[22] The ignorance of those who doubt or deny the existence [or operation] of actions as good [and bad] is designated ignorance associated with doubt and with false view respectively.

'Ignorance of cause' means ignorance of result, cause, and the like. 'Ignorance of fruit' means ignorance of result, fruit, and the like. It also includes the ignorance of those who teach that the world is without any cause.[23] One who denies cause does not
107 accept the prior cause of a result. Therefore, ignorance of those who deny the cause and its fruit is associated with a false view. 'Ignorance of cause and fruit' is to be understood in the same way.

'[Ignorance of phenomena] produced by causes' means ignorance of conditioned dharmas. '[Ignorance of] conditioned co-production' means ignorance of the conditioned constituents such as ignorance. '[Ignorance of phenomena] conditionally co-produced' means ignorance of constituents such as ignorance that are conditionally co-produced causes due to being produced in concert. '[Ignorance of phenomena] produced conditionally' (pratītya) refers to any constituent that has become a fruit [by] being produced conditionally. Thus all the constituents are proved to be both cause and fruit. There is no contradiction here as [shown] in the example of [something that is at once] cause and fruit or the example of one who is both father and son.[24]

Ignorance through not understanding, doubting, or denying is called respectively special (āveṇikī°) ignorance, ignorance associated with doubt, and ignorance associated with false views.

'Ignorance of Buddha, Dharma and Saṅgha'. Having heard of the enlightenment of the Buddha, that the Dharma is well taught, and that the Saṅgha practices well the Dharma, and either not understanding, doubting, or denying this: these are known respectively as ignorance [of the three kinds mentioned].

'Ignorance of suffering'. Having heard the characteristics of 108
the truth of suffering—impermanence, suffering, emptiness and absence of self—and not understanding them—[the three kinds of ignorance arise].

'Ignorance of origination'. Having heard the characteristics of the truth of origination—cause, origin, arising, and condition—[the three kinds of ignorance arise].

'Ignorance of cessation' Having heard the characteristics of the truth of cessation of suffering—cessation, quietude, sublimity, and escape (niḥsaraṇa)—[the three kinds of ignorance arise].

'Ignorance of the path'. Having heard the characteristics of the truth of the path—path, method°, and practices conducive to deliverance—[the three kinds of ignorance arise].

'Ignorance of the wholesome and unwholesome' means ignorance of dharmas that act as aids to enlightenment (bodhipakṣya dharmas°) along with their opposites (vipakṣa). The dharmas acting as aids to enlightenment are the foundations of mindfulness, the right efforts, the bases of psychic powers, the faculties, the powers°, the constituents of the [Eightfold] path, and the constituents of enlightenment. Their opposites are ignorance, sloth, forgetfulness, mental disturbance, lack of clear consciousness, and latent defilements (anuśaya°), which are to be abandoned by insight and meditation (darśana-bhāvanā-heya°).

The aids to enlightenment are wholesome (kuśala), since they signify peace and security (kṣema°) and produce the desired fruit. Their opposites are unwholesome (akuśala) because they indicate lack of peace and security and produce fruit that is not
109 desired. There are three kinds of ignorance with regard to them, as above, based on not understanding, doubting, and denying.

'[Ignorance of] the blameworthy and the blameless'. Blameworthy [dharmas] counteract the dharmas that act as aids to enlightenment, as stated above. Owing to being contemptible, the killing of living beings is said to be blameworthy. Because this is the work of negative (vipakṣa) dharmas, they are blameworthy. Opposed to the blameworthy (sāvadya) is the blameless (anavadya). These dharmas alone act as aids to enlightenment, and are praised by the wise.

'Ignorance of what should be practiced (sevitavya) and what should not be practiced (asevitavya)'. The dharmas [that] are aids to enlightenment (bodhipakṣya), being experienced personally [literally, face to face] and being beneficial, are said to be worthy of practice. And anything beneficial deserves practice again and again. Opposed to these are dharmas that are not to be practiced. As they are not beneficial, they are not worthy of practice.

'[Ignorance of] what is inferior' refers to what opposes [the aids to enlightenment]. As they are instrumental in debasing the mind and body [these dharmas are inferior]. 'The superior' [or sublime] are the bodhipakṣya dharmas, which exalt the body and mind. When one is collected (samāhita), they exalt the body and mind, which become highly charged with tranquility (praśrabdhi).

'The dark' (kṛṣṇa) refers to opponent [dharmas], for they are full of outflows (sāsravas°) and are not free from muddiness. '[Ignorance of] bright dharmas' refers to the dharmas that act as aids to enlightenment, and are pure and immaculate (nirmala). The outflows are muddy; they soil the mind and mental states. [In bright dharmas] these outflows disappear.

110 Ignorance 'concerning all the six sense fields of contact°'—the eye and so forth—signifies non-penetration. The base of ignorance is divided in terms of the activity of life and of cessation (nivṛtti).

The activity of beings is the coming and going from a past which is known through the appearance of the continuity of consciousness—one's own as well as others—in accord with the arising of results of actions. [All] this is an aspect [pakṣa] of the activity of life (pravṛtti).

The true support (āśraya) for cessation [of suffering] is the triple refuge. This support of the triple refuge is—in brief—the Four Noble Truths, and comprehensively [it is] conditioned co-production. The equipment (sambhāra) [required] are the dharmas that act as aids to enlightenment. The impediments (antarāya) are the opposite states (vipakṣas). And [realization of] the nature (svabhāva) of the six sense fields of contact is true penetration and is the aspect of cessation. [It] contradicts the view that maintains the existence of the self (ātmadṛṣṭi) and the false view of eternal individuality (satkāyadṛṣṭi), from 'I see', ['I hear',] to. . . 'I know'.

What is the purpose for giving seven synonyms ['absence of knowledge and insight' and so forth]? This is done so that if one's mind was disturbed at some particular point, one can still hear at least one of the synonyms (paryāyas°). With that one word, the meaning may become clear. There are other purposes not stated here, owing to the fear that this work may become too voluminous [literally, burdensome].

[Objection:] In the Abhidharma, ignorance is said to animate
all defilements in the previous life. Here, ignorance is said to 111
continue in all the three periods of time [past, present and future]. [Reply:] This is presented in view of the inclination of trainees. The explanation is intentional, not definitive (lākṣaṇika). The definitive explanation is given in the Abhidharma.

The constituent of ignorance has been explained.

Subtopic Two: Karma Formations

"Karma formations are conditioned by ignorance. 7

"What are the karma formations? There are three: karma formations of body, speech, and mind.

"What are the karma formations of the body?

"Breathing in and breathing out. This is a phenomenon of the body; it depends on the body and is linked to the body; it occurs in dependence upon body. Therefore breathing in and breathing out is called karma formations of the body.

8 *"What are the karma formations of speech?*

"One speaks after applying the mind and investigating, but not otherwise. Therefore initial application of mind and investigation are called karma formations of speech.

"What are mental karma formations?

"The volition of one who is under the influence of passion, of ill-will or of infatuation is a mental phenomenon. It depends upon mind, is fastened to mind and occurs in dependence upon mind. Therefore, volition is called a mental karma formation.

"These, monks, are the three karma formations."

Having explained ignorance, an exposition of the karma formations° is next: 'Karma formations are conditioned through ignorance. What are the karma formations?' The question arises due to a lack of clarity, for the word saṁskāra (karma formations) is used [in various ways. It is used] concerning all conditioned states; as in "All conditioned things are impermanent." It is used in a compound in referring to the aggregate of karma formations (saṁskāra-skandha); and is used in the sense of 'volition' (cetana): "What is the aggregate of clinging to karma formations (saṁskāra-upādānaskandha)? The six classes of volition."[25] It is also used in the sense of the faculty of life (jivitendriya), as [in the statement,] "karma formations of life and
112 lifespan." But it is not known what 'karma formations' are meant here.

In order to specify, it is said there are three karma formations. To make these known, it is said, 'karma formations of the body°, speech, and mind'.

Here the Blessed One explains the division of karma formations but not their nature. He divides them in relation to the body and so forth in accord with the different inclinations [literally, tastes] of trainees. Now, [to begin] to describe the nature of each [division], the question is asked, 'What are the karma formations of the body?' The reply: 'Breathing in and breathing out' (āśvāsa-praśvāsa).

[Question:] Elsewhere, the Blessed One first explains the innate nature (svabhāva) and then the division. For example, [he asks] "What is feeling? That which experiences (anubhava)." [Then comes the division] into happiness, suffering, and neutral feeling. Here, the division comes first, and then its innate nature is explained. [Reply:] There is no inconsistency. Here and elsewhere the exposition is given in accordance with the dispositions of trainees. Therefore is it said:

> Your manifold appearances, speeches, and deeds are activated to be ever in accord with the dispositions of trainees°.

'Breathing in and breathing out'. [Question:] Why [are these
karma formations of the body? Reply:] They are physical phenomena, and they are linked to and exercise the body (kāyabhi- 113
saṁskṛtatvāt°). Since breathing in and breathing out exercise the
body, 'breathing in and breathing out' are designated karma formations of the body.

Regarding vocal karma formations, the question is put: 'What are karma formations of speech? [Reply]: 'One speaks after applying the mind and investigating'. The meaning is that one speaks in this manner. Having explained karma formations of speech, the concluding [part of the sentence states] 'Initial application of mind (vitarka°) and investigation (vicāra°)']. This being so, it should be known that this is exercising [the activities of] speech.

On mental karma formations, it is said 'of one who is under the influence of passion, etc.' The volition of one who is passionate is associated with passion (rāga), that of one who is malignant with ill-will (dveṣa) and that of the infatuated person with infatuation (moha).

The concluding portion regarding mental karma formations begins with 'therefore'. Here the inclusion of the volition associated with passion and so forth implicitly means inclusion of wholesome (kuśala) and imperturbable (āniñja) volition also. Otherwise, wholesome volition and the rest would be excluded from the discussion of karma formations. This would also lead to inconsistency in the Sūtras, which is unacceptable. Therefore this explanation should be implied, and thus it should be known that these [mental karma formations] fashion [or exercise°] the mind as well as bringing about rebirth.

[A further discussion on karma formations of the body, speech, and mind:]

Here it may be asked: Elsewhere the Blessed One has explained particular deeds relating to body, speech and mind as karma formations of the body and so forth.[26] Here breathing in and breathing out are explained as karma formations of the body. Should these particular deeds be implied here, or only acts of breathing in and breathing out? [Reply:] Both are to be
114 included. Breathing in and so forth exercise° the body, and so are called karma formations, [while] in a different context particular deeds [are called] karma formations because they lead to rebirth. How is this known? From the Sūtras and by reasoning (yukti).

[Establishing this point through the Sūtras:]

The Blessed One has declared in the Kumbhopamasūtra:[27]

"Conditioned by ignorance, he forms the karma formations of merit; he forms the karma formations of demerit; he forms the karma formations of the imperturbable."[28]

Breathing in and breathing out are [included] neither in merit nor demerit, nor are they imperturbable, for they are of the nature of great [primary] material elements. And this is an established doctrine: that the primary material elements are undefiled (anivṛta) as well as neutral (avyākṛta).

115 Again it has been stated that if one forms the karma formations of merit, he will be accompanied with rebirth conscious-

ness of merit° . . . up to . . . rebirth consciousness of the imperturbable. It has been stated here that consciousness is conditioned by karma formations. Thus it is settled that [rebirth] consciousness is conditioned by karma formations.

Again it is said that if one forms injurious karma formations of the body, one will reborn in world of harm. Breathing in and breathing out are not the cause of rebirth because they are of nature of the primary material element and wholly undefiled and neutral. What is undefiled and neutral is like rotten seed, incapable of producing result-karma. [Question:] If this is so, why are they explained here as karma formations of body? [Reply:] As stated in detail, it is because they exercise [fashion] the body.

[An example to clarify this point:] Both the initial application of mind and investigation are explained as [karma formations of speech] because they cause the production of speech and bring about speech. But they are not of the nature of speech. The karma formations of mind can be explained in the desired manner without inconsistency.

[Question:] If this is so, why does the Blessed One not teach 116
the karma formations of the body as the characteristics of karma in this Sūtra? [Reply:] This is done in view of the dispositions of the particular trainees present at that time. These karma formations of body take the characteristics of karma with reference to subsequent teaching, and [this] is supported by another Sūtra. It is not expressed [here] in consideration of future trainees. With the support of that [Sūtra], [this] nature [karma characteristics] will be understood, for the author of the [two] teachings is one and the same.

Reason also [establishes this point]:

The intention is [to establish] karma formations as a condition (pratyaya) of consciousness (vijñāna). Breathing in and breathing out as karma formations of body characterize [literally, accompany] even an Arhat. [In that case], they would bring about his rebirth consciousness. Moreover, being undefiled and neutral, they cannot be conditions of rebirth consciousness, just as a rotten seed has no reproductive capacity. Therefore, particular karma formations of the body and so forth in the form of merit and the like are to be understood as karma formations of the body.

The constituent of karma formations has been explained.

Subtopic Three: Consciousness

8 *"Consciousness is conditioned by karma formations. What is consciousness? There are six groups of consciousness. What six? Eye-consciousness, ear-consciousness, nose-consciousness, tongue-consciousness, body-consciousness and mind-consciousness. These are the six groups of consciousness called consciousness."*

After karma formations, the constituent of consciousness (vijñāna) is explained.

'What is consciousness conditioned by karma-formations?' Here follows the explanation of consciousness conditioned by karma formations.

Other Sūtras state [literally, establish] [it] differently. Therefore it is not determined whether all consciousness is conditioned by karma-formations or only a part of it.

117 Therefore it is stated, 'six classes of consciousness'. Here also the Blessed One has explained the classification [division] of consciousness in accord with the classifications of the faculties of the eye and so forth, not the innate nature (svabhāva). Again, this exposition accords with the [requirements of] trainees at particular times.

Elsewhere even the classification [or analysis = vibhaṅga°] of consciousness is not stated; only a list is given; namely, six classes of consciousness. The word 'class' (kāya) also refers to the different activities of eye consciousness and the rest toward their objects; namely, form and the rest. The [activity of] eye consciousness and the rest toward their objects, such as blue and the rest, is presented in multiple ways. Otherwise he [the Blessed One] would have spoken of six consciousnesses only, because it served no purpose to use the word 'class'.

In listing 'eye consciousness through mind° consciousness', the word 'six' is given only for enumeration and not for explanation. And why in listing the class of eye consciousness through the class of mind consciousness is no explanation given? Reply: through enumeration the differences in the activities regarding objects are shown as well. This is to clarify that there is no 'class' separate from consciousness.

In other places, concerning eye consciousness through mind consciousness it is said, "Specific recognition of form based on the eye is eye consciousness." Likewise it is said elsewhere that
the [specific] recognition of sound, odor, taste, touch and mental 118
objects based on ear, nose, tongue, body and mind° is ear-consciousness and so forth. And why is this not stated in the Sūtra here? [Reply:] It should be implied.

[Question:] Elsewhere it is stated that rebirth consciousness is conditioned by karma formations. According to scripture, "The aggregates at conception [relinking birth] are consciousness."[29] [Reply:] In accord with actions, there is linking of consciousness in the next birth. It is also said in a Sūtra:

"Ānanda, if consciousness were not to descend into the mother's womb, would name and form be constituted in the embryonic stage of kalala?"

"No, Lord."[30]

Consciousness, however, is here to be taken as mind consciousness. According to scripture, "Breaking up, reunion [taking up again], detachment, loss, death, and rebirth are all [properly] considered mind consciousness.[31]

[Question]: Here in [this Sūtra] in the analysis of mind consciousness, it is said, 'What is consciousness? It is six classes of consciousness.' [However,] the rebirth bond is concerned with the mind consciousness, not with six [classes of consciousness). How can this view go unopposed?

[Reply:] There is no point of opposition. In [explaining] the classification of consciousness, the Blessed One has divided the

whole complex of consciousness. As 'conditioned by karma formations', it should be understood in the context of [literally, as far as possible] conception (pratisandhi). It is like the classification of name and form [that follows]. There, indeed°, it is said 'What is the material (rūpa)? Whatever is material, including the four great elements and all that is derived from the four great elements.' In this way the whole of the material is analyzed [lit-
119 erally, divided]. When name and form are presented as conditioned by consciousness, the presentation is as complete as possible.

Thus the explanation of the classification of constituents of consciousness is intentional, not definitive. The definitive [explanation] is given elsewhere.

The Sautrāntikas[32] maintain that there is no inconsistency because 'consciousness conditioned by karma formations' is intended to refer to the six classes of consciousness, and not only to the rebirth consciousness pervaded by (paribhāvita) karma formations.

The constituent of consciousness has been explained.

Subtopic Four: Name and Form

8 *"Name and form are conditioned by consciousness.*

"What is name?

"It is the four formless (mental) aggregates. What four? The aggregate of feeling, aggregate of perception, aggregate of karma for-
9 *mations, and aggregate of consciousness. This is 'name'.*

"What is form? Whatever is material includes four great elements and all that is derived from the four great elements. What four? The elements of earth, water, fire, and air.

"What is the earth element? That which has heaviness and hardness. What is the water element? That which is fluid and drenched. What is the fire element? That which is hot and cooks. What is the air element? That which is compressible, can spread, and has lightness and motion.

"This, the material, and the former, the mental, are both called collectively 'name and form'."

After explaining the constituent of consciousness, the constituent of 'name and form' is presented. Name and form are conditioned by consciousness. It is stated in this way: "Through consciousness are conditioned name and form."[33]

The word 'name' (nāma) is used in the sense of 'appellation' (adhivacana), [but] it can also refer to the unassociated (viprayukta) categories of dharmas and to the four formless [mental] skandhas. Hence the question: 'What is name?' To exclude the unassociated categories, it is explained as four formless skandhas. [As for 'name' as] appellation, according to the Sautrāntika view [literally, method (naya)], since it is of the nature of speech it is included in form (rūpa). According to the view of the Vaibhāṣikas[34], since it is an unassociated category, it comes under karma formations.[35]. But in the Sūtra, the whole of nāma [i.e., mental categories] is conditioned by consciousness, and not only appellation.

'Feeling, perception, and so forth'. Such experiences as happi- 120
ness [unhappiness, and neutral feeling] are feelings (vedanā). The grasping of characteristics is perception. The aggregate of karma formations includes other mental states (caitasika dharmas) and unassociated [dharmas]. Consciousness is the apprehension of the object.

Why are all non-material aggregates called name? Because they are saturated with craving (tṛṣṇā) and bend toward defiled karma. It further signifies 'going to the next rebirth'. Again, it is called 'name' because it bends towards the object—form, etc.—or because it refers to grasping the modes (ākāra) of objects.

In the scriptures whatever belong to form is called 'material'. Therefore, the reply to the question, 'What is form?' is 'Whatever is material.' The explanation 'Whatever is [material]' shows that there is no form other than the physical (inanimate) element (bhūta) and that which belongs to it (bhautika°).

121 'Derived from' means having as a cause, as when some says that fire derives from fuel, conveying that fire has fuel as its cause. Similarly the words 'derived from the great [primary] elements' convey that the four great elements are the cause. The five skandhas (aggregates) are called 'name and form conditioned by consciousness' when in the embryonic stages of kalala°, arbuda, ghana, peśī, śākhā, and praśākhā, the six sense fields are in an undeveloped stage.

The material elements [or matter = bhūtani] are [now] stated: 'What are the material elements?' The reply: the elements of earth and so forth. The choice of the word 'dhātu' (element) excludes visible matter (rūpa) whose nature is to have the color or shape of earth or any other [element]. 'Dhātu' is so called because it bears its own [unique] characteristics as well as [those of] derived matter. In [the phrase] 'and the element of air', the word 'ca' (and) is used to limit [the enumeration].

The great [primary] elements (mahābhūta) are four only—
122 not three or five. This is due to purposelessness and incapacity: It is like the legs of a bed [where four legs will suffice].

Not understanding the own-nature [of the elements], the question is put, 'What is the earth element?' The reply: 'Whatever has heaviness.' Heaviness is derived matter. Since [the meaning] may not be understood [from this single word], the synonym 'hardness' [is given], meaning toughness.

'Light' refers to the element of air, which has the characteristic of lightness, which is also derived matter (upādāyarūpa); through its activity [functioning] the nature of the air element is expressed. Whatever has the nature of lightness, has air as its [primary] element of air, for lightness is its derived matter.

This name and form are both put in the same place. This shows their togetherness.

Now, it may be asked: Subsequent to the moment of rebirth, name and form are conditioned by name and form; how [can it be said] they are conditioned by consciousness? Reply: In the constituents [of conditioned co-production], conditionality is not indicated as to moments of the same kind but rather as to [moments of] different kinds. Otherwise it could [always] be said that ignorance is conditioned by ignorance and consciousness by consciousness.

Name and form have been explained.

Subtopic Five: The Six Sense Fields

"The six sense fields are conditioned by name and form. 9

"What are these six sense fields?

"The six internal sense fields: eye, ear, nose, tongue, body and mind. These are the six sense fields."

After the explanation of name and form come the [six] sense 123
fields (ṣaḍ āyatana): 'Conditioned by name and form', etc.

In the Sūtra it is stated, 'The six sense fields are conditioned by name and form.' 'Name and form' are of two kinds: internal and external. To exclude the external, it is said, 'six internal sense-fields'. The meaning of 'sense field' has been explained above.

Now, it may be asked: Since the possibility of the sense fields of body (kāya) and mind (manas) is present in the state of 'name and form' from the time of conception, how can it be maintained that six sense fields are conditioned by name and form? It should be stated that only four sense fields are conditioned.

[Reply:] This [objection] is well-taken, but it has been stated [in this way] to complete the series [set] of supports (āśraya°) and that which is supported (āśrita). The sense field of the body will be complete only when the eye and the other [sense organs] supported by the body have been produced. And being the entry (dvāra) of support [= body], the sense field of the mind is also complete. When the sense field of mind takes form as six kinds of consciousness, then the supports—the eye, etc.—are complete. The meaning is that [then] it is possible to have a full-fledged [complex of] supports [with all the sense organs produced].

The six sense fields have been explained.

Subtopic Six: Contact

10 *"Contact is conditioned by the six sense-fields.*

"What is contact?

"The six classes of contact are eye contact, ear contact, nose contact, tongue contact, body contact and mind contact. This is contact."

124 Next is the explanation of contact (sparśa°). Hence it is stated: 'Contact is conditioned by the six sense fields. It is said, 'Contact is conditioned through the six sense fields'.[36]

Contact, however, is referred to in scripture both as 'the tangible' (sparṣṭavya), and as a mental state (caitasika) characterized by coming together (saṅgati). From this it cannot be determined which 'contact' is conditioned by the six sense fields. To determine [this], it is said: 'Six kinds of contact'.

Within this division, a further question is asked: What six? The reply: 'Eye contact . . . through mind contact'. Here the Blessed One has explained contact by categorizing it in terms of the eye and so forth, dividing it in terms of the support (āśraya°) and so forth. [He does] not explain its innate nature. This explanation is frequently given, in view of the disposition of trainees at a particular time. As to the innate nature of [contact], this has been stated elsewhere: "Whatever is the aggregate of feeling, aggregate of perception, aggregate of karma formations, all this is conditioned by contact."[37]

[Question:] If [contact] is not perceived by mind as are feeling and the others, how is it apprehended? [Reply:] Like the eye, in view of the statement in the scriptures, "What is eye? It is the sensitive material element°, the support of eye-consciousness."

[Question:] But the characteristic of sensitivity is not apprehended. [Reply:] Although it is acquired by class of consciousness and is not apprehended, [it] is known by its own group [of elements] (svayūthya°) . [Contact is to be taken] in the same way.

125 The innate nature of contact is [again] stated by the Blessed One in the scriptures:

"Conditioned by the eye and form, eye consciousness is produced. The coming together (saṅgati), meeting (samavāya), and assembly (sannipāta) of those three is contact."

This is a metaphor for [discovering] the effect in the cause, as in the expression, 'the fire is happiness'.[38] This is a refutation of those who consider 'contact' a category apart from [the coming together of the three]. It should be understood that the nature of contact is explained in taking it as [this] assemblage.

Here the Sūtra says 'contact of eye . . . through . . . contact of mind'. [The contacts] supported by the faculty of the eye and so forth, together with the [respective] encounters are called 'the five encounter contacts'. The encounter of the mind, [however,] is known as 'appellation (adhivacana) encounter'. It is called appellation encounter because the activity of mind-consciousness is in relation to expression [or speech] towards their objects, not [in relation to the] five [other] classes of consciousness. The contact 126
associated with it is mind contact. The former is strongly activated by support; the latter by association (samprayoga).[39]

'Contact' has been explained.

Subtopic Seven: Feeling

"Feeling is conditioned by contact. *10*

"What is feeling?

"There are six classes of feeling. Feeling that arises through eye contact is of three kinds: pleasurable, painful, and neutral. Similarly, feeling arising through the contact of ear, nose, tongue, body, and mind is pleasurable, painful, and neutral. This is feeling."

Next, the explanation of feeling (vedanā), [starting] with the words, 'Feeling is conditioned by contact.'

[In the Sūtra] it is declared, 'Feeling is conditioned by contact.' [And] feeling is of three kinds. What [sort] of feeling conditioned by contact is intended here? The reply: 'six classes of feeling'. What six? The reply: 'Feeling produced by contact of eye

. . . through . . . produced by contact of mind.' Here the classification of feeling is explained rather than its nature, with regard for trainees uncertain as to the classification. [As for] the nature of feeling, it has already been discussed.[40]

As was said earlier, eye-consciousness arises conditioned by eye and material form, through the coming together of three factors. The feeling produced in this way is called feeling born of contact of eye. And this is of three kinds. 'Pleasurable' (sukhā)
127 means agreeable: that which is favorable to the sense organs and the primary elements. 'Painful' means disagreeable: hurting to the primary elements. 'Neutral' (aduḥkhāsukhā) is opposed to both. The same applies to the ear and the rest.

'Pleasurable [feeling] produced by contact of mind'. Due to the characteristic of being agreeable, gladness is produced, as indicated by the word 'happiness' (sukhā). 'Painful' means that which has the characteristic of being disagreeable; that is, what is unpleasant.

[Question:] If there are three [kinds] of feelings, this contradicts what the Blessed One has stated in another Sūtra: "Whatever is felt here [in this world] is all pain." [Reply:] There is no contradiction. [This statement] is said with specific intention (abhiprāya). And what is the intention? [The Sūtra explains it:]

"Ānanda, concerning the impermanence of compounded things (saṁskāras), concerning their being subject to change, I have said that whatever is felt here, is all pain."

The gāthā (verse) says this as well:

Having known the impermanence of compounded things,
as well as their being subject to change, the perfect Buddha,
who wisely knows, has declared feeling to be pain.

128 Thus the Blessed One himself has indicated his intention. Accordingly, there is no innate painfulness of pleasurable and neutral feelings. Only intentionally [i.e., for a particular purpose] has their painfulness been indicated.

Feeling has been explained.

Subtopic Eight: Craving

"Craving is conditioned by feeling. 10

"What is craving?

"There are six classes of craving: craving for form, craving for sound, craving for smell, craving for taste, craving for touch, and craving for mental objects."

After feeling comes the opportunity of [explaining] craving (tṛṣṇā). Thus it is said: 'Craving is conditioned by feeling.'

[Now, as to] the phrase 'craving conditioned by feeling'. According to its support, [craving] is of six kinds. In another Sūtra it is [said to be] of three kinds: craving for sense pleasures, craving for existence, and craving for non-existence.[41] And according to its object (ālambana), it is of six kinds. Since it is not apparent what sort of craving is conditioned by feeling, it is said that there are six classes of craving.

Here also, in view of the particular types of trainees, the Blessed One has explained the divisions of craving with reference to attachment to form and the other objects, rather than [explaining] its innate nature. Elsewhere it is stated that the nature of all kinds [of craving] is attachment (abhiṣvaṅga°). This attachment is a constant activity (pravṛtti°) of the mind continuum with regard to material form and the other objects. It results from craving. Without attachment, no such activity is produced. It [attachment] is absent in those who have eradicated craving.

[Question:] If craving is conditioned by feeling, then since everyone experiences feeling, the occasion (prasaṅga) will arise for an Arhat also to experience craving. [Reply:] This is not the case. If rain is conditioned by clouds, and if clouds form, will it
necessarily rain? Similarly, though feeling arises, it is not neces- 129
sary that craving will follow.

Why is this so? Because the opponent force [or adversary] has been destroyed. Here the particular opponent is the seed of craving. [Once this] is uprooted, then in spite of the existence of feeling, the non-existence of any seed means that [craving] is not produced. An analogy: Though the conditions such as [fertile] fields are present, the sprout will not grow in the absence of the seed.

Elsewhere the Blessed One has stated that craving is born conditioned by feeling produced by its association with ignorance. Its absence is because it is not produced when it is not associated with ignorance[42], for the opponent forces have been removed. Therefore, craving does not arise in an Arhat.

Now, why is it not also specifically stated here that craving is conditioned by feeling produced by its association with ignorance? Because ignorance is the general condition of karma formations. [Thus] the significance of this statement is known in that context elsewhere.

[Question:] If craving is conditioned by feeling, why has the Blessed One elsewhere declared it to be conditioned by ignorance: "Ignorance, monks, is the cause (hetu) of craving; ignorance is the condition (pratyaya) of craving; ignorance is the origin (nidāna) of craving." Again, at another place contact is declared [the condition]: "Craving is produced by contact of the eye." Yet here it is said to be conditioned by feeling. How can there be no inconsistency?

[Reply:] There is no [inconsistency]. The difference is one of intention (abhisandhibheda°). Ignorance and contact are named as general conditions. Ignorance is the general cause of all crav-
130 ings in all the different realms (dhātu), stages (bhūmi), and destinies (gati), and also [the general cause] of all the other defilements. In this regard it has been stated, "Ignorance, monks, is the cause of craving."

Contact[43] is likewise a general cause of craving, for all the mental states (caitasikas) are general [common] conditions. As has been stated: "Craving is born of the six contacts, starting with the eye." Thus contact is also stated to be the cause of craving.

Feeling [on the contrary] is intended as a special condition, for the cause of craving for the realm of desire is a feeling for that realm, and [likewise] the cause of craving for the first stage of dhyāna [in the realm of form] is feeling for that stage. In each stage, feeling—divided into weak, [medium, and strong] by reason of a particular craving being activated—should be understood to be intended as a special condition.

[The constituent of] craving has been explained.

Subtopic Nine: Clinging

"Clinging is conditioned by craving. 10

"What is clinging?

"There are four kinds of clinging. What four? Clinging to sense desires, clinging to views, clinging to ceremonial practices and observances, and clinging to belief in the existence of the self."

Now the explanation of clinging (upādāna°), [introduced with] the statement, 'Clinging is conditioned by craving.'

Clinging, which is said to be conditioned by craving, is fourfold: clinging to sense pleasures, clinging to [wrong] views, clinging to ceremonial practices and observances, and clinging to belief in the existence of a self.

Commonly, clinging is known as that which grasps things to possess them. [To explain] what 'clinging conditioned by craving' is intended [as] here, it is said, 'four kinds of clinging' and so forth. Clinging is what takes hold of or grasps rebirth or continuity of mind in the world of sense desires.

What are the four clingings? Clinging to sense desires . . . through . . . clinging to belief in the existence of a self.

'Clinging to sense desires'. Attachment, hatred (pratigha), pride, ignorance to be abandoned by insight (darśana) and meditation (bhāvanā), four doubts to be abandoned by insight, and 131
ten outbursts [of defilements] (paryavasthānas°): These constitute clinging to sense desires.

'Clinging to [wrong] views'. Seeing individuality as eternal, holding extreme views (antagrāhadṛṣṭi)[44], and clinging to the

esteeming of wrong views (dṛṣṭiparāmarśa)[45] in all the three
132 realms (kāma, rūpa and ārūpya): These constitute clinging to [wrong] views.

'Clinging to ceremonial practices and observances' (śīlavratopādāna°). The esteeming of ceremonial practices and observances belonging to the three realms. Śīla (morality) is abstinence from immorality. Vrata (religious observance) is restraining the action of body and tongue as well as non-indulgence in wrong practice and the wearing of [special] dress and ornaments.[46]

133 Why is clinging to ceremonial practices and observances separately mentioned, distinguishing it from clinging to [wrong] views? Reply: This is to contrast the path (mārga) to the paths of the Sāṁkhya, Yoga, Jñāna[47], and others, which present an attainment of liberation that deludes householders as well as recluses. Householders are deluded [into thinking] that fasting leads to the path of heaven, while recluses [think] that by renouncing agreeable things one restores purity. Hence fasting and the like[48] are included in ceremonial practices and observances.

134 'Clinging to belief in the existence of the self'. This constitutes lust (rāga°), pride, and ignorance belonging to the realm of form and the formless realm, to be abandoned by insight and meditation as well as eight doubts to be abandoned by insight. This is clinging to belief in the existence of the self.[49]

The [constituent of] clinging has been explained.

Subtopic Ten: Becoming

11 *"Becoming is conditioned by clinging.*

"What is the process of becoming?

"There are three processes of becoming. What three? Coming to be in the realm of sense desire, coming to be in the realm of form, and coming to be in the formless realm.

"What is coming to be in the realm of sense desires?

"[First] there is coming to be in the eight hot hells. What eight? Samjīva, the hell where pain revives; Kālasūtra, the black-string hell; Saṅghāta, the hell of intense oppression; Raurava, the hell that causes screaming and weeping; Mahāraurava, the hell of intense screaming and weeping; Tāpana, the heater hell, Pratāpana, the intense heater hell, and Avīci, the hell of endless torture.

"There is also coming to be in the eight cold hells: Arbuda, where tumors form due to the cold; Nirarbuda, where a multitude of tumors form due to the cold; Aṭaṭa hell; Hahava hell; Huhava hell; Utpala, the hell of blue lotus-like ulcers; Padma, the hell of red lotus-like ulcers; and Mahāpadma, the hell of great lotus-like ulcers.

"Also within the realm of sense desire are ghosts, animals, human beings, and the six classes of desire-realm gods. What are the six classes of gods? The four great kings, the thirty-three gods, the Yāmas, the gods of Tuṣita paradise, the Nirmāṇaratis, and the Paranirmitavaśavartins.

"And what is coming to be in the form realm? Among the gods 12
of this realm are the Brahmakāyikā, who belong to the company of Brahmā; the Brahmapurohitā, who serve as priests of Brahmā; the Mahābrahmā gods, who follow Mahābrahmā; the Parīttābhā gods, whose splendor is limited; the Apramāṇābhā gods, whose splendor is immeasurable; the Ābhāsvarā gods, who shine in splendor; the Parīttaśubhā gods, who are limited in auspiciousness, the Apramāṇaśubhā gods, who are unlimited in auspiciousness;[50] *the Śubhakṛtsnā gods, who are wholly auspicious; the Anabhrakā, gods of the cloudless heaven; the Puṇyaprasavā; gods of virtuous birth; the Bṛhatphalā, gods of great reward; the Abṛhā gods, whose greatness is limited; the Atapā gods, of serenity; the Sudṛśā, gods of excellent appearance; the Sudarśanā, gods excellent to gaze upon; and the Akaniṣṭhā, highest of the gods.*

"And what is coming to be in the formless realm? This is as follows: the sphere of infinity of space, the sphere of infinity of consciousness, the sphere of nothingness, and the sphere of neither perception nor non-perception. For the gods of the formless realm, who take consciousness alone as the object of meditation,

there are thus four kinds of existence.[51] *This is called the formless existence°.*

"These are the three kinds of becoming."

After explaining clinging, the constituent of becoming (bhava°) is elucidated, [introduced by the phrase], 'Becoming is conditioned by clinging'. What is becoming? The answer is given: 'Becoming is conditioned by clinging.'

Becoming [in general], without any classification, refers to the five aggregates of clinging. In another Sūtra, it is stated there are seven different kinds of becoming [existences], beginning with existence in hell, etc.[52] Therefore, the word 'becoming' does not establish which kind of existence is indicated. [To clarify], it is replied, 'There are three kinds of becoming.'

What three? The reply: The realm of sense desires (kāmabhava), etc. Existence in the realm of sense desires refers to existence associated with sense desires. [A grammatical clarification:] The middle term 'associated with' (-pratisaṁyuka) is dropped [in compound phrases], as in the phrase 'black pepper drink', meaning 'drink associated with black pepper (marīcapānaka)'.
135 Similarly, existence (bhava) associated with the realm of form and with the formless realm are called respectively existence in the form realm and existence in the formless realm.

The classification of existence into the desire realm and so on has been given, but not its innate nature. To clarify its nature, the question is put: 'What is coming to be in the desire realm?' The reply: [There are] eight hot hells. Here the word 'hot' is used to separate; there are cold hells also, which will be designated subsequently.

A hell is [a realm] to which beings are led [taken] due to their demerits (apuṇya).[53]

'Saṁjīva', etc. The hell where airs bring the dying back to life is Saṁjīva, the Fresh Revival Hell. In Kālasūtra, the Black String
136 Hell, beings are ripped apart by black strings that descend upon them.[54] In Saṅghāta, Intense Oppressor Hell, mountains in the

form of rams fall down from both sides, tormenting beings.
Raurava, the Hell of Screams and Weeping is one where beings 137
are made to fall and cry to excess. In Mahāraurava Hell, this occurs still more. In Tapana, the Heater Hell, beings are burnt by blazing fire and other torments; when this is done still more strongly, it is Pratāpana Hell. Avīci Hell is where beings encircled by the flames of hellfire have not [the slightest] interval of happiness.[55]

What are the eight cold hells? 'Arbuda', etc. Those born in 138
Arbuda, the Tumor Hell, have tumorous ulcers on the body due to the cold. In Nirarbuda, the Hell of Profuse Tumors, the quantity of ulcers is multiplied. In Aṭaṭa° Hell, [beings] seized with
cold make sounds with no control over their tongues. In the 139
Hahava° and Huhava° Hells, uncontrollable sounds come from the innermost part of the tongue. In the Utpala°, [Padma, and Mahāpadma] Hells, the flesh and bones of the body crack open in shapes that look like flowers: the blue lotus (utpala) and so forth. Thus, [all] these hells are named for the bodily and vocal deformities [of those born there].

Preta (ghosts) are those who, having fallen from here, have gone and shall not return. Again, pretas are so called because they are always consumed by thirst. Animals are beings that do not stand erect [literally, who walk horizontally]. According to scripture, human beings (manuṣya) are those who are born from mind (manas). According to the popular view, human beings are the progeny of Manu°.

'The six classes of desire-realm gods (devas)'. Devas° are so 140
called due to their radiance.

[The classification of devas:]

Cāturmahārājikā (retinue of four great kings).[56] The four great kings, protectors of world, are Virudhaka, Virūpākṣa, Dhṛtarāṣṭra and Vaiśravaṇa.[57] Those who are among them are called 'Cāturmahārājikā'; this is like the expression 'He is born in devas', meaning he is born among the devas. [The expression thus refers to] those devas who are in the seat of four great kings, with the middle word being elided. Others explain this through the example of the word 'cow cart' (goratha).[58]

Trayastriṁśā. Gods who do good deeds collectively and are born in the [Heaven of the Thirty-Three (Trayastriṁśa)].[59] Among them are eight Vasus, two Aśvinikumāras, eleven Rudras, and twelve Ādityas. According to the popular view, it is only because of the eminence of these gods that this Heaven is [known as] the Heaven of the Thirty-Three. They are spoken of accordingly in the scriptures as well.

141 Yāmā. [Devas] who reach [the god realms] according to their merit. Again, those are called Yāmā who in each watch of the day or night (yāma°) proclaim, "What happiness! What happiness!"

Tuṣitā.[60] Those endowed with happiness and satisfaction or in whom happiness is born are called 'The Contented Ones' (Tuṣitā), 'Those Delighting in Creations' (Nirmāṇarati). They delight in objects of enjoyment that they themselves create.

Paranirmitavaśavartin. Their characteristic is to bring under control objects of enjoyments created by others.

[Now, regarding those who come to be in the realm of form:]

Namely, the Brahmakāyika gods. Brahmā is so called because of being perfectly skilled in [perfecting] vast [numbers of] roots of wholesome actions (kuśalamūla). And who is this [Brahmā]? He is [also] called Mahābrahmā, for he has gained intermediary dhyānas,[61] and because [in this world] he is the last to die and the first to take birth. The assembly of Brahmā is known as the Brahmakāyika, and comprises a body vast in dimension.

142 Brahmapurohitā°. As they are placed before Brahmā [as his ministers or counselors], they are called Brahmapurohitā.

Mahābrahmāṇaḥ. They belong to the company of Mahābrahmā, who is distinguished from others by special features such as age, color, and power.

Parittābhā (of limited splendor). Their splendor is limited in comparison to their position.[62]

Apramāṇābhā. The range of their splendor is impossible to measure.

Ābhāsvarā. They are called Ābhāsvarā gods because they flash radiance in all directions, illuminating all locations.

Parīttaśubhā (gods of limited auspiciousness). The mental 143
happiness on [reaching] this stage is called auspicious (śubha°). The auspiciousness [of these gods] is limited in comparison to their position.

Apramāṇaśubhā°. The auspiciousness of [these gods] is unlimited.

Śubhakṛtsnā. [These gods are] wholly auspicious; hence they are called Śubhakṛtsnā. This signifies that there is no higher happiness anywhere.

Anabhrakā. The gods [float] like clouds, never in contact with the earth. Hence they are Anabhrakā gods, the Cloudless heaven gods. According to scriptures, celestial palaces appear and disappear with their coming into being and [their disappearance].[63]

Puṇyaprasavā. Gods of virtuous birth, who take birth from imperturbable (āniñja) karma. Their birth (prasava°) is due to merit.[64]

Bṛhatphalā. Gods destined to take birth in an ordinary place [among ordinary beings], who nonetheless obtain the great and best reward.

Abṛhā (not great). From Abṛhā to Akaniṣṭha, there are five stages of pure abode (śuddhāvāsa). Śuddhāvāsa is so called because those belonging to this stage are not corrupted by contact with ordinary beings and their abode is pure. Their greatness does not exceed that of the Śuddhāvāsa stage, and this is
why they are called Abṛhā. Again, they are called Abṛhā° because 144
they do not leave their abode [for even a short time].

Atapā. The gods who acquire through special samādhi immunity from the searing heat of the defilements are called the Atapā° gods.

Sudṛśā. Those who through pure vision see rightly are [called] Sudṛśā gods.

Sudarśanā. Gods in this realm are delightful in appearance.

Akaniṣṭhā. There being no higher stage than this, the gods of this realm, being the eldest, are call the Akaniṣṭhā.

[As for coming to be in the formless realm, first there is] the realm of infinity of space. [This is the realm of becoming of those] who attain through practice of higher meditation (samā-
145 patti) the [clear] vision (ākāra°), "Space is infinite! Space is infinite!" and make this their abode (āyatana).

(Vijñānānantyāyatana). Similarly at the time of the practice of attainment, there are those who attain the clear vision, "Consciousness is infinite! Consciousness is infinite!" and make this their abode.

(Ākiñcanyātana): The abode of those who when practicing attainment have the intense thought (manasikāra),[65] "There is nothingness!"

(Naivasaṁjñānāsaṁjñāyatana). The abode of those who produce a dull perception of 'the realm of neither perception nor non-perception'. [They think as follows:] "Perception is a boil,
146 perception is a dart,[66] and non-perception is a delusion (saṁmoha) as well.[67]

[This concludes the account of the god realms.]

This is 'becoming (bhava) conditioned by clinging'.

Here the word 'bhava' signifies the fruit of action as a future existence in the triple world (traidhātuka). [Etymologically explained], 'becoming' or 'existence' is that which rebirth [immediately] follows, as a vehicle (vaha) is that which carries [anything).[68] Another Sūtra states:

147 "Whatever deed, Ānanda, produces rebirth in the future, is of the nature of bhava.[69] It is said in the Prakaraṇas[70] also:

"What is existence linked to sense desires (kāmabhava)? The deed associated with sense desires conditioned by clinging produces a new existence. What is existence linked to form (rūpa-bhava)? The deed associated with form, conditioned by clinging, produces a new existence. What is existence without form (ārūpya-bhava)? The deed associated with the formless, conditioned by clinging, produces a new existence."

Therefore, [in this quotation the reference to] kāmabhava, etc. indicates the fruit of action as a future existence in the triple world. The explanation of the place of rebirth is to show the different deeds [producing] rebirth.

[Question:] If bhava is of the nature of karma, what is the difference between saṁskāras (karma formations) and bhava? [Reply:] Karmas relating to the past are saṁskāras and those relating to the present are bhava. This is the difference between the two.

The constituent of becoming has been explained.

Subtopic Eleven: Birth

"Through becoming, birth is conditioned. What is birth? That which, for various beings and groups of being, progresses through conception, production, coming into existence, descent, rebirth,
appearance, obtaining aggregates, obtaining elements, obtaining 13
sense fields, reproduction of aggregates, production of vital organs, and the coming together of similar species. This is birth."

After exposition of the constituent of becoming, the explanation of birth (jāti) is introduced with the words, 'Through becoming, birth is conditioned. The phrase 'for them (various beings)' refers to different beings, distinguished in terms of realm, destiny, (gati), place of birth, and personality [individuality = ātma-bhāva]. The phrase 'various groups of beings' refers to the particular origin [or birth] taken by beings, as for example the gods.

The words 'conception (jāti), production (saṁjāti), and so on' are synonyms uttered to show specific stages [in the process of birth]. When one is thrown [into the world], there comes first the arising in the mother's womb of name and form, with [the

skandha] of feeling the final element. At this point one is born into a particular class of beings, and this is called birth.[71] [Next
148 comes] the completion of name and form, which is termed production. [The usage here is] similar to the popular expression which designates as one endowed with full power one in whom power is fully produced (saṁjātabala).

Upapatti (coming into existence) is reaching the specific state of embodiment with name and form complete. Avakrānti (descent into the womb) is attaining the specific stage of possessing all the remaining sense organs. Abhinirvṛtti (rebirth) is birth (nirvṛtti°)—coming out of the mother's womb—when the [newly born] being, already endowed with the six āyatanas, comes face to face with object[ive reality] and apprehends it: It is emerging (prasava) from the womb [or uterus]. Prādurbhāva (appearance) is to be [in the world] after being born. When these aspects of birth (janma) have come together (saṅgrahīta), the process of birth is fully accomplished. These are the characteristics of the different stages of birth.

149 The particular (sva) characteristic of birth is obtaining one's own individual being (ātmabhāva°) among beings (sattva). Personality or individual being is explained as 'obtaining the aggregates' and so forth. This ātmabhāva of beings has three aspects, [founded in] strong attachment (abhniveśa°) to the perception of [permanent] being in the continuity of aggregates and other [elements and sense fields].

To refute this threefold imaginary construct (kalpanā) of ātman or self as one, as embodied, and as apprehender of the object, the three categories of skandhas, [dhātus, and āyatanas] are employed. The acceptance of skandhas in the sense of heaps (rāśi) is to refute the imaginary construct of ātman as one (eka). The explanation (nirvacana°) of dhātu as just a state (dharmamātram) and as an empty element (tucchadhātu) is to refute the imaginary construct of ātman as embodied. Since the eye and other sense fields apprehend the object with no [separate] apprehender of an object, acceptance of the āyatanas is to refute the third imaginary construct of ātman as apprehender.

Having explained the characteristics of the different stages of birth, a brief explanation of the phrase 'reproduction of aggregates and production° of vital organs' (jīvitendriya) [is in order].

In this way even the characteristics of birth of beings born
from moisture and born through apparition[72] can be clarified. In
this context, to come forth into being refers to rebirth. The 'life 150
faculty' is the power through which deeds set in motion in a previous existence link being of the same continuity [of mind] and the same class (sabhāgasantāna) and give birth to skandhas [that take form] in the same species of being and continue to act [in the present existence]. That state is called the life faculty.[73] Similarly, in brief, a linking in the same species of beings through conception in continuation [from the previous existence] is 'birth'.

[Question:] It may be right that in the five kinds [stages] of birth, the first stage of birth (conception) is conditioned by the process of becoming (bhava), and that after that each stage conditions the next stage. [In that case, however,] how can the successive stages be [said to be] conditioned by becoming? [Reply:] The 'process of becoming' has inherent in it the power to condition the first stage of birth. The different stages are specially conditioned by each other successively, although fundamentally they are conditioned by the process of becoming.

Birth has been explained.

Subtopic Twelve: Decay and Death

"Through birth, decay and death are conditioned. *13*

"What is decay° [or old age]?

"It is broken teeth, graying hair, a multitude of wrinkles in the skin, decrepitude, a stooped and bent posture, a rattling noise in the throat when breathing, black moles on the limbs, reliance on the support of a staff, the bending over of the body, ripening and disintegration of faculties, decay of karma formations, wreckage, blurring, sluggishness, wasting away, and loss. This is decay.

14 *"What is death?*

"It is the fall of beings from a group of similar species of being, the passing away, breaking up, disappearance, and demise, the completion of time span and finishing of age, the loss of vital heat, the cessation of vital faculties, the laying down of aggregates. This is death. Together with decay, it is known by the collective name, 'decay and death'.

"This, monks, is Twelvefold Conditioned Co-production."

151 Decay and death (jarāmaraṇa) are conditioned by birth. The explanation is given in the order the terms [appear in the Sūtra). Therefore, explaining decay (jarā°), it is asked: 'What is decay?' Loss of hair (khālitiya°), graying of hair and so on: eighteen different terms [expressing] the sevenfold changing nature of disintegration and decay (paribhedajarā°). The changing nature of form is seen by the loss of hair and its changing nature [i.e., change in color]. The term 'khālitya' refers to loss of hair.

[Question:] It is proper that a change in hair color [is seen as showing] the characteristic of change in material form in [regard to] disintegration and decay (paribhedajarā) because [it is said], "to alter is to change," and change is decay. But how can loss of hair [be seen as indicating] decay? Reply: Not due to loss of hair in itself, but because without change [or transformation] loss of hair does not occur.

'Wrinkles in the skin' refers to shrinkage of the skin, for wrinkles do not occur without shrinkage of the skin. 'Decrepitude' refers to phased disintegration, while 'curvature' refers to looseness of the flesh, meaning curvature of body. To illustrate the deformity in the shape of body, the phrase is used, 'stooped and bent posture like a rafter (gopānasī°). 'Gopānasī' is a wooden structure, curved like a bow, that supports a peaked roof. [The meaning is that] with old age, the body becomes like that. Others say that the term refers to a curved wooden beam used by cowherds for carrying things on the shoulders (gopālavāhiṅgikā°).

152 'Black moles'. This refers to an alteration in color. In old age such moles on the body are common.

'A rattling noise in the throat when breathing (khuru-khuru-praśvāsakāyatā°). This refers to wheezing [literally, 'breathing with excessive words']. [It] indicates a change in stamina.

'The unsteadiness [literally, 'leaning forward'] of the body'. This refers to the increased danger of falling while standing or moving. Here it refers to [falling] while standing.

'Reliance on the support of a staff'. This refers to [falling forward] while moving.

'Blurring' refers to the onset of dullness due to a change in the signs of wisdom. It is called blurring because one is unable to understand the meaning of words that are well-spoken and stainless [i.e., words of Dharma], and [cannot distinguish them from words] that are falsely spoken and impure. Also, one is incapable of knowing what should be done and what should not be done.

'Sluggishness' refers to the characteristic in disintegration and decay by a change in [the power of] recollection (smṛti-vipariṇāma), manifesting in quick forgetfulness and indistinct recollection.

'Loss' refers to loss of virility and sexual impotence, for [in advanced age] there is a loss of manliness and deprivation of pleasure and enjoyment in sexual intercourse.

'Decrease' refers to the mark of change in decay that manifests as loss of appetite and of pleasure and enjoyment of food.[74]

'Over-ripeness and disintegration of the sense faculties'. This refers to the marks of disintegration and decay that manifest as weakness in apprehending the object and [the resulting] loss. Disintegration is loss when it is not considered a part of decay. 'Disintegration' is synonymous with decay.

'Decay of karma formations.' This refers to the mark of a 153
change in the life-force[75] extending to the embrace of death. Therefore it is said, 'decay of karma formations'.

'Wreckage' refers to the inability to move even a little. This is said with regard to karma formations.

[Now, as to death]:

154 'What is death' (maraṇa)?' Here ten synonyms are given, [beginning with] 'fall' and 'passing away'.

'Fall' signifies a fall of being from a [particular] class of being and separation from that class of being (nikāyasabhāga). At the point of death one 'falls', and that is the fall. To be in this state is 'passing away' (cyavanatā).

'Breaking up' is the separation of the group of mental states from that of material states. What is its nature? The mutual responsiveness of receptivity and encounter with objects loses its efficacity.

'Disappearance' is the destruction of the organic sense faculties, as with the eye, the ear, and so on of a corpse.

'Loss of life and loss of vital heat'.[76] These terms indicate that at the time [of death] everything is completely destroyed in two successive stages.

155 [Now to explain the interrelation of these synonyms]: 'Breaking up' refers to the cessation of life set in motion by previous existence, while 'disappearance' refers to [loss of] the support of food; together, the two words show the meaning of the term 'fall'. The two phrases ['loss of life' and 'loss of vital heat'] show the meaning of 'passing away'. [More generally,] death signifies two states: the fall of a being whose life span has gradually ended and its passing away (cyavanatā). It is called cessation of the life faculty, [for] at that time a being with a residue of life suddenly dies[77] and the life faculty comes to an end. It is [also] called laying down the aggregates, [for] it is laying down the aggregates of the life faculty. Thus 'death' has been explained in brief.

[Question:] What is cessation of the life faculty? [Reply]: The 'fixed time [of death]'.[78] It refers to halting [literally, destroying] the momentum of the karma formations of life acquired from previous existence.

156 The constituent of decay and death has been explained.

Topic Six

The Four Noble Truths

"What are the Four Noble Truths? The Noble Truth of Suffering, 14
the Noble Truth of the Arising of Suffering, the Noble Truth of the
Cessation of Suffering, and the Noble Truth of the Path Leading to
the Cessation of Suffering."

After conditioned co-production, [the four noble] 'truths' (satya) 157
are explained, in accord with the list of topics (uddeśa). To
explain this, the question is put: 'What are the Four Noble
Truths?' [Reply:] They are the truths of the Noble Ones (āryas°);
therefore, they are called the 'noble truths' in the Sūtra itself.

[Question:] Are they not true for others? [Reply:] They are true
for all [beings], for they are not contrary (aviparīta°) [to what is].
However, they are seen rightly (yathā) by the Noble Ones; they 158
are not seen by others. Therefore they are called truths of the
Āryans, and not truths of the non-Āryans, who see quite contrary
[to what is]. As a verse [uttered by the Blessed One] states:

"What Noble Ones call 'happiness', others know as 'suffering';
what others call 'happiness', the Noble Ones know as 'suffering'."[79]

Now, what accounts for the order in which the truths [are presented], starting with 'suffering' and ending with 'path'? The
159 reply: The truth that is explained first is the truth that is the first to be realized (abhisamaya°). The order of explanation accords with the [manner of] realization.

[Question:] How is it that truth is realized in this sequence? Reply: One who is caught in suffering, is afflicted by it, and seeks deliverance from it, first examines it and afterwards [asks]: What is its cause (hetu)? This is the 'truth of arising'. Next [he asks]: what is its cessation (nirodha)? This is the 'truth of cessation'. Then [he asks]: What is the path? This is the 'truth of the path' (mārga). It is like recognizing [the symptoms of] a disease:[80] One searches for its origin (nidāna°), extinction , and remedy.

This simile for the truths is further explained in a Sūtra:

160 "A physician and surgeon deserves the king's favor, qualifies for the king's council, and is reckoned a member of the king's retinue when he is endowed with four qualities. And what are these four qualities? He is an expert in [diagnosing] disease, in the etiology of disease, in eradicating disease, and [in ways] to prevent the future occurrence of disease that has been eradicated. Likewise, the Tathāgata, the Arhat°, the Fully Awakened One (samyaksambuddha°) the incomparable physician and surgeon, is said to be endowed with four qualities. And what are these four? Here, monks, the Tathāgata, the Arhat, the Fully Awakened One knows truly (yathābhūtaṁ): This is the noble truth of suffering (duḥkhaṁ āryasatyaṁ); this is the arising of suffering; this is the cessation of suffering, and this is the noble truth of the path leading to the cessation of suffering."[81]

Subtopic One: The Truth of Suffering

"What, then, is the Noble Truth of Suffering? Birth is suffering, old age is suffering, disease is suffering, death is suffering, separation from what is pleasant is suffering, association with what is unpleasant is suffering. What one desires and searches for, if it is not obtained, is also suffering. In brief, all the aggregates of clinging are suffering. This is the Noble Truth of Suffering."

Birth is suffering because all karma formations (saṁskāras) are suffering. Decay [or old age] is suffering due to change (vipariṇāma = transformation). Disease is suffering because of the suffering inherent in suffering (duḥkhaduḥkhatā). The rest is clear. In brief, all the five aggregates of clinging are suffering because they are the outcome [of suffering] and are inseparable from [literally, sprinkled with (upamṛṣṭatvāt°)] the three [types of] suffering.

[Question:] Since suffering [or pain] is considered an aspect of feeling [and feeling is considered one of the skandhas], why are all the five skandhas called suffering? [Reply:] They are called suffering because they are associated with the three types of suf-
fering: suffering as suffering (duḥkhaduḥkhatā°); suffering born
of conditioned things (saṁskāraduḥkhatā); and suffering pro- 161
duced by change (vipariṇāmaduḥkhatā°).[82] It is due to [the respective operation of] these [three] that all the impure (sāsrava°) aggregates are called suffering.

[Question:] Since there is also happiness (sukha), why is suffering alone called a noble truth?[83] [Reply:] Because happiness is 162
of such short duration. Although a small proportion of green pulse (Hindi, mūṅga) is mixed in with a heap of black pulse (māṣa; Hindi, uḍada), the heap will [still] be called a heap of black pulse. [It may be asked:] What wise being would consider a wound as bringing happiness because it gives a slight joy to sprinkle it with water?[84]

The truth of suffering has been explained.

Subtopic Two: The Truth of the Arising of Suffering

"What is the Noble Truth of the Arising of Suffering? The crav- *15*
ing that leads to rebirth and is accompanied by pleasure and attachment, finding pleasure now here and now there. This is the Noble Truth of the Arising of Suffering."

Wishing to explain the truth of arising, the question is put, 'What is the Noble Truth of the Arising of Suffering?' The term 'arising' indicates that from which suffering arises. It refers to the universal production [of suffering]. The arising of suffering is 'arising suffering'; that is, the cause of suffering.

'The craving that leads to rebirth and is accompanied by pleasure and attachment.' [Here] 'rebirth' means birth in the future, and 'craving that leads to rebirth' refers to that which directs toward rebirth. 'Pleasure' refers to defiled joy. Attachment (rāga) is well known as a characteristic of addiction.

The craving that leads to rebirth is also known as the desire (prārthanā) to be reborn without any specification (abhedena); that is, the desire simply to become again, with no specification as to whether the birth shall be in the domain of humans or of
163 gods.[85] Craving is accompanied by pleasure and attachment when it is [directed] toward present objects of enjoyment for oneself, [associated] with pleasure and lust (nandīrāga), and is alternately activated and interrupted (vyavakīrṇatvāt°).

The word 'accompanied' indicates immediate succession. It means that pleasure is produced after attachment. [Grammatically,] this is like when the phrase 'cultivation of the enlightenment constituent of mindfulness' (smṛtisambodhyaṅga) [is joined with the term 'friendliness' in saying]: "He cultivates the enlightenment-constituent of mindfulness with friendliness." This is understood to mean that friendliness is cultivated in immediate succession [to mindfulness], for friendliness possesses outflows (sāsravatvāt) and mindfulness does not (anāsrava°), so that there can be no simultaneity of association (sahakālāyoga). [Similarly, craving and attachment cannot be simultaneous,] due to the antagonism of entities of the same species. [Rather,] pleasure and attachment are caused by craving, and since the latter is the [actual] cause of rebirth, it is said to be 'accompanied' by pleasure and attachment.

'Finding pleasure now here and now there' means [in general] longing to acquire a variety of unobtained enjoyments for oneself. It is explained as craving with the characteristic of longing for rebirth in which one wishes (prārthayate°) specifically for birth as a god or a human being.

[Question:] But (nanu°) in another Sūtra, the Blessed One has declared karma° to be the truth of the arising [of suffering]. How can this [be true for] both karma and craving? [Reply:] Ignorance (avidyā) is the cause of karma formations [that arise] in a future state of birth, for ignorance and other [defilements] are the cause of future birth. And the cause is [called] 'the arising'. 164

Again, it has been declared by the Blessed One:

"Monks, five types of seed—those which are not smashed, intact, not rotten (apūtīni°), unharmed by wind and heat, and not without sap—when well-embedded [in the soil][86] become the earth element, water element, and fire element. Seeds of this type grow, develop and increase.[87] Monks, this simile has been employed to express the meaning of this [declaration regarding karma]."

Here the meaning should be understood as follows: 'Five types of seed' refers to consciousness associated with clinging. The earth element refers to the four abodes of consciousness. 'Seed' refers to a cause. And that which is a cause is the arising. 165
Thus, the abodes of consciousness (vijñānasthiti°) are the causes of firm grounding (pratiṣṭhāhetu).

[Question:] As it is established in the scriptures that karma and ignorance and [other defilements] are the cause of the truth of arising, why in [this] Sūtra is craving alone given as the truth of arising? [Reply:] [The point] is well taken, but the statement here is given in this way because craving is the main cause. Moreover, [only] karma saturated with craving has the power to 166
throw one into a new birth, not karma alone. When one is cast into a new birth, craving is the root (mūla). Therefore it is a special cause (viśeṣa pratyaya°), while ignorance and karma are general causes, for latent defilements cannot be present without delusion. Thus, in the three realms of existence Arhats possess no karma which is not of unfixed nature (aniyatavedanīya),[88] but due to the absence of craving karmas have no power to effect rebirth. This is the reason it is stated [in the scriptures] that the roots of existence are latent defilements (anuśaya).[89]

Subtopic Three: The Truth of Cessation

15 *"What is the Noble Truth of the Cessation of Suffering? Complete abandonment and relinquishment, bringing to an end, destruction, removal of attachment, cessation, quietude, disappearance of that very craving which leads to rebirth and is accompanied by pleasure and attachment, finding pleasure now here and now there. This is the Noble Truth of the Cessation of Suffering."*

Next, to explain the truth of cessation, the question is put: What is the Noble Truth of the Cessation of Suffering? The cessation of suffering is 'suffering-cessation', signifying the abandonment of those things with outflows. The explanation of the concluding terms [from 'craving which leads to rebirth'] is as given in the previous topic.

From 'complete abandonment' through 'disappearance' there are eight terms. 'Complete abandonment' is the indication in
167 brief (uddeśa°); the rest is exposition (nirdeśa). How so? Because it sets forth the abandonment of all the states (avasthā) of craving. This is the meaning of 'relinquishment'. The total abandonment of all [such] states means their removal. 'They are being relinquished' is equivalent to 'They are being removed'. 'Removal' signifies throwing off by averting regenerated defilement.

'Bringing to an end' signifies setting an obstruction through the state pertaining to penetration and the like.[90] [Again], 'bringing to an end' signifies 'subduing'.

'Destruction' (kṣaya) refers to the path of vision (darśanamārga). As with the maxim on breaking the slab of stone (śilābhaṅganyāya),[91] [destruction refers to] the states to be abandoned by vision. [In the same way], 'removal of attachment' (virāga) refers to the path of meditation (bhāvanāmārga), for here attachment is completely removed. And 'cessation' (nirodha) refers to the path of the one who no longer needs training (aśaikṣa),[92] because the latent defilements have been abandoned without any remainder.

'Quietude' (vyupaśama) signifies [not only] the absence of any
168 veil or obstruction (āvarṇa) to higher meditative attainment

(samāpatti) [but also] the absence of even those obstructions that are free from defilements (akliṣṭa). It is absolute calm. (Finally,) 'disappearance' indicates the absence of any clinging or attachment (upadhi°)

[Question: Why are so many terms required? Reply:] No one term can show all the different states of abandonment.

Other masters interpret some of these terms differently. 'Relinquishment' is explained as nirvāṇa, through whose realization the accumulation of all latent defilements is relinquished. 'Bringing to an end' [is said to] signify a precise end, meaning thereby the end of the continuity of becoming. [Here] 'bringing to an end' means that what has no end comes to an end: This is nirvāṇa. 'Cessation' is understood as abandonment of whatever has the characteristics of the five aggregates of clinging, while 'quietude' signifies that through its attainment all forms of distress are specifically and wholly quieted.

[In this view,] 'disappearance' refers to the absence of all that is conditioned or non-conditioned, what is pure as well as what is impure, for it is said in a Sūtra:

"As [explained] in the parable of a raft, those who have learnt the Dharma teaching (dharmaparyāya) should abandon even good things (dharmas), all the more evil ones (adharmas)"[93]

[Notwithstanding this alternative interpretation] the exposition of the list of terms is [to be understood] as stated before.[94]

Through these terms, the nirvāṇadhātu is explained [in its 169
two aspects:] with the remainder of attachment (upadhiśeṣa°) and without the remainder of attachment (nirupadhiśeṣa).

The Truth of Cessation has been explained.

Subtopic Four: The Truth of the Path

"What is the Noble Truth of the Path Leading to the Cessation of 15
Suffering? This is the Noble Eightfold Path beginning with right view; namely, right view, right thought, right speech, right action,

right livelihood, right effort, right mindfulness, and right concen-
16 *tration. This is the Path Leading to the Cessation of Suffering.*

"These, monks, are the Four Noble Truths."

Next comes the path (mārga), introduced with the phrase, 'the Path leading to the cessation of suffering'. [Here] 'cessation of suffering' means that suffering has ceased. This signifies [the stage of] nirvāṇa.

The 'path leading to the cessation of suffering' refers to that which has the nature [literally, conduct (śīla)] of 'going to' or 'reaching' [the goal]. This signifies the noble way (āryamārga). The way (mārga) is stated to be identical (eva°) with the path (pratipad°), for the aim [in both cases] is achieving nirvāṇa. [In the term] 'noble eightfold', 'noble' (ārya) means without outflows or pure (anāsrava), while the 'path' is so called because yogins [make use of it] to seek [the goal].

[Question:] In what manner is it eightfold? [Reply:] 'Right view' through 'right concentration', indicating a threefold path. 'Right speech', 'right action', and 'right livelihood' pertain to the branch of morality (śīlaskandha°). 'Right concentration' and 'right mindfulness' pertain to the branch of meditation (samādhi-skandha); since mindfulness is favorable to meditation, it is said to come within the branch of meditation. Moreover, one who is ever mindful has a concentrated mind due to nondisturbance (avikṣepa). 'Right view,' 'right thought', and 'right effort' are included in the branch of wisdom (prajñāskandha).

[One may point out:] 'Right thought' and 'right effort' are not of the nature of wisdom, since they have the nature respectively of 'initial application of mind' (vitarka) and 'energy' (vīrya). [Reply:] They are classified in this way because their qualities are those that belong to wisdom.[95]

The Four Noble Truths have been explained.

Topic Seven

The Twenty-Two Faculties

“Now, monks, what are the twenty-two faculties? These are as fol- 16
lows: the faculty of sight, the faculty of sound,the faculty of smell, the faculty of taste, the faculty of touch, the faculty of mind, the female faculty, the male faculty, the faculty of vitality, the faculty of physical pain, the faculty of mental pain, the faculty of physical pleasure, the faculty of mental pleasure, the faculty of equanimity, the faculty of faith, the faculty of energy, the faculty of mindfulness, the faculty of concentration, the faculty of wisdom, the faculty of knowing what is unknown, the faculty of perfect knowledge, and the faculty of one whose knowledge has been perfected. These, monks, are the twenty-two faculties.”

After the noble truths, to explain the faculties (indriyas), the 170
question is put, ‘What are the twenty-two faculties?’ The faculties [are so called] because they exercise supreme authority, signifying that they rule over their own domain.

‘The faculty of sight, and so forth’. Which faculty rules in which domain? From sight to touch, each has authority° over apprehending its own [respective] object. However, the mind has

171 [authority] over all objects. The 'female faculty' has [authority] over female characteristics and the 'male faculty' over male ones. The 'faculty of vitality' (jīvitendriya) has [authority] over maintaining the sameness of class. The five faculties of feeling [have authority] over defilements as it is stated:

"In pleasure, lust (rāga) lies dormant; in pain, malice (dveṣa); and in neutral feeling, ignorance (avidyā)."[96]

The faculties beginning with 'faith' have authority over the
172 equipment for purification, for on the worldly path they block° the defilements and in the state belonging to penetration (nirvedhabhāgīya°) they lead to the path. 'The faculty of knowing what is unknown' (anājñātam ājñāsyāmīndriya) has authority over eradication of the defilements that can be abandoned through vision (darśanaheya), and the faculty of perfect knowledge (ājñendriya) over the defilements that can be abandoned through cultivation of meditation (bhāvanāheya). 'The faculty of one whose knowledge has been perfected' has authority over living happily (sukhavihāra°) in this very life (dṛṣṭadharma), due to experiencing (saṁvedanāt°) liberation (vimukti), joy (prīti), and happiness (sukha°).

173 Now, 'faculty of sight' through 'faculty of touch' can exist [literally, are possible] in the realm of sense desires and the realm of form, but not in the formless realm, because there is an absence of form in the latter and these [faculties] are of the nature of form. The male and female faculties can exist in the realm of sense desire only. The faculties of mind (manas) and vitality can exist in all the three realms.

The faculty of pain signifies disagreeable feeling pertaining to
174 five classes of consciousness[97] in the sphere of sense desire. The faculty of mental pain signifies a disagreeable mental feeling in one who is not free from attachment to the sense pleasures. The Sūtras say that one not free from attachment to the sense pleasures is pierced with two kinds of pain: bodily pain (duḥkha) and mental pain or distress (daurmanasya°). But for one who is free from attachment, only a one-pronged feeling, i.e. bodily pain, is named in the scriptures.[97a]

The faculty of pleasure denotes agreeable feelings pertaining to the five classes of consciousness in the sphere of sense pleasures and in the first dhyāna, where it pertains to three classes of consciousness. In the third dhyāna, agreeable mental feelings are [likewise called] the faculty of pleasure. The faculty of mental pleasure refers to agreeable mental feelings in the kāmadhātu and in the first and second dhyāna.

The neutral feeling of neither pain nor pleasure [is both] bodily and mental; it has been put together in [one] 'faculty of equanimity' (upekṣendriya) because there is no intellectual operation (avikalpa) [in either case].[98] It exists in the three realms. How is
[this neutral feeling] known? As a Sūtra says, there is a third 175
experience besides pleasure and pain. And there is a rational basis (yukti) also.

[As to scriptural authority], it is stated in a Sūtra: "There are three types of feelings: pleasant, painful, and neutral." Again, the scriptures say: "By giving up pleasure as well as pain, a [state] devoid of pleasure and pain [is obtained], purified by equanimity and mindfulness."[99]

[As to] reason: No [moment of] mind can arise without a feeling, and it is well known that there exists a mind that is free from pleasure and pain.

[Regarding] faith and the others [of the five faculties], they are found in all the three dhātus, except in a person who has completely cut off all roots of merits. Faith (śraddhā°) is serenity of mind; energy (vīrya) is determination° to do meritorious
deeds; mindfulness (or recollection, smṛti°) is the expression of a 176
[mental] object that has been experienced; concentration (samādhi) is one-pointedness of mind; wisdom (prajñā) is investigation° of dharmas.

The three faculties beginning with 'knowing what is unknown' are pure (anāsrava), and they are absent in any of the [three] dhātus. Their nature should be explained as follows:

On the path of vision, nine entities (dravyāṇi)—mind [manas or manodhātu], bodily pleasure, mental pleasure, equanimity, faith, energy, mindfulness, concentration, and wisdom—are established as the faculty of knowing what is unknown. Why? Because the function of knowing the Four Truths, which were [previously] unknown, begins on the path of vision.

177 Here the faculty of knowing what is unknown is [thus] said to be the faculty of one [who has entered the path of vision]. Nine [entities or faculties] are mentioned in view of the different groups, but not all nine can exist in a single group. [For example,] regarding pleasure, mindfulness, and equanimity, only one [of the three] is present [at one time]. If the path [has developed to] the stage of anāgamya° meditation, dhyānāntara°, the fourth dhyāna, the sphere of infinity of space, the sphere of infinity of consciousness, or the sphere of nothingness, then only the faculty of equanimity is present, not the faculty of bodily pleasure or mental pleasure. If the path is at the stage of the first or second dhyāna, only the faculty of mental pleasure is present, not any other faculty of feeling. If it is at the stage of the third dhyāna, only the faculty of bodily pleasure is present, not any other faculty of feeling.[100]

On the path of meditation, [after the path of vision], all these nine entities beginning with the faculty of mind are established as the 'faculty of perfect knowledge'. Why? Because on the path of meditation (bhāvanā) there is nothing further to be known,[101] for the set of Four Noble Truths is known.[102] [This is the time] for giving up the remaining latent defilements that can be abandoned through meditation. The faculty of one who has thus perfected knowledge is called the 'faculty of perfect knowledge'.

178 On the path of one with no more to learn, these nine faculties are established as the 'faculty of one whose knowledge has been perfected'. Why? On the path of the perfect one, he obtains knowledge (avabodha°) that is perfect. One who possesses this is a person of perfect knowledge, or is one who possesses the nature of knowing. For such a one has gained knowledge of cessation as well as of non-origin (kṣaya-anutpādajñānalābha°). That person's faculty is the 'faculty of one whose knowledge has been perfected'.

For these latter two, the nomenclature is given in view of their being a separate group. If they are at the stage of anāgamya, intermediate dhyāna (dhyānāntara), the fourth dhyāna, the sphere of infinity, the sphere of consciousness, or the sphere of nothingness, the faculty of equanimity is present in them. If they are at the stage of the first or second dhyāna, the faculty of mental pleasure is present in them. And at the stage of the third dhyāna, the faculty of bodily pleasure is present.

The faculties have been explained.[103]

Topic Eight

Four Meditations

17 *"And further, monks, what are the four meditations?*

"Here, monks, a monk aloof from sense desires and aloof from evil and unwholesome thoughts attains the first meditation born of aloofness and accompanied by initial thought and sustained thought, and he attains the first meditation with rapture and joy and abides there.

"Putting to rest initial and sustained thought, with mind made inwardly tranquil and absorbed in a single object, he attains the second meditation, devoid of initial and sustained thought, and he abides there.

"Being detached from rapture, he abides in equanimity, mindful and clearly conscious, experiencing in his person that joy of which the Noble Ones say: 'Joyful abides a person who has equanimity and is mindful.' Thus he attains and abides in the third meditation.

"Giving up pleasure as well as pain, with disappearance of previous feelings of mental pleasure, he attains and abides in the

fourth meditation, which is devoid of pleasure and pain and is purified by equanimity and mindfulness.

"These, monks, are the four meditations."

After the faculties, the (four) meditations (dhyānas) are explained. To elucidate them, the question is put: 'What are the four meditations?' 179

Now, what is the meaning of meditation (dhyāna°)? Meditation is that by which one [literally, they] meditates. It means 'to know or comprehend' (prajānanti°), for true knowledge (yathābhūtaprajñāna) [arises] in one whose mind is concentrated (samāhita).[104] The root (dhātu: pra+jñā) in fact signifies 'reflection' (cintana), (for) it is an established norm (siddhānta) that reflection is wisdom. Thus it has been stated, "One pointedness of wholesome mind is meditation." [This is so] because meditation has the innate nature of concentration (samādhisvabhāva).

Explaining the first dhyāna, it is stated: 'Here, monks, a monk' and so on. 'Here' means in the realm of the sense desires (kāmadhātu). Meditation (samāpatti°), being an antidote (pratipakṣa) to the defilements of the kāmadhātu, is produced in one who is free from the lust [generated] in the kāmadhātu, and not in any one else. Therefore, it is said, 'aloof from sense desires', etc. 'Aloof' (vivikta°) means 'devoid of', while 'sense desires' signifies latent defilements (anuśayas) such as lust. 'Free from evil and unwholesome thoughts' (pāpaka, akuśaladharmas°) means [free] from thoughts having characteristics such as malice (pratighādi).

'With initial and sustained thought' (savitarka, savicāra°) indicates that one remains with initial and sustained thought. 'Born of aloofness' means born from aloofness. And what is this aloofness (viveka°)? It is the quiescence of five hindrances (nīvaraṇas).[105] When these are quiescent, one obtains pure meditation (śuddhaka-dhyāna). 180

'Rapture (prīti°) and joy (sukha°)'. Rapture and joy [collectively] are 'rapture-joy'. 'Rapture' means mental pleasure and

'joy' means the joy of tranquility (praśrabdhi-sukha°) signifying lightness [or workability] of the mind (cittakarmaṇyatā).
181 'Attaining' means 'entering into' (samāpadya°). 'Abides' indicates continuity of meditation.

This completes the description of the first attainment of meditation as endowed with five constituents: initial thought°, sustained thought°, rapture, joy, and concentration. [Here] the word 'meditation' (dhyāna) stands for concentration.

[Question:] The word 'joy' [is said to] signify the joy of tranquility. Why is it not joy of feeling (vedanā-sukha)?[106] [Reply:] At the time of meditation, bodily joy is not possible (na yujyate°), due to the absence of the five groups of consciousness [from consciousness of sight to consciousness of touch]. Mental joy is also not possible, since the use of the term 'rapture' already indicates mental joy and there can be no simultaneity (yaugapadya°) of joy and rapture, [both] having [the same] characteristics of feeling. Neither is it tenable that they function in rotation, due to the mention of 'five constituents'.[107]

182 [Now] the second meditation is explained. 'Putting to rest initial thought . . . he . . .' 'He' means the yogi° 'Putting to rest' refers to disappearance. Since in the second attainment, the disappearance of the disturbance (kṣobha) [inherent in] 'initial and sustained thought' makes the mind calm (praśānta), both are said to be put to rest.

'Inwardly tranquil'. What is this inward tranquility (adhyātma-samprasāda°)? It is tranquility born of faith. A yogi who attains the second meditation produces in that concentrated state of freedom a conviction (or faith) called inward tranquility.

'With mind . . . absorbed in a single object°'. The word 'single' signifies exclusion of any other. 'Ūti°' means movement towards an object. Where there is unity of function [directed toward an object], this is called the becoming of one function (ekoti° = absorption in a single object). To become absorbed in a single object is ekotībhāva, signifying singleness of function [literally, movement] or [a single] objective support of mind.

Since in the second dhyāna and beyond, concentration 183
(samādhi°) is sought that is without initial and sustained thought, therefore it is stated [in the Sūtra] to be 'devoid of initial and sustained thought'. 'Rapture and joy' are as above.

Thus the second attainment of meditation is shown, endowed with four constituents: rapture, joy, one-pointedness of mind, and inward tranquility.

Explaining the third attainment of meditation, it is stated: 'Being detached from rapture' and so on. Since the third attainment of meditation is produced by detachment from mental pleasure, it is said: 'Being detached from rapture, he abides in equanimity.' This should be understood as the equanimity of conditioned states (saṁskāropekṣā°), which by nature does not
incline towards (anābhogalakṣaṇā°) rapture. [That is, it is] nei- 184
ther equanimity of feelings nor the equanimity of the four immeasurables (apramāṇas°), for neither is possible here.

'Mindful'. Mindfulness is the non-loss of the marks of equanimity (upekṣānimitta°). 'Clear awareness' (samprajanya°) is wisdom (prajñā).[108] [In this meditative state] there is clear awareness of mindfulness and other [faculties].

'[Experiencing] in his person (kāyena) that joy.' Here 'kāya' (body) means 'mental body' [or grouping],[109] for [here] mental
joy is sought, not physical pleasure. [Moreover], the five classes 185
of consciousness (vijñānakāyas)[110] pertaining to the body are absent in one who has entered into meditation. To indicate this, the phrase is used, 'of which the Noble Ones (Āryas) say'. Āryas means anāgāmins° (non-returners) and others who have abandoned the defilements of the realm of sense desires. Etymologically speaking, those who have gone far (ārāt yātāḥ) away from unwholesome states are Āryas.[111] The meaning of the rest is clear.

Thus the third attainment of meditation is said to be endowed with five constituents: equanimity, mindfulness, clear
awareness, joy, and concentration. 186

[Now] to explain the [description of the] fourth attainment of meditation: 'Giving up pleasure', and so on. [Here] 'pleasure' means bodily pleasure and 'pain' means bodily pain only,[112] because with entry into the first dhyāna, bodily pain (duḥkha) and mental pain (daurmanasya°) disappear; with entry into the second dhyāna, bodily pleasure disappears; and with entry into the third dhyāna, mental pleasure is absent. This is why the Sūtra speaks of 'giving up pleasure, etc.' Since bodily feelings are in balance, [both] pleasure and pain are abandoned, and because mental feelings are in balance, mental pleasure and pain are given up [as well].

'Devoid of pleasure and pain'. This feeling, which has the characteristics of neither pain nor pleasure', is mentioned [in the texts].[113] In the fourth attainment of meditation, there is an absence of pleasure and [pain], but it would be improper [to hold that there can be] a meditative state in which feeling is absent. Thus there remains the feeling that possesses the indicated characteristics.

'Purified by equanimity and mindfulness' means purified by equanimity and purified by mindfulness. As the phrase 'purified by' occurs at the end, it refers to both [terms]. The word 'equanimity' (upekṣā) here refers to the equanimity of conditioned states (saṁskāras) rather than immeasurable equanimity (apramāṇopekṣā), for the latter is inapposite.[114] [This is because]
187 the purification of equanimity and mindfulness [at issue] here arises through the disappearance of faults (apakṣālas°) [found] in the lower stages. These faults are of eight types: initial thought (vitarka), sustained thought (vicāra), breathing in and breathing out, and the four beginning with happiness [i.e., bodily happiness and pain, mental happiness, and mental pain].[115]

Thus, in the fourth attainment of meditation there are four constituents: the feeling of neither pain nor pleasure, purification of equanimity, purification of mindfulness, and purification of concentration.

188 [Question:] Why are initial [and sustained] thought and the others named as constituents of meditative states, but not other dharmas, such as contact? Reply: Because these constituents are

sufficient to perform the function of being hostile (pratipakṣāṅga), the function of being favorable [or supportive] (anuśaṁsāṅga°), and both functions. [Let us investigate this.]

In the first dhyāna, initial and sustained thought are hostile constituents. They work against thoughts (vitarka) linked to sense desire, malice, and violence. Rapture and joy are favorable [or advantageous] constituents. After initial and sustained thought have defeated their opponents, seclusion, joy and happiness are attained. One-pointedness of mind is both [hostile and favorable]: Because of [its] supporting power, initial thought and the others do not function.

In the second dhyāna, inward tranquility is hostile to initial and sustained thought, for they are eliminated [literally, opposed]. Rapture and joy are favorable constituents. One-pointedness of mind is as above.

In the third dhyāna, equanimity, mindfulness and clear awareness are hostile constituents, for they eliminate rapture. Joy is a favorable constituent. One-pointedness of mind is as above.

In the fourth [dhyāna], purification of equanimity and mindfulness are both hostile constituents, for they eliminate joy. The feeling of neither pain nor pleasure is a favorable constituent. One-pointedness of mind is both [a hostile and a favorable constituent].[116]

Meditation has been explained.

Topic Nine

The Four Formless Attainments

18 *"What, monks, are the four formless attainments?*

"Monks, a monk passes wholly beyond the perception of form by eliminating all perception of resistance and paying no attention to different perceptions. [Maintaining the awareness:] 'Space is infinite', he attains and abides in the state of infinity of space.

"Having fully transcended the state of infinity of space, he becomes aware as follows: 'Consciousness is infinite'. Thus he attains and abides in the state of infinity of consciousness."

"Having fully transcended the state of infinity of consciousness, he [maintains the awareness:] 'There is nothing'. Thus he attains and abides in the state of nothingness.

"Having fully transcended the state of nothingness, he attains and abides in the state of neither perception nor non-perception.

"These, monks, are the four formless attainments."

189 Just as the knowledge associated with the rūpadhātu is an antidote to the latent defilements associated with kāmadhātu, so

knowledge associated with the ārūpyadhātu [the formless realm] is an antidote to the latent defilements associated with rūpadhātu.[117] Therefore, it is said: '[passing] wholly [beyond] the perception of form'. 'Wholly' indicates that gross form [totally] disappears.

Some maintain that subtle form continues to exist in the ārūpyadhātu, but this is not so, for it is explained in a Sūtra that 'formless' signifies escape [or release] from form°.[118] As expressed 190
by the word 'wholly' (or 'totally'), not even subtle form remains.

'[Eliminating all] perception of resistance (pratighasaṁjñā°)'. The perception of resistance has the nature of striking. That is possible when one form hinders another, [but] is not possible in the [higher] meditation (samāpatti°) in which perception of form is eliminated. Through taking the form or formless states as objects, there are different perceptions.[119] As the object is space, there is non-attention to different perceptions.

[For one who] practices formless meditation in this way, the consummation of his resolve (adhimokṣa-niṣpatti°) is unbounded space. Hence it is called 'infinity of space'. 'Attaining', i.e., obtaining, he 'abides'. Desiring to go beyond the state of infinity of space [the meditator] grasps the characteristics of pure consciousness, the consummation of his resolve being [attainment of] infinite consciousness. Hence it is called the state of infinity of consciousness.

When the meditator whose mind has experienced infinite
coarse materiality (anantaudārika) has no delight in it, and when 191
with equanimity he reaches the consummation of his resolve to be detached (viveka°) from perception, this is called 'nothingness' (nāstikiṁcit).

'State of nothingness' (ākiñcanyātana) means there is nothing [at all]. Not experiencing (anabhisaṁvedanāt°) infinite forms, they [meditators] do not direct their mind° towards anything [i.e., they are impassive]. Therefore they are in the state of nothingness.[120]

[When], the functional application [in meditation] becomes indistinct, there is neither perception nor non-perception, for its

function is weak. There is neither the absence of perception as in
the case of those who are not conscious, such as the non-conscious gods,[121] nor is there sharp perception as in the four
dhyānas and the three [previous] formless meditations (ārūpya-
192 traya samāpatti). Although possessed of perception, owing to its
weakness the [meditators] remain in this state as though not
possessing any perception.[122]

Topic Ten

The Four Sublime States

"What, monks, are the four sublime states?

"Monks, a monk with well cultivated, extensive, lofty, non-dual, and immeasurable mind, endowed with loving kindness that is free from enmity, jealousy and harmfulness, applies great zeal in pervading [with loving kindness] a quarter of the world, and attains and abides in that state. 19

"Likewise, with mind well cultivated, extensive, lofty, non-dual, and immeasurable, endowed with loving kindness that is free from enmity, jealousy and harmfulness, he applies great zeal in pervading [with loving kindness] the second, third, and fourth quarters of the world; and so also above, below and across the whole world, in all regions. And he attains and abides in that state.

"In the same way, a monk with well cultivated, extensive, lofty, non-dual, and immeasurable mind, endowed with compassion that is free from enmity, jealousy and harmfulness, applies great zeal in pervading [with compassion] a quarter of the world, and attains and abides in that state.

"Likewise, with mind well cultivated, extensive, lofty, non-dual, and immeasurable, endowed with compassion that is free from enmity, jealousy and harmfulness, he applies great zeal in pervading [with compassion] the second, third, and fourth quarters of the world; and so also above, below and across the whole world, in all regions. And he attains and abides in that state.

"In the same way, a monk with well cultivated, extensive, lofty, non-dual, and immeasurable mind, endowed with sympathetic joy that is free from enmity, jealousy and harmfulness, applies great zeal in pervading [with sympathetic joy] a quarter of the world, and attains and abides in that state.

"Likewise, with mind well cultivated, extensive, lofty, non-dual, and immeasurable, endowed with sympathetic joy that is free from enmity, jealousy and harmfulness, he applies great zeal in pervading [with sympathetic joy] the second, third, and fourth quarters of the world; and so also above, below and across the whole world, in all regions. And he attains and abides in that state.

"In the same way, a monk with well cultivated, extensive, lofty, non-dual, and immeasurable mind, endowed with equanimity that is free from enmity, jealousy and harmfulness, applies great zeal in pervading [with equanimity] a quarter of the world, and attains and abides in that state.

"Likewise, with mind well cultivated, extensive, lofty, non-dual, and immeasurable, endowed with equanimity that is free from enmity, jealousy and harmfulness, he applies great zeal in pervading [with equanimity] the second, third, and fourth quarters of the world; and so also above, below and across the whole world, in all regions. And he attains and abides in that state.

"These are the four sublime states."

193 After the formless [attainments], the four sublime states (brāhmavihāras°) are explained. To explain them, the question is put, 'What are the four sublime states?' The answer: 'Monks, a monk . . . endowed with loving kindness (maitrīsahagatena)'. 'Loving kindness (maitri°)' is an earnest intention to work for the

benefit and happiness of other beings. "May all beings be happy!" Having this thought in mind, one cultivates loving kindness. 'Associated with loving kindness' [indicates] a mind focused° on loving kindness; [i.e.,] with such a mind.

The words 'free from enmity, jealousy and harmfulness (avairaṁ, asapatnaṁ, avyābādhena°)' respectively counter the three adherences (upaśleṣas°). [The first is] enmity toward equal and higher harmful (apakāri°) beings. 'Free from enmity' is the counter. [Second,] there is jealousy towards equal and higher beings who do no harm. 'Free from jealousy' is the counter. [Third,] there is hatred toward lower, harmful, and [even] harmless beings, because of which one oppresses these beings. 'Free from harmfulness' is the counter.

'Extensive'. Because [its practice bears] great fruit, it is called extensive. This is a metaphorical expression that indicates a result for a cause. Again, it is because the object (viṣaya) [of loving kindness] is extensive. . . .° 'Lofty' (mahadgata°) indicates that loving kindness extends into the [higher] sphere of forms. 'Non-dual' indicates that it directs the same [friendly] thoughts
toward all. 'Immeasurable' (apramāṇa) indicates that its object is 194
the innumerable beings of the kāmāvacara sphere. 'Well cultivated' indicates that it has conquered its opponents, malice being a [major] opponent.

Thus the mind [of loving kindness] has been displayed as to its opposite, its fruit, its sphere, range, object, and purification.

'One direction'. [Here] the receptacle [or container] stands for [literally, shows] the things contained, as in the examples, 'the benches are crying' [i.e., those seated on them are crying]; 'the mountains are burning'.[123] 'Applies zealously' shows the direction [or disposition] of the mind. 'Pervades' shows both the pervasion and the disposition toward all beings. 'Attains' means practicing
[literally, face to face with] the basic meditations.[124] 'Abides' 195
(viharati°)shows continuity and repetition of meditation.

'As in one [quarter°], likewise in the second', etc. Explaining this it is stated: 'and he pervades the second [quarter]'. 'Across the whole world' signifies the realm of sense desires, because the beings of the desire realm are his object of thought (ālambana).

What has been stated above is also to be applied to compassion (karuṇā) [and the other sublime states]. This is shown by the phrase, 'likewise endowed with compassion'.

Having explained this conclusion, it is stated: 'These are the sublime states (brāhmavihāras). [Here] brāhma means 'great' (bṛhat). The cultivation of loving kindness and the others brings a great fruit; therefore they are called brāhmavihāras.

These sublime states are also called immeasurable (apramāṇas) because immeasurable [innumerable] beings are the object of thought of one who practices the sublime states.

196 [Question:] Why are there only four? [Reply:] Because they are antidotes in sequence to [four unwholesome thoughts]: malice, cruelty, discontent, and [both] attachment to sense desires [and] malice. Loving kindness is an antidote to those who are dominated° by malice (vyāpāda), compassion is an antidote to those dominated by cruelty (vihiṁsā°), sympathetic joy (muditā) to those dominated by discontent (arati°), and equanimity to those dominated by attachment to sense desires and by malice.[125]

[Question:] As an antidote to the attachment to sense desires (kāmarāga), what is the difference between [meditation on] repulsiveness (aśubha°) and equanimity (upekṣā)? [Reply:] Repulsiveness (aśubhatā) is an antidote for sexual lust and equanimity for attachment to mother, father, son and relations.

Now, these are the aspects of loving kindness and the other [sublime states]:

"Let beings be happy!" With this thought in mind, one cultivates loving kindness.

"Beings are suffering!" With this thought in mind, one cultivates compassion.

"Let beings be joyful!" With this thought in mind one cultivates sympathetic joy.

"They are simply beings." With this thought in mind, one cultivates equanimity (upekṣā°) due to impartiality.

How does the beginner apply himself to loving kindness? As 197
he finds himself happy or hears of the happiness of others such as Buddhas, Bodhisattvas, and noble disciples, he likewise earnestly applies his mind with zeal toward the happiness of beings [with the thought]. "May [all] beings be thus happy!"

If he is not able to do this due to a state [of mind] in which defilement has arisen, he separates his loving intention into three parts. First, he directs his intention for happiness toward his very intimate friend, after that to the friend for whom he has moderate liking, and then to those friends for whom his liking is weak. If he can balance his loving intention [toward all three] then he cultivates the aspect of neutrality, making the same division.

Afterwards he makes a threefold division with regard to his enemies. First, he directs his intention for happiness toward a lesser enemy, then to a moderately [disliked] enemy and then to his intense enemy. Here he cultivates intense loving kindness toward his intense enemy. And when his earnest intention of giving happiness (sukhādhimokṣa°) has been activated, then in sequence he applies the thought of loving kindness toward his family, village, and country, first pervading one direction until finally he pervades the whole world.

One who can appreciate the qualities [of others] (guṇagrāhin) everywhere will quickly produce loving kindness. However, one can learn to appreciate the qualities° even of one whose roots of merits have been cut off (samucchinnakuśalamūla°) by seeing [in good features of his body] the result of good deeds performed
in the past; in the same way one may find fault with a Pratyeka- 198
buddha by seeing [in deformities of his body] the result of bad deeds performed in the past.[126]

One applies onself in the same way to [producing] compassion. "These beings are submerged in a flood of various distresses (vyasanamagna). May they be free from suffering!" Similarly for sympathetic joy: "May these beings be joyful!" Equanimity, however, begins from the aspect of neutrality.

Topic Eleven

Four Courses [of Meditation]

"And what are the four courses [of meditation]?

"There is a course, monks, that is painful and sluggish in intuition; there is a course that is painful and swift in intuition; there is a course that is pleasant but sluggish in intuition; there is a course that is [both] pleasant and swift in intuition.

"And what is the course that is painful and sluggish in intuition? Here a person is by nature extremely lustful, extremely hateful, extremely infatuated. Because of his extremely lustful nature, born of lust, he experiences in every moment pain and dejection. Likewise, because of his extremely hateful nature, born of hatred, and because of his extremely infatuated nature, born of infatuation, he experiences in every moment pain and dejection. Moreover, his five transcendental faculties are weak, not sharp, and slow in accomplishing the destruction of defilements. And what are these five? The faculties of faith, energy, mindfulness, concentration, and wisdom. Because these transcendental faculties are weak and slow, he reaches only slowly the immediate succeeding meditation that destroys the defilements. This is the painful course sluggish in intuition.

*"Now, what is the course that is painful but swift in intuition?
Here a person is by nature extremely lustful, extremely hateful,
extremely infatuated. Because of his extremely lustful nature, born
of lust, he experiences in every moment pain and dejection.
Likewise because of his extremely hateful nature, born of hatred,
and because of his extremely infatuated nature, born of infatuation, he experiences in every moment pain and dejection. His five
transcendental faculties, however, are predominant, sharp, and
swift. And what are these five? The faculties of faith, energy, mind-* 21
*fulness, concentration, and wisdom. Because these transcendental
faculties predominate and are sharp and swift, he reaches quickly
the immediate succeeding meditation that destroys the defilements.*

"Now, what is the course that is pleasant but sluggish in intuition? Here a person is almost free from lust, hatred and infatuation. Being free from lust, hatred, and infatuation, he does not experience in every moment pain and dejection born of lust, hatred and infatuation. His transcendental faculties, however, are weak, not sharp, and not swift. And what are these five? The faculties of faith, energy, mindfulness, concentration, and wisdom. Because these transcendental faculties are dull, not sharp, weak, and slow, he reaches only slowly the immediate succeeding meditation that destroys the defilements. This is called the course that is pleasant but with sluggish intuition.

*"Now, what is the course that is pleasant and swift in intu-
ition? Here a person is almost free from lust, hatred and infatuation. Being free from lust, hatred, and infatuation, he does not
experience in every moment pain and dejection born of lust, hatred
and infatuation. Moreover, his five transcendental faculties are
predominant, sharp, and swift. And what are these five? The faculties of faith, energy, mindfulness, concentration, and wisdom.
Because these transcendental faculties predominate and are sharp
and swift, he reaches quickly the immediate succeeding meditation
that destroys the defilements. This is called the course that is [both]* 22
pleasant and swift in intuition.

"These, monks, are the four courses [of meditation]."

199 After the sublime states, the four courses (pratipad°) are explained, starting with the phrase, 'And what are the four courses?'

'Painful (duḥkhā) and sluggish (dhandhā) in intuition (abhijñā°).' In the anāgamya° and intermediate dhyānas° and the three formless attainments, the path is called a painful course. It is called painful because these [meditations] are not endowed with the constituents (aṅgāparigrahāt), because calm (śamatha) and insight (vipaśyanā) are deficient, and also because effort is required.

Effort is required in the anāgamya° and intermediate dhyānas° because calm is deficient and because [these states] are not endowed with the constituents° (aṅgas). Effort is required in the formless dhyānas because again they are not endowed with the constituents, and because insight is deficient. Therefore the preliminary path [of dhyāna] in the anāgamya stage is a painful course.

'Sluggish in intuition' refers to a course in which intuition is sluggish [or weak]. This is dull wisdom (mandaprajñā°), or the intuition of a dull person.

200 To explain this in detail, it is stated: 'Here a person' and so on. 'By nature' means by temperament. 'Extremely lustful' means 'of intensely lustful temperament': a person whose lust arises [immediately] in respect of even a small thing. 'Extremely hateful' and 'extremely infatuated [deluded = tīvramoha] [are to be understood] in the same way. Each arises in accord with differences in the stream of personality (santāna-bheda°). 'His' refers to that specific person. 'Five' indicates faith and the other [faculties]. 'Transcendental' signifies that the faculties are pure. 'Dull' means sluggish [or slow].

'Now, what is the course that is painful but swift in intuition?' [This is] as explained above. 'Swift intuition' is a swift intuition in a [particular] course. It means sharp wisdom (tīkṣṇa-prajñā°). Again, swift intuition is the intuition of a swift or sharp person. The rest is as above.

'Now, what is the course that is pleasant but sluggish in intuition?' The course is called pleasant in the first, second, third and the fourth basic dhyānas° because it is endowed with the constituents, calm and insight are balanced, and [the course] is effortless. 'Sluggish' is explained as above.

'Now, what is the course that is pleasant and swift in intuition?' [This is] as explained above. 'Immediate succeeding meditation (ānantarya-samādhi°) signifies the characteristics of the path of abandonment, through which the defilements are abandoned.

Topic Twelve

Four Ways of Cultivating Concentration

22 *"There is, monks, a way of cultivating concentration that when practiced, developed, and repeatedly followed, leads to destroying sensual lust.*

"There is, monks, a way of cultivating concentration that when practiced, developed, and repeatedly followed, leads to living happily in this very life.

"There is, monks, a way of cultivating concentration that when practiced, developed, and repeatedly followed, leads to acquiring knowledge and vision.

"There is, monks, a way of cultivating concentration that when practiced, developed, and repeatedly followed, leads to acquiring wisdom."

201 After the four courses, the cultivation of concentration (samādhibhāvanā) is taught. To explain it, the question is put, 'Now monks, what is the way of cultivating° concentration?'

'Practiced'. Here 'practiced' means developing by practice. 'Developed' means abandoning the opposing forces. 'Repeatedly followed' signifies keeping away (dūrīkaraṇa°) from the opposing forces. Alternatively, 'practiced' refers to the path of application (prayogamārga°), 'developed' refers to the uninterrupted path (ānantaryamārga°), and 'repeatedly followed' indicates the path of deliverance (vimuktimārga).[127]

"Now, monks, what is the way of cultivating concentration that 23
when practiced, developed, and repeatedly followed, leads to destroying sensual lust?

"Monks, a monk goes into the forest or to the root of a tree or to an empty, uninhabited, sheltered place and reflects rightly and with wisdom on the body as it really is, well placed and situated, enclosed in skin and full of various impurities from the soles of the feet upward and from the top of the head downward, [reflecting thus:] 'Here in this body there are the hairs of the head, hairs of the
body, nails, teeth, dirt, filth, skin, flesh, bones, sinews, nerves, kid- 24
neys, heart, spleen, pleura, intestines, mesentary, upper and lower stomach, bladder, liver, excrement, tears, sweat, saliva, snot, grease, synovic fluid, marrow, fat, bile, phlegm, pus, blood, head, and brain.'[128]

"Monks, Just as a man with keen eyes looking into an open
storehouse full of various grains such as rice°, sesame seeds, mus- 25
tard seeds, beans°, barley, and māsa recognizes these as the grains of barley, these as the grains to be plowed, [and so on,] so, monks, the monk [engaged in reflection] sees his body as it is, situated and well placed. Thus he reflects on the body as it is, [full of impurities].

"This, monks, is the way of cultivating concentration that is practiced, developed, and repeatedly followed to destroy sensual lust."

To elucidate these states of cultivation of concentration in 202
sequence, it is said, 'Here', etc.

'Goes into the forest'. These three phrases (pada°), indicate seeking physical seclusion. One who dwells alone is [said to have] withdrawn in his physical person (kāyavyapakṛṣṭa), because he is far away from contact with the public.°

'He reflects . . . as it really is'. This signifies pure penetration with proper insight.

'Hairs of the head', 'hairs of the body', etc. These words show withdrawing mentally for one is far away from evil thoughts. 'Hairs of the head' are those that grow on the head. 'Hairs of the body' are the beard and those that grow on the body.

203 'Earthen storehouse open on both sides°' (ubhayato mutoḍi°). [The practice of] storing rice in an earthen storehouse is well known in the middle country (madhyadeśa).

'Performed to destroy sensual lust'. This refers to abandoning sensual lust (kāmarāga°), because a beginner is instructed in disgust for the body.[129]

25 *"Now, what, monks, is the way of cultivating concentration that is practiced, developed, and repeatedly followed to live happily in this very life?*

"Monks, a monk goes into the forest or to the root of a tree or to an empty, uninhabited, sheltered place, and drenches, saturates, permeates, and suffuses the inner body with rapture and joy, born of aloofness and concentration. There is not a single part of his body that is not suffused and permeated with rapture and joy, born from inner aloofness and concentration.

"Monks, just as in a pond, lotuses of various colors° are born in water, grow up in water, and are sunk in water, all of them drenched, saturated, permeated, and suffused by cool water, so a monk goes into the forest or to the root of a tree or to an empty,
26 *uninhabited, sheltered place and drenches, saturates, permeates, and suffuses the inner body with rapture and joy born of aloofness and concentration. There is not a single part of his whole body that is not suffused with rapture and joy, born of inner aloofness.*

"This is the way of cultivating concentration practiced, developed and repeatedly followed for living happily in this very life."

204 Explaining the second stage of the cultivation of concentration, it is stated: 'For happiness in this [very] life.' This [very] life (dṛṣṭadharma°) means this [present] birth. 'Happy dwelling' is 'living happily'. In this life, living happily is 'happiness in this life'; [thus the phrase] 'for happiness in this [very life]'. In the

term dṛṣṭadharma, the word 'seen' (dṛṣṭa) indicates what is before the eyes or visible, while the word 'dharma' signifies 'birth'. [Thus] the sense is that in this life before one's eyes [there is] the experience of happiness of concentration.

'[Suffuses] the inner body'. This inner (adhyātma°) body is born of aloofness or seclusion. 'Born of seclusion' signifies 'seclusion-born'. What is [thus born]? Rapture and joy. 'Through that seclusion'. What, indeed, is this seclusion? Through the power of [this] stage of concentration, a special quality is produced.

[Question:] What is the special advantage to the body of this felicity? Reply: From the soles of the feet up to the head, this whole body composed of the four [primary] elements is filled and pervaded with [felicity]. As lotuses that spring from the water are filled and drenched within and without with the moisture of water, likewise there is no part of the body that is not in contact with felicity.

This stage of cultivation 'for living happily in this very life' should be known as the stage of the first dhyāna. It is a pure and undefiled state. The first dhyāna coming at the outset, the other dhyānas should be understood in the same way.[130]

[Question:] Why does the [second] stage of cultivation (bhā- 205
vanā) not [also] offer future happiness? [Reply:] Because for the anāgāmins (non-returners) who have abandoned the first dhyāna and are born in the subsequent dhyānas above, future happiness is not at issue, [for they will not be reborn]. Likewise for Arhats who have abandoned the latent defilements of the three realms in their meditation, [concern with] future happiness is out of the question.

"What is the way of cultivating concentration that is practiced, developed and repeatedly followed to acquire knowledge and vision?

"Herein, Monks, a monk develops well° a perception of light. He attends to it mentally, sees it and penetrates into it. Sustaining the perception of daylight, he develops the luminous mind: as by day,

so by night; as by night, so by day; as in front, so behind; as behind,
27 *so in the front; as below, so above; as above, so below. Thus with an open and unhampered mind, a monk sustains the perception of daylight and develops a mind that is evenly luminous, pervading the whole world.*

"Monks, as in the last month of summer on a clear, cloudless day, at high noon, when the clouds in the sky have disappeared and light is pure, radiant, and bright, with no darkness, so, monks, a monk develops well the perception of daylight. He attends to it mentally, sees it, and penetrates into it. He develops a mind that is evenly luminous: as by day, so by night; as in front, so behind, as behind, so in front; as below, so above; as above, so below. With an open and unhampered mind, a monk sustains the perception of daylight and develops a mind that is evenly luminous.

"This is the way of cultivating concentration that is practiced, developed, and repeatedly followed to acquire knowledge and vision."

Explaining the third stage of cultivation, it is stated: 'For the acquisition of knowledge (jñāna) and vision (darśana°)'. [Regarding] 'knowledge and vision', knowledge is itself vision°, being directly experienced. [For] in ordinary speech, a direct experience is called vision; likewise, since knowledge is itself directly experienced, it is also called vision.

In attending to the perception of light, there is application (prayoga) of the higher knowledge (abhijñā) of the divine eye. Therefore it is said, 'perception of light' (ālokasaṁjñā). As long as the instruction [for cultivation at this level] is not well grasped, practice will not lead to attaining the state of cultivation. To ensure that the instruction[130a] does not simply slip away [literally, 'is not washed off'], it is [elaborated in the passage] 'perception of light' through 'penetrates into it'. When the instruction as it is given is heard respectfully, it is called well grasped (sūdgṛhītā°). At the time of reflection, not forgetting whatever is well grasped is called 'well attended to'. At the time of cultivation, because it is being specificially produced, it is called 'well seen', in the sense of 'well sustained' (susevitā°).[131]

When the instruction has been accomplished, it is [called] 'well penetrated'; that is, personally realized.

[Question:] What is that [perception of light]? [Reply:] It is 206
explained [literally] as 'perception of daylight', meaning 'perception of illumination: 'evenly luminous' [mind].[132] The yogi cultivates his mind with luminous [bright] light.

[Question:] In what way? Reply: 'As by day, so by night', [throughout] 'the whole world'. The meaning is that when the practice of cultivation reaches its culmination, he radiates (sphurati°) throughout and pervades the whole world. 'Cloudless' means when clouds have dispersed.

"Now what, monks, is the way of cultivating concentration that 28
is practiced, developed, and repeatedly followed to acquire wisdom?

"Monks, a monk goes to a forest or the root of a tree or an empty uninhabited sheltered place, giving up [bodily] pleasure and pain, and with the disappearance of previous feelings of mental pleasure he attains and abides in the fourth dhyāna, which is devoid of pleasure and pain and is purified through equanimity and mindfulness.

"This is the way of cultivating concentration that is practiced, developed, and repeatedly followed to acquire wisdom.

"These are the four ways to cultivate concentration."

Explaining the fourth stage of cultivation, the phrase is used, 'to acquire wisdom' (prajñā-pratilambhāya°). The acquisition of wisdom signifies 'wisdom acquisition': it is mentioned to indicate gaining special [or excellent] wisdom or gaining the consummation of wisdom. To explain this further, it is said, 'What is the way of cultivating concentration' through 'he attains and abides in the fourth dhyāna'.

[Question:] Why is the cultivation of the fourth dhyāna [an appropriate means] for the acquisition of wisdom? Reply: Because the fourth dhyāna is free from the eight faults[133] and is the foundation for all qualities of practice.[134] And all these qualities develop [the capacity for] gaining special wisdom or reach- 207
ing its consummation.

Topic Thirteen

Four Foundations of Mindfulness

28 *"What then, monks, are the four foundations of mindfulness?*

"Monks, here a monk abides contemplating the body internally: ardent, clearly aware, and mindful, neither covetous nor dejected with the world. Likewise, he abides contemplating the body as body externally: ardent, clearly aware, and mindful, neither covetous nor dejected with the world. Likewise he abides contemplating the body as body both internally and externally: ardent, clearly aware, and mindful, neither covetous nor dejected with the world.

"He abides contemplating feelings as feelings internally: ardent, clearly aware, and mindful, neither covetous nor dejected with the world. He abides contemplating feelings as feelings externally: ardent, clearly aware, and mindful, neither covetous nor dejected with the world. He abides contemplating feelings as feelings both internally and externally: ardent, clearly aware, and mindful, neither covetous nor dejected with the world.

"He abides contemplating the mind as mind internally: ardent, clearly aware, and mindful, neither covetous nor dejected with the world. He abides contemplating the mind as mind externally:

ardent, clearly aware, and mindful, neither covetous nor dejected with the world. He abides contemplating the mind as mind both internally and extremely: ardent, clearly aware, and mindful, neither covetous nor dejected with the world.

"He abides contemplating mental objects as mental objects internally: ardent, clearly aware, and mindful, neither covetous nor dejected with the world. He abides contemplating mental objects as mental objects externally: ardent, clearly aware, and mindful, neither covetous nor dejected with the world. He abides contemplating mental objects as mental objects both internally and externally: ardent, clearly aware, and mindful, neither covetous nor dejected with the world.

"These, monks, are the four foundations of mindfulness."

After the [four] cultivations of concentration, the foundations of 208
mindfulness (smṛtyupasthānas°) are explained. To explain them [the question is put]: 'What then, monks, are the four foundations of mindfulness?' 'Four' refers to mindfulness of body, feeling, mind, and mental objects. [Question:] Why four, and neither more nor less? [Reply:] Because these are antidotes to the four perversions respectively: [belief in] the purity of things (śuci), pleasure (sukha), permanence (nitya), and the self (ātman).[135]

Now, concerning the mindfulness of body, it is stated:
'Monks, here a monk . . . .' 'Here' means in this world of sense 209
desires. 'Internally in the body' means in one's own body. 'Contemplates the body': Contemplation (anudarśana) is wisdom; it is also that which belongs to one who is a contemplator (anudarśī°), as in the example of daṇḍin [as one who possesses a daṇḍa = stick]. [Gramatically speaking], this is [a locative compound named] saptamītatpuruṣa. [Thus], 'contemplates the body' refers to the one who contemplates the body. (In this contemplation), the body is to be distinguished by its own [innate] and general characteristics (sva-sāmānyalakṣaṇa).[136]

'Ardent' (ātāpī) means energetic. 'Mindful' means endowed with the faculty of mindfulness. 'Clearly aware' (samprajānan) means endowed with wisdom (prajñā). 'Neither covetous nor dejected' means discarding [these aspects].

27 [Question:] Why are only the removal of covetousness and dejection mentioned, and not all of the hindrances [āvaraṇas, literally, 'covering']. [Reply:] By implication, removal of all [the hindrances] should be understood. Alternatively, removal of covetousness includes removal of sensual desires and removal of dejection includes removal of malice.

[Another interpretation:] 'Ardent' signifies the removal of sloth and torpor, 'mindful' signifies the removal of excitement and remorse (auddhatya-kaukṛtya°), and 'clear awareness' signifies the removal of doubt (vicikitsā). By eliminating the hindrances in this way, 'the foundation of mindfulness of contemplation on the body as body°' develops.

210 Thus the foundation of mindfulness of the body pertaining to one's own stream of consciousness (svasantati) has been explained. In reference to the stream of consciousness of others (parasantati), it is said, '[one contemplates] the body externally'. Pertaining to both [one's own and others' bodies], it is said, 'internally and externally'.[137]

[Question:] What is the purpose (abhiśaya°) of referring to 'internal', 'external', and 'both'? Reply: 'Internally' signifies that a practitioner uproots internal defiled entities (vastus) and 'externally' signifies those entities that are outside. 'Both' means both types of entities.

[Question:] What is the meaning of 'body' (kāya)? [Reply:] [In this context] it means 'collection' (saṅghāta).

[Question:] [In the phrase] 'contemplates the body as body', what is the purpose of mentioning [the body] twice? Reply: If he contemplates (anupaśyī°) feeling, mind and mental objects as [literally, 'in'] the body, his mind will become perverted (or con-
211 fused). 'Contemplating the body as body' means one contemplates as it really is. It should be understood in the same way with respect to feelings, mind, and mental objects.

In each stream of personality [and] for each foundation of mindfulness, [and] in connection with [focusing on] one's own, others', and both, there are three types of practice: hearing (śruta), reflection (cintā), and meditation (bhāvanā). All have the nature of wisdom (prajñā svabhāva).[138]

[Question:] Why are the foundations of mindfulness [said to have] the nature of prajñā? Reply: Because prajñā serves (uptiṣṭhate°) mindfulness of the body: As [prajñā] sees, so it is expressed. This is why the foundation of mindfulness is called wisdom.[139] When the body is the object of wisdom, this is called 212
the foundation of mindfulness pertaining to body [and so on] up to 'dharmas' as the object of wisdom, which is called 'foundation of mindfulness pertaining to dharmas'.

Wisdom investigates the body and the other [objects of mindfulness] with regard to their unique and general (svasāmānya°) characteristics. Here the unique characteristic of 'body' is its innate nature (svabhāva) [as] the primary and their derived elements; the unique characteristic of feelings is experiencing (anubhava); of mind is apprehension (upalabdhi). The rest of the dharmas° leaving aside these three constitute the foundation of mindfulness of mental objects. [Each] of them accordingly has its innate nature. 'Impermanence', 'suffering', 'emptiness', and 'selflessness' (anātmakatva) are general characteristics of all [four] foundations of mindfulness.[140]

[Question:] Why does the order of the [four foundations] fol- 213
low the order given? Reply: The order is in accord with their [mode of] arising. And why do they arise in this sequence? Whatever is more gross appears first. Again, it is because the body is the abode of sensual lust, which [manifests] on account of desire that arises through feeling, which in turn arises because the mind is untamed, and this is owing to the non-abandonment of defilements.[141]

As to their nomenclature, it is according to their objects (ālambana). The foundation of mindfulness of the body has the body as an object; the same applies to feelings and the others.

The foundations of mindfulness have been explained.

Topic Fourteen

Four Right Efforts

29 *"Now, monks, what are the four right efforts?*

"Monks, a monk generates desire, endeavors, stirs up energy, exerts his mind, and rightly makes a vow to rid himself of evil and unwholesome thoughts that have arisen.

"He generates desire, endeavors, stirs up energy, exerts his mind, and rightly makes a vow not to allow the arising of evil and unwholesome thoughts that have not arisen.

"He generates desire, endeavors, stirs up energy, exerts his mind, and rightly makes a vow for the arising of wholesome thoughts.

"He generates desire, endeavors, stirs up energy, exerts his mind, and rightly makes a vow to maintain, preserve, protect, repeatedly enact, increase, and consummate wholesome thoughts that have arisen.

"These, monks, are the four right efforts."

214 Next, right efforts (samyakprahāṇas°) are explained. Regarding them, the question is put, 'Now, monks, what are the four

right efforts?' They are called 'efforts' (pradhānāni°) because they rightly tame the body, speech and mind.[142] By this is meant that they generate[143] the arising of wholesome thoughts and cessation of unwholesome thoughts.

'Evil [and unwholesome thoughts] that have arisen' and so 215
on. Evil (pāpaka) signifies the inherent nature, association, and arising of lust and so forth. 'Ridding oneself' means abandoning their practice. 'Generates desire': Desire is a part of energy (vīrya). Thus in the beginning he generates the desire (chanda°) to abandon them, which is of the nature of 'wishing to do'. 'Endeavors' indicates that in the initial, preparatory state when concentration is not present, he makes use of means (upāya) that will lead to abandoning them.[144]

When he has developed these means through frequent practice and through strengthening [his effort], he activates energy. Here 'strengthening' is a continuing activity [that depends] on
frequent practice. By zealously [literally, respectfully = satkṛtya°] 216
practicing concentration and removing sluggishness (laya°) when it arises, he exerts his mind. By developing resistance to excitedness, he rightly makes a vow (cittam praṇidadhāti°).

[Now for the other three of the four right efforts:]

'[Thoughts] that have not arisen'. Which are those? Regarding the non-arising of these very evil latent defilements, their true nature of utter non-arising is set forth. 'He generates desire'. This is as above.

'The arising of wholesome [thoughts] which have not arisen'. Here too he generates desire, as above.

'Wholesome [thoughts] that have [already arisen]'. [These are] faith (śraddhā) and the like. 'He generates desire . . . to maintain'. This is as above.

An alternative [explanation:]

'He generates desire' means generating the application of energy (vīrya-prayoga). By bringing application to consummation, he endeavors. In not relaxing his striving to generate bodily

and mental development [literally, sequence], he activates energy. By preventing the [arising of] secondary defilements [that obstruct] mental calm (śamatha), he exerts his mind. [And] by preventing the [arising of] secondary defilement [that obstructs]
217 insight (vipaśyanā), he rightly makes a vow. As for these [two] secondary defilements (upakleśas)[145], they are sluggishness (laya) and excitedness (auddhatya) respectively.

[The special terms of the fourth right effort:]

By zealously practicing development of energy, 'he generates desire'. By abandoning indolence, he endeavors; that is he fixes [his intention] upon the body and mind. By removing sluggishness and excitedness, 'he activates energy'.

How does he begin? He stirs up the sluggish [or sinking] mind with thoughts (manaskāra) of religious devotion [literally, emotion] [toward the teachings of the Buddha, contemplating the miseries of the world] and arousing delight (pramodanīya).[146] By fixing the excited mind on its object (ālambana), he 'rightly makes a vow' (samyakpradadhāti°). This means that he takes hold [of the mind] and sets it in [right] motion. Likewise he protects (aparihāṇi°) and maintains wholesome [thoughts] that have arisen. 'Repeatedly enact' indicates continuous arising and 'consummation' indicates reaching the apex. All of this explanation (vyākhyā) of the words [of the Sūtra] has been given by our teacher°.

218 With these four [terms] the fourfold functioning of energy is explained. Thus the [four] right efforts (samyakpradhānas°) are known to possess the nature of energy.

[Question:] Why is the present dark aspect the first to be presented? Reply: The present (pratyutpanna) is easily understood, not that which is not present (anutpanna°). Again, the dark aspect is easily understood by persons [setting out] to be trained.

Topic Fifteen

Four Bases of Psychic Powers

"Now, monks, what are the four bases of psychic power? 30

"Monks, a monk cultivates the basis of psychic power possessed of concentration born of zeal. Endowed with action involving effort, based on detachment, dispassion, and the cessation [of defilements] that ripens into renunciation, his zeal is° neither too sluggish nor too strenuous.

"He cultivates the basis of psychic power possessed of concentration born of energy. Endowed with action involving effort, based on detachment, dispassion, and the cessation [of defilements] that ripens into renunciation, his energy is neither too sluggish nor too strenuous.

"He cultivates the basis of psychic power possessed of concentration born of consciousness°. Endowed with action involving effort, based on detachment, dispassion, and the cessation [of defilements] that ripens into renunciation, his consciousness is neither too sluggish nor too strenuous.

"He cultivates the basis of psychic power possessed of concentration born of investigation. Endowed with action involving 31

effort, based on detachment, dispassion, and the cessation [of defilements] that ripens into renunciation, his investigation is neither too sluggish nor too strenuous.

"These, monks, are the four bases of psychic powers."

219 After 'right efforts' [come] the four bases of psychic power (ṛddhipāda°) To expound them, the question is put, 'Now, monks, what are the four bases of psychic power?'

Psychic power (ṛddhi) is the abundance or affluence (smṛddhi°) of all qualities of higher knowledge (abhijñā°) and the like.[147] They [are] feet (pāda) as [they are] the foundation (pratiṣṭhā) of psychic power; hence they are called 'the bases of
220 psychic power'. This means they are the cause of psychic power.[148] They have [four] characteristics: 'zeal' (chanda°), energy (vīrya°), mind [or consciousness] (citta°), and investigation (mīmāṁsā°).

Explaining them in order, it is stated: 'Monks, a monk . . . [possessed of] concentration [born of] zeal ... [involving] effort....'

Concentration caused by zeal is 'concentration-zeal' (chandasamādhi), meaning that it is produced by the predominance of zeal, which is the desire [to do]. Here the term 'chandasamādhi' indicates this predominance. Zealously one develops his effort and advances to attain the concentration of mind.

The actions for abandonment (prahāṇasaṁskāra°) are 'abandonment actions'; that is, they are to be abandoned°. What is to be abandoned? The five faults (doṣas): indolence, confusion (saṁmoṣa), sluggishness, excitedness, and lack of effort (anabhisaṁskāra°).

Again, there are eight karma formations involving effort
221 (prahāṇasaṁskāra) are mentioned in a Sūtra. They have the characteristics of desire, effort (vyāyāma), faith, tranquillity (praśrabdhi), mindfulness, clear awareness, volition (cetanā) and equanimity.[149]

Concentration born of zeal and karma formations involving effort (prahāṇasaṁskāra) are [to be understood as] concentration-zeal and karma formations of effort. 'Endowed with' means that he [the yogi] is accompanied by or joined by; [on this basis] he cultivates psychic power through his practice. 'Based on detachment': Detachment (viveka°) is a path (mārga), and it gets its name because through it defilement (kleśa) is isolated (vivicyate) and thus abandoned (prahīyate). 'Based on' indicates that detachment and the rest are favorable or serve to support.

'Based on dispassion'. Dispassion is the abandonment of passion (rāga°); it signifies nirvāṇa°. 'Based on cessation'. Separation from impure entities is cessation, [and this] is a [further] support. 'Ripens into renunciation'. 'Renunciation' (vyavasarga) means that conditioned entities (samskṛtavastu) are abandoned,
given up, cut off. 'Ripening into' means confirming (anukūla°). 222

The second [base of psychic power]: The phrase is given, 'concentration of energy' (vīryasamādhi°). 'Concentration of energy' indicates reaching one-pointedness of mind through applying energy to constant practice. The rest is as above.

The third [base of psychic power]. The phrase is given, 'concentration of mind'. 'Concentration of mind' means that when [the yogi] has obtained the seed of previous samādhi, holding mind as mind, he reaches one-pointedness of mind. The rest is as before.

The fourth [base of psychic power]. The phrase is given, 'concentration of investigation' (mīmāṁsā-samādhi°). Investigation is [characteristic of] wisdom (prajñā). Here 'concentration of investigation' indicates that when selecting an object, he does so with one-pointedness of mind. The rest is as before.

In this way, it is shown that the bases of psychic powers have the nature of samādhi.

Topic Sixteen

Five Faculties

31 *"Now, monks, what are the five faculties?*

"The faculty of faith, the faculty of energy, the faculty of mindfulness, the faculty of concentration, and the faculty of wisdom.

"Now, what is the faculty of faith? It is the faculty by which [a monk] has confidence in four things. What are these four?

"He believes in the right view concerning transmigration in the
world. He takes refuge [in the view] that every karma has conse-
quences, [thinking]: 'Whatever action I take, whether virtuous or
sinful, I shall have to experience the result of that action.' There-
32 *fore, he does not commit sin even for the sake of his life.*[150] *This is*
the faculty of faith.

"And what is the faculty of energy? It is the faculty through which he acquires the qualities that he accepts through the faculty of faith. This is the faculty of energy.

"And what is the faculty of mindfulness? It is the faculty through which he guards from loss the qualities that he acquires through the faculty of energy. This is the faculty of mindfulness.

"And what is the faculty of concentration? It is the faculty through which he fixes his mind on the qualities that he guards from loss through the faculty of mindfulness. This is the faculty of concentration.

"And what is the faculty of wisdom? It is the faculty through which he thoroughly understands and deeply reflects on the qualities on which he fixes his mind through the faculty of concentra- *33*
tion. And he cultivates the nature of deep reflection on these qualities. This is called the faculty of wisdom."

After the bases of psychic powers, the faculties (indriyas) are 223
explained. To expound them, the question is put: 'Now, monks, what are the five faculties?' They are the faculty of faith through the faculty of wisdom: 'Faith' is serenity of mind (prasāda°); 'energy' is enthusiastic determination (abhyutsāha°) to perform meritorious deeds; 'mindfulness' is non-forgetfulness (apramoṣa°) of the object°; concentration is one-pointedness of mind; and wisdom is investigation of dharmas (dharmapravicaya°).

Now, the order of the faculties. One who has faith activates 224
energy to obtain the result. One who has activated energy is well-established° in mindfulness. One with mindfulness well established is free from distraction, and one who has a concentrated mind knows reality.[151]

'Concerning transmigration in the world' means that which includes or belongs to the world of transmigration°. 'Worldly' is that which arises from the world and concerns it. 'Right view' (samyagdṛṣṭi) means [accepting] the [order of] existence of the other world. 'Virtuous' means wholesome. 'Sinful' (pāpaka) means unwholesome. 'Result of karma' (vipāka) means results that have the nature of being desired (iṣṭa) and undesired (aniṣṭa), which 'I shall experience' (pratisaṁvedayiṣyāmi).

'Acquires° by energy' indicates energy, characterized by enthusiastic determination to perform meritorious deeds. He prevents 225
this from being lost through the faculty of mindfulness, for mindfulness has the characteristic of not losing (asampramoṣa) its object.

Commentary on Topic XVI

'Fixes [his mind]' indicates that because of the characteristic of concentration, there is one-pointedness of mind. 'Thoroughly understands' (literally, penetrates) means to realize directly, face to face, due to the faculty of wisdom (prajñā), having the nature of discernment of dharmas.

Topic Seventeen

The Five Powers

"Now, monks, what are the five powers? Power of faith, power 33
of energy, power of mindfulness, power of concentration, and power of wisdom. These, monks, are the five powers."

After the faculties, the powers. To explain them, the question 226
is put, 'What are the five powers? [The reply:] the power of faith' through 'the power of wisdom.' These are the five faculties, beginning with faith, [but] when they become powerful they are called powers (balas).

How does their power develop? When the opposing forces—lack of faith (aśraddhā), indolence (kausīdya), loss of awareness (muṣitasmṛti), distraction (vikṣepa), and lack of clear awareness (asamprajanya°)—are not activated [even] intermittently, they [the
five powers] are not crushed, and for this reason they are called 227
powers. [In contrast], the faculties continue to be intermittently overpowered; not having conquered their opponents, they are [simply] called faculties.[152]

The powers have been explained.

Topic Eighteen

The Seven Constituents of Enlightenment

"What, monks, are the seven constituents of enlightenment?

"Mindfulness, the investigation of dharmas, energy, rapture, tranquility, concentration, and equanimity.

34 *"Monks, a monk cultivates the enlightenment constituent of mindfulness based on detachment, dispassion, and the cessation [of defilements] that ripens into renunciation.*

"Likewise, he cultivates the enlightenment constituent of investigation of dharmas based on detachment, dispassion, and the cessation [of defilements] that ripens into renunciation.

He cultivates the enlightenment constituent of energy based on detachment, dispassion, and the cessation [of defilements] that ripens into renunciation.

"He cultivates the enlightenment constituent of rapture based on detachment, dispassion, and the cessation [of defilements] that ripens into renunciation.

"He cultivates the enlightenment constituent of tranquility based on detachment, dispassion, and the cessation [of defilements] that ripens into renunciation.

"He cultivates the enlightenment constituent of concentration based on detachment, dispassion, and the cessation [of defilements] that ripens into renunciation.

"He cultivates the enlightenment constituent of equanimity based on detachment, dispassion, and the cessation [of defilements] that ripens into renunciation.

"These, monks, are the seven constituents of enlightenment."

Next, the constituents of enlightenment (bodhyaṅgas). To ex- 228
plain them, [the question is put]: 'What are the seven constituents of enlightenment?' The reply: 'enlightenment constituent of mindfulness' through 'enlightenment constituent of equanimity'.

[Question:] What is [the relation between] 'enlightenment' (bodhi°) and 'constituent of enlightenment' (bodhyaṅga) Reply: 'Investigation of dharmas' (dharmapravicaya°) is both enlightenment and a constituent of enlightenment. The rest are constituents of enlightenment only.

[Now, regarding] a Bodhisattva's [journey leading to] enlightenment (bodhisattvābhisambodha°): To accord with different [kinds of] individuals (pudgalabhedena°), there are three [types of] enlightenment: the enlightenment of a disciple (śrāvaka°, literally, hearer); that of a 'buddha by himself' (pratyekabuddha°); and that of the Perfectly Awakened One (samyaksambuddha).

The investigation of dharmas (dharmapravicaya) is said to be 229
'enlightenment' because it is of the nature of bodhi (bodhyātmaka). Mindfulness and the others are associates of bodhi, and so are 'constituents'. [They are] also [constituents] because these six are favorable to [the gaining of] bodhi.

[To explore this further:] 230

Mindfulness is a support constituent to bodhi. Through the power of mindfulness, one is not distracted in concentrating on an object.[153]

Investigation of dharmas is a constituent in its own being, because the nature of enlightenment is knowledge (jñāna).

Energy is a constituent of 'going forth' (niryāṇāṅga). By it one crosses over from the stage of being a worldling (pṛthagjanabhūmi).

Rapture is a favorable constitutent, because by it body and mind are benefitted.

Tranquility, samādhi, and equanimity are constituents free from defilements, because they work as antidotes to the defilements.[154]

[Regarding equanimity,] the reference here is to equanimity of conditioned states, not equanimity of feelings. This is because 'rapture' is mentioned, and rapture is of the nature of mental happiness. In a single grouping of mind and mental states, two entities of feeling cannot co-exist; therefore, the constituent of equanimity here is [to be taken as] the equanimity of conditioned states.[155] Since these constituents [when cultivated] on the path of meditation (bhāvanāmārga), are close to bodhi,[156] they are regarded as constituents of enlightenment.

The constituents of enlightenment have been explained.

Topic Nineteen

The Noble Eightfold Path

"Now, monks, what is the Noble Eightfold Path? 35

"Right view, right thought, right speech, right action, right livelihood, right effort, right mindfulness, and right concentration.

"And monks, what is right view? 'There is this world and the next; there are mother and father; there is the giving of alms and the making of sacrifices. There is the ripening fruit, pleasant and unpleasant, of good and evil deeds. There are in this world persons who have rightly gone and are well practicing'.[157] *This, monks, is the right view, and what is opposed to it is the wrong view°.*

"What is right thought°? It is doing virtuous and generous deeds [with the aim that they] ripen into attaining Buddhahood rather than leading to universal sovereignty.[158] *This is right thought.*

"What is right speech? Monks, it is [speech] free from rudeness, falsehood, slander, and frivolity. This, monks, is right speech.

"What is right action? It consists in performing ten wholesome 36
ways of action, through body, speech, and mind. Action of the body

is of three kinds: Abstinence from killing a living being, from taking what is not given, and from wrongful conduct in seeking sensual pleasures°. Action of speech is of four kinds: Abstinence from falsehood, from slander, from harsh speech, and from frivolous talk. Action of the mind is of three kinds: Abstinence from covetousness, malice, and wrong views.

"And what is meant by 'killing a living being'? A living, sentient being is present, and someone generates the intention to kill, attacks, and takes away its life. This is called killing a living being. It is not 'killing a living being' when the act is done through carelessness or oversight.

"What is stealing? Intending to take to own the wealth of others is called stealing. Taking small portions of the property of mother, father, or brother, or of one's own relations or friends without causing any hindrance is not stealing.[159]

"And what is wrongful conduct in seeking sexual° pleasures? Enjoying the women of others, such as those who are under the guardianship of master, king, mother, or father. It is also wrongful conduct to seek sexual pleasure in an improper place, where one
37 *should not go, or at the wrong place and time. This is called wrongful sexual conduct.*

"These are the three actions of body.

"Now, what is falsehood? When one is asked to bear witness and says what is not really so, this is falsehood. [An example:] Claiming to be an Arhat when one is not. To speak in jest is not falsehood.[160]

"What is slander? Speech that is not truthful and causes dissension is slander. This is called slander.

"What is harsh speech? To address hurtful words to another
38 *desiring to cause anguish is harsh speech. This is called harsh speech.*

"What is frivolous talk? Talk concerning kings, thieves, war, intoxicants, gambling, women, legends, and stories. This is called frivolous talk.

"These are the four actions of speech.

"What is covetousness? To desire to own others' wealth is covetousness. [The wish:] 'May whatever wealth he has belong to me': This is called covetousness.

"What is malice? The thought of taking away the life of others, of injuring or torturing them, and so forth: This is malice.

"What is wrong view? [To maintain views opposed to right view, such as] 'Neither this world nor the next exists', as well as the other views already indicated°. [This is wrong view.]

"These are the the three actions of the mind.

"Now, what is right livelihood? [It is breached when] a monk 39
indulges in hypocrisy, chatter, hinting, extortion, or exhibiting gain to seek gain.

"Now, what is hypocrisy? A monk having seen a generous donor coming, immediately sits in the cross-legged position at the side of the road or in an empty, uninhabited, sheltered place, thinking that the donor will take him to be a meditator and an Arhat and will honor him with gifts. This is called hypocrisy.

"And what is chatter? A monk intent on receiving gifts and honor speaks [to donors in this way]: 'O! You are my mother, my father, my sister, my daughter', and other sweet words. This is called chatter.

"And what is hinting? A monk having taken a meal repeatedly says: 'The likes of this meal that I have taken is not served in the houses of other laymen.' If said with no intention of seeking gain and honor, this is not a fault; [otherwise] this is called hinting.

"And what is extortion? A monk does not receive food at a 40
house and wishes to be given it. He says to the householder, 'Those who are not liberal donors go to hell. You are not a liberal donor and you will certainly go to hell.' The donor out of fear of hell makes an offering of food and the monk eats it. This is called extortion.

"And what is exhibiting gain to seek gain? A monk purchases beautiful robes with his own money and shows them to laymen,

saying 'We received such robes as offerings.' Out of shame, the laymen also give robes, and the monk makes use of them. This is called seeking gain by exhibiting it.

"This, monks, is wrong livelihood. To abstain from such action is right livelihood.[161]

"Now, as to wrong livelihood for laypeople: The sale of poison, weapons, living beings, intoxicants, or flesh, and the crushing of sesame and mustard without first examining them—these are wrong livelihood. To abstain from it, [monks, is right livelihood.]

41 *"This, monks, is called right livelihood.*

"What is right effort? Acting rightly through salutation, veneration, rising from a seat to bid welcome, raising the open hands placed side by side in respect. This, monks, is right effort.[162]

"And what, monks, is right mindfulness? "Monks, a monk sees a woman and passion arises in him. Now he looks at her body externally and internally in its reality and its impure form, [calling to mind:] 'In this body are hairs of the head, hairs of the body, nails, teeth, dirt, filth, skin, flesh, bones, sinews, nerves, kidney, heart, spleen, pleura, upper and lower stomach, intestines, mesentary, bladder, liver, excrement, tears, sweat, saliva, snot, grease, synovic fluid, marrow, fat, bile, phlegm, pus, blood, head, brain,
42 *feces, urine, and a full array of impurities.' This, monks, is called right mindfulness.*[163]

"Now, what is right concentration? The four meditations. Here, monks, a monk aloof from sense desires and from evil and unwholesome thoughts attains the first meditation born of aloofness and accompanied by initial thought and sustained thought, and he attains the first meditation with rapture and joy and abides there.

"Putting to rest initial and sustained thought, with mind made tranquil and absorbed in a single object, he attains the second meditation, devoid of initial and sustained thought, and he abides there.

"Being detached from rapture, he abides in equanimity, mindful and clearly aware, experiencing in his person that joy of which the

Noble Ones say: 'Joyful abides a person who has equanimity and is mindful.' Thus he attains and abides in the third meditation.

"Giving up pleasure as well as pain, with previous feelings of mental pleasure and pain having disappeared, he attains and abides in the fourth meditation, which is devoid of pleasure and pain and is purified by equanimity and mindfulness.

"These, monks are the four meditations. This is called right concentration.

"This, monks, is the Noble Eighfold Path."

After the constituents of enlightenment, the constituents of 231
the [Noble Eightfold] Path (mārgāṅgas) are explained. The question is put: 'What is the noble eightfold path (ārya-aṣṭāṅga-mārga)?' The explanation (in reply): from 'right view' through 'right concentration'.

Here the arrangement of the constituents of the path, starting with 'right view (samyagdṛṣṭi), has been ordered in sequence in relation to their opponents, from wrong view through wrong concentration.[164]

[Question:] One who is in the state of samādhi on the noble [eightfold] path [is said] to gain in one moment simultaneously all eight constituents of path. This is appropriate for the constituents starting with right view. But how could a person in
meditation (samāpanna°) gain right speech, right action and right 232
livelihood? While in meditation does he speak, act, go in search of robes, and so on? Reply: Never.

[Question:] Then how can these [three constituents] be included within [what is gained] in a meditative state? [Reply:] When [the meditator] is [engaged] in the path, then through the power of the path he gains a pure non-communicated state (avijñapti°). Having this in his possession, when he arises [from samādhi], he continues to engage in right speech rather than wrong speech, and so on. The explanation on this point is given metaphorically, the cause (nimitta) taking the form of its result (naimittika).[165]

Commentary on Topic XIX

According to the view of the Sautrāntikas, a meditator who is in the state of samādhi on the noble path, even without avijñapti, gains through the power of the noble path a type of intention
233 (āśaya°) and a personality (āśraya°) that he continues to possess when he rises from samādhi, and therefore he does not engage in wrong speech but engages in right speech, and so forth. Thus by metaphoric substitution of a cause for its result, the eight constituents are established [through the samādhi of the noble path]. In fact, they do not exist apart [from this].

Topic Twenty

The Sixteenfold Mindfulness of Breathing In and Breathing Out

"Now, what, monks, is the sixteenfold mindfulness of breathing in and breathing out?

"Monks, a monk, breathing in mindfully, truly knows: 'I am 43
breathing in.' Breathing out mindfully, he truly knows: 'I am breathing out.'

"Breathing in a long breath, he truly knows: 'I am breathing in a long breath.' And breathing out a long breath, he truly knows: 'I am breathing out a long breath.' Breathing in a short breath, he truly knows: 'I am breathing in a short breath.' Breathing out a short breath, he truly knows: 'I am breathing out a short breath.'

"Experiencing all the activities of body he breathes in and truly knows: 'I am breathing in experiencing all the activities of body.' Likewise, he breathes out experiencing all the activities of body and truly knows: 'I am breathing out experiencing all the activities of body.'

"Experiencing rapture he breathes in and truly knows: 'I am breathing in experiencing rapture.' Likewise, he breathes out experiencing rapture and truly knows: 'I am breathing out experiencing rapture.'

44 *"Experiencing happiness he breathes in and truly knows: 'I am breathing in experiencing happiness.' Likewise, he breathes out and truly knows: 'I am breathing out experiencing happiness.'*

"Calming the activities of the body, he breathes in and truly knows: 'I am breathing in calming the activities of the body.' Likewise, he breathes out and truly knows: 'I am breathing out calming the activities of the body.'

"Experiencing the activities of the mind, he breathes in and truly knows: 'I am breathing in experiencing the activities of the mind.' Likewise, he breathes out and truly knows: 'I am breathing out experiencing the activities of the mind.'

"Calming the activities of the mind, he breathes in and truly knows: 'I am breathing in calming the activities of the mind.' Likewise, he breathes out and truly knows: 'I am breathing out calming the activities of the mind.'

"Experiencing the mind, he breathes in and truly knows: 'I am breathing in while experiencing the mind.' Likewise, he breathes out and truly knows: 'I am breathing in while experiencing the mind.'

"With the thought, 'My mind rejoices', he breathes in and truly knows: 'I am breathing in while thinking, "My mind rejoices."' Likewise, he breathes out and truly knows: 'I am breathing in while thinking, "My mind rejoices."'

"Concentrating the mind, he breathes in and truly knows: 'I am breathing in while concentrating the mind.' Likewise, he breathes out and truly knows: 'I am breathing out while concentrating the mind.'

"With the thought, 'My mind is free,' he breathes in and truly knows: 'I am breathing in while thinking, "My mind is free."' Likewise, he breathes out and truly knows: 'I am breathing out while thinking, "My mind is free."'

45 *"Thus, contemplating impermanence, he breathes in and truly knows: 'I am breathing in contemplating impermanence.' Likewise, he breathes out and truly knows: 'I am breathing out contemplating impermanence.'*

"Contemplating dispassion, he breathes in and truly knows: 'I am breathing in contemplating dispassion.' Likewise, he breathes out and truly knows: 'I am breathing out contemplating dispassion.'

"Contemplating cessation, he breathes in and truly knows: 'I am breathing in contemplating cessation.' Likewise, he breathes out and truly knows: 'I am breathing out contemplating cessation.'

"Contemplating renunciation, he breathes in and truly knows: 'I am breathing in contemplating renunciation.' Likewise, he breathes out and truly knows: 'I am breathing in contemplating renunciation.'

"This, monks, is the sixteenfold mindfulness of breathing in and breathing out."

After expounding the path, in order to explain mindfulness of 234
breathing in and breathing out (ānāpānasmṛti), the [topic is introduced with the question]: 'Now, what, monks, is the sixteenfold mindfulness of breathing in and breathing out?'[166]

'Breathing in' (āna) refers to air that is taken in—air that is caused to enter. 'Breathing out' (apāna) is the air that is let out or expelled°. Mindfulness based on this [process] is 'mindfulness of breathing in and breathing out'. It has the nature of wisdom.[167] The word 'mindfulness' indicates that through the power of mindfulness, the process of wisdom is directed toward the object (ālambana) of mindfulness.

A yogi practicing mindfulness of breathing in and breathing
out should search for a spiritual guide (kalyāṇamitra°) to attach 235
himself to for instruction in the practice. He should also be of pure conduct, fond of learning [literally, listening] and reflection, and bodily and mentally aloof. Only in this way can the practice be done.

The sixteen aspects are explained by the words: 'Monks, a monk, breathing in mindfully, truly knows (yathābhūtam prajānāti), "I am breathing in." Breathing out mindfully, he truly knows, "I am breathing out." This is the [main] program generally implied in every aspect of breathing in and breathing out.

The rest is exposition (nirdeśa). 'Long and short breathing' and so on are the special implied aspects.

Here 'mindfully' indicates [a person] who is mindful. 'Knows' indicates one who is thus engaged in the meditation (bhāvanā); because of its practice his thought (mati°) is established in concentration.

[Now for the sixteen aspects:]

'Breathing in a long [breath]' 'Long' means extensive.

'Short [breath]' means opposed to 'long'. 'Knows' means he observes the movement of breathing in and breathing out.

'Experiencing all the activities of body'. All activities of the body are [encompassed in] 'all the activities of body'. They involve breathing in and breathing out. One whose nature it is to experience this becomes focused on it (tadanuyogāt°). Doing it constantly, he becomes aware° that [these activities] pervade the whole body.

'Experiencing rapture'. Rapture is experienced because in the
236 first and second attainments of dhyāna there is experiencing°
(saṁvedana) of mental happiness.

'Experiencing happiness'. In the first and second dhyāna, there is the happiness of tranquility (prasrabdhisukha°). In the third attainment of dhyāna there is mental happiness.[168]

[Question:] Since the mindfulness of breathing in and breathing out is associated with equanimity, how can one breathe in experiencing rapture and happiness? Reply: There is no difficulty. Turning away from thought (buddhi°) fixed on air, breathing in while observing (pratyavekṣamāṇa) rapture and happiness, he is called 'one who experiences rapture and happiness'.

A further question arises: If this happens, he may break off the practice of mindfulness of breathing. [Reply:] No, this will not happen, for he has not finished° with the intended exercise; moreover, he can quickly return to the object of meditation.

'Calming the activities of body' means tranquilizing through quietude (praśama), gradually attenuating and abandoning [the activities of the body]. Attenuation is obtained on gaining the third dhyāna. Abandoning is gained on entering the border (sāmantaka°) of the fourth dhyāna.

'Experiencing the activities° of mind' refers to one whose nature is to experience activities of mind; namely, perception and feeling. According to suitability, [one of] these finds a place in the dhyānas and formless attainments.

'Calming the activities of mind' means making them more 237
subtle and gradually transmuting them to formless attainments, and [finally] abandoning all of them in the [dhyāna] attainment of cessation (nirodha-samāpatti°).

'Experiencing the mind' means experiencing purity of mind through the power of attaining the fourth [dhyāna]. [There is] turning away from the thought fixed on air, due to attaining the fourth dhyāna.

'Rejoicing' indicates that the signs of sluggishness (laya) and exertion (pragraha°) are absent. Alternatively, 'rejoicing' means being endowed with joy. On account of sloth and torpor the mind is sluggish, and by reason of excitation it exerts itself. By their disappearance, one comes face to face with with joy (mudā yujyate). Therefore this is called 'rejoicing'. This is [because] mind is directed [literally, takes hold of] toward an object [of meditation] (nimitta) that is joyous [such as the Buddha]. A [third] alternative: 'Rejoicing' is experiencing [the sublime state of] sympathetic joy (muditā°).

'Concentrating the mind' means holding it quietly in samādhi. This is to experiencing it with equanimity (upekṣā°).

'Freeing' [the mind] means freeing it from fetters (prati- 238
bandha°) through gaining later [stages of] samādhi, or freeing it from the defilements of the rūpa and ārūpya stages.

'Contemplating° impermanence' means observing in each moment that [every] object (artha°) is impermanent. [This] is contemplating impermanence, and this contemplation concerns all processes (sarvasaṁskāras) in breathing in and breathing out.

'Contemplating dispassion'. Dispassion (virāga°) signifies that passion or lust for the three realms has been turned away. It is quietude of all processes (sarvasaṁskāropaśama°). That is what one realizes.

'Contemplating cessation'. Cessation means the entire extinction of all defilements. It is an absence of continuity due to the rooting out of all states (sarvadharmopaccheda).

'Contemplating renunciation' Renunciation is abandonment. It is casting off the burden of the skandhas acquired since beginningless time.

'Contemplating that, he breathes in' means that he trains; he strives.

239 Other [masters] explain [as follows]: "Breathing in long and short' means that while practicing, [when the breath] exceeds the natural [rhythm], it is called long, and when it is less than natural, it is called short." 'Knows' (prajānāti°) indicates that the practice is without any delusion.

[Further,] the beginner, with body and mind tranquil, mindful of breathing in and breathing out, reaches 'while breathing' a subtle state.[169] On account of the subtleness [of breathing in and breathing out],the breath cannot be found. At that time the yogi should discern° it [or mark° it] by taking long breaths until the object of meditation is [again] established (nimittaṁ saṁtiṣṭhate). When the object of meditation (nimitta°) is established, he should breathe in a natural way. This is a practice that is free from delusion (asammohakriyā).

The rest [of the explanation] is as stated above.

In this regard, when the object [of meditation practice] does not display either breathing in or breathing out, it should be understood that the object is in transition (ālambanasaṁkrānti).[170]

Topic Twenty-One

Four Constituents of Attaining the Stream

"Now, monks, what are the four constituents of attaining the 45
stream?"

After the mindfulness of breathing in and breathing out, the 240
constituents of attaining the stream° (srota apattyaṅgas°) are explained. To explain them, [the question is put]: 'What are the constituents of attaining the stream?'[171]

'The constituents of attaining the stream' means those [constituents] that are the cause of obtaining the fruit of stream-attainment.[172] They are [four aspects of] faith based on comprehension (avetyaprasāda°): faith in the Buddha, the Dharma, the Saṅgha, and in the moral precepts (śīla) dear to the Noble Ones. They are explained in order:

Subtopic One: Faith in the Buddha

"Monks, a noble disciple with faith in the Buddha based on comprehension [reflects]: 'Thus indeed is he the Blessed One, the Tathāgata, the Perfected One, the Rightly and Fully Awakened One, endowed with knowledge and right conduct, well gone, the Knower

of the World, the incomparable charioteer of men to be tamed, the teacher of gods and men, the Buddha, the Blessed One.'"

'Faith in the Buddha based on comprehension', and so on.

The dharmas of one who is no longer in training (aśaikṣa°) belong to the stream of personality° of a Buddha. [Here] 'Buddha' signifies the dharmạs which make one a Buddha.[173] Faith (prasāda) in these [dharmas] is faith in the Buddha based on comprehension.

241 What is the meaning of 'faith based on comprehension' (avetyaprasāda)? A conviction (sampratyaya°) that arises after comprehending the [four] truths as they truly are is a faith based on comprehension. It is established at the time of realizing (abhisamaya) the truth of the path. As one rises [from meditation] and experiences this directly, he proclaims°: 'Thus indeed is the Blessed One', and so on.

The words 'thus indeed is he the Blessed One' and so forth indicate the qualities and glory [of the Blessed One] in order. He has broken the fetters, and he possesses the attributes of the Teacher, a good speaker and one who practices [what he teaches]. For these reasons he is [called] the Blessed One, who surveys the fit and the unfit and establishes in discipline (vinayati) all who are fit. The epithets of the Teacher, well-known [literally, established] in regard to [these trainees], are [now] explained [in sequence].

242 Etymologically, the word 'bhagavān' (Blessed One), indicates the breaking of fetters. Having broken [them] (bhagnavān), he is called bhagavān°. But what, in this regard, is the obstacle (or fetter) to achieving [the status] of Teacher (śāstṛ)? [Reply:] It is Māra, the son of a god. When this [obstacle] is removed [literally, broken], the achievement of being Teacher has first been gained.

'Tathāgata', Perfected One (Arhat), 'Rightly and Fully Awakened One' (samyaksambuddha): These words indicate the achievements of being the Teacher. These are of two types: having the characteristics of a [good] speaker and of a practitioner.

Being a speaker means teaching Dharma that is not false. Because of this, the Blessed One is called Tathāgata°, for he speaks truly (tathaiva gadati) and not to the contrary.

The achievement of practice is [also] of two kinds: achievement of abandonment (prahāṇasampad°) and achievement of knowledge (jñānasampad°).

Because he has achieved abandonment, the Blessed One is called Arhat. Etymologically, [Arhat signifies] one who has killed his enemies (ari). And the enemies are the defilements, for they destroy all wholesome dharmas.

Because he is accomplished in knowledge (jñānasampad), he is called "Rightly and Fully Awakened One" (samyaksambuddha°), for he has comprehended without error dharmas all 243
round (samantāt°).

The achievement of being the Teacher is perfected in this way: teaching without falsehood, abandoning all defilements, and thoroughly realizing° all dharmas. These three achievements are found in the Blessed One only. Therefore is it said that the Blessed One possesses the achievement of being the Teacher (śāstṛtvasampad) in all its aspects.

'Endowed with knowledge and right conduct' (vidyācaraṇasampanna°). This [epithet] indicates the cause for the [Blessed One] gaining the achievement of being the Teacher. Knowledge (vidyā) and right conduct (caraṇa) [together] signify the Noble Eightfold Path. Right view is knowledge, [which is like the eyes]; the remaining constituents are taken as the feet, for without eyes (lit. 'sight') and feet, one cannot move.

An alternate explanation: 'Knowledge and right conduct refer to the three trainings (śikṣās°). The training in wisdom is knowledge, while the trainings in morality and mental development or meditation (adhicitta) signify 'right conduct'. Since wisdom is [both] preparation and an advancing movement (puraścaraṇa), [the word] caraṇa is justified. Knowledge is mentioned first because when it is purified, morality and meditation are purified [as well]. And also because by seeing with the eye of wisdom (prajñā) and by moving with the feet of morality (śīla) and meditation (samādhi), one reaches the destination. Thus knowledge and right conduct point to the three trainings.

244 [The epithet] 'sugata°' indicates reaching the destination. One who is 'well gone' is sugata in the sense of not returning again to this world. It is like a fever that has vanished forever. Alternatively, sugata means one who has fully gone, i.e. has reached completely the [highest] knowable state [or the apex of knowledge]. It is like a jar full to the brim.

These two interpretations differentiate [the Blessed One] from the disciples and from outsiders. Outsiders° are not well gone because they return again [to saṁsāra]. The disciples, though they are well gone—for they cannot any longer return to the state of worldling (pṛthagjanatā)—are not fully gone, for they are obstructed in their knowledge of all that is knowable (sarvajñeya). Thus, through achieving 'knowledge and right conduct', [the Blessed One] posesses rightly and fully the achievement of being the Teacher [of gods and men].

The work of the Teacher is [further] shown by these terms: Knower of the World (lokavid) and incomparable (anuttara) Charioteer of men to be tamed°.

[In this regard,] the work of the Teacher is twofold: to survey those in the world who are capable (bhavya) and incapable (abhavya) [of following the path] and to establish in discipline
245 those who are capable. The epithet 'Knower of the World' indicates surveying the world [to discover] the capable and the incapable. One who knows the world with this special knowledge is called Knower of the World.

In addition, the Blessed One [has this name because he] surveys the world with the Buddha eye (buddhacakṣu) three times each night and three times each day [to determine] as follows:

> Who diminishes°; who increases; who is in distress; who has met misfortune; who is sunk in the state of woe that I

can bring out from the state of woe to establish in heaven and liberation; whose roots of merits are not yet planted, that I can cause to be planted; whose roots [of merit] have been planted, that I can mature (paripācayeyam°); and whose [roots] have matured, that I can liberate." [174]

'Incomparable Charioteer of men to be tamed' (anuttara-puruṣa-damyasārathi°), indicates establishing in discipline those who are capable. The Blessed One, as the [Great] Charioteer, having surveyed the capable and incapable, tames those [worthy or] capable of being tamed, for taming is the role of a charioteer.[175] 'Incomparable' serves as a qualifying word, due to [his] taming persons who are difficult to be tamed, due to their intense attachment, hatred, and infatuation. Examples include Ārya Sundarānanda, Aṅgulimāla, Uruvilvākāśyapa, and others.[176] 246
Again, he is called 'incomparable Charioteer of men to be tamed' because he disciplines beings to reach the highest goal, and not to return to [this world]. It is for disciplining the capable that he is so described.

And how does the Buddha act toward those who are not capable? He protects them from miserable and woeful states, as well as from suffering, and establishes them in the comfort of pleasure and happy states.[177] Those who are capable and definitely destined for a [particular] family [or clan, gotra°], such as the enlightenment of the disciples, he establishes according to their capacity. And through the power of conditions (pratyayabala),[178] he turns those who are not so destined away from the lower states and establishes them in the higher states of existence.

'Teacher of gods and men' (śāstā devānām ca manuṣyāṇāṁ° ca) indicates the work of teacher, which operates with regard to [sentient] beings. Although the Blessed One is especially° the teacher of [all] beings°, since he instructs them regarding the path [leading] to heaven and beatitude, [those who share] the noble vision and seek the fruit of the reclusive life (śrāmaṇyaphala)
have the [first] claim. In this regard, right instruction (yathār- 247
thānuśāsana°) is considered [lit., desired] the work of the teacher. 'Gods and men' are mentioned because they are recipients.

Commentary on Topic XXI

Now, for what purpose are the two words 'Buddha' and 'Bhagavān' used [at the end]? The nine epithets [already given] explain all that is intended regarding the qualities and glory [of the Buddha]. Whenever these qualities and glory [are found], they signify 'Buddha and Bhagavān'

[A verse] to sum up: 'Having broken the fetter, all the achievements of a teacher; by whom and how he has come; all the work
248 of a teacher and by whom gained.' Thus it is explained.[179]

Subtopic Two: Faith in the Dharma

"He has faith in the Dharma based on comprehension [and reflects]: 'The Dharma is well proclaimed by the Blessed One; it is realized [by oneself] in this very life; it is free from the fever [of defilement]; it is timeless, leading onwards [to nirvāṇa]; it is [truly, as the Tathāgata has said,] a thing to "come and see" [for oneself].
46 The wise experience it for themselves as the crushing of pride, the removing of thirst, the destruction of attachment, the cutting off of conditioned existence°, the realization of the void; as the destruction of craving; as freedom from the passions, as cessation, as nirvāṇa'."

'Faith in the Dharma based on comprehension', and so on.

Here 'Dharma' signifies the path of the Bodhisattva and Pratyekabuddha° and the three truths.[180] Thus, faith in the Dharma based on comprehension is attained through comprehending the four truths. As one rises from meditation° and experiences this directly, it is made manifest: 'The Dharma is well proclaimed by the Blessed One; it is realized' and so on. Here the main topic is 'well proclaimed'. The rest is exposition.

'Well proclaimed' indicates that it is free from error (aviparīta°), rightly proclaimed. Because it can be seen [directly], it is said to be 'realized [in this very life]' (sāndṛṣṭika°), [for] it is not known only on faith. As an antidote to defilements (kleśas) and latent defilements (anuśaya°), it is called 'free from fever'. As it is unfailing (aparihāṇīyatvāt°), it is timeless (ākālika°). Alternatively, [it is called 'timeless'] because it can never fail, and because there are no temporal limits [on its power] for the abandonment of defilements.

[The Dharma] 'leads onwards' because it leads to complete release (niryāṇa) from suffering. It is [an experience to] 'come and see' (aihipaśyaka°) because it is extraordinary. It is a state (bhāva) to be seen here in this very existence, since it manifests suchness of phenomena (tathātva; i.e., tathatā°) here (and now). 249

'The wise (vijñas) understand it for themselves'. Since it is beyond logical reasoning (atarkyatvāt°), it is to be known directly; the wise are the Āryas. Alternatively, the wise must know it for themselves; it cannot be expressed [in words].[181]

With these [words], the Eightfold Path[182] is well expounded; again, with these [words] the special (viśeṣa) qualities of the Bauddhadharma° have been clearly explained in comparison to other dharmas. The religions (dharmas) of outsiders, because of wrong [misleading] proclamations, cannot be called 'well proclaimed'. Because [their followers] have not seen reality [the truth] (artha°), their dharma cannot be experienced here and now°. Similar explanations can be applied [contextually] elsewhere.[183]

Subtopic Three: Faith in the Saṅgha

"He has faith in the Saṅgha based on comprehension [and reflects], 'The Blessed One's Saṅgha of disciples is well established in practice; it is on the way to nirvāṇa; it is upright in views; it is on the proper path; it is on the path of Dharma in all its aspects; it follows the Dharma in all its aspects. Within the Saṅgha are those 47
who are practicing to realize the fruit of attaining the stream and those who have attained this fruit; there are those who are practicing to realize the fruit of the once-returner and those who have attained this fruit; there are those who are practicing to realize the fruit of the never-returner and those who have attained this fruit; there are those who are practicing to realize the fruit of Arhathood and those who are Arhats. Thus the Saṅgha includes the four pairs of persons; the eight classes of individuals.'

"[He reflects that] this is the Saṅgha of disciples of the Blessed One, endowed with moral conduct, endowed with concentration, endowed with wisdom[183a]*, endowed with faith, endowed with learning by oral tradition, endowed with deliverance, endowed with deliverance obtained by knowledge and vision. It is worthy of offerings, worthy of providing hospitality, worthy of obeisance, worthy of paying homage. It is a matchless field of merit, worthy of the offerings made by the world."*

'He has faith in the Saṅgha based on comprehension', and so on.

The Saṅgha collectively constitutes those to be trained
250 (śaikṣa) and the adepts (aśaikṣa), persons who with regard to the path are beyond conquest by enemies such as Māra. Faith in the trainees and the adepts, born of the continuity of stream of the Saṅgha, is faith in the Saṅgha based on comprehension. It is established (vyavasthāpyate°) at the time of comprehension (abhisamya) of the path of the truth: Arising from meditation, one comes face to face with [its truth], seeing it [for oneself].[184]

'The Saṅgha of disciples (śrāvakas°) of the Blessed One is well established in practice (supratipanna°)'. Here 'well established in practice' is the main topic; the rest is explanation. The description given here shows the Saṅgha's progress [on the path], the object of the religious life, the right course for those who follow the religious life, and an exposition (upadeśa°) of the religious life of the Saṅgha of the Buddha's disciples.

Here nirvāṇa is the object (artha) of those who enter the religious life[185] and 'being well established in' refers to progress toward nirvāṇa (nyāyapratipanna°). As it is said in the scriptures:
251 "He indeed wins° the transcendental (anuttara) dharma." Here nyāya means nirvāṇa dharma. As is stated in the scriptures:

"Place (ayanaṁ) means where one arrives (āyaḥ); the place of permanent arrival (nityam āyaḥ) is nyāya°."

Entry into the religious life (śrāmaṇya°) is the Noble Eightfold Path.[186] And one who is well established in practice is proceeding uprightly. It is said in the scriptures:

"The door to immortality is open and the upright way is illumined."[187]

In another verse (gāthā), it is put as follows:

"What is the upright noble path°, and what the twisted [crooked], evil view?[188]

Among those in the religious life, being well established in practice means progressing properly. And righteousness is being endowed with loving kindness [towards beings, expressed] by actions of body, speech and mind. This [comes about] through equality [or sharing] (samānatā°) in the use or enjoyment of objects, moral precepts, and views. In this regard, equality in the use of objects refers to material things, equality [or similarity] of precepts refers to [common] precepts, and equality [or similarity] of views refers to [common] beliefs.[189]

'The exposition of the religious life' is a dharma that has the 252
characteristics of instruction: This explains the obtaining [of instruction]. Therefore the Saṅgha 'is on [the path of] Dharma in all its aspects (dharmānudharma°-pratipanna)'. It performs what is prescribed to be done. [Thus] it is practicing in accord with the Dharma (anudharmacārī°).

'Within the Saṅgha are those who are practicing to realize the fruit of attaining the stream', and so on. While on the path of vision (darśanamārga), in fifteen moments of patient acceptance and knowledge (kṣāntijñānakṣaṇa)[190], one is said to be 'progressing towards the fruit of the stream-winner'. On the path of meditation (bhavanā-mārga) in the subsequent knowledge of the path (mārgānvayajñāna°), in the sixteenth moment, one becomes a stream-winner (srota āpanna).[191] After the sixteenth moment of knowledge until reaching the moment when defilements of the sixth type are extinguished, one is said to be progressing toward the 'fruit of the once-returner". And at the moment of extinction of the sixth type of defilement, one becomes a 'once-returner' (sakṛdāgāmi). Beginning with the extinction of the seventh type of defilement until the moment of extinction of the ninth type of defilement, one is progressing toward [or obtaining] the fruit of the non-returner. And when the ninth type of defilement is extinct, one is called a non-returner (anāgāmi) to the realm of desire, because the five lower (avarabhāgīya)[192] defilements are extinct.

From the detachment of the first stage of meditation (of the rūpadhātu) up to the last stage of worldly existence (bhāvāgrika, in the ārūpyadhātu), as long as the ninth type of defilement is not extinct, one is said to be 'progressing toward [obtaining] the fruit of an Arhat'. When the ninth type of [defilement] is extinct in the highest stage (bhāvāgrika), one has become an Arhat.[193]

Thus there are four pairs (yuga) [in the Saṅgha], as stated immediately above°: the first pair is one progressing toward the
253 fruit of the stage of stream-winner and one who is a stream-winner; the second pair is one progressing toward the fruit of the stage of once-returner and one who is a once-returner; the third pair is one progressing toward the fruit of the stage of non-returner and one who is a non-returner; and the fourth pair is one progressing towards the fruit of the stage of an Arhat and one who is an Arhat. This comprises the eight types of persons or individuals (puruṣa-pudgala°).

[As to the term 'puruṣa-pudgala',] pudgalas° are [etymologically] so called because they are fully endowed with (pūryante) the accomplishment (prāpti) of accumulation (upacaya) of pure (anāsrava) dharmas, or else because acquisition of the major and secondary defilements (kleśopakleśa) vanish through melting away. These persons (puruṣa) and individuals (pudgala) are puruṣa-pudgalas. The [compound term] is an appellation for the appearance of the five skandhas.

'This is the Saṅgha of disciples (śrāvakas, literally 'hearers') of the Blessed One'. 'This' refers to [the persons] mentioned immediately above. 'Śrāvakas' are so called because they are subsequently (pareṇa°) brought to hear [the teaching] of the Buddha, the Blessed One. The Saṅgha constitutes the assembly of these [śrāvakas], without any distinction. The use of [the phrase] 'of the Blessed One' (bhagavato) is to distinguish it from other Saṅghas.

'Endowed with virtue' (śīlasampanna) means free from any faults (or flaws) [lit. 'gaps']; in other words, endowed with the accomplishment of virtue.

It is stated [in a gāthā]:

> 'Endowed with right view and right thought,' the nature of the assembly (gaṇa) of the Noble Ones (āryas) is [distinguished through] its virtuous moral conduct (śīla°)". The conduct (śīla) of others [who are not followers of the Buddha] lacks virtue and morality—their range of moral conduct is often cut off by immorality°.

'Endowed with concentration'. This means endowed with or 254
rightly engaged in (yukta°) the concentration of a trainee or an adept.

'Endowed with wisdom'. This means being possessed of wisdom having the characteristic of understanding of truth (satyāvabodhalakṣaṇa).

'Endowed with faith'. This means being endowed with or possessed of faith having the characteristic of faith based on comprehension.

'Endowed with learning' (śrutasampanna°). This means being endowed with learning that conforms to [or aids in] the abandonment of latent defilements and taking [the path of learning].

'Endowed with deliverance'. 'Deliverance' (vimukti) is the abandonment of defilements (kleśaprahāṇa). The Saṅgha is endowed with that deliverance.

'Endowed with deliverance, knowledge, and vision'. One who is delivered by abandoning the latent defilements (anuśaya) obtains knowledge and vision. 'Knowledge' signifies knowledge of extinction (kṣayajñāna°) etc., and also vision (darśana).

Alternatively, 'knowledge' signifies such [aspects] as right view of an adept (aśaikṣa),[194] which itself is vision, since it can be experienced directly (pratyakṣavṛttitvāt°). What can be experienced directly is known in common speech as vision, and knowledge should be understood accordingly. To be endowed with it is to be 'endowed with deliverance, knowledge and vision'.

'Worthy of gifts [āhavanīya, literally, of offerings]'. One who deserves offerings is called worthy of offerings. Here all types of offerings should be given, for the Saṅgha is worthy of all special [offerings].

'Worthy of providing hospitality (prāhavanīya°) [Just as] consecrated fire is [considered] truly special [for offerings], so whatever is [offered the Saṅgha] with profound faith gives immeasurable fruit of merit.

It is said as well:

> Month after month for a hundred years, one may make offerings with value of thousands, yet [such a] one is not worth even one-sixteenth part of one [with] faith (prasāda) in the Saṅgha.[195]

255 'Worthy of obeisance' (añjalīkaraṇīya). Since the [Saṅgha] is a field of merits, it is worthy of obeisance.

'Worthy of paying respect' (sāmīcīkaraṇīya°). This refers to taking a humble position while following [members of the Saṅgha].

'Matchless field of merit'. It is matchless and incomparable because there is none higher. 'Field of merit' (puṇyakṣetra): The field filled with merit is a field of merit, for even a minute meritorious deed (kuśala) [done for it] bears immeasurable fruit.

'Worthy of the offerings of the world'. [This is said] because [the Saṅgha] is worthy of offerings from the whole world, [and] such offerings bear immeasurable fruit.

As it is said in a gāthā:[196]

> Monks, those who have offered gifts to the Saṅgha have
> 256 served and offered well. The gift [given to the Saṅgha] excels all [gifts] given to [other] assemblies. The knower of the world has described it as bearing great fruit.

Subtopic Four: Moral Conduct

"This Saṅgha of disciples is endowed with moral conduct dear to 47
the Noble Ones, which is unbroken, flawless, pure, and unblemished; which leads to freedom and cannot be tarnished, which is well finished and well begun, praised by the wise, and not subject to denunciation.

"These, monks, are the four constituents of attaining the stream."

Moral conduct dear to the Nobles Ones (āryakāntāni° śīlāni), being beloved of the Noble Ones, is [by nature] pleasing. Moral conduct (śīla) is [etymologically] so called because it cools[196a] the stream of personality (santāna°).

Know that these words indicate the training in morality (adhiśīla-śikṣā). To explain further:

'Unbroken' means not violating the seven limbs of morality, beginning with abstinence from killing a living being.[197] 'Flawless' (acchidra) means not being set aside from time to time. 'Pure' (aśabala, lit. 'unspotted') means not being mixed with immorality. 'Unblemished' means not interrupted (avyavakīrṇa°) by any arising thought (or scruple) (tannidāna-vitarka°).

'Leading to freedom' (bhujiṣya°) indicates the freedom to acquire the antidotes (pratipakṣa) to moral laxity; namely, the power of careful consideration (pratisaṁkhyāna-bala°) and the power of meditation (bhāvanā-bala°). Acquiring them means coming face to face with them, again and again. In this way freedom [is obtained].

Freedom is not to be sought by such means (pratyaya°) as evil
friends. Thus, when the opponents [evil friends, etc.] are con- 257
quered, 'leading to freedom' is called 'free' (svatantra).

'Bhujiṣya' [in essence] means 'free', as is known from the Sūtra:

"From today, my son, you are no servant and no messenger; [you are] free, free to go as you please (yathākāmaṅgama°)."

'Untarnished' means not tarnished by a wrong view and a wrong vow (kudṛṣṭipraṇidhāna°). Here wrong view means belief in the existence of individuality (satkāyadṛṣṭi°), and wrong vow is [for example] as follows: "By this [vow of] celibacy (brahmacarya), or by this practice or rite, may I become a deva (god) or one in the [retinue of] devas."

[Question:] What is the quality through which the moral practices are called untarnished by these two [wrong views and wrong vows]? [Reply:] By going forth (nairyāṇikatā°), which is the way to deliverance from this world.

[An alternative explanation:]

'Unbroken', 'flawless', 'pure': These terms indicate that immor-
258 ality (dauśīlya) cannot overpower (anupahataṁ°) [the śīlas]. 'Unblemished' shows that the causes of immorality—the primary and secondary defilements (kleśopakleśas°)—also cannot overpower them. 'Leading to freedom' means supported by antidotes to these [defilements], and 'untarnished' indicates that [the antidotes] do not depend on rebirth in [celestial] realms.[198] In [clarifying] these terms, non-overpowering by immorality and its causes and right support from the antidotes to defilements are to be applied as is suitable.

The moral practices are 'well finished' on account of their perfection in being 'unbroken', 'flawless' and 'pure'. They are 'well begun' on account of their purity, being unblemished, free [from hindrances], and unsoiled. 'Praised' [by the wise] indicates that they are well approved by the Noble Ones for their wholesomeness. They are 'never denounced' due to their purity always (paryāyenāpi°) being uncensured.[199]

This faith in the moral precepts or virtues, based on comprehension and dear to the Noble Ones, is established at the time of seeing the [four] truths. It arises through pure restraint (saṁvara)[200] of the ever-changing mind (cittānuparivartitvāt). Arising from meditation (vyutthita), one experiences [its truth] face to face, in accord with the description given.

[Question:] What accounts for the sequence of the [four] faiths based on comprehension? [Reply:] It accords with the direct experience of a yogin as he arises from meditation. And how does he directly experience? [In accord with the insights as they have been indicated above]: 'Thus the Blessed One' and so on; 'Well-proclaimed is the Dharma', and so on; 'Well established in practice (supratipanna°) is the Saṅgha of disciples of the Blessed One', and so on—these [objects of faith] being respectively the physician, the medicine, and the attendant°. And that which clarifies or purifies the mind, the faith in moral conduct, 259
coming fourth, has been stated at the end.[201]

Topic Twenty-Two

Ten Powers of the Tathāgata

48 *"Now, what, monks, are the ten powers of the Tathāgata?*

"Herein, monks, the Tathāgata knows truly what is possible and what is not possible.

"He knows truly the results of actions and undertakings of the past, future, and present.

"He knows truly the different and diverse dispositions of other beings and of persons.

"He knows truly the world of different and diverse elements.

"He knows truly the higher and lower faculties of other beings.

"He knows truly the way leading to all destinies.

49 *"He knows truly the faculties, powers, constituents of enlightenment, meditations, deliverances, concentrations, and attainments of other beings as well as their differences in defilements and purity.*

"And also with regard to the former existence of beings, he well remembers their size, their place of birth, and the causes for their

birth, [not just] for one, two, three, or four existences, but for myriads of existences and so on.

"And further, with his heavenly vision, pure and superhuman, he sees beings dying and taking birth in good and bad states in accord with their good and bad deeds of body, speech, and mind, and so on.

"He knows truly and with wisdom the undefiled deliverance of mind through the destruction of defilements.

"These, monks, are the ten powers of the Tathāgata."

After 'faith based on comprehension', the ten powers (daśa 260
bala) are explained.[202] After putting the question, "What, monks, are the ten powers of the Tathāgata?" the reply is given.

(1) He knows truly the 'possible' (sthānaº) as possible and the 'impossible' as impossible (asthānaº). 'This is the Tathāgata's [first power], and so on'.[202a] [Here] 'possible' means the potential (sambhava) for knowledge through discernment (viniścaya-jñāna) of the nature (svabhāva) and power (śakti) of all dharmas.
'Impossible' means the impossibility that neither this innate 261
nature nor this work [or action = kriyā] is possible. This is the knowledge that is called knowledge of 'what is possible and what is not possible'.

Instances of this are given by the Blessed One himself. [Thus:]

"It is impossible when paying improper attention (ayoniśo manasikurvataḥº) for the defilements (āsravas) to become extinct. It is possible when paying proper attention."

This declaration has also been made: "It is possible for this cause and condition to bear this fruit. It is impossible for this cause and condition not to bear this fruit."

The possible and the impossible cover [all] knowable conditioned and unconditioned things (saṁskṛta and asaṁskṛta-jñeyavastu). Knowledge regarding them is considered a power because it is [wholly] unobstructed.[203]

262 Now, the question may be asked: Concerning the words 'possible' and 'impossible', when one is explained, the other is explained as well. What is the use of explicating both? [Reply:] The point is well-taken, but [there is a deeper meaning]. Knowledge of the possible refutes belief in the theory of non-causation (ahetuvāda);[204] i.e., that things occur without any cause; and knowledge of the impossible (refutes) belief in a mistaken causal theory (viṣamahetuvāda). This is why both have been explained.

More particularly, here the omniscience (sarvajñatā) [of the Buddha] is indicated. To comment briefly, a person who does not make great efforts will not be able to understand [the omniscience of the Buddha]; therefore [in listing the powers of the Tathāgata] nine [further] aspects [of his power or omniscience] are mentioned.

'Of the Tathāgata': These words are not explained, as they are easily understood.

This is [the explanation of] the power of knowledge of the possible and the impossible, concerning both sentient and nonsentient [entities].

(2) 'Results of actions and undertakings of the past, future, and present' and so on. The dharma of action is known as 'dharma action'. It is of [three] kinds: meritorious (puṇya), nonmeritorious (apuṇya) and without karmic consequence (āniñja).[205] It is stated [in scripture]: "He knows truly [all] types of actions and undertakings of the past," and so forth.

'According to place' (sthānataḥ°) means according to [a particular] place. In one place one karma will mature; in another, another. And this action done as a god will bear fruit [later] for the human being, since that is his circumstance (ity ava-
263 dhāraṇāt°); [while this action done as a human being will bear fruit later for the deva or non-human being, for this is his circumstance.]°

'As to the cause (hetutaḥ°)' means 'as to the reason'. Due to one reason, it will mature thus, and due to another, [it will mature] so. Conditioned by this assemblage [of causes], one kind of karma will arise, and conditioned by that, another kind. 'This [the Buddha] knows truly'.

'As to things' (vastutaḥ) means as to entities (dravyataḥ). From which action which entity will mature in form, smell, taste, and so on [he knows rightly]. Alternatively, knowledge in respect of innate nature is knowledge of things; [since] this karma is of this innate nature, thus [he] has knowledge of [this entity] in all respects.

'As to the karma result' (vipākataḥ). The result of this karma will certainly mature or will certainly not mature. Regarding this [action] the continuum of its karma results (vipākānubandha°) will last until such a time, and of this [action] until such [a time]. This karma will mature with a remainder of karma results and this without any remainder. Minutely and incomparably, he knows truly concerning the results of karma. In brief, [he knows] the result of this action in this state will be thus and of this karma, so. The unobstructed knowledge of skill in classifying karma results and knowledge of [particular results of] karma is the power of knowledge of karma results.

(3) '[He knows truly the different and diverse dispositions] of other beings' and so on. 'Diverse' signifies various types of dispositions (adhimukti°); i.e. a variety of dispositions, there being diverse dispositions [of beings]. This is clarified: 'Persons of
diverse dispositions'. [An example of] a diverse disposition: taste 264
or liking (ruci) for lower or higher things, and so on. 'Taste for' and 'disposition' (adhimukti) are synonyms.

Unobstructed knowledge of the variety of tastes of beings and their classification is the power of knowledge of diverse dispositions. It is also stated that the Blessed One alone knows the powerful attachment and discord that beings feel toward one another.

(4) '[He knows truly] the world of different (aneka) elements'. This refers to [knowledge of] the various elements. Here 'elements' (dhātu) means the particular set of mind [literally, mind

cultivated in a particular way] and mental states (citta-caitta-viśeṣa) of beings that come from [the past] through perfuming impressions (vāsanās°). Only unobstructed knowledge in this regard [is considered a 'power']. The phrase 'diverse (nānā) elements' is added for clarification. This is the power of knowledge of diverse elements.

(5) 'He knows [truly] the higher and lower faculties of other
265 beings'. 'Faculties' refers to faith (śraddhā) and so on. 'Higher' means superior, 'lower' means inferior, and 'middle' means higher in relation to the inferior and lower in relation to the superior. These [middle faculties] are not separately mentioned in the Sūtra. Unobstructed knowledge of the faculties of faith and the rest, their being superior and inferior [and] their division into weak, middling, and strong [categories] is called the power of knowledge of higher and lower faculties. As it is said:

"The excellence and inferiority of faculties—their weakness, middling power, and strength, their differences part by part, and their boundlessness—none but you, [O Blessed One], can [truly] understand."[206]

(6) 'The path leading to all destinies'. There are many paths; they lead to cessation (nirodha) and to the various realms, from the god [realm] to the hell [realms]. The paths (pratipads) are the cause, because [by them] one progresses° towards the god (deva) [realms, etc.]. 'The path leading to cessation' is the [Noble Eightfold] Path (mārga): One progresses° toward cessation through being led to obtain disjunction (visaṁyoga°) [from all of the defilements].

In brief, there are two kinds [of path], one leading to the arising of the individual body (satkāya°) and one leading to the cessation of the individual body. Here 'individual body' means the five skandhas. Arising refers to the cause that brings about arising, while cessation of the individual body is disjunction. That
266 whose characteristic is to go everywhere is called the path leading to all destinies. When knowledge thereof is unobstructed, it becomes a power.

(7) 'He knows truly the exact° distinction of defilement and purification, meditation, deliverance, concentration, and attainment.' [Here] 'defilement' (saṁkleśa) is that which is an obstacle in the attainment of meditation, while purity (viśuddhi) is immaculateness.

There is another reading°: 'the purification of faculties, powers, constituents of enlightenment, meditation, deliverance, concentration, and attainment'.

Here 'faculties' (indriyāṇi) refers to faith and the others, 267
which [as discussed above] become 'powers' when they conquer their opponents (vipakṣa). The constituents of enlightenment (bodhyaṅga) are investigation [or discernment] of dharmas (dharmapravicaya) and so forth.[207] 'Meditations' means the dhyānas, starting with the first. 'Deliverances' (vimokṣa) refers to the eight [deliverances]: one possessed of form sees form, and so on; 'concentrations' refers to [concentration on] emptiness (śūnyatā), and so on; and 'attainments' (samāpattis) refers to the attainment of cessation, and so on. Regarding these faculties, meditations, and so forth the power (dhyānādijñānabala) [at issue] is the unobstructed knowledge of fall, of duration, of distinct progress, of that which belongs to penetration, of enjoyment, of purity, and so on, up to undefiled attainment[208] and so on.

(8) 'And also' and so on. '[With regard to the former existence of beings, he remembers their size, their place of birth, and the causes]'. [Here] 'size' refers to [size] at the time of coming into existence: long, short, dwarfish, and so forth. The word 'place'
indicates 'place of birth', as when people say, "In what place did 268
you see me?" meaning, 'in what location? 'And 'with cause' (sanimittam) refers to reason (sahetukam, lit. 'with reason'). 'In diverse ways' means 'in manifold ways'. 'Former existence' means 'former birth', [and] this is further clarified through the phrase 'one birth' and so on. It is stated: The unobstructed knowledge of recalling the succession of the past births of others and one's own [past births as well] is the power of knowledge of recollecting former existences.[209] It is knowledge concerning the past.

(9) 'And further' and so on. '[With his heavenly vision]'. 'With heavenly eye' (divya-cakṣu). When the object of the eye is not

within reach, the human eye can still see the form at some distance, but not when it is far away. (In contrast to this mode of seeing), the term 'heavenly' is used, indicating that which accords with the heaven realms.

[The term 'heavenly'] may also be used of devas who have attained rebirth [in the heaven realms]. That is not meant here, and therefore the phrase is added, 'pure' (lit., 'with pure'), meaning that which consists of super-knowledge (abhijñāmaya). [In this sense] it accords with the heaven realms and is heavenly (divya).

[Question:] What is the difference between that which accords with the heaven realms and that which consists of super-knowledge? Reply: A being that dwells in the heavens can see a form in a realm lower than its own but not in a higher realm. But one endowed with super-knowledge can see everywhere. Worldlings who are free from lust (laukikavītarāga°) can [thus] take hold of their respective object through super-knowledge. The objects available effortlessly to Śrāvakas, Pratyekabuddhas, and Buddhas respectively are one thousand, two thousand and three thousand or many thousands of world systems. By making effort, the Arhat, the Rhinoceros° (Pratyekabuddha), and the Master [daiśika = the Buddha] can see two thousand, three thousand and innumerable world systems.[210]

269 Unobstructed knowledge of beings concerning their rebirth in the future is the power of knowledge of death and birth.[211] This knowledge concerns the future.

(10) 'Destruction of defilements' (āsravakṣaya). [Here] the term 'outflows' (āsravas°) means defilements (kleśas); 'extinction' [or 'destruction'] means abandonment of the āsravas. 'Deliverance of mind free from outflows' means immaculateness of mind, which he knows with noble 'wisdom'. Unobstructed knowledge in respect of extinction of outflows is the power of knowledge of destruction of defilements.

'These, monks, [are the ten powers of the Tathāgata].' This is a concluding sentence.

This tenfold knowledge of the Tathāgatas is applied to examine those persons who are being trained. Through knowledge of the possible and impossible, [the Tathāgata] investigates the fitness and unfitness of trainees. Through knowledge of the specific nature of karma (karmasvakajñāna°), [he investigates] the obstruction of karma; through knowledge of dharmas and so on, [he investigates] enjoyment; through knowledge of faculties, the power of purification; through knowledge of disposition [or aspiration], the preparatory effort through which one obtains special attainments; through knowledge of dhātus [elements, realms], intention (āśaya). Through knowledge [of the path] leading to all destinies, he acts rightly (samyagvidhatte), leading beings to benefit (hita) and preventing them from doing harm (ahita). Through knowledge of previous existences, he knows the final attainment (samudāgama°); with the divine eye [he knows] rebirth; through knowledge of the destruction of defilements [he knows] deliverance [vimukti]. One who was deficient in any of these [powers] would not be able to perform the entire work of the Teacher. 270

Topic Twenty-Three

Four Grounds of the Tathāgata's Self-Confidence

"Now, what, monks, are the four grounds of the Tathāgata's self-confidence?

"The Blessed One, the Tathāgata, the Arhat, the Rightly and Fully Awakened One, firmly maintains as follows:

50 *"If someone charges, 'You have not realized these dharmas°', I find no ground for such a charge—not in the whole world of devas, Māra, Brahmā, with all its inhabitants, including ascetics, brahmins, gods, men and demons. And finding no ground, the Tathāgata abides calmly and fearlessly. He knows his distinguished place. Having rightly gone to the assembly, he utters the lion's roar and sets rolling the Brahma wheel, not previously set in motion in accord with the Dharma° by any śramaṇa or brahmin or by anyone in the world.*

"Regarding those things that I have called stumbling blocks, if someone charges, 'For one who practices these things, they are not stumbling blocks', I find no ground for such a charge—not in the whole world of devas, Māra, Brahmā, with all its inhabitants, including ascetics, brahmins, gods, men and demons. And finding

no ground, the Tathāgata abides calmly and fearlessly. He knows his distinguished place. Having rightly gone to the assembly, he utters the lion's roar and sets rolling the Brahma wheel, not previously set in motion in accord with the Dharma by any śramaṇa or brahmin or anyone in the world.

"If some one charges that the noble path leading to deliverance, which I have taught to the disciples, does not, when followed, lead to the right extinction of suffering, I find no ground for such a charge—not in the whole world of devas, Māra, Brahmā, with all its inhabitants, including ascetics, brahmins, gods, men and demons. And finding no ground, the Tathāgata abides calmly and fearlessly. He knows his distinguished place. Having rightly gone to the assembly, he utters the lion's roar and sets rolling the Brahma wheel, not previously set in motion in accord with the Dharma by any śramaṇa or brahmin or by anyone in the world.

"Having myself destroyed the defilements and having firm 51
knowledge that this is so, if someone charges, 'These your defilements are not extinct', I find no ground for such a charge—not in the whole world of devas, Māra, Brahmā, with all its inhabitants, including ascetics, brahmins, gods, men and demons. And finding no ground, the Tathāgata abides calmly and fearlessly. He knows his distinguished place. Having rightly gone to the assembly, he utters the lion's roar and sets rolling the Brahma wheel, not previously set in motion in accord with the Dharma by any śramaṇa or brahmin or by anyone in the world.

"These are the four grounds of self-confidence."

After the powers [come] the four grounds of self-confidence. 271
To explain them [the question is put], 'Now what, monks, are [the four grounds of self-confidence]?' As for 'self-confidence' (vaiśāradya°): The state of being self-confident (viśārada°) is 'self-confidence'. It means the absence of hesitation in assemblies; in other words, 'fearlessness°'.

(1) 'The Rightly and Fully Awakened One (samyaksambuddha°) firmly maintains°'. This phrase indicates perfect comprehension of all dharmas (sarvadharmābhisambodha°).

'"You have not realized [comprehended] these dharmas."' If
272 someone out of delusion (moha) makes a charge° concerning
[the Buddha's] perfect comprehension of all dharmas, the Buddha
replies to him, "I do not find any ground [for such a charge]."
This is the first [ground of self-confidence].

(2) 'Those dharmas that I have called stumbling blocks'. This
refers to putting obstruction (antarāyakara°) in [the path] to realization of the goal (adhigama°). Examples are dharmas that
bring immediate retribution (ānantaryādilakṣaṇa).[212] 'For one
who practices these things' refers to any such course of action in
one of its three aspects: preparatory, the action itself, and the
273 consequent action.[213] 'They are not real stumbling blocks' refers
to one who thinks while practicing that [such actions] are not
stumbling blocks. For one who has this doubt, it is stated, '(I do
not find any) ground'. This is called the ground of self-confidence
concerning perfect comprehension of obstructive dharmas.

(3) '[The noble path] . . . which I have taught to the disciples'. 'Path' (pratipad) means the noble path (āryamārga); noble (ārya) means pure (anāsrava). 'Leading to deliverance'. That which shows the way out [of saṁsāra] (niryāṇa°) and leads to deliverance. 'When it is followed' refers to coming face to face with the noble path; the word 'it' (tat) has 'the noble path' as its referent. 'That is not the path', and so on, is easy to understand. This is called the ground of self-confidence characterized by perfect comprehension of the path of deliverance.

(4) 'One whose defilements are extinct' refers to one whose defilements are eliminated. 'These your defilements are not extinct'. This is as [explained] above. With this, the ground of self-confidence characterized by knowledge (bodha°) of elimination of defilements has been explained.

Here the first ground of self-confidence is a special one and the rest are [simply] grounds of self-confidence. In view of the special [needs of] persons to be trained they are set forth by the Blessed One in four parts. And like powers, their division (vyavsthāna°) is fourfold.[214]

As regards the order of knowledges concerning one's own 274
accomplishment and that of others,[215] there is an absence of assertion. With the first ground of self-confidence, [the Buddha] has declared (udbhāvita°) his own accomplishment of knowledge, and with the second one, [his] accomplishment of abandonment (prahāṇasampad°). Through accomplishing knowledge and abandonment, one's own accomplishment becomes complete. Now, as to the accomplishment that concerns others (parasampadatvaṁ°), this signifies preventing others from taking a wrong path and showing them the right path.

Here a disciple (śiṣya) has [truly] set forth on the way to mastering the skill of accomplishing abandonment by avoiding obstructive dharmas, taught by the Tathāgata. When he follows that teaching, he is rightly on the way to the Dharma that brings about deliverance. Then he progresses toward the accomplishment of knowledge. Thus the four grounds of self-confidence represent the consummation of accomplishment of knowledge and abandonment. This is the accomplishment of being onself a teacher of others to the fullest possible extent.

Here the special knowledge is called [either] a power° or a ground of self-confidence. [Question:] What is the distinction between power of knowledge and a ground of self-confidence. Reply: Not being overpowered (anavamṛdyatā°) is the ground of power of knowledge, while absence of hesitation [or diffidence] (asaṁkoca°) is the ground of self-confidence.

Topic Twenty-four

Tathāgata's Four Kinds of Special Knowledge

"Now, what are the four kinds of special knowledge of the Tathāgata?

52 *"Special knowledge of categories, special knowledge of Dharma, special knowledge of languages, and special knowledge of ready exposition.*

"What is special knowledge of categories?

"Unshakable knowledge of ultimately real categories.

"What is special knowledge of Dharma?

"Unshakable knowledge of undefiled dharmas.

"What is special knowledge of languages?

"Unshakable knowledge of speeches and usages.

"What is special knowledge of ready exposition?

"Unshakable knowledge of speech that is fitting, unhindered, and clear[o] *due to mastery in concentration."*

After the grounds of self-confidence have been explained 275
[four] kinds of special knowledge (pratisaṁvid°) are stated. [The
question is put]: 'What are the four kinds of special knowledge?'
and so on.

(1) 'Knowledge of dharmas concerning ultimately real categories (paramārthajñāna°)'. Unobstructed (avyāhata) knowledge of dharmas concerning ultimate categories is special knowledge of dharmas. [It] refers to [knowledge] of unique (sva) and general characteristics.[216] No comment is given for the words, for 276
fear of the treatise being [unduly] enlarged.

(2) 'Special knowledge of Dharma'; 'That which concerns all dharmas' and so on. Here the word 'Dharma' is to be taken as 'the Dharma that is taught' (deśanādharma). [For] the word 'dharma' has many meanings. For instance, [there is the statement of the Blessed One], "Monks, I will teach the aggregate of dharma (dharmaskandha),[217] virtuous in the beginning." This is the Dharma that is taught (deśanādharma).[218] Again, [there is the statement of the Blessed One], 'What is the Dharma? The Noble
Eightfold Path." Here the meaning is the Dharma that is to be 277
practiced. (pratipattidharma°). Again, [when one says] "I take refuge in the Dharma," this signifies nirvāṇa, the fruit of the Dharma.[219] [But the special knowledge referred to here] should be understood as that which penetrates (anupraveśa°) all dharmas—wholesome, unwholesome, and so forth—and the understanding of the wholesome ones.

(3) 'Special knowledge of languages'. 'Language' (nirukti°) means linguistic expression. What is indicated is [the knowledge] that delves into all languages [forms of speech] (sarvaruta), [including those] of the devas and so forth.

(4) 'Special knowledge of ready exposition'. Ready exposition 278
(pratibhāna°) signifies 'fitting and unhindered expression' (yuktamuktābhilāpitā°). 'Fitting' means related to the meaning and 'unhindered' means without faltering. The state of fitting and unhindered expression is fitting and unhindered expression. The rest being easy, no explanation is given.[220]

Topic Twenty-Five

Eighteen Special Dharmas of the Buddha

"What are the eighteen special dharmas of the Buddha?

53 *"The Tathāgata never takes a false step.*

"His speech is neither rash nor noisy.

"He is never deprived of mindfulness.

"His mind is never unconcentrated.

"He has no perception of multiplicity.

"His equanimity is not due to lack of consideration°.

"His zeal is unflagging.

"His energy does not diminish.

"He never loses his mindfulness°.

"He never loses his concentration.

"His wisdom never fails.

"His deliverance never fails.

"He has absolute and infallible knowledge and insight concerning the past.

"He has absolute and infallible knowledge and insight concerning the future.

"He has absolute and infallible knowledge and insight concerning the present.

"All his actions of the body are preceded by knowledge and accord with knowledge.

"All his actions of speech are preceded by knowledge and accord with knowledge.

"All his actions of mind are preceded by knowledge and accord with knowledge."

"These are the eighteen special dharmas of the Buddha."

After the explanation of 'special knowledge' [come] the spe- 279
cial [dharmas of the Buddha].[221] The question is put: 'Now, monks, what are the special [dharmas] of the Tathāgata°'?

[As to the meaning of 'special']: The word veṇi° signifies the state of admixture (miśrībhāva). That which is not mixed is 'unmixed' (āveṇika°), i.e., extraordinary (asādhāraṇa = special, unique). These [dharmas] are possessed by the Tathāgata and by no one else. And that which is extraordinary (asādhāraṇa) is 'special' (āveṇika).

(1) 'The Tathāgata takes no false step°'. This is due to having 280
abandoned all the major and secondary defilements (kleśopakleśas), along with the perfuming impressions (savāsanā°) giving rise to bodily and vocal depravities. Others, such as the disciples (śrāvakas), may commit bodily faults and the like when they are inattentive (asamanvāharataḥ°). Also it is said [as an example of faulty bodily movement]: "One moves leaping like a monkey." And [there is] also the episode of Ārya Pilindavatsa calling Gaṅgā by the abusive appellation 'outcaste' (vṛṣalī).[222]

(2) 'Rash and noisy speech' (ravita°) means sudden vocal 281
activity.

(3) 'Loss of mindfulness' (muṣitasmṛtitā°). The state of loss of mindfulness is called 'loss of mindfulness'. It is not found [in the Tathāgata].

(4) 'His mind is never unconcentrated', due to being ever concentrated. This has been stated in a verse [from scripture]:

> The elephant (nāga°) remains concentrated while moving, standing, sleeping, and sitting.[223]

(5) 'He has no perception of multiplicity (nanātvasaṁjñā°)'.
282 The manifestation (pravṛtti°) of pleasure, pain, and neutral feelings, felt respectively through attachment, hatred, and delusion], is the perception of multiplicity. This the Tathāgata is free from°.

(13–15) ['Absolute and infallible knowledge'.] Whatever happens depending on a cause is said to be 'attached', while that which happens without depending on a cause is considered 'unattached', and thus is called 'absolute'. That which happens at one place and not at another is called 'obstructed', while that which happens everywhere, offering no obstacle of knowability (jñeyavibandhābhāva°) is considered 'unobstructed', explained here as 'infallible' (apratihata). Knowledge (jñāna) is vision (darśana), by reason of being experienced [literally, seen] directly (pratyakṣavṛtti°).

(16–18) 'All the actions of body, [speech, and mind]' are 'preceded by knowledge', for the mindfulness of the Blessed One is well established.[224]

Topic Twenty-Six

The Tathāgata's Thirty-Two Marks of a Great Personage

"Now, what are the Tathāgata's thirty-two marks of a Great Personage? Namely:

"Well-placed feet; the soles of the feet marked with a wheel; the 54
heels of the feet large and the ankles prominent; the fingers long; the
hands and feet webbed; the hands and feet soft and tender; seven
convex surfaces on the body; legs like those of the antelope; the pri-
vate organ concealed in a sheath; the upper part of the body like
that of the lion; the space between the shoulders well-filled; the
shoulders evenly rounded, long arms when standing erect; pure
limbs; a neck shaped like a shell; a jaw like that of the lion; forty
even teeth; even teeth that are without spaces; teeth that are mar-
velously white; a long tongue; an exquisite sense of taste; a voice
like that of Brahma and like that of the Kalaviṅka bird; dark blue
eyes; eyelashes like those of a cow; smooth skin; golden skin; a hair
in each pore of the skin; hair that is raised and turns to the right;
hair having the color of the sapphire; brilliant white hair growing 55
on the head between the eyebrows; a protrusion at the crown of the
head; and a body of well-proportioned symmetry, like the banyan
tree; (and a body pleasing from all sides, like that of Mahānārayaṇa°).

"These are the thirty-two marks of a Great Personage.

[Meritorious Deeds that Account for the Arising of the Marks]

"Having well-placed feet: This mark of a Great Personage arose because in former existences [as a Bodhisattva] the Tathāgata firmly undertook [always to do meritorious deeds].

56 *"The soles of the feet marked with a wheel: This mark of a Great Personage arose because in former existences the Tathāgata accumulated merit by giving various kinds of gifts.*

"The heels of the feet large and the ankles prominent: This mark of a Great Personage arose because in former existences the Tathāgata did not disappoint° other beings.

"The fingers long: This mark of a Great Personage arose because in former existences the Tathāgata protected and guarded the Dharma.

"The hands and feet webbed: This mark of a Great Personage arose because in former existences the Tathāgata brought no dissension to the families of others.

"The hands and feet soft and tender: This mark of a Great Personage arose because in former existences the Tathāgata donated many kinds of robes.

"Seven convex surfaces on the body: This mark of a Great
57 *Personage arose because in former existences the Tathāgata gave abundant food and drink.*

"Legs like those of the antelope: This mark of a Great Personage arose because in former existences the Tathāgata acquired dharmas special to the Buddha.

"The private organ concealed in a sheath: This mark of a Great Personage arose because in former existences the Tathāgata protected the secret mantra° and abstained from the sexual act.

"The upper part of the body like that of the lion: This mark of a Great Personage arose because in former existences the Tathāgata practiced good deeds in regular succession.

"The space between the shoulders well-filled: This mark of a Great Personage arose because in former existences the Tathāgata practiced wholesome deeds.

"The shoulders evenly rounded: This mark of a Great Personage arose because in former existences the Tathāgata gave fearlessness and consolation to others.

"Long arms when standing erect: This mark of a Great Personage arose because in former existences the Tathāgata always sought to ascertain how he could help others. 58

"Pure limbs: This mark of a Great Personage arose because in former existences the Tathāgata undertook to practice to his satisfaction the ten wholesome deeds.

"A neck shaped like a shell: This mark of a Great Personage arose because in former existences the Tathāgata donated various medicines to the sick.

"A jaw like that of the lion: This mark of a Great Personage arose because in former existences the Tathāgata practiced to their culmination the wholesome deeds.

"Forty even teeth: This mark of a Great Personage arose because in former existences the Tathāgata practiced consoling all beings.

"Even teeth that are without spaces: This mark of a Great Personage arose because in former existences the Tathāgata united those who were disunited.

"Teeth that are marvelously white: This mark of a Great Personage arose because in former existences the Tathāgata guarded well his actions of body, speech, and mind. 59

"A long tongue: This mark of a Great Personage arose because in former existences the Tathāgata well protected truthful words.

"An exquisite sense of taste: This mark of a Great Personage arose because in former existences the Tathāgata performed inestimable merit° and transferred [it] to others.

60 *"A voice like that of Brahma and like that of the kalaviṅka bird: This mark of a Great Personage arose because in former existences the Tathāgata always maintained [the practice of] telling sweet and truthful words and words that caused delight.*

"Dark blue eyes: This mark of a Great Personage arose because in former existences the Tathāgata protected other beings as his friends.

"Eyelashes like those of a cow: This mark of a Great Personage arose because in former existences the Tathāgata's intention was never inauthentic°.

"Smooth skin: This mark of a Great Personage arose because in former existences the Tathāgata was always inclined° to participate in the councils of the Dharma°.

"Golden skin: This mark of a Great Personage arose because in former existences the Tathāgata gave beds, rugs, and pleasing garments.

"A hair in each pore of the skin: This mark of a Great Personage arose because in former existences the Tathāgata shunned crowded gatherings°.

"Hair that is raised and curls to the right: This mark of a Great
61 *Personage arose because in former existences the Tathāgata com-*
prehended with perfect competence° the instructions of his teach-
ers°, preceptors, and spiritual guides.

"Hair having the color of the sapphire: This mark of a Great Personage arose because in former existences the Tathāgata, with compassion for all beings, laid aside sticks, stones, and other weapons.

"Brilliant white hair on the head between the eyebrows: This mark of a Great Personage arose because in former existences the Tathāgata praised those worthy of praise.

"A protrusion at the crown of the head: This mark of a Great Personage arose because in former existences the Tathāgata respected his teachers and made obeisance to them.

"A body of well-proportioned symmetry, like the banyan tree:
This mark of a Great Personage arose because in former existences 62
the Tathāgata motivated himself and others in concentration.

("A body pleasing from all sides, like that of Mahānārāyaṇa: This mark of a Great Personage arose because in former existences the Tathāgata made images of the Tathāgata, repaired broken stūpas, consoled beings who were fearful, and helped different beings cross [the ocean of saṁsāra].)

"The Tathāgata demonstrated mastery over innumerable roots of good. This is the reason that the thirty-two marks of a Great Personage were produced in his body."

With regard to the marks (lakṣaṇas), [the question is put]: 283
'What are the thirty-two marks?'[225]

Now it may be asked (nanu°): The marks have already been
mentioned (uddiṣṭa°) in giving the list of topics (uddeśa°), so why
is the list presented again by way of putting this question? Reply:
Earlier they were mentioned in a general way, and now they are
presented in a specific [detailed] way. Again, the listed topic
might be lost [sight of] if obstructed by multiplicity of items.
Therefore [this topic] is again stated [separately], so that listeners whose minds were disturbed may pay proper attention, and 284
those who paid attention may readily understand. The list of topics is set out for those who understand through brief explanation
(udghaṭitajña°); who have a penchant for brevity (saṁkṣipta-
ruci°); the exposition is set out for those who comprehend
through a detailed explanation (vipañcitajña°); who are fond of
details. This is the view of [my] teacher.

The [thirty-two] marks (lakṣaṇas) are possessed by universal monarchs (cakravartins)[226] as well [as Buddhas], but [in the former case] they are not properly placed (deśastha°), bright, and complete, as with the Blessed One. Therefore they are said to belong to the Tathāgata (tathāgatasya°).

To determine the exact number and exclude any other enumeration, it is stated: 'Thirty-two marks'. There are thirty-two

marks, neither more nor less°. It is stated that they are the marks of a Great Personage because they indicate the reason for attaining the state [position] of a Great Personage (mahāpuruṣa-bhāva). A Great Personage is one who is great because he is endowed with such qualities as great compassion (mahākṛpādi°). His marks, known as the marks of a Great Personage, are called
285 marks because they indicate an outcome of future prosperity.

The marks are [now] enumerated, starting with 'the state of having well-placed feet'. The explanation follows:

(1) 'The state of having the well-placed feet of the Tathāgata°'.

The state of well placed feet is the state of having well-placed feet (supratiṣṭhitapādatā°). The suffix 'state' (bhāva) should be understood to apply to the subsequent marks [as well]. Because the feet are soft, of even sole, and not [too] large (anutkaṭa°), the Blessed One touches the earth evenly. Others are of the view that owing to the softness of the Blessed One's feet, the lower and upper portions of the feet adjust according to the ups and downs of the ground.

Wishing to hear the splendor of this mark with regard to the karma-result (vipāka) on account of which this [particular] mark appears, and seeking° a way to bring this about,[227] the cause
286 through which this particular karma matured° is stated.

'Formerly [the Tathāgata] firmly undertook'. 'Formerly' means in former times, i.e., in a [previous] life as a Bodhisattva. 'Because of firm undertaking' means that constantly and zealously (satkṛtya°) he was endowed with the practice of performing wholesome deeds, or else that he firmly undertook to follow the [prescribed] trainings.

(2) 'The soles of the feet marked with a wheel'. On the soles of the feet of the Blessed One there is a wheel[228] with spokes, a rim and a nave, beautiful and perfect in every respect, like one made by an expert artisan. When the Blessed One walks on the ground, an impression in the shape of a wheel is formed in the earth.
287 Others, [however], say that the Blessed One walks above the

ground at the height of one vitasti° [the distance between the extended thumb and the little finger]. The impression of the soles of his feet is produced through [his] miraculous power (adhiṣṭhāna°).

The cause of [this] karma-result is given. 'Appeared owing to accumulation of generous deeds of many types'; that is, owing to accumulation of merits by giving abundantly various gifts of solid and liquid food°, beds and chairs (śayyāsana°). 'Appeared' means 'produced'. A wheel appears not only on the soles of the feet but also on the palms of the hands. This is not indicated since it is readily visible°.

(3) 'Having large heels and prominent ankles°'. The heels of
the Blessed One are large and fleshy, and the feet are fleshy also. 288
The explanation of past action is clear.

(4) 'Having long fingers'. A person disfigured by short fingers and toes is not pleasing [literally, radiant] in appearance. Accordingly [the mark] is noted, 'having long fingers'. The soft, creeper-like fingers of Buddhas, developed in regular shape, are long. The explanation of [past] action is clear.[229]

(5) Having webbed hands and feet'. On the sides of each
finger of [the Blessed One's] hand, there is beautiful and very del- 289
icate skin, which joins with the fingers to either side when the hand is closed, but which spreads out when the hand opens, as with a royal swan or the drawing in of the expanded hood of a cobra. The same holds for the toes of the feet.[230] The exposition of [past] action: 'In former lives, he united the families of others.' By cultivating well abstinence from slander in former lives, he united the families of other beings.

(6) 'Having soft and tender hands and feet'. Soft to the touch and fresh in complexion like the hands and feet of a new born baby. The hands and feet of the Tathāgatas are tender in this way: In youth, maturity, and old age, they are free from both
weakness and hardness. In another Sūtra this (mark) has been 290
compared to cotton wool, using an example of something well-known that is very soft. 'Cotton wool' (tūlapicu°) refers to cotton

of the silk-cotton tree. The [explanation of past] action is quite° clear.

(7) 'Seven convex surfaces on the body'. Convex (utsada°) means properly raised through being fleshy, [for on the body of the Tathāgata] these seven parts are fleshy. The seven parts are the upper portions of the hands and feet, the back of the neck, and the upper shoulders. On the hands, from the wrist to the tips of the fingers [the surface] is fleshy as though filled in with cotton. The same is true for the feet, commencing from the ankles to the soles. The back of the neck and the tips of the shoulders are also well raised.[231] The past [action] is clear.

291 (8) 'Having legs like an antelope'. An antelope is a kind of deer (mṛga°). The Blessed One is said to have legs like an antelope (eṇeyajaṅgha°) because his legs are circular and taper in extent and flesh. The exposition of past action: 'In a former life he had acquired Buddha dharmas'. Acquisition of the 'dharmas of the Buddha', powers, and grounds of self-confidence means acquiring that which is the cause of producing those dharmas. It is known [lit. said] [traditionally] that as a Bodhisattva, [the Buddha] acquired the equipment of merit and knowledge (puṇyajñāna-sambhāra), leading to this mark of having legs like an antelope.

292 (9) 'Having a private organ concealed in a sheath' (kośagata-vastiguhyatā°). The private organ in a sheath means the private organ (pudendum) is concealed in a sheath; the sheath (vasti°) encloses the male organ. The pudendum is the male organ, and the membranous sheath is that in which the private organ is found. One whose private organ is in a sheath is one having the private organ hidden in the sheath. This condition of having the private organ concealed in a sheath is called 'the state of having a private organ concealed in a sheath'. For the Blessed One, the Buddha, it is as for a horse of the noble breed (aśvājāneya°).

(10) 'The upper [literally, first] part of the body like that of a lion'. The half that is first is the first half. Here the term 'first' (pūrva) refers to the upper part of the body. [The body of] a lion has two parts, the upper and lower; the upper part is large, and

this is the comparison here, for the upper body of the Blessed 293
One is likewise large. The [past] action is clear.

(11) 'Having the space between the shoulders well filled°'. A person is said to have level shoulders when the space between his shoulders is well filled in. 'Filled in' (cita°) means 'well leveled', not having [some parts] low and some high.The [past] action is clear.

(12) 'Having the shoulders evenly rounded°'. 'Even' means level, while 'rounded' means circular, with no parts higher or lower. This signifies that the shoulders are entirely round.

[Question:] What is the difference between round and convex 294
shoulders? [Reply:] Convex means well filled, while roundness of the shoulders indicates circularity. 'Exposition of [past] action': To give fearlessness (abhayadāna°) to others means refraining from killing any living being. To give 'consolation' (āśvāsadāna) [refers to comforting] those who are fearful.

(13) 'Having long arms when standing erect°'. While standing, the two hands of the Blessed One touch the kneecaps. The past [action] is to be applied (yojya°).

(14) 'Having pure limbs'.[232] Because of the absence of impu- 295
rity and perspiration, the limbs are pure [or spotless°]. The [past] action [is clear], as before.

(15) 'Having a neck shaped like a shell.[233] A shell is a conch. His neck is like that of shell, (and) this state is called having a neck shaped like a shell. The neck is adorned with three beautiful wave-like folds. The exposition of [past] action is clear.

(16) 'Having a jaw like that of the lion'. Since it is round, strong at the base, and tapers in shape, the Blessed One is described as having a jaw like that of a lion. The exposition of (past) action is clear.

(17) 'Having forty even teeth'. Through sameness of shape, 296
quality, and color, they are even (sama), neither raised [high] nor low, neither facing downwards nor curved (vakrībhūta). [There

are] forty, neither more nor less.[234] The exposition of [past] action is clear.

(18) 'Having even teeth that are without spaces°'. Due to the absence of any deformity (vikaṭādyabhāvāt°), the teeth are even. As they are close together, there are no gaps (avirala). The exposition of [past] action is clear.

297 (19) 'Having marvelously white teeth'. Being completely free from taints, the teeth are very white like a garland of mallikā jasmine flowers (vārṣikī°) in full blossom. The [past] action is clear.

(20) 'Having a long tongue.[235] The tongue of the Blessed One measures a hand in length and also in breadth. It is tender like the petal of a red lotus. When it is extended, it covers the area of the whole face. [Question:] If it is so long, how does it remain in the mouth? Reply: Though large, it is delicate, tender and soft, and so does not obstruct the mouth. The exposition of [past] action is clear.

298 (21) 'Having an exquisite sense of taste' (rasarasāgratā°) [no commentary].[236]

(22) 'Having a voice like that of Brahmā and the kalaviṅka°'. The word 'brahma' is an appellation signifying great qualities. By reason of its greatness°, the voice of the Buddha is called a sublime voice (brahmasvara°). It is said in the scriptures that (the
299 Buddha fills with his voice the three-thousand many-thousand
[world systems].[237] The voice of a kalaviṅka is a sweet voice. The exposition of past action is clear.

(23) 'Having dark blue eyes'. This mark is explicit in meaning.[238]

300 (24) 'Having eyelashes like those of a cow°'. [This mark is also] explicit in meaning.

(25) 'Having soft° skin'. [This indicates] absence of hardness, like the petal of a lotus or red lotus. Our teacher° speaks of the delicacy (tanutva°) of the body (tanu°) of the best among men[239] (narottama = Buddha). The exposition of [past] action is clear.

(26) 'Having golden skin. The word 'gold' indicates the purity of color. It signifies that the [body of the] Blessed One is beautiful, shining like gold.[240] 301

(27) 'Having one hair in each pore. In each pore there is only one stalk of hair and not a second.[241] The exposition of [past] action is explicit.

(28) 'Having hair that is raised and curls to the right'.[242] Since 302
hair might curl to the left, here it is stated, 'curling to the right'. The hair has the lustre of sapphire, and is very tender, like the fiber of a lotus, rising upwards.[243] In some texts, the reading is 'curling like a bracelet'; [here] 'bracelet' is a special form of measure (parimāṇasanniveśaviśeṣa°).

(29) 'Having hair the color of sapphire. The exposition of 303
[past] karma is explicit.[244]

(30) 'Having brilliant white hair between the eyebrows on the head'. In the space between the eyebrows is a circle of hair, curling rightwards, [the color being] as white as a crystal pill (sphaṭikaguḍikā°) or the rays of the moon.[245] The exposition of
[past] karma: [The mark] appeared [on the body of the Buddha 304
in a former life] for speaking in praise of those who were worthy of praise.

(31) 'Having a protrusion at the crown of the head'. Some (masters) say that it is a rounded cranial crest in the middle of the head of the Blessed One, while others (anye) interpret [lit., wish] it as a piled-up growth of hair in the middle of head, arranged aloft like a [royal] turban (uṣṇīṣa°).

(32) 'Having a body of well-proportioned symmetry, like the 305
banyan tree' (nyagrodhaparimaṇḍala°). [Etymologically] 'nyag' means 'below'. That which grows downwards is nyagrodha°, the banyan tree. The measure of the body of the Blessed One is similar: The height is equal to the fathom measured by his outstretched arms (vyāmaparimaṇḍala°). While standing, the long arms of the Blessed One, like the tusk of an elephant, reach his knees.[246]

[Additional mark] (33) 'Having a body pleasing from all sides, like that of Mahānārāyaṇa'. Mahānārāyaṇa is a name of physical [bodily] power. One who possesses a body of Mahānārāyaṇa has
306 such [power]. For it has been stated that the Blessed One possesses the [physical] power of Mahānārāyaṇa. Others speak of the power of [the god] Nārāyaṇa [being found] in every joint of the body of the Blessed One.[247] 'Pleasing from all sides'. This refers to his pleasing complexion (asecanakarūpatvāt°) from all sides.[248]

307 'Innumerable' [roots of good]. Each one [of the marks] is produced owing to [the performance of] hundred of meritorious actions (puṇyaśataja°), as it is said in the Scriptures.[249] The 'roots of wholesome [actions]' (kuśalamūla) produce [or cause the appearance of] the marks.

Topic Twenty-Seven

Eighty Minor Marks

"What are the eighty minor marks? The Buddhas, the Blessed Ones, 63
*have (1) copper-colored nails, (2) glossy nails, (3) elevated nails,
(4) regular lines in the palm of the hand°, (5) round fingers, (6)
large fingers°, (7) regular fingers, (8) hidden veins°, (9) veins without knots, (10) hidden ankle bones, (11) level feet, (12) a stride like
that of a lion, (13) a stride like that of an elephant, (14) a stride like*
that of a swan, (15) a stride like that of a bull, (16) an upright gait, 64
(17) an elegant gait, (18) straight limbs, (19) round limbs, (20) smooth limbs°, (21) regular limbs, (22) a broad and elegantly rounded body, (23) fully developed sexual organs, (24) even steps, (25) pure limbs, (26) soft limbs, (27) bright limbs, (28) limbs that are unimpaired, (29) prominent limbs, (30) firm limbs, and (31) well-proportioned limbs. They (32) cast an aura of pure light that dispels darkness, and have (33) a round belly, (34) a soft belly, (35) an unbent belly, (36) a slender belly, (37) a deep navel, and (38) a navel that turns to the right. They are (39) pleasing to behold from all sides and are (40) pure in conduct°. They have (41) limbs free from black moles, (42) hands soft like cotton wool, (43) glossy lines in the palm, (44) deep lines in the palm, (45) extensive° lines

*in the palm, (46) a face that is not long, (47) looks that produce an
original and reflected image[o], (48) a soft tongue, (49) a slender
65 tongue, (50) a copper-colored tongue, (51) a voice like the roaring
of an elephant and like thunder, (52) a sweet, agreeable, and pleasing sound, (53) round eye-teeth, (54) sharp eye-teeth, (55) level eye-teeth, (56) regular eye-teeth, (57) a prominent nose, (58) a clean nose, (59) wide eyes, (60) large eyes, (61) raised eyelashes, (62) eyes like the petals of a blue lotus, (63) a chest that is wide and long, (64) elongated eyebrows, (65) soft eyebrows, (66) eyebrows with level hairs, (67) glossy eyebrows, (68) long and fleshy ears, (69) level ears, (70) an unimpaired faculty of hearing, (71) a well-
66 shaped forehead, (72) a wide forehead, (73) a full-grown head, (74) hair that is dark like a black bee, (75) raised hair, (76) soft hair, (77) hair that is not shaggy and (78) hair that is not rough, (79) fragrant hair. (80) The hands and feet of the Buddhas, the Blessed Ones, possess auspicious markings such as the śrīvatsa, svastika, Nandyāvarta, wheel, vajra, lotus, and fish.*

"These are the eighty minor marks."

308 The eighty minor marks are explicit in meaning.[250]

[Regarding the last of the marks], 'śrīvatsa' and so on. The mark of śrīvatsa is said to appear on the breast [of the Buddha, though] others speak of it as being on the sole of the feet. The svastika is found on the bottom of the heel. The nandyāvarta is on the inner surface of the fingers, and above it is a pair of fish. The wheel is said to be on the hands and feet.[251] The vajra (diamond) is on the palm of hands. The padma (lotus) is found on the palms of the hands and the soles of the feet.[252]

Conclusion

"The Blessed One [previously[o]] said, 'The Dharma, monks, that I shall teach you is virtuous in the beginning, virtuous in the middle, virtuous in the end, good in sense and letter, most perfect, pure, clear, leading to the highest path. This is the Dharma discourse that I shall explain, the Compendium of Categories.'

67 *"This has now been said again.*

"[The Blessed One also said]: 'Monks, there are forest haunts, roots of trees, secluded uninhabited sheltered places, mountain caves, heaps of straw, open spaces, cemeteries, jungles, and remote places. Arrange your lodging° there. Meditate monks, do not be indolent. Be not remorseful later.' This is the instruction."

While this Dharma discourse was being presented, the minds of five hundred monks became free from defilements, free from grasping.

Thus the Blessed One spoke. Delighted, those monks and that whole assembly and the world of gods, men, demons, and gan- 68
dharvas° rejoiced in what the Blessed One had said.

Here ends the Dharma discourse, the Compendium of Categories.

Those things which proceed from a cause,
of these the Tathāgata has told the cause,
and that which is their cessation.
The great ascetic proclaims such a teaching°.

So that disciples [may be encouraged to] follow with ease the 309
path of practice°, what has been previously said is now recalled.

[At the outset of the Sūtra], it was said, 'virtuous in the beginning', and so forth [i.e., 'virtuous in the middle, virtuous in the end'].

'Virtuous in the beginning°' highlights characteristics of the training in prātimokṣa,[253] meditation, and pure morality. Here the classification of right action through [phrases] such as 'abstinence from killing a living being' highlight the characteristics of prātimokṣa restraint. Through the exposition of meditation and meditational attainments, the restraint of dhyāna [is indicated]. And though the exposition of moral practices dear to the Noble Ones (āryakānta) pure morality (anāsravaśīla°) is indicated. Thus the training in morality is explained.

'Virtuous in the middle' sets forth the training concerning the mind. Here the explanation concerns cultivation of concentration.

['Virtuous in the end'] The remainder of the exposition of the Sūtra presents [the training in] wisdom.

In conclusion, it is stated: 'This has now been said again°'

Commentary on Conclusion

'Thus, monks, the teacher for disciples' and so on. The Blessed One is [called] 'teacher' (śāstā°) by reason of teaching without falsehood.

310 Those who are led [lit. caused] to hear by others are 'disciples' (śrāvakas°), the followers of teachings [of the Buddha imparted] by others. Disciples should be given right admonition (avavāda) and instruction (anuśāsana°), for it is by right instruction that the Blessed One is called teacher. The Blessed One, whose intention is full of compassion (karuṇāśaya) gives aid [lit., gives a hand] by teaching the true Dharma. [He] saves [those] beings capable [of being saved].[254] Therefore he is called the Compassionate One (anukampaka). The Śrāvakas and Pratyekabuddhas are Sages (ṛṣis), but because of such extraordinary qualities as great compassion (mahākṛpā), the Blessed One is exalted among [Sages]. Therefore he is called the Great Sage (maharṣi).

It is through twofold detachment alone [literally, not by anything else] that one cultivates meditation (bhāvanā) with success. [Therefore] it is said, 'Monks, there are [forest haunts]'. The
two kinds of detachment are bodily detachment (kāyaviveka)
and mental detachment° (cittaviveka). Bodily detachment means
avoiding contact with people; to indicate this it is said, 'Monks,
there are forest haunts' and so on. Mental detachment (citta-
311 viveka) may be explained in the manner a person finds agreeable,
[and] he may cultivate it [accordingly]. However, mental detachment [in brief] is avoidance of unwholesome thoughts (akuśalav-
itarka). To accomplish this, it is said, 'Meditate, monks, do not
be indolent (mā pramādyata°). I am only the teacher (upadeśaka): You must gain [the benefit] through your own practice
(pratipatti).'[255] Hence it is stated, 'Be not remorseful later.'

It should be known that the rejoicing of the disciples, gods, and others came after penetrating [or fully comprehending] the instruction given [by the Blessed One].

Colophon in Verses by Vīryaśrīdatta, the Commentator

Having compiled the Commentary (Nibandhana°) on the Artha-viniścaya [Sūtra] in detail (bahuśaḥ°), [I dedicate the benefits:] Whatever merit, white like autumn moonlight. I have earned by generating this wholesome effort, may living beings thereby quickly wash away accumulated blemishes through repeated [meditational] practice (abhyasāhita°), and may they gain the three kinds of bodhi[256] in accord with their lineage (gotra°).

Whatever I have stated here wrongly out of ignorance, may the wise make it faultless. What is well spoken may be spoken [merely by chance], like the [popular] saying regarding 'letters bored in wood by an insect'[257] and not through any wisdom (bodhayogāt°) [of mine].

May the nectar-like words of the son of Śuddhodana [the Blessed One], the tamer of passionate desires (manmatha-śāsana°), the dust from whose feet is worshipped by gods and men, forever lead [beings] in this world to the final eradication° of all diseases in the form of vices (doṣa), and may they be the instrument (nimittabhūta) for attaining the happiness of final beatitude (niḥśreyaso) and [worldly] prosperity (abhyudaya°).

[Let it be known] that there once reigned a most powerful 312
Buddhist king, lord of his people, famed as Dharmapāla.[258] And in the kingdom of this preeminent (mahodaya°) [king] in the monastery of Śrī Nālandāvihāra, lived a bhikṣu, subduer of the sense faculties (jitendriya°), named Vīryaśrīdatta, who compiled this Commentary (Nibandhana).

The measure of this text is to be known precisely as one thousand three hundred seventy-five ślokas°.

Colophon by Vīryaśrīmitravīra, the Copyist

(in prose)

The Nibandhana° to the Arthaviniścaya-sūtra was finished in saṁvat 319, in the month of śrāvaṇa (July–August) on the first day of śukla (pakṣa) [the bright half of the lunar month].[259]

(in verse)

In the year 319, in the month of śrāvaṇa, on the bright half of the lunar month, this copy was written by Vīryaśrīmitravīra, who wishes for the welfare of [all] other beings (parahitaiṣī°).

Notes

1. 'Sugata-sūtra-padārthavijña'. To our great loss and disappointment, we have no information about this anonymous great teacher of Vīryaśrīdatta, who must have resided at Śrī Nālandā Vihāra, the seat of the great Nālandā University.

2. One who has attained the status of an Arhat has access to means of understanding that do not depend on sensory consciousness; thus, the reference to hearing shows the lack of this attainment. However, even an Arhat does not reach the state of being a Buddha. On the powers, confidences, and special dharmas of the Buddha, see sections 23–25.

3. Māra is the god of evil, the tempter. 'Devaputra' refers to Māra as the son of a deva (god), 'kleśa' refers to the Māra of defilements, skandha refers to the Māra of the aggregates, and mṛtyu refers to the Māra of death. See the discussion of the four Māras (referred to as Mārayas) in WE, pp. 246–50. The Pāli tradition adds a fifth Māra; see Māro in DPL, pp. 240–41.

4. Cf. Abhis Ā., p. 272; Vism. VII.61

5. Jetavana Park was built through the munificence of Anāthapiṇḍika, great patron of Buddhism, a leading banker of his time and a lay follower of the Buddha. On Jetavana and Anāthapiṇḍika, see DPPN, pp. 963ff.; 67ff.

6. During the last twenty years of his life, the Buddha divided his time at Śrāvasti between the Jetavana of Anāthapiṇḍika and the palace of Mṛgāramātā. Cf. the legends about the Pūrvārāma in DPPN, pp. 628–29.

7. Śrāmaṇyaphala. A major Sutta in the Suttapiṭaka of the Pali canon. It discusses the fruits of the life of a recluse (śramaṇa). Cf. DN I. pp. 47ff.

8. The fivefold voice of the Buddha is mentioned in Adv. p. 189. It is deep (gambhīra), pleasant (valgu), heart-stirring, (hṛdayaṅgama), very clear (vispaṣṭa), and worthy to be heard (śravaṇīya). Cf. MN II, p. 140 for eight qualities of the Buddha's voice; also MLS II, p. 326.

9. The meaning of the verse is not very clear, but its source has now been identified as Mātṛceṭa's Varṇārhavarṇastotra. See Jens-Uwe Hartmann

(ed. and tr.), Das Varṇārhavarṇastotra des Mātṛceṭa (Göttingen, 1987), p. 175, with German rendering and notes. PED, p. 76a, renders araṇa as 'quietude', 'peace' and in in its adjectival form 'peaceful'. Cf. the same source for araṇavihārin. See also raṇa = sound in SED, p. 864. Compare raṇa as defilement (kleśa) in AKB I.8, p. 5 and VII.35cd, pp. 416–17.

10. The source of this quotation (inadvertently put into prose in the published edition), has not yet been traced. Buddhaghosa also tries to prove the preeminence of the bhikkhus in his comment on the word bhikkhu, but not after the manner of Ācārya Rāhulabhadra. In the Sumaṅgalavilāsinī (p. 756, PTS ed.), he comments on the vocative bhikkhave: "This is an address to persons who are recipients of dhamma" (dhamma-paṭiggāhaka-puggalālapanam etaṁ). But Buddhaghosa also says that the word 'bhikkhus' include the other assemblies, just as when "a king goes, [the] king's retinue is also included." Ibid.

11.Compare Dhammapada 276: "You yourself must strive. The Tathāgatas are (only) teachers."

11a. Cf. AK IV.1.

12. See Vibh., p. 1; BA, p. 1; ASM, p. 15.

13. There is a great controversy over whether it is the eye or eye-consciousness that sees. Cf. AKB I.42a, AKB(E), p. 114ff.

14. Cf. AKB(E), p. 78. See also Nyanamoli, Path of Purification, XV. 4. See also WE, ch. 24, p. 170.

15. The Buddha under the Bodhi tree realized the truth of the law of pratītyasamutpāda in both direct (anuloma) and reverse (pratiloma) order. See Mhvg. p. 1; The Book of the Discipline, p. 1. The present text likewise gives the sequence in both orders.

16. The explanation of this important term in AKB III.28, p. 138, is as follows: 'prati' means 'to obtain', 'to attain', in the sense of prāpti. The root 'i' signifies 'to go', but with the prefix modifying the sense of the root (prati+i) signifies 'to obtain'. So pratītya (which is a gerund) signifies 'having attained' (obtained). 'Pad' signifies existence (sattā) and with the prefix 'sam+ut', it means 'to appear' = prādurbhāva. Thus the term pratītyasamutpāda signifies 'having attained appearance'. It conveys the idea of appearance or manifestation of (separate) entities in relation to causes and conditions. See AKB, pp. 138-39; AKB(E) pp. 413-15. But the explanation given in our text is ascribed to Śrilābha, a Sautrāntika teacher. See AKV (Dwa), p. 456. Cf. Stcherbatsky, The Conception of Buddhist Nirvāṇa (Leningrad, 1927) p. 86ff.

17. The AKB refers to 'prakaraṇeṣu' (treatises). This means the seven Abhidharma treatises, for which see AKB(E), Introduction by de la Vallee Poussin, p. 17.

17a. Cf. AKB III.28cd. where it is said "The non-friend (amitra) is the opposite of a friend. [It is] not a non-friend, that is, any one other than a friend, nor the absence of a friend. . . . Thus avidyā is the opposite of vidyā, (and is) a real separate dharma." AKB(E), pp. 419–20.

18. In Buddhist teachings the 'personality' or 'individuality' is spoken of in terms of 'continuity (santāna) of consciousness'. Each moment of consciousness is impermanent, and no two moments of consciousness share the same identity.

19. Also spoken of as 'within our personal continuity'. Pali ajjhattika santāna. See S.Z. Aung, Compendium of Philosophy (London, 1963), p. 161.

20. Cf. AKB I.39; AKB(E), p. 27. Twelve dhātus are internal: the six organs (eye, etc.) and their six kinds of consciousness (eye-consciousness, etc.) Here the word āyatana is used for dhātu, as the twelve āyatanas are included in the eighteen dhātus. If the source quoted in the Nibandhana refers to AKB I.39, the AKB does not refer to two continuities of consciousness (santatis) of self and others. On the twelve āyatanas, see Topic Four, supra. The twelve āyatanas (sense fields) are divided into six internal (ādhyātmika) sense fields (eye, ear, etc.) and six external (bāhya) sense fields (form, sound, etc.).

21. See the explanation of right action in Topic Nineteen, infra; AVS, p. 36.

22. I am not sure that I have been able to convey clearly the import of the textual explanation. The phrase 'mixed continuity of consciousness' may indicate that which performs now good and now bad actions.

23. On ahetujagadvādin, note that Makkhali Gosāla was one of those who did not believe in any cause of purification or impurification of beings. Cf. DN I. p. 53. See also AKB III.28, p. 136; AKB(E), p. 416.

24. Cf. AKB III.28ab; AKB(E) p. 411.

25. Cf. AKB I.15; SN III, p. 60.

26. Cf. AVS, p. 36 on bodily, vocal and mental actions.

27. This quote is found in SN V, p. 48, and also in AN II, p. 104. The title of the Sūtra is the Kumbhasutta.

28. See PP XVII.64. Vism does not refer to the Kumbhasutta for the above quotation.

29. Cf. AK III.21c. Sandhi = pratisandhi (Pali paṭisandhi) for which a good explanation by Nyantiloka can be found in Buddhist Dictionary, p. 171.

30. Cf. DN II, p. 63, Dialogues of Buddha II, p. 60. Cf. excellent analysis with vast reference materials on this important canonical quotation by L. Schmithausen in AV p. 37, section 3.3.1 and notes 238–44.

31. Cf. AKB III, 42abc.

32. The Sautrāntikas (literally, adherents of doctrines as explained in the Sūtras only) were an important school of Buddhism. Their controversies with the Vaibhāṣikas, adherents to the views found in the commentaries known as the Vibhāṣā, abound in the Abhidharmakośa Bhāṣya of Vasubandhu. On the Sautrāntikas, see the excellent article by L. de La Vallée Poussin in Encyclopaedia of Religion and Ethics (ed. J. Hastings) Vol. XI. The Arthaviniścaya-sūtra was a leading Sūtra in the Abhidharma style. Yaśomitra refers to it in his explanation of the word Sautrāntika. Cf. AKV on AKB I.3, p.15 (Dwa. ed.)

33. Although the phrasing here is repetitious, I have retained it in translation. Repetitions are sometimes purposeful, and may be sacred as well! Although sometimes irritating to the modern reader, they are sacrosanct to the devoted. Aśoka in his edicts says repetitions are sometimes given for the melody of the speech, and also so that people may act accordingly. Kalsi Edict, in R.G. Basak, Asokan Inscriptions (Calcutta, 1959), p. 77.

34. Vaibhāṣikas are followers of Vibhāṣā Śāstras (Abhidharma treatises explaining doctrines in Buddhist Canon). They are also known by another name, Sarvāstivādins.

35. Cf. P.S. Jaini, "Vaibhāṣika Theory of Words and Meanings." Bulletin of the School of Oriental and African Studies, Vol. XXII, Pt. I, 1959.

36. See note 33.

37. The source of this quote has not been traced.

38. This refers to a point of controversy, for which see AKB III.30b, p. 143; AKB(E), p. 424. See also AKV (Dwa), p. 470.

39. Cf. AKB III.30, pp. 143–44; AKB(E), p. 425.

40. See AVSN, p. 112.

41. See DN III, p. 216.

42. Cf. AKB III.27, p. 135. Also Cf. AKB(E), p. 409.

43. Cf. AKB II.24 for contact as a mental state (caitasika) found in every moment of mind.

44. I.e., belief in permanence (dhurvadṛṣṭi) and annihilation (ucchedadṛṣṭi). AKB V.7, p. 282; AKB(E), p. 777.

45. Esteeming of wrong or bad views is explained in AKB(E), p. 778 as the "esteeming of that which is low, beginning with erroneous views."

46. The explanation of śīla is the usual one given in Buddhist texts, although it is not in conformity with the concept here. More peculiar is

the explanation of vrata, which I have not found elsewhere. The text reads: vratam veśālaṅkārād asadabhyāsācca kāyavākkarmaṇaḥ, kāyavākprabhṛtiniyamaḥ. AVSN, p. 132. In discussing mental defilements in regard to the explanation of auddhatya (mental excitement), AKV lists dance, music, decoration, dress, and ornament. AKV on AKB II.26, p. 191 (Dwa. ed.). Vrata in AKB III.28, p. 140 is the vow to act like a dog or bull, to practice nudity, etc. See also AKB(E), p. 418.

47. This list of schools is not found in AKB, but AKV (Dwa) refers to it (p. 833). See also Nib, p. 133 nt. 2.

48. On 'fasting and the like', AKV explains further by adding practices such as throwing oneself into water or into fire, maintaining silence (mauna), and wearing rags (cīrādāna [misprinted as vīrādāna]). See AKV (Wog. ed.), p. 487. Cf. also Dhammapada verse 141 (tr. by Khantipalo, Dhammapada (The Path of Truth) [Bangkok 1977]), p. 110: "Not going naked, nor coiling up hair, nor filth, nor fasting nor lying on the ground, nor striving while squatting, nor ashes, nor dust can purify a mortal who has not crossed over doubt."

49. This explanation is in light of various latent defilements (anuśaya). I have not been able to trace the list of categories such as the eight doubts. But cf. Dhs. 1004. An entire chapter of AKB deals with these various defilements and their abandonment through the path of meditation (bhāvanā) and insight (darśana).

50. The Sūtra here omits a class of gods traditionally mentioned as apramāṇṣubhā (gods of limitless aura or limitless delight). Ferrari's text records this class of devas. Arthaviniścaya (Testo e versione). (Rome: Reale Academia D'Italia, 1944), p. 559. The Nibandhana (see p. 143) mentions them and adds comments.

51. This sentence is a kind of gloss on the four kinds of ārūpya bhavas. It may be a later addition. See AVS, p. 12, note 5.

52. These seven forms of existence (bhavas) are hell-realm existence, devas, animals, pretas, human beings, existence of karma (karmabhava), and intermediate existence (antarābhava). See AKB III. 4, p. 114, AKB(E), p. 372.

53. For a detailed description of the following hells, see A. Waddell, Buddhism and Lamaism of Tibet, (London, 1985), pp. 93ff.; W. M. McGovern, A Manual of Buddhist Philosophy (London, 1923) pp. 61 ff.; Zhechen Gyaltsab, Path of Heroes: Birth of Enlightenment (Berkeley, 1995), pp. 148–60.

54. The term 'string' may also mean 'wire', 'measuring line', or 'wire rule'; hence a black marker put around a log to guide the saw. Cf. Mahāvastu (trans.) J. J. Jones, Vol. I, p. 6, n. 3.

55. J. J. Jones, in his translation of the Mahāvastu (London 1949) Vol. I, p. 21, remarks: "It is so called because of the unremittent nature of its torments." He considers this likely to be popular etymology.

56. The four kings inhabit the lowest of the six devalokas. See the entry for 'cātur', PED p. 264b. For other translations of the proper names of the gods of Buddhist cosmology, see MBP, p. 64.

57. Dharmasaṅgraha, entry no. 7, gives Kubera in place of Vaiśravaṇa. On these four gods in early Buddhism, see J. R. Halder, Early Buddhist Mythology (Delhi, 1977), pp. 80-81; Alice Getty, Gods of Northern Buddhism (Delhi, 1978), pp. 166–68.

58. This is not further explained in the text. Perhaps the meaning here is not 'in' (madhya) but 'of' ('cow cart' means 'cart of a cow'). Thus, the phrase would mean 'of' or 'belonging to the class of' the four great kings.

59. The chief of the thirty-three gods is Indra (Śakra = Pali Sakka). See Tāvatiṁsa, PED, p. 300b. Also see DPPN, p. 1002. The thirty-three gods of Traystriṁśaloka are also found in the Vedic tradition and are likely borrowed from the Vedic conception. Cf. J. R. Halder, EBM, p. 24; M. Winternitz, History of Indian Literature (Delhi, 1977), Vol. I, p. 76.

60. Tuṣita heaven is ruled by Śakra (Indra). All Bodhisattvas are born in Tuṣita heaven prior to their final descent into the human world to become a Buddha.

61. On the intermediary stage between dhyānas, see AKB VIII. 22 and copious notes by L. de La Valle Poussin. See also controversies between Andhaka and Sammitya Schools on this issue in Kathāvatthu, XVIII 7, Points of Controversy (London, 1960), p. 329. Cf. AKB VIII.23b, p. 448 for the explanation of Brahmā achieving his status as the fruit of 'performing intermediary dhyānas'.

62. In other words, one might expect their splendor to accord more fully with the exalted stage they have reached.

63. AKV indicates that there is no higher stage than this. In contrast, some (apare) interpret the name to mean that like a cloud these gods have no connection to any stage above them. AKV (Dwa), p. 382.

64. The devas of this world are born from imperturbable (lit. immobile) karma; that is, karma which is neither meritorious (puṇya) nor unmeritorious (apuṇya), neither kuśala nor akuśala. See āniñjya in BHSD, p. 24b. There seems to be a contradiction. How can they be born from puṇya when they are born from āniñjyakarma! McGovern renders the name of this realm as 'heaven of fortunate birth'. MBP, p. 67.

65. We have the phrase manasikārāt in this samāpatti (attainment), whereas earlier it is ākāratvāt. Manasikāra is often used in Buddhist texts.

For the meaning, see BHSD, p. 418a; CP, p. 283. It is generally translated as "attention." Z.A. Aung writes: "Mind indeed always gets at its object, its constant companion being attention (manasikāra) without which it would be like a rudderless ship, drifting on to *any* object." CP 283, italics in original.

66. Cf. MN II, p. 231; Vism. X.40.

67. Cf. AKB VIII.4, p. 436.

68. Cf. AKB III.24ab; AKB(E), p. 403

69. Cf. AKB(E), p. 419, n. 225.

70. On the seven prakaraṇas (Abhidharma commentaries = Vibhāṣās), see L. de La Valle Poussin's Introduction to Vasubandhu's Abhidharmakośa; AKB(E) pp. 17ff.

71. This explanation of birth is important and throws light on the concept of pratisandhi (linking consciousness). However, it is a debatable point in Buddhist thought whether feeling is active initially. There were controversies over the first stage of entry of consciousness into womb and its biological functioning. Probably the most recent discussion, focusing on the famous statement of the Buddha, "If consciousness, Ānanda, were not to descend into mother's womb . . ." (see AVSN, p. 118), is by L. Schmithausen. His excellent and detailed analysis, with an abundance of material, can be found in AV (Tokyo, 1988), pp. 37ff., and the accompanying notes at pp. 301ff. See also note 30, above.

72. For an explanation of beings born from moisture, see AKB(E), p. 380; for apparitional or 'spontaneously generated' beings, see AKB(E), p. 381.

73. See AK II45a; AKB(E), p. 234 for discussion of the life faculty (jīvitendriya). The interpretation here is that of the Sautrāntikas, who speak of a certain power of action from previous existences leading to a renewal of skandhas in the new birth. On birth in the same species of being, see Walpola Rahula, Le Compendium de la Super-doctrine (philosophie) (Abhidharmasamuccaya d'Asaṅga) (Paris, 1971).

74. The order of words in the Sūtra in this section differs from that of the Commentary. Such discrepancies in readings are due to the fact that the commentary is not based exactly on the copy of the Sūtra printed in the volume edited by me. See my Introduction to AVSN, p. 157ff.

75. Cf. AKB II.45a on the concept of āyu (life) and the controversies on this point between the Sautrāntikas and Vaibhāṣikas. See AKB(E), pp. 233ff.

76. On the loss of life and heat (or warmth) of a being, cf. AKB II.45b; AKB(E), pp. 233ff.

77. On sudden death or death before its proper time (akālamaraṇa), cf. AKB II.345; AKB(E), p. 235. Also see AKB III.55; AKB(E), p. 473.

78. On a fixed time of death (kālakriyā), it may be pointed out that the Sautrāntikas believed that at the moment of conception of a being, a power (sāmarthyaviśeṣa, āvedha = motion) inherent in actions taken in previous existences causes the skandhas to renew themselves for a determined length of time, ". . . in the same way as a shot arrow (kṣipteṣu) has a certain power which causes it to travel for a certain period of time." See AKB II.45, p. 74; AKB(E), p. 234.

79. Cf. AKB VI.2, p. 328; also SN IV, p. 127.

80. Cf. Vism, XVI 87; PP, p. 586; BDSL, pp. 158–59.

81. For comparison of the Buddha to a physician, cf. Śikṣ, p. 243. See also Bendall and Rouse: Śikṣāsamuccaya: A Compendium of Buddhist Doctrine (Delhi, 1971), p. 225; cf. SBT, p. 73; Buddha C. XIII, 61; Bodhic. II, 57.

82. On the three types of suffering, see AK VI 3; SN V, p. 259; Vism. XVI. 35; SP, p. 108.

83. Vasubandhu discusses in detail the controversy between the Sautrāntikas and the Vaibhāṣikas as to whether there substantially exists such an entity as sukha (happiness). The Vaibhāṣikas believed in the existence of sukhā vedanā, while the Sautrāntikas (like Śrīlāta and others) denied it. See AKB VI. 3, pp. 329–33; AKV (Dwa), p. 880 ff.; AKB(E), pp. 901–10. See also Kathāvatthu II.8; Points of Controversy, pp. 127ff.

84. Cf. AKB VI.3 p. 329; AKB(E) p. 901.

85. AKB VII.13, p. 400 lists four kinds of desire (chanda): (i) the desire [through which one thinks] 'I am' (asmi), which does not distinguish a separate form of being (abhedena ātmabhāva-chandaḥ); (ii) the desire 'May I exist', which does not distinguish the type of rebirth (abhedana punarbhava-chandaḥ); (iii) the desire 'May I be born there', which specifies the place of rebirth (bhedena punarbhava-chandaḥ); and (iv) the desire for 'bondage with reunion'. (pratisandhibandha-chanda). Cf. AN II, p. 212. See Vibhanga, p. 392ff. for 18 types of desire. Cf. AKB(E), p. 1188, fn. 93.

86. Cf. sukhasayita, PED, p. 716b.

87. Cf. SN III, pp. 54ff.

88. On unfixed or indeterminate actions (aniyatavedanīya karma), see AKB IV.50, p. 229; AKB(E), p. 625ff. See also Points of Controversy (tr. of Kathāvatthu) (London, PTS, 1960), pp. 355–57.

89. Cf. AKB V. 1, p. 277; AKB(E), p. 767.

90. On nirvedhabhāgīya, cf. AKB VI, 20, p. 346; AKB(E), p. 935. See AVSN, p. 167, n. 5; BHSD, p. 305a; cf. also nibbedha, PED, p. 366b.

91. This maxim (nyāya), not traced in the Sanskrit classical literature so far, signifies complete destruction beyond repair. For a similar idea, cf. seyyathāpi nāma puthusilā dvedhā hutvā bhinnā appaṭisandhikā hoti, Vin. III, p. 74. Also cf. aśmā vā bhinno' pratisandhiko bhavati, YB, p. 151.

92. The one who no longer needs training is the Arhat or the Buddha. Cf. 'aśaikṣa', BHSD, p. 80b; 'asekha', PED, p. 89b. See also the articles on arahatta and arahant, PED, pp. 76b, 77a, as well as the explanation of nirodha, AVSN, p. 238.

93. For this famous quotation, see MN I, p. 135. Cf. also Vajracchedikā (ed. Max Muller, Oxford, 1881), p. 23. See also MLS I, pp. 173-174; SBE, Vol. 49, p. 118. The terms 'impure' and 'pure' in the text render sāsrava and anāsrava. Following Conze, the phrasing would be 'with or without outflows'.

94. In citing these alternative explanations, the author may be continuing to endorse the earlier explanations and only incidentally referring to those of others (anye). However, one is curious to know who these 'others' are and to which school they belong. I have not been able to trace the reference for these explanations to any school.

95. Cf. AKB II.25, p. 55. AKB(E), p. 192 appears to render both the passage and the terms incorrectly. In the Pali tradition, 'right effort' (sammāvāyāma) is put under the division of meditation (samādhiskandha). Cf. MN I, p. 301. The omission of any explanation of the constituents of the eightfold path is noteworthy. Is it because the Sūtra has already given explanations?

96. Cf. AKB II.3, p. 39; AKB(E), p. 157; SN IV, p. 208.

97. The five consciousnesses: eye, ear, nose, tongue, and body consciousness. But AK II.7ab defines 'disagreeable bodily feeling' as the faculty of pain, and AKB likewise does not refer to five classes of consciousness.

97a. Cf. Sellasutta, SN IV, p. 208, where the simile of being pierced with two barbs is used. Cf. AKB(E), p. 329, n. 64.

98. Cf. AK II.8; AKB II.8, p. 42; AKB(E), p. 162.

99. DN III, p. 222; AVS, p. 17. The quote deletes from the passage the words 'feeling of pleasure and displeasure already absent' (pūrvameva ca saumanasya-dauramanasyor astaṅgamāt). The words are found in other texts as well.

100. The various dhyānas and associated topics are discussed elsewhere in the commentary. See next topic, on meditation.

101. Cf. AKV (Dwa) II.9, p. 148; At AKB(E), p. 163, the translation of this passage is defective.

102. Rendered 'newly knows' in AKB(E), p. 163, but this translation is not correct. The period (virāma) in the text of AVSN should be dropped. Cf. AKV (Dwa) II, 9, p. 148.

103. For further references and discussion on the indriyas, see WE, pp. 192–98; cf. list at pp. 341–42, ibid.

104. Cf. Samādhi-sutta, SN III, p. 13; cf. also samāhitacitto yathābhūtam prajānāti, AVSN, p. 224.

105. The five hindrances are sense desire (kāmacchanda), malice (vyāpāda), sloth and torpor (styānamiddha), restlessness and worry (auddhatyakaukṛtya), and doubt (vicikitsā). See also AKB V.58, p. 318; AKB(E), p. 851 (different renderings); also AVSN, p. 180, n. 3; PP IV.104.

106. This is a controversial point. See the discussion of praśrabdhisukha in Terms and Variants for folio 180, below. The commentator seems to refer to bodily joy; hence the question arises why it is not the joy of feeling (vedanāsukha).

107. Cf. AKB VIII.9, p. 438; AKB(E), p. 1231–32.

108. This is an unusual explanation. Perhaps 'prajñā' is used here for samprajñāna or prajñāna.

109. AKV (Dwa), p. 1143 clearly interprets 'mental body' (manaskāya) as manaḥsamudāya (mental grouping). There is a long controversy between the Sautrāntikas and Vaibhāṣikas on the nature of joy in the first three dhyānas. A subsect of the Sautrāntikas contends that in the first three dhyānas bodily joy is implied, not mental joy. The controversy arose over the word kāyena in the Sūtra phraseology: sukham ca kāyena pratisaṁvedayata (vl. pratisaṁvedayati). See AVS, p. 17; AKB VIII.9, p. 439, AKB(E), p. 1233.

110. The exception is the sixth grouping, or mental consciousness (manovijñānakāya).

111. Compare, "And how, monks, is a monk an ariyan? Evil, unskilled states that are connected with defilement . . . are far from him." Middle Length Sayings, Vol. I, p. 334. Cf. AKB III. 44, p. 157; AKB(E), p. 450.

112. The word 'only' (eva) adds emphasis, which the Author justifies by pointing out that bodily pain already disappears in the very first stage of dhyāna, together with bodily pleasure. Cf. PP IV.184.

113. Cf. AVS, p. 10; AKB I, 14, p. 10.

114. The equanimity of conditioned states (saṁskāropekṣā) is described in AKB as mental balance or evenness (cittasamatā) by which the mind remains in balance and free from partiality (literally, 'not leaning' [anābhoga]). Cf. AKB II.29, p. 55. See also La Valle Poussin's n. 130, AKB(E), p. 337. Concerning immeasurable equanimity, see term notes for folio 184.

115. See AKB VIII.11, p. 441.

116. Cf. AKV (Dwa), p. 1147; AKB(E), p. 1291, n. 77.

117. This section of the commentary opens in an unusual way, departing from the phraseology found elsewhere. Perhaps it did not originally form an independent section. It is missing from some manuscripts. See AVSN, p. 189, n. 1.

118. Cf. DN III, p. 275. On the controversy over whether some subtle form persists in the formless attainments, see AKB VIII.3, p. 431; AKB(E), p. 1221. See also Points of Controversy, p. 220.

119. I have given an exact rendering of the phraseology in the text. This may also be rendered as 'differences (nanātva) in perceptions (saṁjñā)', 'perceptions of variety', or 'perception of multiplicity'; 'multiplicity of perception. See PP. X.20 for a detailed explanation of this phraseology. The term is also used in the explanation of the āveṇikadharmas (See Topic Twenty-Five below.)

120. Ākiñcanyāḥ(?). The construction of this sentence is peculiar and the reading uncertain. See AVSN, p. 191, n. 6.

121. Among beings who take birth among the non-conscious gods, there is a dharma that arrests the mind and mental states which is called 'non-consciousness'. Cf. AKB II, 41, p. 68; AKB(E), p. 221.

122. As with the beginning of this section, so here at the end the usual phraseology is missing.

123. Cf. AKB VIII.30, p. 453; AKV (Dwa), p. 1172. The simile of chairs and mountains is not given in these texts.

124. Basic meditations or dhyānas = maulasamāpattis. On these, see AKB V. 66, p. 323; AKB VIII.5, p. 436; AKB(E) pp. 862, 1227. They are the four dhyānas of the rūpāvacarabhūmi and the four formless attainments (ārūpyasamāpattis). See the two preceding topics.

125. Cf. PP IX.108.

126. Cf. AKB VIII.31, p. 454. AKV (Dwa), p. 1174 comments that the result of good action in the past is visible in the body of the samucchinna-

kuśalamūla in that he possesses a body with good features, while in the body of a Pratyekabuddha, the result of bad action in the past is visible in the deformity of body. See also AKB(E), p. 1270, which adds the comments from the AKV in the translation of the AKB passages.

127. On the mārgas (paths), see AKB V.61, p. 320; AKB(E), p. 855.

128. Cf. Buddhaghosa on the explanation of these parts of body. Vism. VIII, 83–138, Path of Purification, VIII, 83-138. On lasikā ('watery humor in the body, serum'), see SED, p. 899. It is better rendered 'synovial fluid'. See PED, p. 582a.

129. Vasubandhu says that the antidote of practicing disgust (vidūṣaṇā-pratipakṣa) is performed on the preparatory path (prayogamārga). AKB V 61, p. 320; AKB(E), p. 855.

130. Cf. AKB VIII.27, p. 451; AKB(E), p. 1262.

130a. On forgetting the instruction or advice (avavāda), see Hopkins, ME, p. 73.

131. Hearing the teachings, one should reflect on them and cultivate them as well. This gives rise to three kinds of prajñā. Cf. AKB VI.5; WE pp. 90–91. See also the discussion of wisdom in the next topic, at note 138.

132. The idea of evenly luminous mind is close to the idea of very bright, resplendent (pabhassaracitta) mind in the early Pali tradition, AN I, p. 10. Compare the later teachings of the Mahāyāna Yogācāra school, based on the theory of 'mind only' (citta-mātratā). Cf. D.T. Suzuki, Studies in the Laṅkāvatāra Sūtra (Boulder, 1981), p. 241.

133. On the eight apakṣālas, cf. AVSN, p. 187; also term notes to folio 187.

134. On the prāyogikaguṇas, cf. AK VI. 69; AKB, p. 384; AKB (E), p. 1025. They are smṛtyupasthāna, samyakprahāṇa and ṛddhipāda, which comprise the next three topics.

135. Cf. AKB VI 15, p. 343; AKB(E), p. 929. Cf. also PP XXII.34.

136. On the svasāmānyalakṣaṇas, see AKB .I 14, p. 341; AKB(E), p. 925. For example, the svabhāva (own nature) of the body (kāya) is the primary elements and their derived elements, while the general characteristics (sāmānyalakṣaṇas) are suffering, impermanence, emptiness, and the non-self-nature of all conditioned (samskṛta) dharmas. See also AVSN, p. 212.

137. Cf. AKB VI.15, p. 342; AKV (Dwa), p. 905–6.

138. Cf. AKB VI.15, pp. 341-42, AKB(E), p. 927.

139. In fact, wisdom is the foundation of mindfulness. As the object is seen or observed by prajñā, so it is expressed (grasped) by smṛti. Cf. AKB(E), p. 928. See also "prajñā" in AKB VI.15b, p. 342; AKV (Dwa), p. 905.

140. Cf. AKB VI.14, p. 341; AKB(E), p. 925.

141. According to Vasubandhu, this explanation of the order of smṛtyupasthānas is ascribed to the Vaibhāṣikas. AKB VI.15, p. 342; AKB(E), p. 929. AVSN has a misprint here: kleśaprahāṇāt should read kleśāprahāṇāt. See AVSN "Corrections," pp. 179ff. (after Introduction; see esp. p. 183).

142. Vasubandhu's explanation is almost the same. Cf. also AKV (Dwa), p. 1019; Vism. XXII.35.

143. The order of the four right efforts is different in different texts. Some begin with akuśalas that have arisen and some with akuśalas that have not arisen. The Pali tradition generally follows the reverse order in the first two statements. Cf. DN III, p. 221.

144. According to Yaśomitra, when the mind is not yet concentrated and meditation is not established (asamāhita), one is in the stage of the Kāmadhātu. AKV (Dwa), p. 1173.

145. On upakleśas, see AK V.46; AKB, p. 312; see also AKB(E), p. 841, n. 66. They differ from kleśas and are included in the saṁskāraskandha. According to the AKV, upakleśa is that which is found near (upa) a defilement (kleśa) or close to which a kleśa is found (i.e., which is produced following a kleśa). It does not have the nature of a full kleśa (paripūrṇakleśa). Cf. AKV (Dwa), p. 843. AKB also cites the Kṣudravastuka text where upakleśas are enumerated. See AKV (Dwa), p. 844. In that list, 'auddhatya' is not found, but 'cetaso linatvam' represents 'laya', mentioned in our text. For auddhatya as an upakleśa along with laya, see ASM, p. 72, where other upakleśas are also found. BHSD, p. 134a has a good note on upakleśa, p. 134a. For a listing and exposition of the upakleśas from a Mahāyāna perspective, see H.V. Guenther and L. Kawamura, trs., Mind in Buddhist Psychology (Berkeley, 1978). See also Pali 'upakilesa', PED, p. 139b. It can be rendered as "secondary or minor defilement."

146. The eight objects that produce religious devotion (saṁvejanīya) are found in the Pali; cf Pali saṁvega, PED, p. 658a. They turn the mind from the world by highlighting its miseries and turn the mind toward the Dharma, awakening delight in the opportunity to practice it in accord with the teachings of the Buddha.

147. Compare the explanation of ṛddhi (Pali iddhi) in Vbh. A, p. 304.

148. According to Vasubandhu samādhi is ṛddhi and the ṛddhipādas are samādhis. AKB VI. 69, p. 384. According to Yaśomitra this view is ascribed to the Vaibhāṣikas. Cf. AKV (Dwa), p. 1019.

149. For a list of the eight prahāṇa-saṁskāras, see MVS, p. 131. On five doṣas and eight prahāṇasaṁskāras called antidotes, see ME, p. 172.

150. Jīvitahetorapi. This passage is quoted in the Śiksāsamuccaya (ed. P.L. Vaidya), p. 316; however, there three additonal beliefs with a clear Mahāyāna import are added. Here is a translation: "He believes in the path of the Bodhisattva and having entered that path he does not wish for any other vehicle. Hearing all the teachings regarding the profound law of dependent origination, truth in the ultimate sense, having definite meaning, non-selfhood, non-being, non-soul, non-personality, lack of substance, void, absence of attributes, and freedom from desire, he has faith in them. He follows none of the heretical views and has faith in all the special dharmas, confidences, and powers of the Buddha; and having faith, his doubts gone, he acquires those qualities of the Buddha. This is called the faculty of faith." Cf. AVS, pp. 31–32, n.5. For the special dharmas, confidences, and powers of the Buddha, see Topics 25, 23, and 22 respectively.

151. Cf. AKB VI. 69, p. 384, for an almost identical explanation of the order (krama). Samāhitacitto yathābhūtaṁ prajānāti (one whose mind is concentrated knows reality) is rendered in AKB(E), p. 1026, as "when the mind is fixed, there exists a consciousness which conforms to the object (prajñā)." On 'a concentrated mind knowing reality', cf. SN III, p. 13; KS III, p. 15. See also AVSN, p. 179.

152. Cf. AKV (Dwa), p. 1020; Vism. XXII. 37; PP XXII.37.

153. Cf. MVS, p. 135.

154. Cf. MVS, pp. 135–36.

155. On saṁskāropekṣā, see AVSN, p. 183. Cf. also AKV (Dwa), p. 1140. On vedanopekṣā = madhyopekṣā, cf. AK II.8, p. 41.

156. Cf. AKB VI.70, p. 384. For an explanation of how the constituents are close to bodhi and the difference between bhāvanāmārga and darśanamārga in this context, see AKV (Dwa), p. 1021.

157. Cf. Pali sammaggata DN I, p. 55. See also DOB I, p. 73, n. 2.

158. The explanation of this member of the Noble Eightfold Path given here is unusual, even novel; I have found it in no other text, and would be grateful for any references from readers. It has a clear Mahāyānic bearing. In my view, it may have been interpolated by later Mahāyāna redactors of the text. Note that this explanation is not found in the Tibetan version of the Sūtra. For the Sanskrit text of the Tibetan version of the Sūtra, see Appendix to AVSN, p. 320ff.

159. This exception is odd and ingenious, possibly a later addition. Its source in other texts has not been traced.

160. Compare this with what the Buddha said in his instruction to Rāhula: Even in jest falsehood should not be spoken. Cf. MN I, 415. See AVS, p. 37, n. 7. It seems these allowances for speaking untruth in jest were made in later centuries.

161. Compare the explanation of hypocrisy (kuhanā), translated as 'scheming' and talkativeness (lapanā), etc., in Vism. I. 71–82; PP, ibid. Also see Vibhaṅga, pp. 352–53; P.A. Thittila (tr.), The Book of Analysis (London, PTS, 1969), p. 459.

162. This explanation of right effort is also unconventional, not found elsewhere in the early Buddhist texts. Right effort is generally explained as abandonment, the non-arising of evil thoughts, and the development and sustaining of good thoughts. See AVS, Topic XIV; DN II, p. 312; DOB II, p. 344. Suggestions from readers for sources of this explanation are most welcome.

163. The list of the parts of the body is the same as in Topic Twelve, with a few differences. There is a change of order in four items: upper and lower stomach come before intestines and mesentery; also, the last two items are additional. But 'excrement' is repeated. The words 'uccāra' (feces) and 'prasrāva' (urine) both come under excrement (purīṣa). This explanation of mindfulness is again somewhat unusual (cf. Topic Thirteen on smṛtyupasthāna). Mindfulness is part of the practice of meditation (samādhibhāvanā); cf. Topic Twelve. Here, however, it is the arising of passion at the sight of a woman that is brought in focus. Compare the episode referred to in the Visuddhimagga I.55 of an elder monk who replies to a request to describe a woman he has seen:

> Whether it was a man or woman
> That went by I noticed not;
> But only that on this high road
> There goes a group of bones.

Tr. by Nyanamoli: The Path of Purification, I.55.

For a detailed explanation of the parts of body, see Vism. VIII.90ff. and XI.48ff. Also see Nyanamoli, PP, ibid.

164. The Sūtra not only explains the constituents of the noble eightfold path, but also refers in some cases to their opposites; e.g., wrong view (mithyādṛṣṭi), which is the opposite of right view (samyagdṛṣṭi). Cf. AVS, p. 35, n. 6. The Nibandhana does not comment on the explanation of the constituents of the path. It takes up only the issue of avijñapti in relation to the three constituents of right speech, right action and right livelihood, a topic hotly debated between the Sautrāntikas and Vaibhāṣikas. The copy of AVS consulted by its author may possibly have made use of opposing

constituents (opponent forces) for explaining the Eightfold Path. See AVSN, p. 231, note 2. In the case of right livelihood, the item (aṅga) is explained negatively, as abstinence from wrong livelihood. See AVS, pp. 38–41.

165. Cf. AKB IV.4, p. 196; AKB(E), p. 566. Cf. also AKV (Dwa), p. 588: Avijñapti is a cause (nimitta) and right speech, etc., are metaphorically used for its result.

166. For a detailed explanation of sixteenfold mindfulness in the Pali tradition, see Vism. VIII. 145–245 (trans. PP). See also Ānāpānasati-sutta, MN III, p. 78 ff. AKB VI. 12, p. 339 does not deal with sixteen aspects, found in the Pali tradition referred to above. For a comparative chart of our text, the other Mss. of AVS, and the Pali tradition, see AVSN, pp. 323–24. Cf. Bhikkhu Buddhadasa, Ānāpānasati (Mindfulness of Breathing) (Bangkok, 1976).

167. Cf. AKB VI.12ab, p. 339.

168. On the controversy over bodily and mental happiness, cf. AKB VIII.9, p. 439; AKV (Dwa), p. 1143. See also AVSN, p. 184, n. 6, and term note below on praśrabdhi-sukha (folio 180).

169. Cf. Vism VIII. 176.

170. For a detailed treatment of the mindfulness of breathing (ānāpānasmṛti, Pali ānāpānasati), with various similes, see Vism VIII. 145–245; PP, ibid. See also Ency. of Bud., fasc. 4, pp. 558 ff.; Piyadassi Thera, Buddha's Ancient Path (London, 1964), pp. 214 ff.

171. According to Vasubandhu, 'stream' (srota) in this context means a way leading to nirvāṇa. AKB, VI. 34, p. 356. See AVSN, p. 240, n. 5. Thus these are the four constituents for entering into the stream of nirvāṇa, the ultimate aim of a Buddhist disciple. On srotaāptyaṅgas, cf. AK VI.73–75, pp. 386 ff.; DN III, p. 227, Vism. VII.1–106; cf. MN I, p. 37; DOB III, p. 218; MLS I, p. 46.

172. Vasubandhu explains the term srotaāpanna as follows: "The stream (leading) to nirvāṇa is a path. One goes by it (to nirvāṇa). One who has attained it, arrived at it, is one who has attained the stream (srotaāpanna)." AKB VI.34, p. 356. Cf. the explanation of sotāpatti in Pali tradition where sota (stream) = eightfold path. SN V, p. 347.

173. On the dharmas by the acquisition of which one is called buddha, see AKB VI.32, p. 216. Also see Adv., pp. 125, 367.

174. For a reference to the Buddha's eye (Buddhacakṣu) and his compassionate survey, see Avadāna-śataka, ed. J.S. Speyer (St. Petersberg, 1906–9) pp. 30–31.

175. The comparison to a charioteer (sārathi) is because a charioteer tames his horses well to assure the safe and smooth running of a chariot.

176. Ārya Sundarānanda (sic) (see Sundarananda, BHSD, p. 599b) is Nanda of the Pali tradition, for whom see DPPN, Vol. II, p. 10. For his story, see E. Burlingame, Buddhist Legends (tr. of Dhammapada Commentary) (Cambridge, Massachusetts, 1921), Vol. I, pp. 217ff. Aṅgulimāla was the great terrorist of ancient India. He wore a garland of 999 fingers cut from the hands of persons he had killed. The Buddha converted him into a peaceful and non-violent monk. For the account, see MN II, pp. 97ff.; MLS II, pp. 284 ff.; Buddhist Legends, vol. II, pp. 6ff. See also DPPN, Vol. I, p. 22. For Uruvilvākāśyapa (Pali Uruvelakassapa), see Vinaya I, p. 24; DPPN, I, p. 434. For a Tibetan source, see W.W. Rockhill, Life of the Buddha (Reprint ed., Varanasi, 1972), p. 40. A reference to all three can be found in Abhis. Ā., p. 352. 'Uruvilva°' in AVSN is a misprint for 'Uruvilvā'.

177. This sentence and the two that follow have an intense Mahāyāna flavor. On the three gotras of Śrāvaka, Pratyekabuddha and Buddha, see AKB VI. 23, p. 348; AKB(E) pp. 940–41. See also gotra, BHSD, p. 216a.

178. On pratyayabala and hetubala see AKB IV.80, p. 250; AKB(E) p. 663.

179. In the above verse (gāthā), our Author has summed up different interpretations briefly by key words occurring in the text. The verse is like an Uddānagāthā, often found in Pali canonical texts, in which the summary of topics or titles is given. Cf. uddāna, PED, p. 135a; BHSD, p. 130a, and Piṇḍoddāna, BHSD, p. 345a.

180. The three truths are the first three of the Four Noble Truths: duḥkha, samudaya and nirodha, discussed in Topic Six. The fourth truth is the truth of the path, just referred to. Compare this statement to AKB VI. 74cd, p. 387. For an explanation, see AKV (Dwa), pp. 1025–26. See also AKB(E), p. 1084, n. 457.

181. To quote Jayatilleke, "This is because of limitations of languages and of empiricism." EBTK, p. 476.

182. Cf. AKB(E), p. 1084, n. 457 for Hsüan-tsang's translation that in a general sense the Dharma as the object of faith is the Four Truths. Compare note 180 above and accompanying text.

183. For other explanations of words that qualify 'Dharma', see Vism VII. 69–88. These explanations often elaborate on our text; in some places they differ. It may be noted that the Commentary does not analyze some words from the AVS: e.g., madanirmadana ālayasamudghāta, etc. See AVSN, p. 249, n. 7. Are they later additions?

183a. Endowed with wisdom (prajñāsampanna). This is omitted in the printed edition of AVS, but noted in the 'Corrections', p. 184.

184. Cf. AKB VI.74ab, p. 386, where it is said that at the time of abhisamaya of the path, one obtains avetyaprasāda in the Buddha and in the Sangha.

185. The Pali Sāmaññaphala-sutta explains the fruits of entering the religious life. DN I. 47–86. The term 'śrāmaṇya' literally means 'life of a recluse or monk', but it has been used here in the more general sense of 'the religious life'.

186. Cf. AKB VI, 51, p. 369, where śrāmaṇya is said to be a pure path (anāsravamārga). Dhp. 265 gives a definition of Pali samaṇa = Skt. śramaṇa.

187. Parallel passages, without any reference to illumination of the upright way (ṛjumārga), are found in LV, p. 400; MN I, p. 168.

188. The source of this gāthā has not been traced. The passage quoted is a question, but is apparently cited for its characterization. The full citation would presumably answer the question.

189. Vīryaśridatta does not give any further explanation of śīla and dṛṣṭisamānatā. Buddhaghosa omits paribhogasamānatā but gives śīla and dṛṣṭi (Pali diṭṭhi). Vism. VII.90.

190. On the fifteen moments of kṣāntijñāna in the darśanamārga, see AKB VI.28, pp. 352–53. On kṣānti as patient acceptance, see MDPL, p. 159.

191. Cf. AKB VI.27, p. 351; Dutta, EMB, p. 269.

192. The meaning of 'avarabhāgīya' is 'belonging to a lower [state]'; here the term has the specific meaning 'belonging to the kāmadhātu', the lowest of the three dhātus. These lower defilements are (1) satkāyadṛṣṭi (belief in a permanent self or individuality); (2) śīlavrataparāmarśa (adherence to mere rules and rituals); (3) vicikitsā (doubt); (4) kāmacchanda (desire for objects of pleasure); (5) vyāpāda (hatred). Cf. AKB VI.36, p. 358. But see the list in AKB V.43, p. 310. See also 'avarabhāgīya', BHSD, p. 73b; 'orambhāgīya', PED, p. 170a.

193. On the concept of the Arhat, see AKB.VI 44–45, pp. 364–65; see also term note below to folio 160. Cf. AVSN, p. 242. Compare the entry for 'ariyapuggala', BD, pp. 23–26.

194. For the samyagdṛṣṭi of an aśaikṣa, see AKB VI.76, pp. 388–89.

195. Two verses from Dhp. (106 and 70), have phrasing similar to the text. The Dhammapada verses do not mention the Sangha directly, but do refer

to those who have developed their mind and comprehended the Dhamma. The Udānavarga (translated by W.W. Rockhill from Tibetan) (London, 1892), at XXIV.20, p. 105 refers to faith in the Sangha. Cf. The Tibetan Dhammapada, tr. Gareth Sparham (New Delhi, 1983), p. 90, verse 20. The earlier portion of Dhp. 70 mentions eating food with the tip of a blade of grass; the whole verse as cited here, however, has not been traced.

196. For references to gifts to the Sangha bearing great fruit, see Ratanasutta, verse 6, Khuddakapāṭha (PTS ed), p. 4. But the identical phraseology to what is quoted here has not been found.

196a. Cf. AKB IV.16ab, p. 20; AKB(E), pp. 583, 715, n. 69.

197. For seven śīlas, see AK IV.78, p. 248. Cf. also Vism. I.17. Here, of ten karmapathas, the first seven are mentioned. For a list of the ten karmapathas, see AVS, p. 36; SN II, p. 168; AKB IV.73–78, pp. 243–48; AKB(E), pp. 650–57.

198. AKB, IV. 123, p. 273 adds viśeṣa (special) to 'upapattibhava', which may mean 'birth in the celestial realms'. See AKB(E), p. 704. According to AKB, such birth will ultimately lead to nirvāṇa.

199. There are additional epithets of the śīlas in the Sūtra that are not commented on. For a Pali listing, see DN III, p. 227.

200. On three kinds of restraints (saṁvara), see AKB IV. 13, p. 205, where 'pure restraint' means 'pure morality' (anāsrvaśīla), arising from the path. See also AKB(E), pp. 580–81.

201. Cf. AKB VI.75, p. 387. Vasubandhu further says that the śīlas (virtues, precepts) are health (ārogya), and the Buddha is a guide or instructor (daiśika); that the Dharma is a path, the Sangha the charioteer or the traveling companion, and the śīlas, dear to the Āryans, are the vehicle (yāna), AKB, ibid. See also the detailed exposition on Vasubandhu's comments by Yaśomitra in AKV (Dwa), pp. 1026–27.

202. On the ten powers (daśabala) of the Tathāgata, see AKB VII.28–30, pp. 411–12; MN I, p. 69ff.; MNA II, p. 28ff.; AKB(E), pp. 1136ff.; Book of Analysis (trans. of Vibhaṅga), pp. 440ff. Cf. also BDSL, p. 20. According to Vasubandhu, the ten balas are included in the eighteen āveṇika (extraordinary) dharmas. The other eight are the four vaiśāradyas (see Topic Twenty-three, infra), three smṛtyupasthānas, and mahākaruṇā. Cf. AKB VII.28, p. 411. This list is prescribed by the Vaibhāṣikas. Cf. AKV (Dwa), p. 1083. Yaśomitra in AKV refers to another set of eighteen āveṇikas, found in AVS, Topic Twenty-five. See also AVSN, p. 260, n. 1.

202a. This phrase is not found in the Sūtra, but it does appear in other copies of the Sūtra. See AVS, p. 48, n. 4.

203. Cf. AKB VII.30, p. 412, which states that knowledge of knowable (jñeya) entities everywhere without any obstacle is a power (bala). This is not so for the knowledge of one who is not a Buddha, for such knowledge is obstructed. Only the Buddhas possess infinite, unobstructed power of mind. An example is cited of Śāriputra's refusal to admit a person into the Saṅgha and the Buddha's power of knowledge regarding that person's potentiality. The AKV explains this further. Cf. AKV (Dwa), p. 1088. See also AKB(E), p. 1197, n. 173.

204. On ahetuvāda, see AKB III.28, p. 139. See also Ency. of Bud., fasc. 2, p. 284; AVSN, p. 106, n. 2; YB, p. 150.

205. On puṇya, apuṇya and āneñja (vl. āniñja) karma, see AKB IV, 45–46, p. 227.

206. This verse has now been traced; see note 9, supra. It is found on p. 156 of the work mentioned in that note. For this bala with different phraseology in the Pali tradition, see Psm I, p. 121; Vbh. p. 340; BA, pp. 445ff.

207. See Topic Eighteen above. Incidentally, the Nib. in its introductory portion explains arthaviniścaya as being equivalent to dharmapravicaya, AVSN, p. 73. Thus arthaviniścaya (the title of this Sūtra) represents a bodhyaṅga.

208. In this paragraph on the seventh bala, see on the vimokṣas AKB VII.32, pp. 454–55; AKB(E), p. 1271; cf. DN III, p. 261; Abhis. Ā, p. 419; notes by La Vallee Poussin, AKB(E), p. 1304, n. 183–86. For three samādhis, śūnyatā being the first, see AKB VIII.23, p. 449; AKB(E), p. 1256. On nirodhasamāpatti, see AKB VI.43cd, p. 336; AKB(E), p. 977; AKB VIII.33, pp. 455–56; AKB(E), 1273ff.; George Grimm, The Doctrine of Buddha: The Religion of Reason and Meditation (Delhi, 1982), p. 250; N. Aiyaswami Shastri, "The Satyasidhi and its Exposition of Buddhism" in Ramchandra Pandeya (ed.), Buddhist Studies in India (Delhi, 1975), p. 97. On hāna-sthiti-viśesa-nirvedhabhāgīya-samāpatti, see AKB VIII. 17–18, p. 445; Vbh. p. 343. On āsvadanā, śuddhakā, anāsravā samāpatti, see AKB VIII.5, p. 436; AKB(E), p. 1227; Adv., pp. 406–07, 418–19.

209. On recollection of past lives, see Vism. XIII. 13-71, PP ibid. 451–64. Early Pali Buddhist texts speak of knowledge of the Buddha's own former existences. See MN I, p. 99; MLS I, p. 94. Concerning the various numerical terms given in the Sūtra passage and their value for computation, see MBP, pp. 39ff.

210. Cf. also AK VII.54–55, pp. 429–30; AKB(E), pp. 1177–78.

211. On this topic, see DN I, p. 82; DOB I, p. 91; Vism. XIII, 72–101.

212. The five ānantarya-karmas that bring immediate retribution are (i) matricide, (ii) patricide, (iii) the killing of an arhat, (iv) causing schism in

the Sangha, and (v) wounding the body of the Tathāgata with malice aforethought. Cf. AKB IV.96, p. 259 and the explanations given there; AKB(E), p. 679–80. Also see AKB IV.80, pp. 250–51. Rendered 'mortal transgression', AKB(E), p. 679; 'deadly sin', 'karma which leads to immediate retribution', MDPL, p. 107. Also see Buddhaghosa's explanation of antarāyika dhamma, MNA II, p. 33; 'antarāyika', CPD, p. 246. Cf. AKV (Dwa), p. 1091, which puts these under the (noble) truth of the arising of suffering (duhkhasamudaya).

213. On prayoga-, maula-, and pṛṣṭha-karmapatha, cf. AKB IV.68, p. 239; Adv. pp. 152–53. See also AKB(E), p. 642. I find the rendering of these terms a difficult task. Here the reference to obstructive dharmas is to the akuśala karmapathas. For kuśala, prayoga-, maula-, and pṛṣṭha-karmapathas, see AKB IV.69, pp. 241–42; AKB(E), p. 647.

214. Cf. AKB VII.32, p. 414.

215. Cf. Adv., p. 390.

216. On sva and sāmānya lakṣaṇas, see above, note 136; AVSN, p. 212; AKB VI.14, p. 341.

217. On dharmaskandha, cf. AK I.25–26, AKB, p. 17; Adv. pp. 10–11. The Buddhist Sanskrit tradition mentions 80,000 dharmaskandhas, the Pali tradition 84,000. Yaśomitra mentions this with the phrase 'other sects' (nikāyāntara) for which see AKV (Dwa), p. 71. See also notes by La Vallée Poussin, AKB(E), p. 86–87, p. 142, n. 114. On the rendering of the term, see also BHSD, p. 281; Pali dhammakkhanda, Childers, DPL, p. 117b.

218. For 'virtuous [or 'good'] in the beginning', etc. cf. the phraseology at the beginning of AVS, p. 2.

219. Cf. AKB IV. 32, p. 216, according to which one who takes refuge in the Dharma takes refuge in nirvāṇa, in the pratisamkhyanirodha (cf. AK I.6). See also AKB(E), p. 602.

220. According to one school (not named, but mentioned by the word kila), the four pratisaṁvids are respectively preparatory exercises for the four special knowledges (or topics for study): mathematics (gaṇita), the words of the Buddha (buddhavacana), sounds (linguistics = śabdavidyā), and logic (lit. study of causes = hetuvidyā). A person who has not worked hard to master these four branches of study is not capable of possessing (literally, producing) these four special knowledges. According to the Vaibhāṣikas, the study of buddhavacana alone is sufficient preparation for possession of the four pratisaṁvids. Cf. AKB VII.40b, pp. 419–20; AKV (Dwa), p. 1105. Reference to the Vaibhāṣika sect is given by Yaśomitra in AKV (Dwa), p. 1105. Cf. AKB(E), p. 1155.

221. The term 'āveṇika-buddhadharma' is rendered 'dharmas unique to the Buddha', AKB(E), p. 1136. For reference to texts mentioning these dharmas, see BHSD, p. 108b. The category is not found in the early Pali texts, but the Milindapañha, pp. 105, 206, 285 (PTS ed.) refers to them. The Milindapañha Commentary (ṭikā), ed. P.S. Jaini (PTS ed., 1961) refers to them (p. 66) without any list. The Pali list is found also in Dīgha-nikāyaṭṭhakathā-ṭīkā, ed. L.D. Silva (London, PTS, 1970), Vol. III, p. 67. The Pali version omits āveṇika. It speaks of 18 Buddha dhammā. See also āveṇi, CPD, p. 231. For translation see BDSL, pp. 21ff. and 326, n. 81ff. Cf. also AVSN, p. 279, n. 1. See also for translation, D.T. Suzuki, Outlines of Mahayana Buddhism (New York, 1967), p. 327, n. 3; cf. also Conze, LSPW, pp. 159–60.

222. I have not found any reference to bodily faults that compares them to a leaping monkey, though the Vinaya rules do forbid monks to enter the house of a layman with body, arms, or head swaying. Vinaya texts, Vol. XIII, pt. I (SBE), sekhiya dhammas, 15–20, pp. 60–61. In modern-day Buddhism in the West, the phrase 'monkey mind' enjoys considerable currency as a description of ordinary consciousness. The story of Pilindavaccha is given as an instant of vocal transgression or imperfection (vāgdauṣṭhulya). According to Pali tradition, Pilindavaccha was in the habit of addressing every one abusively as 'outcaste'. See "Pilindavaccha," DPPN II, p. 209–11. However, this important work on Pali proper names by Malalasekera does not mention any episodes in which Pilindavaccha (Skt. Pilindavatsa) abuses a lady named Gaṅgā. Perhaps there is such a story in the Sanskrit tradition, but I have not yet found it. P.V. Bapat, in his article "Arhat Pilinda-vaccha (Sans. Pilinda-vatsa) and his Unpleasant Mode of Address," in Homage to Bhikkhu J. Kashyap (Commemoration Volume) (Nalanda, 1986), pp. 107–08 refers to another source, the Mūlasarvāstivādī Vinaya-sūtra with Guṇaprabha's Commentary, where mention is made of Pilindavatsa's abusing a lady named Gaṅgādevi. Cf. P.V. Bapat and V.V. Gokhale, Vinaya-Sūtra with Guṇaprabha's Vṛtti (Commentary) (Patna, 1982), Chapter I, sūtra no. 102.

223. Cf. AKB IV.12, p. 204; Also see AN III, p. 346.

224. Cf. AVSN, p. 80, for 'well established mindfulness' (sūpasthitasmṛti) as one of the qualities of bhikṣus. On upasthitasmṛti of the Buddha in the four postures, cf. AKV (Dwa), p. 604.

225. For the thirty-two marks of a Great Personage in Pali sources, see Lakkhaṇa sutta, DN III, pp. 142ff.; also DN II, pp. 16ff.; DN II, pp. 136ff. Explanations of these lakṣaṇas are found in the commentaries on these texts: DNA II, pp. 445 ff., MNA III, p. 374. For Sanskrit sources see MV I, p. 226; LV, p. 105 ff. (English translation, Voice of the Buddha [Berkeley, 1983], pp. 155–56); MVY no. 235ff.; Abhis Ā, pp. 537ff.; Bodhisattvabhūmi,

pp. 259ff.; Dharma S. no. 83; Ratnagotravibhāga (Mahāyanottaratantraśāstra), pp. 94ff.; Gaṇḍavyūha, pp. 309ff.; Adv., pp. 187ff. For translations, see Rhys Davids, Dialogues of the Buddha (London, 1977) Pt. III, p. 137ff.; J.J. Jones (tr.), The Mahāvastu (London, 1973), Vol. I, pp. 180ff.; Dharma S. by K. Kasawara (tr.), ed. Max Muller and H. Wenzel (Oxford, 1885), pp. 53ff.; E. J. Thomas, The Life of the Buddha (London, 1931), pp. 220ff.; Har Dayal, BDSL, pp. 300ff.; Edward Conze, LSPW, pp. 657ff. Also see the entry for 'lakṣaṇa' in BHSD, pp. 458ff., where a comparative list is given. References to some lakṣaṇas are found at various places in AK; particularly notable is AK III.97ab; AKB, p. 186. See also La Vallée Poussin's note in AKB(E), p. 753, n. 483.

226. There are three types of cakravartin kings, the first being a universal monarch. Definitions are given by Buddhaghosa in DNA I, p. 249. Cf. also PED, p.259a, under 'cakka'.

227. This is clearly a Mahāyānic concept, for Bodhisattvas are endowed with the 32 lakṣaṇas. Cf. LV, p. 106; BDSL, p. 300; cf. Kathāvatthu IV. 7, pp. 283ff., for controversy on the theory that one gifted with the 32 marks is a Bodhisattva. There seems to have been some controversy on this issue in early Buddhism. Cf. Points of Controversy (London, 1960), p. 166.

228. On the significance of the wheel (cakra), cf. LOB, p. 219, BDSL, p. 304.

229. Our Commentator sometimes skips over important words —where we would expect comments—by the simple device of calling them 'spaṣṭa' (clear) or 'subodha' (easy to understand). The phraseology 'karmanirdeśaḥ spaṣṭaḥ' ('the exposition of the past action is clear') is used concerning the majority of lakṣaṇas. Sometimes he uses instead the term 'yojya' ('to be applied, related'), or 'pūrvavat' ('as above').

230. See the explanation of this mark in DNA II, p. 446; MNA III, p. 376, where Buddhaghosa says that the four fingers and five toes of the Buddha were of equal length, and that when the Blessed One entwined his fingers, they were like a window with lattice made by an expert carpenter (kusala vaḍḍhaki). It is said at the beginning of this comment that a person whose fingers are 'webbed' (i.e. grown together), like a snake's hood, is not fit for pabbajā (going into the homeless state). In that case, how could webbed fingers be a mark of a Great Personage? Buddhaghosa explains that the Tathāgata's fingers are spaced evenly, as with 'netting' or net-work (jāla). Cf. I.B. Horner, MLS, II, p. 321; cf. also articles by A. K. Coomarswamy and J. N. Banerjea on "webbed fingers" (of the Buddha), Indian Historical Quarterly, Vol. VII, 1931. Also see E.J. Thomas, LOB, p. 222; BDSL, pp. 302–03. On the image of the royal swan, cf. Adv. p. 188.

231. Cf. BDSL, p. 301; Adv. p. 189; also DN III, p. 151; DOB III, p. 144; DNA II, p. 448; MNA III, pp. 378–79; AVSN, p. 290, n. 8.

232. This is one of the minor marks also; see infra, nos. 25 and 27, Topic 27. It is not found as a major mark in other texts.

233. This is considered to be a sign of great fortune. Cf. Apte, 'kambugrīva' in the entry for kambu, PSED, p. 335b. See also PED, p. 189. This lakṣaṇa is not found in the standard lists, but the Gaṇḍavyūha mentions it, p. 400 (D.T. Suzuki ed.). See also AVSN, p. 295, n. 3.

234. This mark represents both samadantatā (even teeth) and catvāriṁśaddantatā (forty teeth), given in some texts as two separate lakṣaṇas. Cf. Adv. p. 189; DN III, p. 144. Abhis Ā (p. 538) fuses both lakṣaṇas, as in our text, but mentions separately 'samadantā'. Ibid., no. 28. Rhys Davids has a footnote on forty teeth in his translation of Mahāpadānasutta, concerning the Brahmin soothsayers who made a prophecy concerning Vipassi Buddha on the basis of his marks: "The Great Man at a more adult stage has eight more than the normal thirty-two. How the learned brahmins saw these signs in the babe is not explained." DOB II, p. 15, n. 9.

235. In the Ambaṭṭha-sutta, it is said that "the Blessed One so bent round his tongue that he touched and stroked both his ears, touched and stroked both his nostrils, and the whole circumference of his forehead, he covered with his tongue." DOB I, p. 131; Cf. DN I, p. 106. See also n. 2, DOB I. loc. cit. The word 'long' (prabhūta) could also be rendered 'extensive'. Rhys Davids has 'long', DOB III, p. 138.

236. The absence of commentary suggests that the copyist of the original manuscript may have overlooked this portion, since there is no remark to the effect that the mark is clear and needs no explanation. And explanation can be found in Adv. p. 189, which indicates that the Buddha's sense of taste is unimpaired by wind, bile, or phlegm. MNA III, p. 381 gives a detailed explanation, stating that 7,000 nerves of taste in the tongue are fastened to the throat. In DN III, p. 166, it is said that the Buddha's taste is supremely acute; "of anything on the tip (of the tongue), sensations of taste are produced in the throat and are diffused everywhere." Cf. DOB III, p. 156. Also compare: "Because his taste is unimpaired by wind, bile or phlegm, because he perceives each individual taste as it occurs, and because his consciousness conforms to it, he possesses a most excellent taste." LSPW, p. 659. See also references in AVSN, p. 297, n. 8 and 9.

237. On the three-thousand and many-thousand (trisāhasra-mahāsāhasra) world systems (lokadhātu), see above, note 210; BHSD, p. 259a.

238. No comments on this mark or the next; in general, the comments are also becoming briefer. Abhis. Ā, p. 538 gives the past karma of this mark as seeing all beings as one sees one's only son (sarvasattvaikaputradarśanāt).

239. Cf. Dhp, 273, "Of bipeds, the one who is gifted with the eye (of wisdom) is the best." The word 'cakkhumā' is taken to mean 'all-wise', an epithet of the Buddha; cf. cakkhumanta, PED, p. 260a. On 'best among men' (narottama) as an adjective of the Buddha, see DN III, p. 147.

240. Cf. Adv, p. 189; DN III, p. 143. See also MNA III, p. 377. "His skin has the hue of the finest burnished gold," LSPW, p. 658.

241. Cf. DN III, p. 144; DOB III, p. 138.

242. Dharmasaṅgraha has 'urdhvāgraromatā' as a separate lakṣaṇa: "having the hairs of the body erect." Dharma S. (tr. K. Kasawara) ed. F. Max Muller and Wenzel (Oxford, 1885), no. 10, p. 53. Pradakṣināvartaikaromatā is listed as no. 16, a separate lakṣaṇa. Ibid, p. 54.

243. In DN III, p. 144, it is said that the hair turns upwards dark blue in color like a collyrium (añjana), in curling rings (cf. English 'ringlets'), curling to the right. Cf. also DOB III, p. 138. See also Adv, p. 188.

244. No explanation is given for this mark. It is possible that the text was missing in Mss. discovered in Tibet and Nepal. Cf. AVSN, p. 303, n. 2. The mark is not mentioned in many texts, including the comparative list given by Edgerton in BHSD, pp. 458ff. However, abhinīlaromatā (dark blue hair) is mentioned in Adv., p. 188. DN III, p. 144 mentions dark blue hair in mark no. 14, which mentions hair rising upwards curling to the right. The Mahāvaṁsa refers to the Buddha's dark blue hair, Mhvs I.34. See also LV, p. 105, which mentions dark blue hair like a peacock's tail or mixed collyrium; cf. BDSL, p. 301.

245. Suśukla-bhrūmukhāntarorṇālalāṭatā. On ūrṇā (circle of hair), between the eyebrows, see BDSL, p. 301. Cf. ūrṇā and ūrṇākośa, BHSD, p. 150a, where Edgerton says that in ūrṇā, hair white in color is prevailingly mentioned. Rendered 'hairy mole', DOB, III, p. 139. Cf. also Adv., p. 189; DN III, p. 144; MNA III, pp. 384–85. In DN trans. (DOB) Rhys Davids renders as follows: "Between the eyebrows appears a hairy mole white and like soft cotton down." DOB III, p. 139. Cf. Har Dayal, BDSL, p. 301. Conze, LSPW, p. 659: "Because his face is adorned with a hair-tuft between his eyebrows, which is a hundred times more brilliant than the moon and sun, and which is white in color, like a jasmine flower, moon, cow's milk or a hoarfrost blossom, his face is adorned with a hair-tuft." The Saddharmpuṇḍarīka-sūtra speaks of a ray of light that issued from the hair growing between the eyebrows of the Buddha, extending over innumerable Buddha-fields which were illuminated by its radiance, from the lowest great hell Avīci to the highest abode in the world, Bhavāgra (SP, p. 6). This lakṣaṇa is represented on statues of the Buddha as a circular lump or by the insertion of a precious gem. Cf. E. J. Thomas, The Life of the Buddha (London, 1969), p. 223.

246. The Pali tradition says "The revered Gotama has the symmetrical proportions of a banyan tree, as is the height of his body so is the length of his arms when stretched out, as is the length of his arms when stretched out, so is the height of his body." I.B. Horner, MLS, II, p. 322. Cf. also DN III, p. 144, MN II, p. 136; BDSL, p. 302; LOB, p. 220; LSPW, p. 659; MNA III, p. 380; Adv, p. 188. In the Gaṇḍavyūha, nyagrodha-parimaṇḍala is explained as samantabhadra and samantaprāsādika (auspicious and pleasing from all sides); compare the mark that follows in our text. For a detailed explanation, see GV, p. 402. See also note on the banyan tree in DOB II, p. 15. Cf. also lakṣaṇa, no. 13, above, AVSN, p. 294.

247. Cf. AKB VII. 31ab, p. 413, where Vasubandhu refers to the view of a Sautrāntika (Dārṣṭāntika) master nicknamed 'Bhadanta' who says that the Buddha's physical power, like that of his mental power, is infinite, otherwise the body of the Blessed One would not be able to hold infinite knowledge. Cf. AKV (Dwa), p. 1089. It is also said that the Blessed One has the power of an elephant (nāgagranthi). On the explanation and controversy over the physical power of the Buddha, see AKB VII.31c, p. 413; AKV (Dwa), pp. 1089–90; Adv., pp. 388–89. See also AKB(E), p. 1198, n. 176 for references to Vibhāṣā on Nārāyaṇabala. The Pali tradition is found in Vibhaṅga Commentary, p. 39; see also DPPN II, p. 54. Also see P.V. Bapat, "Nārāyaṇabala," Studia Indologica Internationalia, I. (Poona and Paris, 1954). For further references on Nārāyaṇabala, see AVSN, p. 306, n. 1. 'Samantaprāsādika' is also one of the minor physical signs (anuvyañjana) of the Buddha. See AVS, p. 64 (no. 39).

248. This last mark is an extra lakṣaṇa, extending the standard number of thirty-two. It is found in all the Mss. of Nib. We have noted earlier Vīryaśrīdatta's remark that there are thirty-two marks, neither less nor more, but still this lakṣaṇa has crept in as an interpolation. I have not included it in the main text of the Sūtra in the first part of the book, but have included it together with its past action, in the text as given immediately above. Cf. AVSN, pp. 305–306. See AVS, pp. 55, 62, n. 3.

The Ratnagotravibhāga, Mahāyānottaratantraśāstra (ed. E. H. Johnston, Patna, 1950), III. 25, p. 95, refers to this lakṣaṇa in the phrase: nārāyaṇasthāma-dṛḍhātmabhāva, rendered by E. Obermiller on the basis of the Tibetan version, 'Sublime and incomparable body of the sage which is firm and possessed of the power of Vishṇu'. The Sublime Science of the Great Vehicle to Salvation (Acta Orientalia IX, 1931), p. 394. This is the last lakṣaṇa in the text of RGV.

249. For the innumerable good deeds = kuśalamūlas = puṇyas or meritorious deeds, see AKB IV.110a, p. 266. Yaśomitra gives a good explanation in AKV (Dwa), p. 737; cf. Poussin, AKB(E), pp. 692, 756, n. 495. The same concept can be found in the Saddharmapuṇḍarīka-sūtra, p. 51 (paripūrṇagātrān, śatapuṇyalakṣaṇān).

250. The list of eighty marks varies in different texts, but many items appear in most lists. For a Pali list, see Milinda Ṭīkā (ed. P.S. Jaini, PTS, London, 1961), p. 17. For a translation of the minor marks, see Dharma S. (tr. K. Kasawara, ed. Max Muller and Wenzel), pp. 55 ff.; E. Conze, LSPW, pp. 661ff.; Mahāvastu II, trans. by J. J. Jones (London, 1976), pp. 40ff. A full list with translation appears in the article on 'anuvyañjana', Ency. of Bud., p. 785.

It cannot be easily explained why the Commentator dismisses this section with a remark at the beginning that the marks are clear in meaning (spaṣṭārthāni), commenting only on the last anuvyañjana. Either the anuvyañjanas did not occupy as much importance in the Buddhist tradition as the lakṣaṇas, or he was in a hurry to bring the Nibandhana to a close. In the Pali canonical texts, although the thirty-two lakṣaṇas are mentioned (the Lakkhaṇa Sutta in the Dīghanikāya is devoted to them), there is not a single reference to anuvyañjanas. Pali commentarial texts do mention them, and they are listed in some late texts, such as the Milinda ṭikā. Buddhist Sanskrit texts, especially of the Mahāyāna tradition, do mention them and some enumerate them. For additional lists, see LV, p. 106; Abhis. Ā, p. 539; Adv., p. 190; MV II, p. 43; Dharma S. p. 84; MVY no. 268ff. For another English translation, see Voice of the Buddha, (Berkeley, 1983), pp. 156–57. Also see BHSD, p. 34a.

251. The second of the thirty-two marks of a Great Personage mentions a wheel on the sole of the feet, and the Commentator points out that the wheel is found on the palms of the hands also. See AVSN, p. 287, and term note to folio 287, below, on 'readily visible'.

252. Śrīvatsa and the other signs mentioned are numbered among the eight auspicious emblems of the Buddhist tradition. They are mentioned in the Pali Commentaries also. Cf. DNA II, p. 445; MNA III, p. 375 (in comments on the second lakṣaṇa). See for citations AVSN, p. 286, n. 4. Cf. also P.V. Bapat, "Four Auspicious Things of Buddhists. Śrīvatsa, Svastika, Nandyāvarta and Vardhamāna," Indian Historical Research Institute Silver Jubilee Commemoration Volume, 1953. There is no reference to the wheel, diamond, lotus, or fish in the lists in Abhi Ā, LV, and Dharma S. The LV list has Vardhamāna (an auspicious diagram), which our Sūtra does not have. Cf. LV, p. 107. For additional reference on these symbols, see AVSN, p. 308, note 6. B.S.L. Hanumantha Rao, in Religion in Andhra (Tripurasundari, 1973) p. 84, says: "Mahāvihāravāsin appear to have recognized the superhuman qualities of the Buddha and began to worship the Buddhapādas with Aṣṭamaṅagalas." In his list of eight auspicious signs he includes the conch, wheel, two fish, two chauris (sic), the water pot [vase], the standard, the lotus, and Śrīvatsa, op. cit., p. 90, n. 144. 'Chauries' perhaps refers to a kind of bushy fan made from the tail of a white cow (or yak) or other animal.

The four auspicious emblems not mentioned among the anuvyañjanas in the AVS are the chatra (parasol), śaṅkha (conch shell), kalaśa (sacred bowl) and dhvaja (flag). Cf. Alice Getty, Gods of Northern Buddhism (Delhi, 1978), Intro., p. 50. Getty does not mention among the eight emblems the svastika. There is some variation among the lists.

253. Prātimokṣa is the code of conduct for monks according to the Vinaya texts taught by the Buddha. On the three kinds of restraints (saṁvara), see AKB IV.13cd., p. 205; cf. Abhidharmasamuccaya (ed. P. Pradhan, Santiniketan, 1950), pp. 57–58; Adv., pp. 128ff.

254. Cf AKB I.1, p. 1; AKV (Dwa), p. 8. The Commentary has earlier discussed the Buddha's concern for all beings, describing how he sees with his Buddha eye persons experiencing difficulties and tribulations and wishes to bring them happiness and deliverance. See AVSN p. 245 and note 174, supra.

255. Cf. AVSN, pp. 83–84 (p. 53 of the present text) for the same instruction. Cf. Dhammapada, verse 276. For similar passages listing places appropriate for meditation, cf. SN IV, p. 133; Kindred Sayings, IV, p. 85. Various terms used in the Sūtra passage are not found together in the Pali tradition. For comments on some of them, see DNA I, p. 210.

256. On the three bodhis, see AVSN, p. 228.

257. "It (ghuṇākṣaranyāya) is the famous maxim (nyāya) of letters bored by an insect in wood. It takes its origin from the unexpected and chance resemblance of an incision in wood or in the leaf of a book made by an insect to the form of some letter and is used to denote any fortuitous or chance occurrence," Apte, PSED, p. 574b. By these remarks the Commentator shows his great humility.

258. On Dharmapāla, the great patron of Buddhism, see AVSN (Introd.), pp. 133–34.

259. Saṁvat 319 refers to the Nepalese era = 1199 A.D. See also AVSN (Intro.), p. 9, n. 1. Thus this copy of the Commentary was written by the copyist Vīryaśrīmitravīra at the end of the 12th century A.D. On the chronogram given in the following verse, see AVSN (Intro.), p. 20, n. 1. The chronogram also gives the saṁvat 319.

TERMS AND VARIANTS

Notes on terms and variants are indicated in the text by the symbol "°". References are keyed to the "folio number" as indicated in the margins of the text (i.e., the page number in the published edition of AVS and AVSN, as given in the bibliography). Folios 1–68 contain the text of the Sūtra. Term and variant notes for the Sūtra are given only for the Sūtra as quoted in the Nibandhana. The letters a, b, and c after page numbers in dictionary references indicate columns on the page.

SŪTRA

Folio 1

Namo Buddhāya. 'Obeisance to the Buddha'. One Sanskrit manuscript, edited by Alfonsa Ferrari (Arthaviniścaya, Atti Della Reale Accademia D'Italia (Serie settima, Vol. V, Fasc. 137, Rome 1944), gives 'Obeisance to the Three Jewels'. The Tibetan version has 'Obeisance to all Buddhas and Bodhisattvas'. Nepalese manuscripts omit the introductory portion but begin with 'Obeisance to Mañjuguru.'

Folio 2

Dharma (Pali Dhamma). The word is untranslatable, so it has been retained. It could be rendered here as 'doctrine', 'law', teaching', 'discourse', etc. For many meanings of the word 'dharma' see AVSN, p. 276. For a good note on the rendering of this all-important term, see K.R. Norman, Elder's Verses (Oxford, 1990), p. 118.

Folio 3

Compendium of Categories. On this translation for 'Arthaviniścaya', see Introduction to AVSN, p. 59.

Folio 6

conditioned co-production. The text gives the term in the plural form: 'pratītyasamutpādeṣu'.

Folio 9

drenches. Abhiṣyandatvam, which may also be translated 'fluid'. Cf. Shanti Bhikshu Shastri (ed.), Pancaskandha-prakaraṇa of Vasubandhu (Kelaniya 1969), p. 2. There the reading is niṣyandatā, which is translated as "fluidity." See p. 25, ibid.

Folio 12

formless existence. Here the Sūtra uses the word 'dhātu' rather than 'bhava'. Dhātu here may be translated as 'existence' or 'world', but not as 'element', as in Topic Three above.

Folio 26

develops well. The words for 'well' are sādhu ca suṣṭhu ca, terms that are almost synonymous.

Folio 30

his zeal is. Literally, 'will be' (bhaviṣyati). So also for the other three bases: energy, concentration, and investigation.

born of consciousness. i.e., of 'natural purity' of consciousness. Cf. Nyanamoli's parenthetical insertion, PP XII.50.

Folio 35

wrong view. The term in Pali is diṭṭhupādāna. Cf. Dhammasangaṇi (= Dhs) article 1215; also A Buddhist Manual of Ethics (tr. of Dhamma-saṅgaṇi), p. 324. Mrs. Rhys Davids translates the term 'grasping after speculative opinion'.

right thought: saṁkalpa. The word is also translated 'resolution', 'resolve', 'intention', 'aspiration'. It is also a synonym of vitarka. See Dhs., article 283; BDSL, p. 162. 'Resolve' may be a better rendering in view of the explanation in the Sūtra, but I have followed the accepted translation.

Folio 36

wrongful conduct in seeking sexual pleasures: kāmamithyācāra. The Pali 'kāmamicchācāra' is translated 'wrong conduct in sensual pleasures' in Expositor, Vol. I, p. 130. Aṭṭhasālini, commentary on the Dhamma-saṅgaṇi, explains: "In the expression 'wrong conduct in sensual pleasures', 'in sensual pleasures' means 'in matters of sexual intercourse'; 'wrong conduct' means bad and truly blameworthy conduct. The characteristic of 'wrong conduct' in sensual pleasure is . . . volition arising in the body-door, through the unlawful intention of trespassing upon a person to whom one has no right of going." Pe Maung Tin (tr.), Expositor (London, PTS, 1920), Vol. I, p. 130.

Folio 46

cutting off of conditioned existence. Cf. 'dharmopaccheda', Lalitavistara, p. 392; Mahāvastu III, p. 200. J.J. Jones translates as 'the breaking up of sensorial states'. The word 'dharma' here means 'phenomena' of the saṁsāric world; it is practically synonymous with skandha. Cf. J.J. Jones (tr.) The Mahāvastu (London, PTS, 1978), vol. III, p. 196, n. 6. Also see the entry for upaccheda, BHSD, p. 135.

Folio 49

dharmas. It is difficult to translate the plural of 'dharma' here. Har Dayal renders "principles and phenomena" and provides a note on the term, BDSL, p. 21.

Folio 50

In accord with the Dharma. Sahadharma. On this term see BHSD, p. 587a; Jones, MV (tr.), Vol. III, p. 328n.

Folio 52

clear. I render samprakhyāna as clarity, obtained through mastery in concentration.Yaśomitra renders it as asammoṣa ('unforgetfulness'). AKV (Dwa), p. 1103.

Folio 53

lack of consideration. Cf. MDPL, p. 55: apratisaṅkhyā = 'not after careful consideration'. See BHSD, p. 48. An alternative rendering would be 'want of judgment'. Cf. BDSL, p. 23.

never loses his mindfulness. This item is almost equivalent to the third. The term in the third item is muṣita (deprivation); here it is hāni (loss).

Folio 56

not disappoint: ajihmakaraṇatayā. Cf. jihmīkaraṇa = disappointing (literally, 'darkening'), BHSD, p. 243b; ajihmīkaraṇa: 'not disappointing', .

Folio 57

secret mantra: guhyamantra. A remark showing Tantric influence.

Folio 59

inestimable merit. apramāṇa-puṇyaskandha. Cf. Pali appameyya mahāpuññakkhanda (boundless great mass of merits), SN. V, p. 400. On the concept of immeasurable merits that accrue to a donor of gifts of food, drink, clothes, etc., see ibid.

Folio 60

never inauthentic. akṛtrima (lit. not artificial, not fictitious). See kṛtrima, PSED, p. 371b.

inclined: karmaṇyatā, see Pali kamaññatā, 'workability', 'adoption', 'readiness', PED, p. 194. I have translated as 'inclination'; here it could also be rendered 'readiness'.

councils of the Dharma. dharmasaṅgīti-cittakarmaṇyatā. Dharmasaṅgīti perhaps refers to the famous Buddhist councils, or else to any assembly in which Dharma is expounded.

crowded gatherings. Saṅgaṇikā = 'society', 'social gathering', 'where people collect'. Bendall and Rouse translate it 'crowd': "A Bodhisattva even in a crowd dwells apart (bodhisattvaḥ. . . saṅgaṇikāyāpi vivekagocaraḥ)." Śikṣāsamuccaya (tr.) C. Bendall and W.H.D. Rouse (Delhi, 1971), p. 197.

Folio 61

comprehended with perfect competence: pradakṣiṇagrāhitayā. Cf. pradakṣiṇagrāhi, BHSD, p. 379b.

teachers, preceptors: ācārya, guru, upādhyāya. These words are used synonymously. See Pali ācariya, PED, p. 96a. On the duties of these two kinds of teachers, see Mahāvagga, pp. 48ff; cf. I.B. Horner (tr.) The Book of the Discipline, vol. IV (London, 1982), pp. 67ff, 79ff. Currently the title 'ācārya' is used in traditional universities in India for 'Professor'. In Thailand 'ācāna', the Thai transliteration for ācārya, is a common word for every class of teacher, irrespective of grade.

Folio 63

regular lines on the palm of the hand. 'tulyapāṇirekhāśca' is rendered 'having regular lines on hand', Dharmasaṅgraha (tr.) K. Kasawara and (ed.) M. Max Muller and H. Wenzel (New Delhi, 1981), p. 59.

large fingers: citāṅgulayaśca. 'Cita' literally means 'piled up', 'heaped up, from which the word 'caitya' is derived. It may also mean 'stout' or 'large'. Cf. BHSD, p. 229.

hidden veins. gūḍhaśirāsca. Cf. Dharma S., but Conze renders 'veins do not bulge out'; LSPW, p. 661 (no. 7).

Folio 64

smooth limbs: mṛṣṭagātrāśca. Rendered, 'having smooth members', Dharma S., p. 56 (no. 19).

pure in conduct. śucisamācārāśca. samācāra = conduct, behavior, PED, p. 684. Cf. kāyasamācāra and vacisamācāra (behavior of body and of speech), DN II, 279. Can it also be rendered here as 'movement'? Cf. PSED, p. 962b.

extensive lines in palms. Read āyata for āyatana (which is a misprint). Āyata means 'long, extensive'. See BHSD, p. 346.

original and reflected image. bimbapratibimbadarśanāśca. On bimba and pratibimba, see SED, p. 731. Dharma S., p. 57 has bimbapratibimboṣṭhatā (no. 49) (having lips red as the bimba berry). Aṣṭasāhasrikāprajñāpāramitā, ed. P.L. Vaidya (Darbhanga, 1960), p. 539 has bimbapratibimbopamauṣṭhatā (no. 48) translated by Conze 'lips are (red) like the Bimba berry." Cf. LSPW, p. 663. In our text the reference is to 'looks', not 'lips'.

Folio 66

previously. i.e., in the beginning of the Sūtra.

Folio 67

lodging. śayanāsana. Lit., sleeping and sitting place. Cf. Pali senāsana, PED, p. 723a.

Folio 68

gandharva. A type of demigod.

such a teaching. This is a very popular verse, found at the end of many Buddhist texts, and used in some traditions as a mantra. The verse in Sanskrit: ye dharmā hetuprabhavā hetū (sic) teṣām tathāgato hy avadat/ teṣām ca yo nirodha evaṁvādī mahāśramaṇaḥ//

NIBANDHANA

Folio 71

Om Namo Buddhāya = 'Om, Obeisance to the Buddha'. The Nepalese manuscript has 'Om, Obeisance to the Omniscient One' (Om namaḥ sarvajñāya).

Kandarpa. A name for Māra. It is generally used in classical Sanskrit literature for the god of love (Kāmadeva). Its use in Buddhist literature is rare. Even the Mahāvyutpatti (=MVY) does not mention it. However, Māra and Kāmadeva are juxtaposed in MVY 163, 18–19.

list of topics. This can also mean 'program'. See MDPL, p. 126.

logical connection: 'anusandhi'. On this word, see BHSD, p. 36a. 'Anusandhi' of a sūtra is referred to in SP, p. 394: A Bodhisattva must know the logical connection in Sūtras.

Folio 72

at the outset. The verse quoted is translated on the basis of reading 'vācyam' in the Nepalese manuscript, which is more correct. See Nib., p. 72, n. 5. The source of this verse has not yet been traced.

dharmapravicaya. This is one of the constituents of bodhi, as well as bodhi itself. See Topic XVIII in Nib., folio 228.

Folio 73

upakleśa. It is difficult to understand why this word is used, rather than 'kleśa', meaning 'defilement'. Cf. AK I.3 for dharmapravicaya and the use of kleśa in this context. I have rendered it here in the sense of 'defilement'.

samāropa. The reading in the printed edition is faulty. It should be samāropāpavāda-parihārārthaṁ vā. I am grateful to the late Prof. J.W. de Jong, who pointed this out in his review of the text in IIJ, Vol. 17, 1975.

sūtra. Here the word is used in the conventional classical Sanskrit usage of 'pithy saying' or aphorism, not in the Buddhist sense of 'discourse' (dharmaparyāya).

Folio 75

absence of attainment. Adhigamābhāva, or non-realization of Arhathood.

Folio 76

bhagavān. It is difficult to render bhagavān into English. I have preferred the rendering "Blessed One" to "Lord" and "Exalted One" generally in vogue in translations. See Nibandhana (= Nib.) pp. 76–77; 241–42 on the interpretation of the term. See also term notes to folio 242, below.

Folio 79

Lord. A translation of bhagavān in the vocative, which I think is in tune with the style of the Sūtra here. Some translators of Pali Sūtras have also used this word.

Folio 81

virtuous: kalyāṇa. Another term that is not easy to translate. I.B. Horner renders it 'lovely', MLS Vol. I, p. 265. The commentaries explain it as synonym of bhadra, meaning good, happy, auspicious, etc. See PED, p. 199, which renders kalyāṇa-mitta 'a virtuous friend'. Other renderings include 'spiritual advisor', 'guide'.

good in sense and letter. The Pali Suttas have literally 'with meaning' (sattha) and 'with letter' (savyañjana) DN I, p. 62. For 'good' (su), the Pali tradition gives 'with' (sa). Rhys Davids renders 'in the spirit' and 'in the letter'. DOB I, p. 78.

brahmacarya. Here the word does not have its common meaning of 'celibacy' but rather signifies 'caryā' (course, path). It is considered to be brahma (the highest) as it leads to nirvāṇa. This is apparently a later interpretation of the term.

Folio 82

opponent of. The text reads kleśapratipakṣa, but should be read kleśāpratipakṣa. See "Additions and Corrections" in AVSN, p. 182 (after Introduction).

Folio 83

category. The term might also mean 'subject matter' (artha).

dharmaparyāya. Cf. the use of this word for canonical texts in Aśokan Inscriptions, Bhabru edict, AI, p. 129.

Folio 84

subject matter or contents. 'Uddeśa' is a technical term. It means 'proposing' or 'setting forth'; doctrinal topics. On this word, see PSED, p. 272c and BHSD, p. 130b.

Folio 85

namely (tadyathā). The usual translation is 'namely', but it may also be rendered in English as "this is, there are," etc.

aggregate (skandha). Among the various renderings of this term by scholars are 'group', 'heap', 'pile', 'mass', and 'agglomerations'. See BHSD, p. 607. For a general discussion, see WE, p. 133ff.

avijñaptirūpa. On this term, see AKB(E), pp. 569–70. This concept occasioned considerable controversy between the Sautrāntika and Vaibhāṣika schools. Cf. AKB(E), p. 560ff. Also see AK I.9ab; I.11; IV.3–4; AKB pp. 5, 8, 196–99. The concept of unmanifested form was a special contribution of the Sarvāstivādins, from whom the Vaibhāṣikas developed. The Sautrāntikas denied its existence. See also McGovern: A Manual of Buddhist Philosophy (London, 1923), p. 128. See also AKB(E), pp. 63, 67, 560 ff.

feeling. The generally accepted translation for vedanā. The other rendering in vogue is 'sensation'. See the good note in DOB II, p. 54, n. 2.

saṁskāra. A most difficult, even untranslatable term. Alternatives to 'karma formations' include 'conformations', 'volitional activities', 'dispositions', 'mental coefficients', and motivational forces. For various renderings and a detailed discussion, see BDSL, pp. 69ff.; WE, p. 144ff. The term is used in several other contexts also.

Folio 86

iti. See Apte, PSED, p. 245a.

Folio 87

tatra. Cf. PESD on tatra and Pali tattha in PED, sub voce, and their various meanings. I have sometimes left this word untranslated.

ṣaṣṭhi (tatparuṣa) samāsa. An example is bhojanavelā (mealtime) which means bhojanasya velā (time of meals). See D.K. Guru, A Manual of Sanskrit Grammar (Bombay, 1938) p. 227.

Folio 88

unmanifested form. Cf. AK I.11. See avijñaptirūpa, notes to folio 85, above.

Folio 91

consumes what is presented. The reading in the footnote of the text in AVSN is correct, and I have translated accordingly.

Folio 92

eighteen dhātus. BMPE, p. 347, gives the translation as follows: sight, visual object, visual cognition; hearing, sound, auditory cognition; smell, odor, olfactory cognition; taste, sapid object, gustatory cognition; body sensibility, tangible, tactile cognition; mind, mental object, representative cognition. On the eighteen dhātus, see also WE pp. 162–68 and sources cited.

āśraya. This term is translated as 'receptacle', 'basis', 'body', 'foundation', etc. See MDPL, p. 114. On this term, see also term notes to folio 233, below.

dharma-dhātu. Here 'dharma' has the sense of 'mental object', 'idea'.

bhautika viṣaya. Derived from primary elements (mahābhūtāni); namely, earth, water, fire and air. Cf. the mahābhūtas, AVS, p. 9.

Folio 93

sensitive. Rendered 'suprasensible subtle material element' in AKB(E) p. 64.

Folio 94

santāna. Conze translates this term as 'continuity'. MDPL, p. 399.

āśraya. See note on this term at term notes to folio 92, above.

Folio 95

āyatana. Also translated as 'base', 'sphere' 'sense and sense objects'. It is interesting that the twelve āyatanas come after the eighteen dhātus. The latter include all the twelve āyatanas, yet they are understood to be different categories. For a discussion, see WE chs. 23–24, pp. 162–74.

ādhyātmika. This term is generally translated 'internal' in contrast to 'external'. See BHSD, p. 95. I have followed this usage in the Sūtra. Here, however, to help bring out the meaning, I have adopted the term 'personal', as given in AKB(E) p. 108. See AKB I. 39. The literal meaning is 'relating to the self'.

Folio 96

upātta and anupātta. Cf. AKB(E) p. 65. Upātta is also translated 'appropriated' and anupātta as 'unappropriated'. See AKB I.34c. AKB(E), p. 98. See also upātta in MDPL, p. 134; PSED, p. 298b.

dharma-dhātu. See the note on this term above, term notes to folio 92.

pratisaṁkhyānirodha and apratisaṁkhyānirodha. On these two important concepts, see AKB I.5-6. See also McGovern, A Manual of Buddhist Philosophy (London, 1923) pp. 111–114.

Folio 98

pratītyasamutpāda. The translation 'conditioned co-production' is taken from Edward Conze, MDPL, p. 279. See also his Buddhist Thought in India (London, 1962) p. 156. Most often the term is translated '(law of) dependent origination'. Other translations include 'law of causation', 'chain of causation', 'conditioned genesis', 'dependent arising', 'formula of causal origin', 'conditioned origination', 'causal production', and 'interdependent co-operation'.

Folio 99

vastu. AKB(E) renders vastu as 'foundation'; cf. p. 407. Also rendered 'base'.

upadiṣṭa. See translation of this term by E. Conze, MDPP, p. 129.

Folio 100

ayoniśo manaskāra. On this term, see P.L. Vaidya (ed.), Madhyamaka Śāstra (Darbhanga, 1960) p. 197. Ayoniśo manas(i)kāra is also rendered 'unwise attention' (MDPL, p. 70), 'disorderly or distracted attention' (PED, p. 560b) and 'incorrect judgment' (AKB[E]), p. 408). See BHSD, p. 418a.

Folio 102

upāyāsa. The translation 'despair' follows E. Conze. See MDPL, p. 135. Other translations: 'irritation', 'disturbance', 'tribulation', and 'vexation'.

entire. kevala, but 'kevalaṁ' means 'only' or 'sole'. The meaning in the Sūtra appears to be 'entire', a rendering consistent with Buddhaghosa's interpretation,. Vism XVII. 50. But Vīryāśrīdatta, following Vasubandhu, explains it as 'without any self or what belongs to the self'. This interpretation may be a later development. Cf. AKB III, 28, p. 140; MMK, p. 558.

prativedha. 'Penetration,' 'comprehension', 'deeper understanding'. Also translated as 'knowledge' or 'insight', PED, p. 399b.

Folio 103

yaduta. The literal meaning is 'as that', 'for example', 'such as.' Cf. Pali yadidaṁ. See PED, p. 554b and BHSD, p. 443b.

ajñāna. I avoid the translation 'ignorance' in order to prevent confusion with avidyā. Conze gives 'non-cognition', but translates 'ajānan' as 'not knowing', MDPL, p. 8. Rhys Davids gives 'ignorance'. See aññāṇa, PED, p. 14. Alex Wayman prefers "nescience" for avidyā. Cf. BI, p. 194.

Folio 106

teach (or preach). Vādin may be translated as "preacher" or "theoretician." See MDPL, p. 348.

Folio 107

āveṇikī. Also translated 'independent'; see AKB(E) p. 788. In AKB(E), p. 417 āveṇikī avidyā is explained by the translator as follows: "The fool (sic) or Pṛthagjana does not understand (aprajānan) that pratītyasamutpāda is merely the saṁskāras, that is, conditioned (saṁskṛta) dharmas—[this lack of prajñā is avidyā āveṇiki, only non-wisdom, not associated with desire]—and this produces a belief in ātman (AK V.7, 12) and egotism (AK V.10a)."

Folio 108

method. Cf. Pali (ñāya), PED, p. 288b.

Bodhipakṣya dharmas. There are thirty-seven items in all, listed and explained in later portions of the AVS, topics XIII–XIX.

powers. Through an oversight the Sanskrit 'bala' is not printed in the published text. The word is in the original Ms. brought from Tibet by Rahul Sankrityayan, on which I worked.

anuśaya. This potent word for expressing a 'layer' of mind is variously translated; e.g, 'bent', 'bias', 'proclivity', 'latent disposition', 'tendency'. Cf. Rhys Davids, PED, p. 44a. Other translations are 'latent bias', 'evil tendency', 'unwholesome tendency' (Conze, MDPL, p. 41), 'latent defilement' (Poussin, AKB(E), p. 767). See also Wayman, who renders it 'trace', BI, p. 193; cf. WE, pp. 238ff.

darśana-bhāvanā-heya. 'Bhāvanā' is often translated 'development (of meditation)', 'mental development', 'meditation', etc. For details see Nyantiloka, Buddhist Dictionary (Kandy, 1980), pp. 36ff.

kṣema. Conze renders kṣema as 'safety' and as 'secure from attack'. MDPL, p. 160. I consider it to mean both 'peace' and 'security'.

Folio 109

āsrava. Pali āsava. A word often used in Buddhist texts. In AKB, the word is explained as follows: "They (āsravas) flow (āsravanti) from the higher realm (bhavāgra = naivasaṁjñānāsaṁjñāyatana) to avīci (the lowest hell); they flow out (kṣar) by the six organs which are as wounds. They are thus called cankerous influences or āsrava," AKB(E) p. 834. The word is variously translated 'canker', 'cankerous influence', 'outflow', 'defilement', 'intoxicant', 'passion', 'influx', 'taint', 'corruption', 'bias', etc. I have used 'outflow' here, though in other places in the text I use 'defilement'.

Folio 110

sense fields of contact. sparśāyatana; i.e., all six faculties of contact, non-mental and mental.

paryāya. This term may also mean 'during the round or course (of teaching the Sūtra). See pariyāya in PED, p. 433b, paryāya, PSED, p. 604a.

Folio 111

karma formations. saṁskāra. For various translations, see Har Dayal, BDSL, p. 69. Alex Wayman, in BI, p. 164, renders it 'motivation'. For more on this term, see term notes to folio 85.

Folio 112

karma formations of the body. Here the term could also refer to the material (physical) aggregates. Cf. PED on kāyasankhāra, p. 209b.

manifold appearances, speeches, and deeds. . . . trainees. The text has gatāni, which may also mean 'spoken' or 'understood'. The Tibetan has been rendered as 'activated'. For this verse, see D.R.S. Bailey (ed.), The Śatapañcāśataka of Mātṛceṭa (Cambridge, 1951), verse 130, p. 134. It is a stotra, or verse of praise, and comes under ch. XIII: Kauśalastava, or praise of the skillfulness of the Buddha. The publication includes the Tibetan translation and commentary and a Chinese translation.

Folio 113

kāyābhisaṁskṛtatvāt. There are a number of renderings of the difficult term 'abhisaṁskāra', 'abhisaṁskāreṇa'. For example: 'bringing about', 'putting together', 'fashioning', 'formative influence', 'exercise', 'accumulation', 'forming'. See MDPL, p. 64; BHSD, p. 57b.

vitarka and vicāra, generally used as a pair, have been translated variously 'reflection and deliberation,' 'initial and sustained application of the mind', 'reflection and investigation', 'thought conception and discursive thought', etc. They are two constituents of the first rūpāvacara-dhyāna ('form' meditation). I.B. Horner renders vitarka 'initial thought' and vicāra 'discursive thought'. See MLS I, pp. 363–64. Bhikkhu J. Kashyap, AP. pp. 53–55 translates these two words "applying and sustaining the mind on the object." See also Bhikkhu Nyanamoli, PP, IV, 88–89. For detailed notes on these two words, see BMPE, pp. 10-11. Vitarka is explained as the directing of concomitant properties towards the object; vicāra is the continued exercise of the mind with regard to that object. See MDPL, p. 353, 352; PED 620a, 615b. PED gives an excellent note on vittaka. See also Path of Purification (tr. of Visuddhimagga) IV.88ff.

Folio 114

exercise. See note on abhisaṁskāra, at folio 113 above.

Folio 115

rebirth consciousness of merit. On the words puṇyopagama vijñāna, see AKB III. 28, AKB(E) p. 412, n. 191.

Folio 117

vibhaṅga. Conze translates vibhaṅga as "classification," MDPL, p. 358. But vibhaṅga is also rendered "analysis." The second Abhidharma text of the Pali Tripiṭaka Vibhaṅga is translated into English by P.A. Thittila as Book of Analysis (London, 1969).

mind. This refers to manodhātu (basic mind element), not manovijñānadhātu (mind consciousness). S.Z. Aung renders manodhātu "element of apprehension" and "manovijñānadhātu" (Pali manoviññāṇa) as "element of comprehension." Cf. CP, p. 123n.

Folio 118

indeed. Sanskrit 'nāma' The usage here seems to be as an expletive, meaning 'indeed', 'however', etc. See nāma in SED, p. 536a.

Folio 120

bhautika. Good material on this term may be seen in BHSD, p. 412b.

Folio 121

kalala, etc. On these different successive embryonic states (difficult to render into English), see the discussion in AKB III.19, p. 130; AKB(E), pp.

395–96. According to the Abhidharma (Vibhāṣā Śāstra), quoted by Schmithausen, mind is faint throughout the embryonic state. AV II, p. 301.

Folio 123

āśraya. On āśraya and āśrita, see AVSN, p. 92. See also AKV (ed. Dwarikadas Shastri), p. 52. AKB, p. 154 explains āśraya as a body with sense organs (sendriyaḥ kāyaḥ).

Folio 124

sparśa. Pali phassa. It signifies mental contact. Also translated 'sense impression'. See phassa, BD, p. 175. Contact is also one of the mental concomitants (caitasika). For contact as a mental factor found in all minds, see AKB II.24, p. 54.

āśraya. Here 'and so forth' refers to āśrita and ālambana. On āśraya, āśrita and ālambana, see AVSN, p. 92; AKB(E), p. 444. See term notes to folio 123, above.

sensitive material element. This is also rendered 'suprasensible subtle material element'. AKB(E), p. 64.

svayūtha. This term could also mean 'our school'; a translation would then be: "But it (sensitivity) is accepted by our school although acquired by its (particular) class of consciousness and is not apprehended."

Folio 128

abhiṣvaṅga. Conze renders abhiṣvaṅga as 'desire': MDPL, p. 64. Edgerton in his dictionary entry on abhiṣvakta gives 'attached'. BHSD, p. 57a. This latter definition of abhiṣvaṅga is important and seems associated with the Yogācāra school.

pravṛtti. Other translations are 'continuance', 'functioning'. See AV, pp. 244, 299.

Folio 129

abhisandhi. See Childers, DPL, p. 7a (quoting Abhidhānappadīpikā 766). BHSD, MDPL, and PED have no entry for this word. Could abhisandhi be rendered here as 'context'?

Folio 130

upādāna. Two other renderings are 'attachment' and 'grasping'. For good notes on this important term, see Childers, DPL, p. 525a and Nyantiloka, BD, p. 228. Alex Wayman renders it 'indulgence', BI, p. 164.

Folio 131

paryavasthāna. 'Outburst' is one of the renderings given by Rhys Davids and Stede. See PED, p. 433b. Others include 'bias' or 'prepossession'. Conze gives 'obsession', 'prepossession'. MDPL, p. 256. Alex Wayman has 'entrapment'. BI, p. 193. AKB(E), p. 841, has 'wrapping'. I have preferred 'outburst' (of a defilement). Cf. Adv., p. 222, which explains it as 'aroused (prabuddha) defilement'.

Folio 132

śīlavratopādāna. Another translation: 'clinging to morality and ascetic practices', AKB(E) p. 832. Cf. also śīlavrataparāmarśa = 'exaggeration of rules and vows', Wayman, BI p. 200. See also endnote 46.

Folio 134

rāga. Other translations include 'greed', 'attachment', 'passion'. See MDPL, p. 335, AKB(E) p. 771, BD, p. 182. See also, N.H. Samtani, "A Study of Aspects of Rāga" in R.K. Sharma (ed.), Researches in Indian and Buddhist Philosophy (Essays in Honor of Professor Alex Wayman) (Delhi, 1993), pp. 61–67.

bhava. Various translations are offered: 'existence', 'becoming', 'state of existence', 'world', 'condition of birth', 'rebirth', etc. Alex Wayman translates it 'gestation' in the context of pratītyasamutpāda, BI, p. 164. I have translated it variously as 'becoming', 'process of becoming, 'existence', and 'coming to be'.

Folios 138-39

Aṭaṭa, Hahava and Huhava Hells. The names of these hells are onomatopoetic, suggesting the sounds made by those unfortunate beings born there.

Utpala. Where the cold sores resemble the buds of the utpala (blue lotus). See McGovern, Manual of Buddhist Philosophy, p. 61.

Manu. According to Vibhāvinīṭikā, the first kṣatriya, or ruler. See Rewatadhamma (ed.), Abhidhammattha-Saṅgaha Vibhāvinī Ṭīkā (Varanasi 1965), p. 116; Nib. p. 139, n. 7.

Folio 140

deva. The entry in PED, p. 329a contains a good note on this term.

Folio 141

yāma. The word 'yāma' can refer to a period of three hours. See Apte, PSED, p. 785a. For the more usual meaning, see PED, p. 554a: "One who belongs to Yama or the ruler of underworld. Usually used in plural, inhabitants of Yama-loka."

Folio 142

Brahmapurohitā. On this term, see McGovern, MBP p. 67.

Folio 143

śubha. Also translated as 'lovely', 'beautiful', 'shining' 'bright', 'pure', 'auspicious'. See entry for subha in PED, 719b. The Tibetan rendering is 'dge', meaning 'virtuous'.

apramāṇaśubhā. This term is inadvertently omitted in the printed edition of the Sūtra text. See AVSN, p. 143, n.4.

prasava. There is a misprint in the Sanskrit text: read prasava for prasrava.

Folio 144

abṛhā. The Sanskrit root 'bṛh' in the sense of 'leaving' or 'giving up' is unusual. SED, p. 735c. gives the meaning of bṛh as 'to grow', 'to increase', which is often used to explain words like 'brahma' and 'brahmā'. A second meaning is 'to tear, 'to pluck', 'to root up,' which may imply 'giving up'. The explanation in the Theravāda tradition is the same. See AVSN, p. 144, n. 2.

atapā. A difficult term to translate, but perhaps best understood in the sense of 'not hot'; thus, cool or serene. Tapa means 'burning', but can also mean 'penance', 'self-control', 'religious austerity'. For various meanings of tapa and tapas, see PSED, pp. 467c and 468a.

Folio 145

ākāra. Literally, appearance. On various meanings of ākāra, see PED p. 93a.

Folio 148

nirvṛtti. An unusual usage, in the sense of abhinirvṛtti (coming into being). See abhinirvṛtta, BHSD, p. 52a; Pali abhinibbati, PED 66a. Nirvṛtti generally means 'extinction', 'cessation'. See BHSD, p. 304b. The Pali 'nibbuti' means 'cooling', 'allaying', 'peace', etc. See PED 366a.

Folio 149

ātmabhāva. Pali attabhāva. A frequently used term in Buddhist texts, meaning 'embodiment', 'person', 'individuality', 'perṣonality', 'body', etc. See ātmabhāva, BHSD 92b; 'attan', PED 22a; attabhāva, CPD, 99b.

abhniveśa. Also rendered as 'settling down', 'adherence to one's doing', 'insistence on erroneous opinion', etc. See MDPL p. 61; BHSD, p. 53a; PED p 66b.

nirvacana. I take this term as used here to mean 'explanation' or 'interpretation'. In some contexts it can mean 'etymology'. Cf. SED, 557a.

production. The Sūtra reads udbhava; the Nib. has prādurbhāva, another instance of discrepant readings.

Folio 151

jarā. I have translated as 'decay' instead of 'old age', although the definition given here refers to old age. In compound form, jarāmaraṇa is better rendered 'decay and death'. See the entry for jarā in PED, p. 279b.

khālitya. Rendered 'morbid baldness' (and spelled khālatya) at SED p. 339c. In Pali we have khaṇḍicca (cf. DN II, p. 305) translated 'breaking-up'. Dialogues of Buddha II, p. 338. But PED, p. 235b also has an entry khallāta, rendered 'bald'.

paribheda. I have translated this term as 'disintegration'. The word is explained in Nib., p. 152 by the commentator as vināśa = 'destruction', 'ruin', 'utter loss', 'decay' (cf. PSED, p. 860a). Monier Williams renders it 'hurt' or 'injury', but renders 'paribhedaka' as 'breaking through'. SED 598b (see 'paribhid').

gopānasī. Cf. gopānasī, BHSD, p. 217a. It is also rendered as "beam supporting the framework of a roof," PED, p. 255b. The simile is often used in Buddhist texts to explain curvature of body as a feature of old age.

gopālavāhiṅgkā. The reading of the text is doubtful. See Nib., p. 152, n. 6. The meaning of the word is also doubtful. Perhaps this refers to what in Hindi is also called bahaṅgī or bahiṅgī. Cf. Pali Vyābhaṅgī, PED 654b.

Folio 152

khuru-khuru-praśvāsakāyatā. The words in Sanskrit are duplicative and onomatopoeic. See 'khurakhura', BHSD 205b.

Folio 157

āryas. On this term, cf. AKB VI.2, p. 328; AKB III.44cd, p. 157; Vism XVI. 20–22, PP, p. 564. See also AKB(E), p. 898 and p. 1042, n. 12. I have translated ārya as 'noble'; another rendering is 'holy'; cf. Tib. 'phags pa. See MDPL, p. 112.

aviparīta. On this term, see SN V, p. 435.

Folio 159

abhisamaya. This term can also be rendered 'comprehension', as in AKB(E), p. 897. Etymologically, it is cognate to 'abhisambodha'. In support of the translation 'realization', see BD, p. 4; BHSD, p. 58a. Cf. also the explanation in AKB VI.2, p. 328; AKB(E), p. 897.

nidāna. In Buddhist texts, a near synonym of hetu and pratyaya (Pali paccaya); also used in the sense of 'introductory portion' as in 'nidānakathā' (introductory story). In the medical treatises of the Āyurveda, its meaning is 'remedy', 'correctness', 'purification', 'diagnosis', etc. See nidāna, PSED, p. 547c.

Folio 160

Arhat. Generally not translated, like 'Tathāgata'. Literally the term means 'worthy one'. It is translated as 'perfect one', 'one who has won perfection', etc., by I.B. Horner in her book, The Early Buddhist Theory of Man Perfected: A Study of the Arahan (London, 1936), pp. 39, 42. Nyanatiloka gives 'holy one', BD, p. 24. For an abundance of material on the concept of the Arhat, see article on Arahant in Encyclopaedia of Buddhism, Vol. II, pp. 41ff; Horner I.B., op. cit., chs. IV and V.

samyaksambuddha. Cf. MDPL, p. 415. The Pali 'sammāsambuddha' is rendered 'perfectly enlightened' (see under 'sammā', PED, p. 696a), and as 'perfectly self-enlightened' in the benedictory homage found in Dhammapada: Verses and Stories (Reprint, Sarnath, 1990), p. XIX.

upamṛṣṭatvāt. The literal meaning is 'sprinkled'. Cf. root 'mṛṣ' (third entry), SED, p. 831a.

duḥkhaduḥkhatā. This could also be rendered 'intrinsic suffering', as given in PP XVI, 35.

Folio 161

vipariṇāmaduḥkhatā. An alternative translation for vipariṇāma is 'transformation', as given at AKB(E), p. 899.

sāsrava. Conze always renders āsrava in its literal sense of 'outflow'; here it may be rendered 'with outflows'. Cf. MDPL, p. 115. I have rendered it in the general sense of being 'impure'.

Folio 163

vyavakīrṇatvāt. Cf. vyavakīrṇa, BHSD, p. 515a, rendered as 'interrupted', 'broken', 'halted'. But the Pali counterpart vokiṇṇa is rendered 'drenched', 'covered with'. PED, p. 651a. In that case, we could replace 'interrupted' with 'being drenched with'.

anāsrava. See AKB(E), p. 430, which renders sāsrava 'worldly' and anāsrava 'transworldly'. For the bodhyaṅgas ('enlightenment-constituents'), see AVS, Section XVIII; cf. AKB.III, 32, p. 146 and AKV (Dwa), p. 478.

prārthayate. In general, 'prays'. In modern Hindi it also has the Buddhist connotation of 'wishing', 'longing', 'desiring'. It is cognate with 'praṇidhi', 'praṇidhāna': 'earnest wish', 'vow'. See BHSD, p. 393a; see also Pali patthanā, pattheti, PED, p. 407b.

nanu. For various meanings of this introductory particle implying interrogation, see PSED, p. 534c. See also folio 283.

karma. For karma as the cause of suffering, AKB quotes Sahetusapratyayasanidāna-sūtra. Cf. AKB VI.3, p. 333.

Folio 164

apūtīni. Translated 'free from mildew', DOB, II, p. 371.

Folio 165

vijñānasthiti. Rendered in PED, p. 619b as 'viññāṇa duration', 'phase of mental life'. PED gives a good note explaining seven types. See also AKB I. 22, p. 15, III.6–7, pp. 115–18; AKB(E), pp. 374–79, and the excellent note by La Vallée Poussin on the vijñānasthitis, p. 503, n. 57.

Folio 166

pratyaya. On various meanings of pratyaya, see BHSD, p. 375b.

Folio 167

uddeśa. See also Pali 'uddesa-niddesa' and 'uddesa-vibhaṅga' (indication in brief and exegetical exposition), CPD, Vol. II, p. 415. Following CPD, I have translated 'uddeśa' here as 'indication in brief' rather than 'list of topics', as above. This frequently used word has many meanings, including 'instruction', 'pointing out', etc. For various renderings and references, see the entry 'Uddesa', CPD, Vol. II, pp. 414–15.

Folio 168

upadhi. An important word having many meanings, including 'clinging to rebirth', 'attachment'. It is a synonym of kleśa and tṛṣṇā. Cf. upadhi, PED, p. 142b; also upadhi as the root of sorrow in Suttanipāta, verses 728, 1051.

Folio 169

upadhiśeṣa. See 'upadhi', immediately above.

eva. For various meanings of this particle, see PSED, p. 316a.

pratipad. In English, both 'mārga' and 'pratipad' are generally rendered as 'path', though pratipad is also translated as 'course', 'destination', 'practice'. Cf. Pali Paṭipadā, PED, p. 396a. To avoid repetition here, I have rendered 'āryamārga' as 'noble way' and retained 'path' for pratipad.

śīlaskandha. Here 'skandha' is used in the sense of 'division', 'branch', 'part'. See 'skandha', PSED, p. 1003a. For the various meanings of the word in the Pali tradition, see the entry for khandha, PED, p. 232a.

Folio 170

authority. ādhipatya is also rendered 'predominating influence'. AKB(E), p. 154.

Folio 172

they block. viṣkambhyante. Cf. viṣkambhana, BHSD, p. 502b. AKB(E), p. 157, renders this term as 'are disturbed' (p. 157).

nirvedhabhāgīya. An alternate translation is 'sharing the quality of penetration'. On nirvedhabhāgīya, see AKB VI.20, p. 346ff., VIII.17, p. 445; AKB(E), pp. 935ff. See also BHSD, p. 305a.

sukhavihāra. See under vihāra, PED, p. 642b.

saṁvedanāt. See saṁvedin, BHSD, p. 542a.

sukha. A possible alternative translation for these last three terms: 'experiencing the joy and happiness of liberation'.

Folio 174

daurmanasya. Also translated as 'dejection'. Cf. F.L. Woodward (tr.), The Book of Gradual Sayings II (London, 1982), p. 153; Pali domanassa, PED, p. 331b; MDPL, p. 207.

Folio 175

śraddhā. Defined in AKB as 'clarification of mind'. AKB(E), p. 191.

determination: utsāha. Also rendered as 'will power' and 'endurance'. MDPL, p. 123; AKB(E), p. 193.

smṛti. AKB explains smṛti (mindfulness) as 'non-forgetfulness of the object' and AKV explains it as 'non-forgetfulness of object by reason of which it expresses it'. Cf. AKB II.24, p. 54; AKV (Dwa), p. 187. See also AKB(E), p. 190. Conze in his review of ASVN (JRAS 1974 Pt. I, p. 76) criticized my rendering (see Introduction to AVSN, p. 89). Referring to Vasubandhu's Triṁśikā, 26, he suggested that abhilapanatā would mean 'repeated recollection.'

Folio 176

investigation: pravicaya. Also rendered 'discernment', MDPL, p. 288; AKB(E), p. 190.

Folio 177

anāgamya. A preliminary dhyāna. See AKV II.16, p. 170; cf. AKB(E), p. 178, which leaves it untranslated. See also AKB VIII.22, p. 448; AVSN,

p. 177, n. 3; AKB(E), p. 716, n. 76, p. 1295, n. 125. On the word 'anāgamya' (not the same as the dhyāna), see MDPL, p. 25.

dhyānāntara. See AKB VIII.22d; p. 448, AKB(E), p. 1254. For discussion of the controversy on its classification, see KV 18.7; Pts. of Contr., p. 329.

Folio 178

avabodha. MDPL, p. 78 renders this term as 'understanding'. Avabodhi is translated 'enlightenment'. Cf. samyagavabodhi, rendered 'perfect enlightenment' in BHSD, p. 582b (but the reading is questioned).

kṣaya-anutpādajñānalābha. On kṣayajñāna and anutpādajñāna, see AKB II.9, p. 42. Cf. AKB VI.45, 50, 67, pp. 365, 368, 382–83; AKB (E), pp. 983, 991, 1023.

Folio 179

dhyāna. This most important term in Buddhist texts has been variously rendered, but cannot easily be translated. Dhyāna is a general term for meditation, but here it is used for a special experience of a mental state when the mind is concentrated. In these four stages of dhyāna, the object of mind is some form (rūpa). Among the translations offered are 'absorption', 'trance', 'contemplation', 'meditation', 'ecstasy'. Cf. Pali 'jhāna', PED, p. 286a. Quoting the etymological explanation, Rhys Davids and Stede state that it is "called jhāna from meditation on objects and from burning up anything adverse." Further, they say, "it is literally meditation. But it never means vaguely meditation. It is the technical term for a special religious experience reached in a certain order of mental states." PED, ibid.

prajānanti. The verb is used in the third person plural. Other meanings of prajānāti are 'understand', 'distinguish', 'discuss'. See also Pali 'pajānanā' which is a synonym of paññā = prajñā. Cf. pajānāti, pajānanā, PED, p. 387a; prajānāti, MDPL, p. 268.

samāpatti. Used here in the general sense for dhyāna, so I do not render it here as 'attainment'. See the next Topic for the more specialized meaning.

vivikta. The literal sense is 'separated'. Cf. viveka (aloofness), at folios 180 and 191, below.

akuśaladharmas. Here 'dharma' has the sense of 'thought', 'phenomenon'. The word 'dharma' has a plethora of meanings; even AVSN (p. 276) says: anekārtho hi dharmaśabdaḥ ('for the word 'dharma' has many meanings.')

Folio 180

savitarka, savicāra. Vitarka is variously rendered as 'thought', 'discursive thought', 'thinking', 'first application of mind'; and vicāra is rendered as 'investigation', 'deliberation', 'examination'. See 'vicāra', PED, 615b. Also see Pali 'vitakka', PED, p. 620a, usually mentioned in close association with vicāra.

viveka. The term signifies separation, either physical or mental with regard to the objects of thought. It can also mean 'detachment', 'seclusion', or 'discrimination'. See PED, 638a. There is a good note on the term in DOB I, p. 84, n. 2.

prīti. Also rendered as 'joy'.

sukha. Also rendered as 'pleasure', 'happiness'. For a discussion of this and the preceding term, see S.Z. Aung, Compendium of Philosophy (London, PTS, 1963), p. 243.

On the difference between prīti and sukha, rendered 'happiness' and 'bliss', see PP (Vism trans.) IV 94–101.

praśrabdhi-sukha. Cf. AKB II.25, p. 55. AKB(E), p. 191 explains, "the dharma through which the mind is clever, light and apt." I am at a loss to understand the source of the word 'clever' in the translation. There is a long controversy concerning whether praśrabdhi is bodily or mental tranquility in the dhyānas. See AKB(E), pp. 191 ff; PP XIV, 144 ff. Cf. Pali 'passaddhi', PED, p. 447. Cf. also AKB VIII.9, p. 439; AKB(E), p. 1231 ff.

Folio 181

samāpadya. Cf. samāpadyate, BHSD, p. 570a; MDPL, p. 407.

initial thought, sustained thought. Another possible rendering of vitarka and vicāra is 'investigation' and 'analysis'.

yujyate. literally, 'tenable'. Cf. various meanings of the root 'yuj', PSED, p. 786c.

yaugapadya. AKB(E), p. 1232 has 'co-existence' for 'simultaneity'.

Folio 182

yogi. The word 'yogi' does not occur in the Pali Nikāyas. See 'yogin' PED, p. 559a. The term refers to a meditator; that is, a yogāvacara who practices dhyāna.

adhyātmasaṁprasāda. On this term, see AKB VIII.9, p. 440. It is rendered as 'internal purity' (or faith) in AKB(E), p. 1236. Vasubandhu remarks that adhyātma-saṁprasāda is free from the agitation of vitarka and vicāra. It is a calm and clear stream or continuity of mind (santati), whereas vitarka and vicāra are like waves that agitate the clear, calm water, making the stream turbid or impure (aprasanna).

single object. In other words, one-pointedness of mind = cetasa ekotībhāvaḥ.

ūti. A difficult term. For Sanskrit 'ūti', see SED p. 221a, but the meaning given there is different. But BHSD, p. 150a, gives the meaning as 'effort', which is closer to our translation as 'movement'.

ekoti. Cf. Pali 'ekodi', 'of one attention', 'limited to one point'. It is suggested that 'ekodi' was Sanskritized to 'ekoti'. PED, p. 160b. The translation is not certain. See also long comment on Pali form in Vism IV.143.

Folio 183

samādhi. Variously rendered 'stability', 'steadiness of mind,' etc. Various explanations are given in PP XIV. 139; AK VIII.8, p. 438; AKB(E), pp. 1229–30.

saṁskāropekṣā. On this term, cf. upekṣā, AKB II. 25, p. 55; for saṁskāropekṣā, see AKV (Dwa), p. 1140.

Folio 184

anābhogalakṣaṇā. On this term, see AKB II. 25, p. 55.

apramāṇas. The four immeasurables are equivalent to the four brahmavihāras; see Topic Ten, below. Upekṣā (equanimity) is the fourth apramāṇa.

upekṣānimitta. For various renderings of 'nimitta', see PED, p. 367a. Cf. Topic Twenty-Five, below, on nāsty apratisaṁkhyāyopekṣā as an āveṇikadharma (no. 6) of the Buddha.

samprajanya. Conze renders this term as 'full awareness'. MDPL, p. 412. The term is very important in vipassanā (Skr. vipaśyanā) meditation. It has been rendered "full awareness" in the translation of the Vism. See PP IV.172. BD (p. 196) gives "clarity of consciousness." In a recent work on vipassanā meditation, I find the following explanation with regard to the Pali form: "sampajañña: understanding of totality of mind-matter phenomenon; i.e., insight into impermanent nature at the level of sensation." Sayagyi U ba Khin Journal (2d ed., 1994, p. 317) (Igatpuri, Vipassanā Research Institute)

Folio 185

anāgāmin. A noble disciple who has reached the third stage of the path to nirvāṇa. Cf. anāgāmi, BD, p. 11.

Folio 186

daurmanasya. Various translations of this term are offered, including 'melancholy', 'unhappiness', 'sadness', 'mental pain', 'distress', 'grief'. Cf. Pali domanassa, PED, p. 331.

Folio 187

apakṣālas. Also rendered 'sins', 'failings', 'transgressions', 'defects'. BHSD, p. 42b. Śikṣ (p. 145) defines it as 'abandoning (vivarjanatā) great and good aspects (udārakuśalapakṣa)'. For more on this term, see AKB VIII.11, p. 441. According to AKB the fourth dhyāna is free from these apakṣālas. Therefore it is undisturbed, unagitated, and stable (āneñjya). Vasubandhu refers to the view of other masters (apare) who compare it to a lamp in a windless (nirvāta) place. See also AKB(E), p. 1239.

Folio 188

anuśaṁsāṅga. Anuśaṁsa is rendered 'advantage' in MDPL, p. 41; it is rendered as 'excellence' by La Vallée Poussin, AKB(E), p. 1291, n. 77.

Folio 190

form. This is also rendered 'material things', cf. DOB III, p. 253; AKB VIII.3, p. 435; AKB(E), p. 1224.

pratighasaṁjñā. Here 'pratigha' means resistance, but it is often translated as 'hatred', 'aversion', etc. Cf. BHSD, p. 362. See also Pali 'paṭigha', PED, p. 393.

samāpatti. Samāpatti, dhyāna, and samādhi are for many purposes substantially the same in meaning. Samāpatti is, however, higher dhyāna, where the object of mind is formless (ārūpya). Dhyāna and samādhi are often used interchangeably. On the difference between samādhi and samāpatti, see AKB VIII, p. 182, n.4; AKB(E), p. 1296, n. 128). It is sometimes said that samādhi is for a shorter period than samāpatti.

adhimokṣa-niṣpatti. On various renderings of adhimokṣa = adhimukti, see MDPL, p. 16; BHSD, pp. 14, 15.

Folio 191

viveka. On viveka as detachment or seclusion, see MDPL, p. 364. Conze quotes one explanation of viveka from Āloka Commentary as śūnyākāraguṇāvāhakatvena vivekaḥ. Cf. Abhis. Ā (P.L. Vaidya ed.), p. 415.

abhisaṁvedanā. The term is not found in dictionaries, although the word saṁvedin = 'experiencing' is there. See BHSD, p. 542a.

do not direct their mind. Cetaso'anābhogagatāḥ. For anābhoga, see MDPL, p. 26 ('impassive', etc.)

Folio 193

brāhmavihāra. More commonly 'brahmavihāra'. The lengthening of the vowel in the initial conjunct is found in a few texts. Edgerton (BHSD,

p. 404a) makes no reference to brāhma but mentions the reading 'brāhmya', for which see Mahāyāna-sūtrālaṅkāra (ed. S. Levi), Comy. on XVII. 17. Brahma or brāhma, translated here as 'sublime', is an important technical term in Buddhism. Cf. N.H. Samtani, "On Some Buddhist Terms Beginning with Brahma," Bharati (V.S. Agrawala Volume), Banaras Hindu University, 1971, pp. 158–64. Generally, the word 'brahma' means 'high', 'supreme'. Brāhmavihāra could thus also be rendered 'supreme state'.

maitrī. This term is also rendered 'friendliness', 'amity', 'love', 'sympathy', etc. See entry on mettā, PED, p. 540b.

focused. literally, 'a mind associated with concentration on'.

avyābādhena. The text at this one place reads 'asambādhena'; elsewhere it is avyābādhena.

upaśleṣa. An alternative translation is 'contagions'.

apakāri. In the text sattveṣūpa° is a misprint. It is sattveṣvapakāriṣūpanāhaḥ. (See "Additions and Corrections" in AVSN.)

. . . . The ellipsis indicates a term whose reading is uncertain. I have not attempted a translation. See AVSN, p. 193, n. 4.

mahadgata. Cf. Pali mahaggata, PED, p. 526a. Also see CP, p. 101n.

Folio 195

viharati. For the interpretation of viharati in different contexts, see AVSN, pp. 77–78 and references.

quarter. This term, 'diśā', also means 'side.'

Folio 196

dominated. Literally, 'have an abundance of'.

vihiṁsā. May also be rendered as 'violence' or 'killing'. Generally in Buddhist texts the terms 'vihiṁsā' and 'avihimsā' are used instead of 'hiṁsā' and 'ahiṁsā', the latter being the word most often used in Jain and Brahmanical texts for 'non-violence'. However, the Dhammapada uses 'ahiṁsā' in verses 261, 270.

arati. It also means 'dislike', 'aversion'. Cf. arati, PED, p. 75b. Arati is the name of one of the daughters (and one of the armies [senā]) of Māra; cf. BHSD p 65a. The reading ārati is also found; BHSD, p. 102b. Rendered 'dissatisfaction' in AKB(E), p. 1264.

aśubha. Cf. aśubha-bhāvanā, BHSD, p. 80a. The word is also rendered 'offensive or loathsome thing(s)'. Cf. AKB VIII. 29, p. 452, AKB(E), p. 1264.

upekṣā. On this term, see AKB II.25, p. 55, where it is explained as mental evenness (cittasamatā) and freedom from any predilection (cittānāboghatā). Cf. AKB(E), p. 192, which has a somewhat different rendering. It is not a question of 'indifference', but of 'detachment'.

Folio 197

sukhādhimokṣa. Adhimokṣa is rendered in various ways: 'intention', 'aspiration', 'resolve', 'firm belief', etc. See MDPL, p. 16. AKB(E) renders it 'aspiration', p. 955. See also BHSD 15a; cf. Pali adhimokkha, PED p. 30a.

appreciate the qualities. Translated 'who takes pleasure in the qualities of others', AKB(E), p. 1269.

kuśalamūla. Rendered as 'basis or root of goodness or merit'. See entry on the term at PED, p. 224a.

Folio 199

pratipad. These are courses directed at the destruction of defilements: "āsravāṇāṁ kṣayāya," runs the common refrain in this section. Cf. AVS, pp. 20–21. Pratipad can also be translated 'method', 'way', 'path', etc. AKB(E), p. 1021 renders it as 'route'. Cf. Pali paṭipadā and its various renderings, PED, p. 396a. F.L. Woodward renders the Pali paṭipadā as 'mode of progress'. The Book of Gradual Sayings (London, 1982), Vol. II, p. 153.

abhijñā. There are various renderings and interpretations of this important word. Cf. Pali abhiññā, PED, p. 64a; BHSD, p. 50b. Conze renders it as 'superknowledge', MDPL, p. 59; AKB(E), p. 1021 gives 'intelligence'. Yaśomitra explains abhijñā as equivalent to prajñā; cf. AKV (Dwa), p. 1015. See also AVSN, p. 199, where abhijñā is also equated with prajñā (dhandhābhijñā = mandaprajñā).

anāgamya. For references to anāgamya, cf. AVSN, p. 177, n. 3; also AKB(E), p. 716, n. 76; p. 1295, n. 125. See also folio 177 above.

intermediate dhyānas: dhyānāntara. See AVSN, p. 177, n. 3; folio 177 above.

constituents. The reference may be to constituents of dhyāna, such as vitarka and vicāra.

mandaprajñā. Another possible rendering here is 'dull intelligence'.

Folio 200

santāna-bheda. For the translation of santāna, see AV, p. 370, n. 580.

tīkṣṇa-prajñā. Again, it seems that prajñā here can better be rendered as 'intelligence' rather than 'wisdom'. Prajñā could also be translated as 'insight', but I have used that rendering for vipaśyanā (Pali vipassanā).

basic (maula) dhyānas. See note 124, above.

ānantarya-samādhi. For this term, cf. Suttanipāta, verse 225; BHSD, p. 96. This meditation is discussed in AKB V.61, p. 320, AKB(E), p. 855. In SBE Vol. X (tr. of Suttanipāta) it is rendered 'uninterrupted meditation' (See translation of verse 225.) PP. XXII. 15 renders it 'concentration with immediate result'. Cf. also Abhis. Ā, p. 302; see also BD, p. 12. There are various interpretations. According to MSA it is called ānantarya because any disturbance (vikṣepa) in the receiver or subject (grāhaka) is destroyed immediately. It is also the stage of the supreme worldly dharmas (laukika-agradharmas). Cf. MSA, ch. XIV, comment before verse 27, p. 93.

Folio 201

way of cultivating. This phrase is a free rendering for bhāvanā, which may also be rendered 'practice', 'development', culture'. Cf. BMPE, p. 261, n. 2.

dūrīkaraṇa. This could also indicate removal or expulsion of the opposing forces. Cf. the use of vipakṣa in pratipakṣa- and vinirdhāvana-bhāvanā in the four types of bhāvanās. AKB VII.27, p. 410; AKB(E), p. 1135.

prayogamārga. Can also be rendered 'path of exertion' (cf. prayoga, MDPL p. 286); 'preparatory path', AKB(E), p. 855.

ānantaryamārga. On this term, cf. AKB V.61, p. 320; AKB(E), p. 855.

rice. The term 'dhānya' actually comprises several kinds of grain. See PED on 'dhañña', p. 334; also 'dhānya', SED, p. 514.

beans: mudga. In Hindi 'mūṅga' is used.

Folio 202

pada. In addition to the phrase, 'goes into the forest', the other two phrases are 'to the root of a tree' and 'to an empty uninhabited sheltered place'. Here 'pada' signifies a part of a sentence. See 'pada', PSED, p. 584b (no. 15).

away from contact with the public. In other words, far from the madding crowds. But cf. Śikṣ (p. 202): a Bodhisattva dwells aloof even when in crowds.

Folio 203

open on both sides. Or 'double-mouthed'. Cf. DOB II, p. 330.

ubhayato mutoḍi. Cf. AVSN, p. 203, n. 1. On this word cf. also MN I p. 57; PED, p. 537a; BHSD, p. 436a. AVS (p. 24) has the reading 'dvāravinirmuktaṁ koṣṭhāgāraṁ' (free from doors [= open] storehouse) instead of mutoḍi. It seems that a gloss on 'mutoḍi' has replaced the original reading in the copy of AVS. Cf. also Śikṣ, p. 210 and Bendall's note. The reading mutoḍi is rendered 'sack'. Cf. C. Bendall and W.H.D. Rouse (tr.), Śikṣā-samuccaya: A Compendium of Buddhist Doctrine (Delhi, 1971), p. 203.

kāmarāga. The Sūtra has kāmarāgaprahāṇāya. The commentary omits kāma in quoting the Sūtra but gives it in the gloss.

lotuses of various colors. The Sūtra mentions various kinds of lotuses or water lilies, each having a different color, by name: utpala, padma, kumuda, puṇḍarīka. See AVS, p. 25. They are generally said to be of three different colors: white, blue, and red respectively. However, interpretation of their colors differs.

Folio 204

dṛṣṭadharma. The term literally means 'seen thing or state', but is used to refer to the present life. For dṛṣṭadharmasukhavihārāya samādhibhāvanā, see AKB VIII.27, p. 451; AKB(E) p. 1262. But in AKB(E), p. 157, dṛṣṭa-dharmasukhavihāra is rendered "Blessedness-in-this- life." Cf. also DNA III, p. 1007.

adhyātma. 'Adhyātma' (with kāya) is what pertains to the innermost or subjective realm. See also note 109 on 'kāya' = grouping.

Folio 205

develops well. sādhu ca suṣṭhu ca. These are almost synonymous words.

darśana. This term is also rendered as 'seeing', but this is too literal a translation. See AKB(E), pp. 775, 895, 994 and passim. Darśana is a technical term; in Sanskrit and modern Hindi alike it is used for 'philosophy'. I have rendered it as 'vision' or 'insight'; however, vipaśyanā is also rendered 'insight'. The pairing of jñāna and darśana occurs often in Buddhist texts. See also AVS, p. 53.

knowledge is itself vision. The particle 'eva' shows emphasis, which I have attempted to convey with 'itself'. Perhaps the sense is better communicated with the term 'direct perception' or 'direct experience' (pratyakṣavṛtti), rather than 'directly visible' or 'direct seeing'. Cf. the identical explanation in AKB VII.7, p. 394; see Yasomitra's comments, AKV (Dwa), p. 1040.

sūdgṛhītā. The Sūtra manuscript reads 'sugṛhītā'. Cf. AVSN, p. 205, n. 9.

susevitā. Alternate renderings: 'well practiced', 'well served', 'well resorted to'. Cf. Pali 'sevati', PED, p. 724a.

Folio 206

sphurati. On this term, see MDPL, p. 436. Cf. also BHSD, p. 613, which gives the meanings 'suffuses', 'pervades', 'fills'. See also AVSN, p. 194.

prajñā-pratilambhāya. AKB reads 'prajñāprabhedāya' in place of this term. AKB VIII, 28, p. 451; cf. AKV (Dwa), p. 1139. AKB (E), p. 1263 renders prajñāprabheda as 'excellent forms of prajñā'.

Folio 208

smṛtyupasthānas. Also rendered 'pillars of mindfulness' (Conze, MDPL, p. 436); 'applications of mindfulness', MLS, I, p. 70, Stefan Anacker, MBM, p. 101; 'stations of mindfulness', Leon Hurvitz, op. cit. p. 207; 'setting up of mindfulness', DOB II, p. 327; 'Establishing of Awareness', Satipaṭṭhāna-Sutta (Igatpuri, 1993).

Folio 209

anudarśī. Vipassanā teachers at present render anudarśī (Pali anupassī) as 'one who observes'.

auddhatya-kaukṛtya. On these two words, cf. Pali uddhacca, PED, p. 136b, and kukkucca, PED, p. 218a.

body as body. literally, 'body in body'.

Folio 210

abhiśaya. This word and the corresponding Pali 'abhisaya' are not found in the dictionaries, but it seems cognate to āśaya and prayojana, meaning 'intention' or 'purpose'. Alternatively, abhiśaya might be a misreading for atiśaya, meaning 'addition'. In that case, the phrase would read, "What is added by mentioning 'internal', 'external', and 'both'?" Cf. "Review of AVS and AVSN" by J. W. de Jong, IIJ, Vol. XVII (1975), p. 117.

anupaśyī is a variant on the usual reading 'anudarśī'. Cf. AVSN, p. 210, n. 5. AKB also uses the same word in the explanation of anupaśyanā = prajñā. Cf. AKB VI.15, p. 342. The form anupaśyanā is criticized in Bhāmati II.32. Cf. La Vallée Poussin, AKB(E) p. 1050, n. 103. Cf. also Yaśomitra's grammatical note on anupaśya, AKV (Dwa), p. 904.

Folio 211

uptiṣṭhate. Rendered 'applied' in AKB(E), p. 927. But see 'upatiṣṭhati', MDPL, p. 128, meaning 'furnish', 'serve upon,' 'waits on'. See also Pali upatiṭṭhati, PED, p. 141b, which gives as the literal meaning, 'to stand by'.

Folio 212

svasāmānya. On sva and sāmānya lakṣaṇas, see note 136, supra. Cf. AKB VI.14, p. 341.

dharmas. The term in this context is especially difficult to translate. Rhys Davids in the Dialogues of Buddha, Vol. III, p. 215 translates as 'ideas'; I have followed I.B. Horner, who uses 'mental objects'. MLS I, p. 77.

Folio 214

samyakprahāṇas. On this word, see AVSN, p. 214, n. 1. The word prahāṇa is a Prakritization of pradhāna = 'effort', 'exertion'; in some texts samyakpradhāna is found with the same meaning. The Pali form is padhāna. Cf. sammappadhāna (PED, 695b) = sammāvāyāma, DN III, p. 221, DN II, p. 312; sammāvāyāma is one of the members of the Noble Eightfold Path. In Sanskrit texts, samyakprahāṇa is the more common form. Cf. pradhāna, BHSD, p. 380b, and prahāṇa, BHSD, p. 389b; also Śikṣ, p. 356. Dharma S., no. 45. But in the Eightfold Path, the term samyagvyāyāma is used. See AVS, p. 15.

pradhānāni. Here the author uses the word pradhāna, not prahāṇa. See also Vasubandhu, AKB VI.69, p. 384. On these two words, see AVSN, p. 214, n. 2.

Folio 215

chanda. The various renderings include 'desire to do', 'will power', 'impetus', 'urge'. Cf. MDPL, p. 178.

Folio 216

satkṛtya. On this word, see BHSD, p. 553b. Cf. also Pali sakkacca-kārin = zealous, PED, p. 660b.

laya. An alternative rendering to sluggishness or laxity is 'process of sinking' or 'sunkenness' of mind. The Tibetan is bying ba.

praṇidadhāti. Nib. wrongly has 'pradadhāti', but the Sūtra has praṇidadhāti, which is correct. Pradadhāti (Pali padahati) means 'exerts', which has already been mentioned before this comment. See praṇidadhāti, BHSD, p. 359b; pradadhāti, BHSD, p. 379b. At the next occurrence, Nib. is correct.

Folio 217

samyakpradadhāti. See the note on this verbal formation, AVSN, p. 216, n. 13, and see preceding note.

aparihāṇi. The Sūtra reading is aprahāṇa, and the order in the Sūtra is different as well. See AVS, p. 29.

our teacher. The plural form 'gurūṇāṁ' for guru (teacher) is used out of veneration for the author's teacher. See also AVSN, pp. 71, 284 for references to his teacher by the author.

Folio 218

samyakpradhānas. The term used here is samyakpradhāna, not samyakprahāṇa, which is used at the beginning of the section.

anutpanna. An alternative rendering of this phrase: "The present (pratyutpanna) is easily understood, but not the future (anutpanna)." This rendering takes 'anutpanna' as being used here for 'anāgata'. The basic meaning is that at the outset of the path, 'sinful and unwholesome thoughts' predominate in the mind; hence the first right effort is directed at these 'dark' aspects. Only later are more wholesome thoughts to be stimulated and increased.

Folio 219

ṛddhipāda. A difficult term to translate. Conze gives 'road to psychic power', MDPL, p. 137. Ṛddhi is rendered 'supernormal power' in AKB(E), p. 1025; 'magic (power)', in SDEBP, p. 319. For various other translations, see BDSL, p. 104.

smṛddhi. Translated as 'success' in AKB(E), p. 1025.

abhijñā. See BHSD, p. 50b. Cf. Pali abhiññā, PED, p. 64a; see also Vism chap. XIII (abhiññā-niddesa).

Folio 220

chanda, vīrya, citta, mīmāṁsā. In the text of the Sūtra, all four of these terms are preceded by the word 'ātma': thus, 'self-zeal', etc. Nib. offers no explanation for this, and the Pali tradition does not mention it. Perhaps the word has been prefixed by a later redactor.

prahāṇasaṁskāra. At this point we encounter what appears to be a confusion based on terminology. Our celebrated commentator interprets the word 'prahāṇa' as having its usual meaning of 'abandonment', understood in the context of faults. However, as stated above (see notes to folio 214; see also AVSN, p. 214, n. 2), prahāṇa is a Prakrit form of pradhāna (= effort, exercise) which does not mean prahāṇa (= abandonment). The eight prahāṇasaṁskāras that are mentioned support this meaning of pradhāna as effort or striving). However, I have translated in accord with the present recension of the Nibandhana. It seems the Commentator relied on another traditional list of prahāṇasaṁskāras. Compare MVS, p. 131, which also assigns the term this connotation.

to be abandoned. The five faults are to be abandoned. Here prahāṇa used in the sense of abandonment is correct. For the five faults, see ME, p. 72.

anabhisaṁskāra. A difficult term to render correctly. The meaning is 'making no effort', which is a fault. Cf. BHSD, p. 20b, no. 2; also AKB VI.37, p. 359; AKB(E), p. 966. In MVS, p. 130 it is mentioned as one of the faults that operates at the time of calming the two upakleśas; i.e., sluggishness and excitedness. For a general note on upakleśas, see endnote 145. ME (loc. cit.) renders anabhisaṁskāra as non-application.

Folio 221

viveka. This term is discussed above; see notes to folio 180.

rāga. Also rendered 'lust'. See term notes to folio 134.

nirvāṇa. Virāga is one of the synonyms or cognates mentioned to explain nirvāṇa = duḥkhanirodha. See the Third Noble Truth, AVS, p. 15; Topic VI in text.

Folio 222

anukūla. Cf. anukūlatā, MDPL, p. 30. The explanation of pariṇata as anukūla is noteworthy. Pariṇata means 'maturing' or 'ripening'. PSED, p. 594a; cf. PED, p. 426a.

vīryasamādhi. Vīrya in this context is practically a synonym of chanda, since both indicate an enthusiasm to do what is beneficial. Other translations include 'vigor', 'strength', 'fortitude'.

mīmāṁsā-samādhi. To the linking of mīmāṁsā with prajñā, compare AVSN, p. 223 (prajñā = dharmapravicaya [investigation of dharmas]).

Folio 223

prasāda. AKB(E), p. 191 gives 'clarification of mind.' Cf. AKB II.25, p. 55. Other renderings include 'tranquility', 'clarity', 'brightness', 'calmness'. The opposite of prasāda is kṣobha (agitation). Cf. Śikṣ, p. 251.

abhyutsāha. See AVSN, p. 175 (where we find the reading utsāha, but see note, referring to AKB).

apramoṣa. Cf. Skt. root pra+mṛṣa, SED, p. 687b. Also see Pali pamuṭṭha, PED, p. 417a. For different interpretations of smṛti, see AVS, p. 32; AVSN, p. 175.

non-forgetfulness of the object. This can also be rendered 'non-loss' of the object. On smṛti, see also passage from Śikṣ., added in AVS, p. 32; cf. Vism XIV, 141; PP, ibid.

dharmapravicaya. On this term, see AVSN, p. 176, n. 3. For Pali sources giving an explanation of wisdom (paññā), see Vism XIV.3ff. PP renders paññā as 'understanding'.

Folio 224

well-established. Upatiṣṭhate literally means 'to serve', 'wait on'; cf. upatiṣṭhati, MDPL, p. 128. But Conze renders upasthitaṁ smṛte 'one whose mindfulness is well-established', albeit with a question mark on the reading. MDPL, p. 133.

world of transmigration. Bendell and Rouse in their translation of the relevant Sūtra portion in the Śikṣāsamuccaya (p. 283), render the apposite sentence as follows: "He believes in right worldly insight in the matter of transmigration in the world." I read saṁsārāvacarā and laukikī as adjectives modifying samyagdṛṣṭi (right view).

acquires: samudānayati. Translated as 'procures', MDPL, p. 410.

Folio 226

asamprajanya. A difficult term to translate. Pali asampajañña is rendered 'lack of intelligence', PED, p. 88. Conze renders its opposite, samprajñatā, as 'self-possession', and gives for samprajāna 'self-possessed', 'clearly conscious', MDPL, p. 412. Pali sampajañña is rendered 'clarity of consciousness', 'clear comprehension'. Cf. BD, p. 196.

Folio 228

bodhi. Also rendered 'awakening'. e.g., Paul Harrison, The Samadhi of Direct Encounter with the Buddhas of the Present (Tokyo, 1990), p. 326. For an explanation of bodhi, see AK VI.67, which defines it as knowledge of destruction (kṣayajñāna) and of non- arising (anutpādajñāna). For these two knowledges, see AK VI.50; VII.4, 7.

dharmapravicaya. Also rendered 'discernment of dharmas'. Cf. pravicaya, MDPL, p. 288. The view that dharmapravicaya is both bodhi and bodhyaṅga is held by the Vaibhāṣikas. Cf. AKB VI.70, p. 384.

bodhisattvābhisambodha. I have not found this compound (bodhisattva + abhisambodha) in any other text. However, Edgerton registers an entry on abhisambodha (BHSD, p. 59b), rendering it 'perfect enlightenment', 'perfect comprehension', 'learning perfectly'. Conze lists abhisambodhanatā (MDPL, p. 65) rendering it 'undergo the process which leads to enlightenment'. I have followed Conze. However, the phraseology is unusual and the reading uncertain.

pudgalabhedena. For various renderings of pudgala, see MDPL, p. 261.

śrāvaka. Cf. Pali sāvaka, PED, p. 707a. See also definition of śrāvaka, AVSN, pp. 253, 310.

pratyekabuddha. This translation for 'pratyekabuddha' was suggested to me by Ven. Prof. S. Rinpoche, former director of the Central Institute for Higher Tibetan Studies, Sarnath. Other renderings include 'Buddha for himself alone', BHSD, p. 379a; 'Enlightened by himself but does not proclaim truth to others', PED, p. 385b; 'Private Buddha'; 'Silent Buddha'; 'Independently Enlightened One;' 'Solitary Realizer'. Cf. the good note in BD, p. 146. I find the translation 'Silent Buddha" in The Opening of the Wisdom Eye by H.H. Tenzin Gyatso, the XIVth Dalai Lama (Adyar, 1977),

p. 112, but it is said there that the literal translation is 'Buddha for himself'. I.B. Horner renders the term 'Buddha for and by himself', Milinda's Questions (London, 1969), Vol. II, p. 5. See also N. H. Samtani, "On Vargacārin Pratyekabuddha(s)" in N. H. Samtani and H. Prasad (ed.) Amalā Prajñā; Aspects of Buddhist Studies (Prof. P. V. Bapat Felicitation Vol.) (Delhi, 1989), pp. 165-170. Alex Wayman renders 'pratyekabuddha' as 'self-enlightened' and 'samyaksambuddha' as 'complete Buddha'. The Lion's Roar of Queen Śrīmālā (New York, 1974), p. 24. The only full-length work on the subject is Ria Kloppenberg's The Paccekabuddha: A Buddhist Ascetic (Leiden, 1974). See also B.C. Law, Designation of Human Types (tr. of Puggalpaññatti) (London, 1979), p. 5, n. 2.

Folio 231

samāpanna. The question is with regard to one who has entered into or attained samādhi or the noble path; generally, the meditator or yogāvacara. Cf. samāpanna, PED, p. 686a.

Folio 232

avijñapti. On this term, see AKB I.11, p. 8. Various other renderings are 'non-information', 'non-communication', 'non-expression'. The concept of avijñapti was denied by the Sautrāntikas, but affirmed and defended by the Vaibhāṣikas. For more on the controversy, see AKB IV.34, pp. 195–99. See also AVSN, pp. 231 n. 4, 232 n. 2; McGovern, MBP, pp. 128–29; AKB(E), p. 709, n. 5.

Folio 233

āśaya. For other renderings of āśaya, see BHSD, p. 109a.

āśraya. Literally, base or support. Here the term possibly refers to change of personality or its radical transformation (āśraya-parāvṛtti), an important doctrine of the Yogācāra (Vijñānavāda) school. On āśaya and āśraya, see AKV (Dwa), p. 588; See also AVSN, p. 233, n. 4; AKB(E), p. 712, n. 33. On āśrayaparāvṛtti, see R. M. Davidson "Āśrayaparāvṛtti and Mahāyānābhidharma," in N. H. Samtani and H. S. Prasad (ed.), Amalā Prajñā: Aspects of Buddhist Studies (Professor P. V. Bapat Felicitation Vol.), Delhi, 1989, pp. 253 ff. See also H.S. Sakuma, Die Āśrayaparivṛtti Theorie in der Yogācārabhūmi (Stuttgart, 1990), English summary pp. 164ff. Parivṛtti is another reading for parāvṛtti.

Folio 234

taken in . . . expelled. On āśvāsa and praśvāsa, see BHSD, p. 110a. For an explanation, see Vism VIII.164, which gives the quite opposite definition: āśvāsa (Pali assāsa) is air issuing out and praśvāsa (Pali passāsa) is air entering in. But Buddhaghosa also refers to the fact that Suttanta

Commentaries give the opposite definition, and this conforms to the explanation given in the Nib. Vism also refers to the infant's first exhalation when coming out of the mother's womb. See also AVSN, p. 234, n. 4.

Folio 235

kalyāṇamitra. Literally, 'well-wisher friend'. PED, p. 199 mentions this word as a technical term and renders it 'spiritual guide', 'spiritual adviser'. Translated as 'good friend' in PP III. 28.

mati. Vasubandhu in AKB II. 24, p. 54 explains mati as prajñā (wisdom) and dharmapravicaya (discernment of dharmas). But in this context mati refers to the mind or mindful thought. Cf. also MDPL, p. 312; PED, p. 517a.

tadanuyogāt. Cf. anuyoga, translated as 'preoccupation', MDPL, p. 40.

aware: saṁvedanāt. Cf. saṁvedin, BHSD, p. 542a, rendered as 'being aware of; 'experiencing'. In the next passage, I have translated the same term as 'experiencing'.

Folio 236

prasrabdhi. Explained in AKB II, 25, p. 55, as cittakarmaṇyatā (workableness, readiness of mind). Cf. Pali kammaññatā, PED, p. 194b. I have followed Conze in rendering it as 'tranquility'. See praśrabdhi, MDPL, p. 289. Both the spellings 'praśrabdhi' and 'prasrabdhi' can be found. The Tibetan term is shin tu sbyangs. See also note to folio 180, *supra*. See WE, p. 324, no. 5.

buddhi. Translated as 'thought', 'intellectual act', MDPL, p. 301.

finished. Cf. pratiprasrabdha-mārga, 'having finished with path', MDPL, p. 274. I too render 'pratiprasrabdha' as 'finished with'.

sāmantaka. On sāmantaka-dhyāna, see AKB III, 5a–6a, p. 116; AKB(E), p. 376; also AKB VI.71, p. 385; AKB(E), p. 1030. Cf. Pali upacāra samādhi, Vism III.6, IV.32.

activities: abhisaṁskāra. On abhisaṁskāra, cf. MDPL, p. 64. The reading in Nib. is cittābhisaṁskāra, not cittasaṁskāra. Here abhisaṁskāra is used in the sense of saṁskāra, as the Author explains. However, abhisaṁskāra has various renderings, for which cf. BHSD, p. 57b. One rendering for 'cittābhisaṁskāra' is 'thought' or 'state of mind', BHSD, ibid. It seems that in this section saṁskāra and abhisaṁskāra are used in the same sense.

Folio 237

nirodhasamāpatti. On this term, see AKB II.43–44, pp. 70–73; Adv. pp. 93–95; AKB(E), pp. 225–35. Cf. also PP XXIII.16ff.

pragraha. The other rendering of pragraha is 'energetic activity', BHSD, p. 357a.

muditā. One of the four sublime states (brāhmavihāras). Cf. muditā, MDPL, p. 323.

upekṣā. Also one of the brāhmavihāras. Cf. AVS, p. 19.

Folio 238

pratibandha. Cf. Pali paṭibaddha, 'bound to', 'in fetters or bonds', PED, p. 397a. I think the 'pratibandha' of our text refers to fetters or obstacles. The reading in the Nibandhana is 'vibandha' (see AVSN, p. 238, n. 1), which also supports the rendering 'fetter' or 'obstacle'.

contemplating. Anudarśī can also be rendered 'realizing', but in this context I find that 'contemplating' seems preferable. Other renderings in Buddhist dictionaries include 'observing', 'viewing'. See anupassanā, PED, p. 39; cf. anudassana, CPD, Vol. I, p. 189. Cf. anudarśana = prajñā, AVSN, p. 209.

artha. On various renderings of this term, see MDPL, p. 71.

virāga. This term can also be rendered 'detachment'. Cf. the explanation of virāga as 'full (or complete) removal (saṁkṣaya) of passion' or 'detachment', AVSN, p. 167; see also term notes to folio 221, above.

sarvasaṁskāra. In this context, the term could also be translated 'all conditioned activities or events'. Cf. saṁskāra, MDPL, p. 390.

Folio 239

prajānāti. For a comment on this term, see term notes to folio 179, above.

discern. Conze renders upalakṣayati as 'distinguish', MDPL, 131. See Vism VIII.176, which uses vicetabba. Cf. Pali vicinati (vl. vicināti) = to investigate, discriminate, PED p. 616a.

mark. See upalakṣaṇaṁ, PSED, p. 292a.

nimitta. For various renderings, see the lengthy entry at PED, p. 367a, and also BHSD, p. 297b.

Folio 240

srota āpattyaṅga. This term can also be rendered 'constituent of entering the stream'.

avetyaprasāda (Pali aveccapasāda). On this term, see K.N. Jayatileke, Early Buddhist Theory of Knowledge (London, 1963), pp. 386ff, 394ff. The term has been rendered as 'unshakable faith' (DOB III, p. 219), 'perfect faith' (MDPL, p. 86), 'unwavering confidence' (MLS I, p. 46). But as appears shortly, our Author explains it as satyāny avabudhya sampratyayaḥ (faith after having understood [the four] truths). I have therefore rendered it 'faith based on comprehension'; another possible rendering would be 'faith preceded by knowledge'. Some scholars have favored 'faith based on understanding'. In AKB(E), p. 1031, the term is peculiarly rendered 'faith (and purity) which accompany intelligence'. During a personal conversation, Prof. Alex Wayman suggested the translation 'rational faith'. See also AVSN, p. 241 n.1 and entry for 'aveccapasāda', CPD, Vol. I, p. 482. It may be mentioned here that 'faith' is also not a satisfactory rendering of prasāda. In some respects 'confidence' would be preferable, but this word is also used for 'vaiśāradya' in connection with the topic of fearlessness (See Topic Twenty-Three).

aśaikṣa. On aśaikṣa as equivalent to the Arhat, see AKB VI.45, pp. 365–66; see also note 92, above.

stream of personality. On santāna and santati, see AV, p. 370, n. 580; see also notes to folio 94 and note 18, above.

Folio 241

sampratyaya. See MDPL, p. 412; cf. sampratyayita, 'trusted', 'reliable', BHSD, p. 577b.

proclaims. Or 'points out'. Cf. nirdiśati, MDPL, p. 228.

Folio 242

bhagavān. See the explanation of the word bhagavān in reference to the destruction of the fourfold Māra, AVSN, pp. 76–77, and term notes to folio 76, above. There our Author refers in the alternative explanation to the six qualities that the Blessed One possesses. For various explanations of bhagavān (Pali bhagavā)—etymological, fanciful, and doctrinal—see Vism VII.53–64.

Tathāgata. For various explanations of Tathāgata (including etymological ones), see Abhis. Ā, p. 351. See also B.C. Law, A History of Pali Literature (Varanasi, 1974), Vol. II, pp. 411ff.; R. Chalmers' article "Tathāgata," JRAS 30 (1898), pp. 103–115; Har Dayal, BDSL, pp. 321 n.25. Ven. Sangharakshita writes: "According to popular Far Eastern exegesis, the Buddha is called Tathāgata, because He (sic) 'thus goes' (tathā-gata) out of the world through wisdom and 'thus comes' (tathā-āgata) back into it through compassion." The Three Jewels (London, 1967), p. 126. Buddhaghosa explains Tathāgata as follows: "having come and having gone like the former Buddhas, i.e., having acquired the same qualities and performed the same essential actions." Cf. E.J. Thomas, The History of Buddhist Thought (London, 1967), p. 151.

prahāṇasampad. AKB(E), p. 1146, renders 'sampad' as 'perfection'. However, Conze, MDPL, p. 411, gives 'achievement' or 'accomplishment'.

jñānasampad. On prahāṇa and jñānasampad, see AKB VII, 34, pp. 415–16; AKV (Dwa), p. 1097, AKB(E), p. 1146. For four kinds of jñānasampad—anupadiṣtajñāna, sarvatrajñāna, sarvathājñāna, ayatnajñāna—see AKB and AKV, loc. cit.

Folio 243

samyaksambuddha. In Vism VII.26 (see also PP), Nyanamoli renders the Pali 'sammāsambuddha' as 'fully enlightened'; AKB(E), p. 1033 gives 'perfect Buddha'; PED, p. 696a gives 'perfectly enlightened', 'Universal Buddha'.

samantāt. A similar etymological explanation for 'samyaksambuddha' is found in Abhis. Ā,. p. 351.

thoroughly realizing. Cf. Pali abhisambuddhatta, 'thorough realization', 'perfect understanding', PED, p. 71b.

vidyācaraṇasampanna. Rendered 'perfect in clear vision and walking' by Alex Wayman. BI, p. 12. Cf. different explanations of the term in the Pali tradition, Vism VII.30–31. Compare the discussion on vijjācaraṇa in the Ambaṭṭha-sutta, DN I, p. 99. See also vijjā and its different connotations, PED, p. 617b.

śikṣās. Also rendered 'discipline'. Cf. Pali sikkhā, PED, p. 708a. For a discussion of the three trainings, see WE, pp. 84–100.

Folio 244

sugata. Abhis. Ā, p. 352 follows the explanation given here. It adds that because he has gone by means of the splendid (śhobana) transcendental path and has the endowments of jñāna and prahāṇasampad, he is sugata, like one having a splendid form (surūpavat).

outsiders. bāhyaka = tīrthika = heretical, BHSD, p. 400a. PED has bāhiraka: 'outsider, non-religious, non-Buddhist, heretic, profane'. PED, p. 486b.

tamed. Rendered also 'tameable'. The wording is specific to men. Alex Wayman points out that in the Chinese version of the Mahāprajñāpāramitāśāstra, the question is raised why women are not included, based on the usual understanding that 'puruṣa' refers only to males. It is replied that women are excluded because they have "detractions;" for example, they cannot become a Cakravratin king, hold the rank of Brahmā, etc. BI, p. 13, Cf. also Vism VII.46–47, where by puruṣa (Pali purisa), taming of males is meant.

Folio 245

diminishes. Or 'is diminished'. Cf. hīyate, MDPL, p. 443; also Abhis. Ā, p. 352.

paripācayeyam. Conze, MDPL, p. 249, has paripācayati = 'matures'.

damyasārathi. Damya is rendered in two ways: 'to be tamed'; i.e., worthy of being established in discipline, and 'tameable'; i.e., capable of being established in discipline. In the text, the first is called damanārha and the second damayituṁ vā śakya. Thus both renderings of damya found in translations are correct. Puruṣadamya-sārathi has been rendered 'leader of all men capable of conversion', Harrison, SDEBP, p. 37.

Folio 246

gotra. For the three gotras of Śrāvaka, Pratyekabuddha, and Buddha, see AKB VI.23, p. 348; AKB(E), pp. 940–41 and 1053ff., notes 142–43.

manuṣyāṇāṁ. It is to be noted that here the word used is manuṣya, not puruṣa as in puruṣadamyasārathi. Manuṣya is rendered both 'man' and 'human'; cf. MDPL, p. 313. Buddhaghosa says that animals are also included here, for the Blessed One as a teacher bestows his teachings upon animals as well. Compare the term note on 'tamed' at notes to folio 244, above. Cf. Vism VII. 50.

especially. In Abhis. Ā, p. 352, in a parallel passage, the words are 'not specially' (na viśeṣeṇa).

beings. The word is 'sattvānāṁ'. It is broader in scope than manuṣyāṇām, used a few lines earlier.

Folio 247

yathārthānuśāsana. Another possible rendering for anuśāsana is 'admonition'. Cf. MDPL, p. 42. There is definitely a difference between śāsana (teaching) and anuśāsana (instruction). In countries like Thailand and Burma, which have borrowed extensively from Sanskrit and Pali, the word śāsana is used not only with reference to 'Buddhist religion', but also in connection with Islam and Christianity. Note that there is no exact equivalent for the English word 'religion' in Indian languages.

Folio 248

cutting off of conditioned existence. Cf. 'dharmopaccheda', Lalitavistara, p. 292; Mahāvastu III, p. 200. J.J. Jones translates as 'the breaking up of sensorial states'. The word 'dharma' here refers to the phenomena of the saṁsāric world; it is practically synonymous with the skandhas. Cf. J.J.

Jones (tr.), The Mahāvastu (London, 1978), vol. III, p. 196, n. 6. See also the entry for upaccheda, BHSD, p. 135a.

Pratyekabuddha. See note on this term at notes to folio 228. This reference to the Pratyekabuddha and Bodhisattva is significant. Cf. AKB VI.74, p. 387, which addresses this same topic; see also AKV (Dwa), p. 1025; AKB(E), p. 1084, n. 457.

rises from meditation. AKB(E), p. 1033 renders this term as 'leaving the contemplation'.

aviparīta. Conze renders this term 'unperverted', MDPL, p. 84. Can it also be rendered 'non-contradictory'?

sāndṛṣṭika. lit. 'visible'. Cf. dṛṣṭadharma, 'in this very birth', AVSN, p. 204.

anuśaya. Vasubandhu devotes an entire Kośasthāna (V) to explaining the latent defilements (anuśayanirdeśa). AKB, pp. 277 ff.

aparihāṇīyatvāt. Cf. aparihāṇi, MDPL, p. 52. Another rendering is 'non-loss'.

ākālika. Rendered 'not delayed' in the Visuddhimagga, in that the fruit of dharma comes immediately. PP. VII.80–81. But in the Path of Purity, an earlier translation of Vism by P.M. Tin (PTS, London, 1971), p. 249, it is rendered 'not subject to time'.

Folio 249

aihipaśyaka. i.e., to experience ('Come and see!'). Cf. PP VII.82.

tathatā. For this concept (here tathātva), meaning the true nature of things, truth, suchness, etc., mentioned in many Buddhist texts, see BHSD, p. 248a. See also D.T. Suzuki, Studies in the Laṅkāvatārasūtra (Boulder, 1981), pp. 404–05; PED, p. 296a.

atarkyatvāt. Cf. Pali takka and its various renderings, PED, p. 292b. For Dharma as outside the scope of reason, see MN I.167 (dhammo atakkāvacaro); Jayatileke, EBTK, p. 431.

Bauddhadharma. The use of this term for the teachings of the Buddha, the religion of the Buddhists, or Buddhism is quite a late coinage in the Buddhist Sanskrit texts. There is no counterpart in Pali. I translate 'dharma' in this context as 'religion' with some diffidence. A more neutral word might be 'teachings', but the term 'religion' for religious systems is common in modern English vocabulary. See also Mrs. Rhys Davids on tr. of dhamma, DOB II, Preface, p. xiii (2nd ed.).

artha. reality or objective reality. Cf. MDPL, p. 71 for various renderings of artha. The term can also signify 'meaning', 'benefit', 'category', 'topic', etc., but not in this context.

cannot be experienced here and now (na sāndṛṣṭikā); literally, 'is not visible'. The term 'dharma' is used in the plural here. Cf. the explanation of Pali 'sandiṭṭhika', Vism VII. 76–79.

Folio 250

vyavasthāpyate. Cf. MDPL, p. 373, for the rendering of cognate verbal formations. Cf. also 'vyavasthāpaka', SED, 1033c.

śrāvaka. See AVSN, pp. 253, 310 and accompanying term notes at the corresponding folios below. The literal meaning is 'hearer'. Cf. śrāvaka, BHSD, p. 535a. See also Pali sāvaka, PED, p. 707a.

supratipanna. An alternative rendering would be 'well on the way'. The term is rendered 'well-practiced', DOB III, p. 219; 'of good conduct', MLS I, p. 47. Compare 'pratipanna', rendered 'progressed', MDPL, p. 273; cf. Pali paṭipanna, rendered as 'going along or by', PED, p. 396a. See also notes to folio 258, infra.

upadeśa. Here the term may be rendered as 'exposition'. Cf. various renderings of the word by Conze, MDPL, p. 129; compare the word upadeśaka as an epithet for the Buddha, AVSN, p. 311.

nyāyapratipanna. On this word, see AVSN, p. 250ff. Cf. Pali ñāya, PED, p. 288b. It is also explained as nibbāna, Vism VII.92, which accords with AVSN.

Folio 251

wins. Cf. ārādhanā, MDPL, p. 111; see root 'ā' + 'rādh', PSED, p. 226a.

nityam āyaḥ. An alternate rendering: Nyāya means the place (ayanaṁ) of arrival, which one arrives at for all time. Cf. explanation of nyāya as an aspect of mārgasatya in AKB VII.13, p. 400. For renderings of 'nyāya', see PSED, p. 573c; SED, p. 572b; see term note on nyāyapratipanna, folio 250, above. See also 'ayana', rendered 'place', 'going', etc., PSED, p. 141a. 'Āya' = arrival, etc. PSED, p. 223c. The quotation has not been traced.

śrāmaṇya. Rendered 'religious life', AKB(E), p. 992; 'living as a recluse', DOB, Vol. I, p. 65, n. 1; in some contexts it can simply mean 'monkhood'.

upright and noble path. 'upright' is literally 'straight'. Cf. Pali ujumagga, DN I, p. 235.

samānatā. Could also be translated 'communality'. Cf. PP VII. 90.

Folio 252

dharmānudharma. Cf. Pali anudhamma, PED, p. 37a. But the interpretation of anudharmacāri (see next note) differs.

anudharmacāri, Conze renders anudharmacāri 'one who courses in the logical sequence of dharma'. MDPL, p. 33. The term appears in a number of texts. Dhp. 20, as translated by D.M. Tin (Burmese ed. Rangoon 1986, Reprint Sarnath 1990), gives 'practices according to dharma'. See also Dhp. Cy. Vol. I (PTS ed.), p. 158 where emphasis is on anurūpam dhammam (according to dharma = living according to dharma). Suttanipāta Cy., Vol. I (PTS ed.), p. 123 refers to 'following the vipassanā-dhamma'.

anvayajñāna. MDPL, p. 47, renders this term 'subsequent cognition'. AKB(E), p. 1124 renders it 'inferential knowledge'.

immediately above. Anantara means 'immediately before or after'. Cf. PSED, p. 52c. Here the former meaning is applicable.

Folio 253

puruṣa-pudgala. A difficult compound to translate. Conze does not have an entry, and BHSD likewise omits. PED, p. 470a, renders the Pali 'purisa-puggala' as 'a man, a human character'.

pudgala. For the root 'gal', with various meanings, see Apte, PSED, p. 401c. Different interpretations of pudgala are given in Abhis. Ā, p. 274 and Vism IX.54. The latter gives a fanciful etymology for pudgala (Pali puggala), referring to the falling of a puggala into hell. See also PP IX.54.

pareṇa. An alternative translation would be 'from others'. Cf. para, PED, p. 418b, and pareṇa, BHSD, p. 333a. In the description of followers of the Śrāvakayāna in SP, p. 80, a reference to the voice of others is found. Kern in his tr. of SP has rendered paraghośa 'authoritative voice' (SBE, Vol. XXI, p. 80), but it is difficult to find the basis for this rendering. According to Sangharakshita, Buddha is also included in para, mentioned in our text; he writes ". . . only after having 'heard', that is to say learned, about the Transcendental Path from a Buddha or Buddha's disciple." A Survey of Buddhism (London, 1987), p. 239. No references are given, but cf. Vism VII.90; see also notes to folio 310, below.

śīla. For various renderings, see śīla, PED, p. 712b. Rhys Davids translated it in a general way as 'virtue'; cf. DOB III, p. 219: "Endowed is it [the Saṅgha] with virtues lovely to Ariyans." But I prefer 'moral practice' or 'moral conduct'.

cut off by immorality. The text has dauśīlyahatāvakāśa. This gāthā is also not traceable in any other text. For hatāvakāśa as an adjective of the best person (uttamaporisa or arahanta), cf. Dhp 97. PED, p. 727b renders the term 'one who has cut off every occasion (for good and evil)'.

Folio 254

yukta. The Sanskrit word has many meanings; here I have rendered it 'endowed with' or 'engaged in'. See 'yukta', Apte, PSED, p. 786a.

śrutasampanna. Endowed with learning. Literally, 'hearing' rather than learning. In the oral tradition in ancient India, one becomes learned by hearing. Ānanda is the chief exemplar in the Buddhist tradition; having heard the Buddha teach extensively, he was 'bahuśruta', or 'one who has heard much' (i.e., was very learned). The 'I' in the usual Sūtra opening, 'Thus have I heard', refers to Ānanda. For reference to Ānanda's bāhuśrutya, see AVSN, pp. 75–76.

kṣayajñāna. On this term, see AK VI.50, pp. 368–69; AKB VII. 7, p. 394.

pratyakṣavṛtti. Literally, 'direct activity'. Conze renders vṛtti as 'the action which works for' MDPL, p. 369. The identical explanation can be found in AKB VII.7, p. 394; AKV (Dwa), p. 1040. See also AVSN, p. 205; AKB(E), p. 1095, renders pratyakṣa-vṛtti 'being directly perceived'.

prāhavanīya. literally, worthy of offering (an oblation). Nyantiloka renders the Pali pāhuneyya as 'fit of hospitality', PP VII. 96.

Folio 255

sāmīcīkaraṇīya. Cf. sāmīci = vandanā, "paying homage," etc. BHSD, p. 592a. See also AVSN, p. 255.

Folio 256

āryakāntāni. Dear to the noble ones. The root 'kam' can also be rendered 'to value highly', for which see Apte, PSED, p. 334c. Cf. AKV (Dwa), p. 1027. See also AVSN, p. 255. F.L. Woodward translates as 'dear to', and I have followed his rendering. Kindred Sayings (London, 1979), Pt. V, p. 342. K.R. Norman renders the term as 'pleasing to'. Elders' Verses I (Oxford, 1990), verse 507.

santāna. See rendering at AV, p. 370, n. 580.

avyavakīrṇa. Cf. vyavakīrṇa, rendered 'interrupted', 'broken up', 'halted', BHSD, p. 515a.

tannidāna. Cf. various renderings of 'nidāna', BHSD, p. 295b.

bhujiṣya. In Divyāvadāna, ed. by E. B. Cowell and R. A. Neil (p. 302), bhujiṣya is given as 'dependent', 'not free', but Vism VII.104, has the same meaning as in our text. See also BHSD, p. 410. See AVSN, p. 257, n. 1 for various references.

pratisaṁkhyāna-bala. On this bala, see BMPE, where it is rendered 'power of computation'. PED, p. 400b gives the same, but see paṭisankhā (p. 400a) = 'consideration', 'judgment', 'reflection'. On this meaning see Dhs. 1353. The explanation is identical with 'faculty of wisdom' (paññindraya = prajñendriya). See BMPE, p. 354, Article 1353.

bhāvanā-bala. On bhāvanābala, cf. Dhs, 1354, which includes within it the seven bodhyaṅgas.

pratyaya. For various meanings of pratyaya, cf. Pali paccaya, PED, p. 384a.

Folio 257

yathākāmaṅgama. See BHSD on kāmaṅgama, p. 177a.

kudṛṣṭipraṇidhāna. On praṇidhāna (vow, resolve), see AKB VI.25, p. 349; also cf. 'praṇidhāna' and 'praṇidhi', BHSD, pp. 360a, 360b. The use of the terms 'kupraṇidhāna' and 'kudṛṣṭi' here is significant.

satkāyadṛṣṭi. On this term see AKB, V.7, p. 281; AKB(E), p. 777, p. 873, n. 27. Conze renders it 'false view of individuality', MDPL, p. 396.

nairyāṇikatā. Cf. Pali niyyānika = 'leading to salvation', PED, p. 369a. See also BHSD, p. 312, which gives as well the reading 'nairvāṇika', found in some texts. See also the explanation in AKB VII.13, p. 400.

Folio 258

anupahataṁ. The term 'anupahata' can also mean 'non-overpowering, non-injurious'. It is rendered 'not troubled' in AKB(E), p. 704. Other renderings: 'not being polluted', 'not vitiated'. Cf. 'upahata' PSED, p. 297a.

kleśopakleśas. Under this term, the AKB states, 'by greed, etc. (lobhādibhiḥ)', AKB IV.123, p. 273.

paryāyeṇāpi. Literally, 'on any occasion'. On various meanings of paryāya, cf. BHSD, p. 335b; PSED, p. 604a.

supratipanna. Rendered 'well cultivating' in AKB(E), p. 1033. See notes to folio 250, above.

attendant: upasthāpaka. Wrongly rendered 'patient' in AKB(E), p. 1033. For upasthāpaka (vl. upasthāyaka) = 'servant', 'attendant', see BHSD, p. 144a.

Folio 260

sthāna/asthāna. On these terms, (Pali ṭhāna and aṭṭhāna), see Vibhaṅga, p. 335ff. and its translation, Book of Analysis, pp. 440-43. These two words have a wide range of meanings; see PED, pp. 289ff; Har Dayal, BDSL, p. 324, n. 64. Yaśomitra gives as an example for sthāna (possible) and asthāna (impossible) that it is possible for a male to achieve Buddhahood but impossible for a female. Cf. AKV (Dwa), p. 1085. See also AKB(E), p. 1197, n. 165. Cf. BDSL, p. 224 for Har Dayal's diatribes against Buddhist monks for lowering the status of women.

Folio 261

ayoniśo manasikurvataḥ. Ayoniśo manasikāra (vl. manasikāra) is rendered 'unwise attention' by Conze, MDPL, p. 70; 'disorderly or distracted attention', PED, p. 560b. Cf. also ayoniśomanaskāra as the cause of avidyā, quoted from a Sūtra in AVSN, p. 100, n. 3. Cf. AKB III, 27, p. 135. Cf. also Nettippakaraṇa. (PTS ed.), p. 79, where ayonisomanasikāra is paccaya of avijjā.

Folio 262

sthānataḥ. Here 'sthāna' has the general meaning of 'place', quite different from the earlier sthāna = possible. This portion of Nib. is quoted from an unknown Sūtra.

Folio 263

ity avadhāraṇāt: circumstance. Cf. avadhāraṇa = 'restriction', 'limitation', 'accurate determination,' PSED, p. 164b. See also MDPL, p. 77.

his circumstance. All Mss. have incomplete readings. The words in brackets are conjectural. See AVSN, p. 262, n. 7–8.

hetutaḥ. This and the following words (vastutaḥ, vipākataḥ) are not found in the Mss. of the Sūtra. Thus the present copy of AVSN is based on some other copy of the Sūtra, which does mention them. For discrepancies between the Sūtra and Nibandhana, see section 13 of the "Introduction" to AVSN, pp. 157 ff.

vipākānubandha. For anubandha as 'continuity' and various other meanings of the word, see PSED p. 69c. Conze renders anubandhayāti as 'move forward', MDPL, p. 39.

adhimukti. Synonymous with ruci, as indicated below. On this term see AKV (Dwa), p. 187. Also see AKB(E) (which renders adhimukti as 'aspiration'), p. 1137, n. 169; Adv. p. 70. Conze renders ruci as 'pleasure', 'a taste for', MDPL, p. 336.

Folio 264

vāsanā. An important term in Yogācāra Buddhism. For various renderings, see BHSD, p. 478b; PSED, 846b. Conze renders it 'residue', MDPL, p. 348. AKB(E), p. 1139 renders it as 'trace'. See also D.T. Suzuki, Studies in the Laṅkāvatāra-sūtra (Boulder, 1981), p. 438. Cf. AKV (Dwa), pp. 1086, 1093; Adv. p. 385. It is translated as 'seed' or 'impression' in A. K. Chaterjee, Yogācāra Idealism (Delhi, 1987) p. 88, and explained in the glossary of that book (p. 232) as "the motive force guiding the evolution of consciousness."

Folio 265

progresses. Cf. pratipadyate = 'progress', 'hasten towards', etc., MDPL, p. 273; Pali paṭipajjati PED, p. 395b.

visaṁyoga. On this term, see AKB I.6, pp. 3–4; also ASVN, p. 265, and the paragraph that follows in the text.

satkāya. See MDPL, p. 396. For satkāya as the five upādāskandhas, see AKB V. 7, p. 281; AKB(E), p. 777.

Folio 266

exact. vyavasthāna = 'definite distinction', 'distinctive definition', etc. MDPL, p. 373.

another reading. This is the reading found in our Sūtra. The Nib. is based on a different recension of the Sūtra. See AVSN, p. 266, n. 5.

Folio 268

laukikavītarāga. On this term see AKB III.94, p. 183. They are called laukikamārga-vītarāga: free from lust but following a worldly path in the kāmadhātu. Cf. AKB(E), p. 483. Pradhan's edition of the AKB has the above reading, but Yaśomitra's Commentary and the Nib. read laukikavītarāga. See AKV (Dwa), p. 549. Yaśomitra in this connection refers to a class of laukikavītarāga beings in contradistinction to that of lokottaravītarāga. AKV, ibid.

Rhinoceros. An epithet for Pratyekabuddhas. See Khaggavisāṇasutta, Suttanipāta (verses 35–75). This Sutta is perhaps the earliest source for the explanation of the ideal of the Pratyekabuddha. See also AK III. 94, p. 183, and Yaśomitra's explanation of khadgaviṣāṇakalpa, AKV (Dwa), p. 548. Also see the monograph by Ria Kloppenberg: The Paccekabuddha: A Buddhist Ascetic (Leiden, 1974); cf. note on this term at notes to folio 228.

Folio 269

āsrava. Various renderings of this often-used term (Pali āsava) are in use: 'outflow', MDPL, p. 115; 'cankerous influence', AKB(E), p. 834; 'noxious influence', SDEBP, p. 319; 'intoxicant', 'evil influence', BHSD, p. 111b; 'bias', 'taint', 'corruption', BD, p. 27.

Folio 270

karmasvakajñāna. On this bala, see AKB VII. 32, p. 414. Rendered 'power of knowledge of the retribution of action', AKB(E), p. 1142, which if based on the above Sanskrit reading is not correct. For the Pali kammassakañāṇa, see PED, p. 194. See also BMPE, p. 356, n. 3; Adv., p. 390; cf. 'karmasvaka', BHSD, p. 171.

samudāgama. Cf. MDPL, p. 409 ('full attainment, final achievement').

Folio 271

vaiśāradya. (Pali vesārajja). Rendered 'confidence in oneself', 'fearlessness', BHSD, p. 512b; 'self-confidence', 'confidence', MDPL, p. 371; 'self-confidence', PED, p. 650b; 'conviction', MLS I, p. 96; 'assurance', AKB(E), p. 1141. See AKB(E), p. 1198, n. 183 for various references; see also MN I, p. 71; BDSL, pp. 20–22.

viśārada. Cf. Bodhisattvabhūmi, ed. N. Dutt (Patna, 1966), p. 277. The text explains viśārada as alīnacitta (of active mind), nirāśaṅka (without doubt), and nirbhi (without fear).

fearlessness. The Vaibhāṣikas interpret vaiśāradya as nirbhayatā. Cf. AKV (Dwa), p. 1092; see also the use of vaiśāradya in the simile of a lion in the Pañjikā Commentary on the Bodhicaryāvatāra VII. 55, p. 130.

samyaksambuddha. (Pali sammāsambuddha). Some renderings: 'Fully Enlightened One', Rhys Davids, SBE Vol. XI, p. 23; Nyanamoli, PP. VII. 26; 'perfectly enlightened one', Edgerton, BHSD, p. 582a; Rhys Davids, W. Stede, PED, p. 696a (see under sammā); 'completely (self) enlightened', Bhikkhu Nanamoli, The Guide (PTS, London, 1977), p. 306; 'Complete Buddha', Alex Wayman, The Lion's Roar of Queen Śrīmala (New York, 1974), p. 24; 'perfectly self-enlightened', Daw Mya Tin, The Dhammapada: Verses and Stories, (Sarnath, reprint, 1990), p. XIX; 'perfectly awakened one', Harrison, SDEBP, p. 37; 'Universal Buddha', PED, p. 696a; BD, p. 195. Yaśomitra explains 'buddha' as svyaṁ budhyata iti 'buddhaḥ' (i.e., 'who is self-awakened'), AKV (Dwa), p. 5. Puggalapaññatti explains sammā-sambuddha as sāmaṁ saccāni sambujjhati ('who comprehends truths by himself') (PTS, London, 1883), p. 14.

firmly maintains. pratijānīte (Pali paṭijānāti) means 'acknowledges', 'approves', 'agrees'. See PED, p. 395a. For Sanskrit pratijānāti, cf. Conze, MDPL, p. 272. He gives renderings such as 'recognizes', 'asserts', 'claims'. I have adopted 'firmly maintains'.

sarvadharmābhisambodha. On abhisambodha, see BHSD, p. 59b, which has 'perfect enlightenment', 'perfect comprehension'.

makes a charge: codayet. The root 'cud' has such meanings as 'reprove', 'accuse', 'question', etc. See Pali 'codeti', PED, p. 273a; Sanskrit 'codayati', BHSD, p. 234b.

Folio 272

antarāyakara. Cf. antarāya as 'obstacle' and 'danger', PED, 48a; antarāyika, BHSD, p. 39a.

adhigama. Rendered 'attainment', PED, p. 28a; 'achievement', 'full attainment', etc., MDPL, p. 15. But BHSD, p. 12b renders it 'spiritual realization', 'attainment of religious goal', etc.

Folio 273

niryāṇa. Cf. niryāṇa = going forth, MDPL, p. 230; Pali niyyāna = release, departure, etc., PED, p. 369a. This reading is not in the Sūtra, which has 'niryāyāt'. See AVS, p. 50.

bodha. PED, p. 491a gives 'knowledge', 'wisdom', 'enlightenment'.

vyavasthāna. For various meanings, see MDPL, p. 373. See term note, folio 266, above.

Folio 274

udbhāvita. On this term see udbhāvanā, BHSD, p. 131a.

prahāṇasampad. For this term, see folio 242.

parasampadatvaṁ. On this reading, which should be either parasampattvaṁ or parasampadātvaṁ, see AVSN, p. 274, n. 2.

power. The term (bala) refers here to the ten powers of the Buddha, each a power of knowledge. See Topic XXII.

anavamṛdyatā. On anavamṛdyatā (non-domination or non-overpowering by any opponent) of balas, cf. . . . tāni navamṛdyante, tasmād balāny ucyante, AVSN, p. 226.

asaṁkoca. Cf. 'non-hesitation (or absence of diffidence) in assembly' as the explanation of vaiśāradya above. cf. AVSN, p. 271.

Folio 275

pratisaṁvid. Rendered by Conze as 'analytical knowledge', MDPL p. 278; by P.A. Thittila, as 'analytic insight', Book of Analysis (London 1969), p. 387. See also Childers, DPL, p. 366a, on the derivation and various explanations of the Pali paṭisambhidā. See also BDSL, pp. 259ff.

paramārthajñāna. Conze renders paramārtha as 'ultimate reality', 'in the ultimate sense', etc. MDPL, p. 241. The term is very important in the Mahāyāna philosophical schools. Here I take 'artha' to mean 'category'. Note the differences in the readings of the Sūtra and Nib. See AVS, p. 52.

Folio 277

pratipattidharma. Conze renders pratipatti 'progressive path', 'progress to'. MDPL, p. 273; PED (p. 396a) renders 'paṭipatti' 'practice', 'performance', 'method', etc. See also term notes to folio 309, below.

anupraveśa = penetrating; cf. BHSD, p. 31b.

nirukti. Edgerton defines nirukti as an explanation, not necessary etymological, of the meaning of a word or text. BHSD, p. 299b. Conze gives 'grammatical analysis', 'language', MDPL, p. 226; P.A. Thittila, 'philology', BA, p. 387. Cf. Pali nirutti ('dialect', 'way of speaking', 'expression', etc.), PED, p. 370. AKB defines nirukti as 'etymological explanation', AKB VII. 40b, p. 419; AKB(E), p. 1154. AKB quotes Prajñapti (-śāstra), which gives various explanations of this pratisaṁvid. Mahāyānasūtrālaṅkāra (MSA), p. 138 explains it as knowledge of the sentences (vākya) of the languages of all regions and countries (janapada). Cf. also Har Dayal, BDSL, p. 265; Vism. XIV.25; Vibh, p. 293; BA, p. 387. Also see AVSN, p. 277, n. 3 for references and quotations.

Folio 278

pratibhāna. Conze gives many renderings, such as 'ready speech', 'inspiration', 'flash of ideas', etc., MDPL, p. 274. He also translates it as 'inspired speech', LSPW, p. 159. See also BHSD, p. 366b; Pali paṭibhāna, PED, p. 397b. AKB VII.38cd, p. 418; AKB(E), p. 1152 ('eloquence'). It may also be rendered 'brilliance'. For Yaśomitra's comments, see AKV (Dwa), p. 1103. See also AVSN, p. 278, n. 2. AKB (p. 419) gives another interpretation of pratibhāna as "rejoinder" (uttarottarapratibhā).

yuktamuktābhilāpitā. La Valée Poussin in his note refers to the explanation of this term by Paramārtha and Hsüan Tsang. According to Paramārtha: "Pratibhāna is to speak victorious words of demonstration and refutation;" according to Hsüan Tsang: "A flow of words without a dike," AKB(E), p. 1204, n. 227.

Folio 279

The word Tathāgata is not mentioned in the Sūtra at this point, though it is found in listing the first āvenika dharma in the beginning. Here again the discrepancy in the readings of the Sūtra and Nib. is evident.

veṇi. literally, 'braiding', 'conflux'. On the derivation, see AKV (Dwa), p. 786; see also BDSL, pp. 21–22; AVSN, p. 279, n. 7.

āveṇika. See in this context the explanation of word āveṇika in the phrase 'āveṇikī avidyā', AK V. 12; AKB, p. 286. Cf. AKV (Dwa), p. 786, where the meaning is 'independent' of any anuśaya (latent defilement).

Folio 280

takes no false step. Conze, LSPW, p. 160 renders as 'does not trip up', but see n. 5.

savāsanā. On vāsanā, see D.T. Suzuki, Studies in the Laṅkāvatāra Sūtra (Boulder, 1981) p. 438. Schmithausen renders this word 'impression, after-effect'. Cf. AV (word index), p. 647. Vasubandhu also refers to sarvavāsanāprahāṇa in connection with three smṛtyupasthānas which are included in the āveṇikadharmas according to another list, cf. AKV (Dwa), p. 1083. Cf. also AKB VII.32, p. 414, and see the explanation of vāsanā, AKV (Dwa), p. 1093. AKB(E) renders vāsanā as 'trace', see index to AKB(E), p. 1420. See also notes to folio 264, above.

asamanvāharataḥ. Cf. samanvāharti, 'focus attention on', BHSD, p. 564a; Pali samannāharti, 'concentrate the mind on', PED, p. 683b.

Folio 281

ravita. Cf. 'rava' = cry, clamor, noise or sound in general, PSED, p. 796a. See also Poussin's note, AKB(E), p. 1195, n. 162; note on ravita, J.J. Jones, Mahāvastu (Eng. trans.), Vol. I, p. 127, n. 3.

muṣitasmṛtitā. Conze renders 'robbed of mindfulness', LSPW, p. 160.

nāga: elephant. Yaśomitra explains the word nāga (used as an epithet of the Buddha) etymologically as the quality of a person who does not commit by body, speech, or mind any sin or offense (āgo na karoty ity aprādhaṁ na karoty ity arthaḥ), AKV (Dwa), p. 604. See also AN III, p. 346; Theragāthā, verses 696–97.

nanātvasaṁjñā. On this term, see AVSN, p. 190; cf. Har Dayal, BDSL, p. 23. The Buddha considers the universe under its aspects of unity and not with reference to the diversity of phenomena and objects.

pravṛtti. This term is rendered differently in different contexts: e.g. 'functioning', 'continuation of saṁsāra', AV, pp. 244, 299; 'appearance', 'manifestation', PSED, p. 670a. See various other meanings, ibid.

Folio 282

is free from. Our text does not comment on the sixth through the twelfth of the special dharmas, and is likewise quite selective in its comments elsewhere in this section. See AVSN, p. 282, n. 1.

jñeyavibandhābhāva. Cf. sarvajñeyeṣu jñānavibandhatvāt, AVSN, p. 244; Abhis. Ā, p. 352.

pratyakṣavṛtti. Cf. the identical explanation in AVSN, pp. 205, 254. Can it be loosely rendered as 'direct experience' or 'direct perception'? Cf. term notes to folios 205 and 254, above; cf. AKB VII.7, p. 394: darśanavacanam tu bhāṣyākṣepāt, pratyakṣavṛttitvād vā. at evoktaṁ yat tāvaj [see fn.] jñānaṁ darśanam api tad iti; also cf. Yaśomitra's lucid explanation of the statement in the Bhāṣya, AKV (Dwa), p. 1040: pratyakṣavṛtti is "direct seeing as by eye-consciousness (tadyathā cakṣurvijñānaṁ)."

Folio 283

nanu. A particle that implies interrogation. Cf. PSED 534c.

uddiṣṭa. Conze renders uddiśati as '(to) point out' also, MDPL, p. 126. Cf. Pali uddiṭṭha, PED, p. 135b.

uddeśa. For an explanation of this term, see text of Nib., p. 46. The list of topics being referred to is found in the Sūtra, p. 4, above. The 'detailed list' is the one found in the Commentary at pp. 37–8, above.

Folio 284

udghaṭitajña. On this term, see BHSD, p. 129b; see also Pali ugghaṭitaññu in Puggalapaññatti (PTS ed., London, 1883), p. 41.

saṁkśiptaruci. This adjectival compound is the Commentator's gloss on the term 'udghaṭitajña'.

vipañcitajña. On this word, see BHSD, p. 491a; cf. vipaññitaññu, Puggalapaññatti, p. 41.

deśastha. Yaśomitra explains deśastha as abhraṣṭasthāna, which signifies proper placement of marks. Cf. AKV (Dwa), p. 553.

tathāgatasya. Cf. AVS, p. 53, last line, for this word.

neither more nor less. Surprisingly, both the Sūtra and the Nibandhana give 33 lakṣaṇas. See AVS, p. 55, n. 3 on the interpolation of the 33rd lakṣaṇa; also "Introduction" to AVSN, pp. 129, 154–55. The additional mark is the last, referring to the Buddha having a pleasing body like that of Mahānārāyaṇa. This later addition may be due to the influence of the devotional school of the Bhāgavatas.

mahākṛpādi. Here 'kṛpā' replaces the more usual 'karuṇa'. Both words are used synonymously to mean 'compassion'. See AKB VII.33, pp. 414–15. In the detailed explanation of the AKB, the comparison is made between 'ordinary' and 'great' compassion. See also AKB(E), p. 1143ff. and Poussin's n. 188, p. 1199; see also Mahāyāna-sūtrālaṅkāra, XVII. 43. Also see Adv., p. 391, which distinguishes the karuṇā of the Śrāvaka and Pratyekabuddha from the mahākaruṇā of the Buddha. On the concept of mahāpuruṣa in the Pali Nikāyas, see Mahāpurisa-sutta, SN V, p. 158. This text does not speak of 32 marks, but mentions emancipation of mind (vimuttacittatta = vimuktacittatva) as a sign of being a Great Personage. See also DOB III, p. 134 for details on the 'theory of the superman' in Buddhist teachings.

Folio 285

of the Tathāgata. These words are not found in the Sūtra, although of course they do appear at the beginning of the section. They are found repeatedly in explanation of past action in the Sūtra.

supratiṣṭhitapādatā. Rendered 'feet with level tread' in some translated texts. Cf. DOB II, p. 14. On 'supatiṭṭhitapāda', Rhys Davids writes: "Literally 'well-planted feet'." The traditional meaning is that the whole under surface of the foot touches the ground at once, instead of proceeding in 'heel and toe' fashion. Cf. DOB II, p. 14, n. 2.

anutkaṭa. For different meanings of utkaṭa = large, spacious, see PSED, p. 258a.

seeking. Cf. paryeṣaṇā = 'search', 'investigation', 'inquiry', PSED, p. 604b. For reference to various kinds of paryeṣaṇā, see Pali pariyesanā, PED, p. 434a.

matured: nirvṛttaṁ = janitaṁ, 'produced'. Cf. nir + vṛt, 'to come forth', 'develop', 'originate'. SED, p. 558a.

Folio 286

satkṛtya. literally, 'respectfully', but it also means 'zealously'. Cf. BHSD, p. 553b.

Folio 287

vitasti. The Pali texts indicate instead a span of 12 aṅgulas or finger breadths. Cf. Pali vidatthi, PED, p. 621b.

adhiṣṭhāna. An alternative rendering: fixed determination or firm resolution. For various meanings of adhiṣṭhāna, see BHSD, pp. 15b–16a; MDPL, p. 17.

solid and liquid food. Ms. reads anupāna, which may be a misreading for annapāna. Cf. the account in the Sūtra regarding the past karma leading to the appearance of lakṣaṇa no. 7, p. 57 (vipulānnapānanupradānatayā nirvṛttaṁ); cf. Abhis. Ā no. 4 praṇītakhādyabhojyādidānāt, p. 537.

śayyāsana. Cf. Pali senāsana, PED, p. 723a.

readily visible. Wheels on the hands are mentioned in many lists (e.g., Adv., p. 188, Dharma S. no. 83). The Commentator explains the omission as due to the fact that one can easily see this mark directly.

prominent ankles: utsaṅgapāda. Cf. Pali ussaṅkha, PED, p. 157a. Various meanings of utsaṅga are suggested; see the long note on ucchaṅkha, BHSD, p. 118a. Also see BDSL, p. 302, no. 28 for various interpretations.

Terms and Variants

The variant reading 'ucchaṅgapāda' is also found in some texts; e.g., Abhis Ā, p. 537. Our text here fuses two marks, a common occurrence in the traditional lists.

Folio 290

tūlapicu. Karpāsapicu is ordinary cotton and tūlapicu is silk cotton of the śālmali tree. Cf. BHSD, pp. 170b, 256a: Edgerton puts a query on the difference between them, BHSD, p. 170b. Cf. Gaṇḍavyūha, ed. D.T. Suzuki (Kyoto, 1949), p. 400, where it is said that the touch (saṁsparśa) of the hands or feet of the Buddha brings extraordinary pleasure to all, like that of kācilindika textile (known for its extraordinary softness). On kācilindika cloth, see BHSD, p. 175b.

quite. The words are 'spaṣṭa eva'.

utsada. Cf. BHSD, p. 126b; Pali ussada, PED, p. 157a.

Folio 291

mṛga. Mṛga means 'animal' as well as 'deer'. For various meanings of mṛga, see PSED, p. 769c.

eṇeyajaṅgha. Apte says eṇa or eṇaka is a kind of black antelope, PSED, p. 315a. See also eṇi, BHSD, p. 155a. In Suttanipāta, verse 165, the Buddha's legs are compared to those of an antelope.

Folio 292

kośagata-vastiguhyatā. Rendered 'male organ concealed in a sheath', DOB III, p. 138. In AKB, we have an interesting reference to this mark of the Buddha, where the question of the ugliness of the sex organ is raised. It is replied that in the case of the Great Personage (mahāpuruṣa) who possesses this mark, it is not by reason of its utility that the sexual organ appears but rather by reason of its cause. Given its cause, it will arise even if it is ugly. AKB I, 30, p. 21; AKB(E), p. 94. In the Ambaṭṭha sutta of the Dīghanikāya, this mark is presented as the subject of curiosity for the young Ambaṭṭha, who is described in the text as finally being allowed to witness it. DN I, p. 106; DOB I, p. 131. Cf. also Milindapañha, where one of the dilemmas put forth by King Milinda to Venerable Nāgasena is with respect to showing this mark to the Brahman named Sela. Milindapañha, pp. 167–68; I. B. Horner, Milinda's Questions (London, 1969) Vol. I, pp. 235–38.

vasti. Cf. Pali vatthi, PED, p. 598b; also vatthaguhya, listed under vattha, PED, ibid. Also cf. kośāvahitavastiguhyatā MDPL, p. 156; kośopagatavastiguhya, BHSD, p. 195a.

aśvājāneya. The comparison is also made to an elephant of noble breed, Adv., p. 188, and to a bull, MNA III, p. 377. Thus the legend expanded even with regard to the private organ of the Buddha once the concept of a Great Personage was developed. Cf. also Gaṇḍavyūha, p. 400. On the concept of a 'noble horse', cf. Dhp. 322 for ājānīyā sindhavā (thoroughbred horses from Sindh).

Folio 293

well-filled. The meaning is that the shoulders are level. DOB III, p. 138 renders this as "There is no furrow between his shoulders."

cita. Cf. 'citāntarāṁsa' in the entry for 'cita', BHSD, p. 229a.

shoulders evenly rounded. This has also been rendered, 'bust evenly rounded'. Cf. MLS II, p. 322; BSDL, p. 301 (no. 14).

Folio 294

abhayadāna. On abhayadāna (bestowing fearlessness), see good article in Ency. of Bud., fasc. A., p. 20. Abhayamudrā (the symbolic gesture of fearlessness) is often found in statues of the Buddha. It signifies abhayadāna.

standing erect. In the Lakkhaṇa-suttanta in the DN, the Pali phraseology of this mark is rendered: "Standing and without bending he can touch and rub his knees with both hands," DOB III, p. 138. See also explanation in MNA III, p. 377, where reference is made to dwarfs and hunchbacks. Cf. also (no. 12) LSPW, p. 658, where Conze renders the phrase, "When he stands up with his thighs straight and without bending the body, he can touch his kneecaps with the two palms of his hands—therefore his arms are long and powerful."

yojya. It seems that here our Commentator uses the word yojya just for variety of expression. Generally he uses spaṣṭa (clear, explicit).

Folio 295

spotless. For various renderings of viśuddha, cf. PSED, p. 875a; PED, p. 640b.

Folio 296

without spaces. BDSL (p. 301) renders this phrase, "There are no gaps or interstices between one tooth and another."

vikaṭādyabhāvāt. 'Deformity' here would mean having some teeth larger or smaller. The word vikaṭa has many meanings: 'ugly', 'frightful', 'broad', 'large', 'changed in appearance', etc., but it also means 'large-toothed'. Cf. Apte, PSED, p. 848a.

Folio 297

vārṣikī. On vārṣikī (jasmine), see BHSD, p. 478a. In Lalitavistara (Lefmann's ed., p. 27) we have 'vārṣikī-suviśuddhadarśanā' as an epithet of Māyā, the mother of the Buddha. Cf. also vassikī and vassikā, Dhp. 55 and 377; see also PED, p. 606a. Mallikā is a kind of jasmine flower, PSED, p. 747a; given as 'Arabian Jasmine', PED, p. 525a. In Dhammapada: Verses and Stories (Rangoon ed., 1986, Reprint Sarnath, 1991), p. 21, n. 3 and p. 22, n. 1, mallikā is identified as Arabian Jasmine and vassikā as Spanish Jasmine (spelled 'jasmin' in the edition).

Folio 298

rasarasāgratā. Cf. rasāgra BHSD, p. 453b, rendered 'excellent taste or flavor', 'supremely acute taste', DOB III, p. 138; 'most excellent taste', Conze, LSPW, p. 659. Har Dayal translates: "Sense of taste is very acute and keen." BDSL, p. 301. The Pali tradition explains: "The 7000 nerves of taste bend towards the tongue." Also see 'rasaggasā', DPL, p. 401a. The Nib. does not explain this mark.

kalaviṅka. A bird famed for its sweet note, called the Indian cuckoo. See also BHSD, p. 172a. Cf. MLS II, pp. 322, n. 5. Cf. MNA III, pp. 382–84; see AVSN, p. 299, n. 2. There is a long gloss on the voice of the kalaviṅka (Pali karavīka) in MNA III, pp. 382ff. The word for 'voice' is ruta ('voice', 'cry', 'sound'); on this term, Edgerton says that in Sanskrit the word "seems to be used only of cries of animals, and esp. birds." BHSD, p. 456a.

greatness. Alternative rendering: Due to its great volume (reaching far-off world systems).

brahmasvara. It is a sublime voice, like that of a Mahābrahmā, cf. MNA III, pp. 382–84; MLS II, p. 322. In AKB I.37, p. 25, it is said that the lakṣaṇa (mark) of brahmasvaratā was the result of Buddha's cultivating the practice of abstinence from harsh speech in past lives. It quotes Prajñapati-śāstra. See also AKB(E), p. 104; also p. 146, n. 159. On brahmasvara having eight qualities, see DN II, p. 211: It is fluent, intelligible, sweet, audible, continuous, distinct, deep, and resonant. Cf. DOB II, p. 245. Other traditions list sixty qualities of the voice of the Buddha.

Folio 300

like those of a cow. Conze's translation in LPSW: "Because his eyelashes, above or below, are just at the right angle and because they are very neat, the Tathāgata's eyelashes are like those of a magnificent heifer." LSPW, p. 659. Cf. also Adv. p. 189.

soft. The Sūtra reads 'sūkṣma' (delicate), but Nib. reads ślakṣṇa (soft). Lakkhaṇa-sutta in DN III, p. 143, has the reading 'sukhumacchavī', rendered 'delicately smooth skin', DOB III, p. 138. The Pali text adds a gloss: "No dust cleaves to his body." DOB, loc. cit. Cf. DN III, p. 143. Cf. also LSPW (no. 15), p. 658, where the smoothness is compared to that of well-worked gold or silver.

Our teacher. The word is put into the plural out of respect. Cf. also other references to the teacher of our Commentator, AVSN, pp. 71, 217, 284; cf. also Intro. to AVSN, p. 127, n. 1; notes to folio 217; cf. endnote 1, above.

tanutva and tanu. The word 'tanu' has various meanings; see PSED, p. 466c. Here there is a pun that plays on two meanings.

Folio 302

parimāṇasanniveśaviśeṣa. Read in the text parimāṇa instead of pariṇāma, the latter being a misprint.

Folio 303

sphaṭikaguḍikā. Cf. guṭikā = ball, pill, pear, etc., SED, p. 356b. Cf. also guḍikā = cluster, BHSD, p. 212a. Instead of 'crystal pill', could we say 'crystal cluster'?

Folio 304

uṣṇīṣa. Cf. BDSL, p. 300, on this mark. Uṣṇīṣa = royal turban, DOB III p. 139; 'Head shaped like a (royal) turban', MLS II, p. 322. Cf. also Dharmasaṅgraha, (tr.) K. Kasawara and (ed.) F. Max Muller and H. Wenzel (New Delhi, 1981), p. 54 (no. 23). There is an interesting comment on this mark in DNA II, p. 452; MNA III, pp. 385–86. Cf. also Adv., p. 189, which speaks of a vajra-like bone, gradually piled up on the head. T. W. Rhys Davids gives the following note on the basis of the Commentary on the Dīghanikāya: "This expression, says the Cy., refers to the fullness either of the forehead or cranium. In either case the rounded highly-developed appearance is meant, giving to the unadorned head the decorative dignified effect of a crested turban, and the smooth symmetry of a water-bubble." DOB II, p. 16, n. 4. Cf. for details, DNA II, p. 452. Dharma S., p. 54 gives a further explanation of this lakṣaṇa; cf. also Conze, LSPW, p. 659: "Because he has on the top of head something like a cowl, which is well-rounded and turns to the right, which is well-formed and beautiful to behold—there is a cowl on his head." On uṣṇīṣa as represented in Buddha's statues and Hellenic influence on it, see A. Grünwedel, Buddhist Art in India (London, 1901), pp. 163–64; E.J. Thomas, The Life of the Buddha (London, 1969) pp. 221–222. Also see articles by A. K. Coomarswamy "The Buddha's Cūḍa, Hair, Uṣṇiṣa and Crown," JRAS 60 (1928), pp. 815ff. and by J. N. Banerjea "Usṇīṣaśiraskatā (a mahāpuruṣa-lakṣaṇa) in the early Buddha images of India," IHQ (Vol. VII, no. 3–4) (1931), pp. 499ff.

Folio 305

nyagrodhaparimaṇḍala (sic). There is no suffix tā added in the text of Nib. The reading is nyagrodhaparimaṇḍala in all Mss. It is only in this case that the abstract form with 'tā' is missing. But in the Sūtra the reading includes 'tā'. Cf. AVS, pp. 55 and 61 (item no. 32).

nyagrodha. See under nyag, SED, p. 571c.

vyāmaparimaṇḍala. Cf. the Buddha's vyāmaprabhā = halo, extending for the distance of a fathom around the Buddha, BHSD, p. 518b.

Folio 306

asecanakarūpatvāt. Another rendering: A form that one cannot be satiated with looking at. Cf. asecanka, BHSD, p. 84b; Pali asecanaka = lovely, sublime, PED, p. 89b. Cf. Pali pasādaniya 'inspiring confidence', 'giving faith', PED p. 446b; see also prasādanīya, BHSD, p. 388b.

Folio 307

puṇyaśataja. Cf. Adv., kārika 242, p. 208; AKV (Dwa), p. 737.

Folio 309

path of practice. Meanings of pratipatti include 'progressive path', 'course of conduct', 'behavior', 'method', 'performance', etc. Cf. Conze, MDPL, p. 273; Edgerton, BHSD, p. 364a; cf. also the cognate pratipad, ibid., p. 364b. Also cf. Pali paṭipatti, PED, p. 396a. See term notes to folio 277, above.

virtuous in the beginning. Explained at AVSN, pp. 80–81.

anāsravaśīla. On this term, see AKB IV. 13, p. 205. For anāsravasaṁvara, see also AVSN, p. 258; also cf. endnote 200, above.

said again. The word is pratyuktaṁ which may be rendered here 'spoken (or taught) again'. Cf. 'prati', PSED, p. 645b; cf. Pali paṭi, which can mean 'again' or 'a second time', PED, 391b (item 3).

śāstā śrāvakāṇām: the teacher for disciples. These and other words are not found in our Ms. of the Sūtra or in the other available copies, but must be recorded in the copy on which the present Nibandhana is based. For discrepancies in the readings of Sūtra and Commentary, see Intro. to AVSN (Chap. 13), pp. 157ff. The terms are explained in the Nib.

Folio 310

śrāvakas. See notes to folio 228, supra. The definition here differs somewhat from that found in Vism VII.90, rendered by Nyanamoli: "They hear attentively the Blessed One's instruction, thus they are his disciples (lit. hearers)." PP VII.90. See also PED, p. 707a; BHSD, p. 535a; SP, p. 80.

anuśāsana. Cf. anuśāsanī, BHSD, p. 35a, where Edgerton remarks that it is hard to distinguish this term from avavāda, with which it is often compounded.

bodily and mental detachment. Compare 'physical and mental withdrawal', discussed at AVSN, p. 202.

Folio 311

mā pramādyata. The word pramāda can be rendered 'negligence', 'carelessness', 'indulgence', 'unmindfulness', etc. Cf. pramāda, MDPL, p. 285; Pali pamāda, PED, p. 416b. Cf. the last words of the Buddha (on apramāda = diligence) before his decease in DN II, p. 156; DOB II, p. 173.

Nibandhana. Here the use of nibandha is metri causa.

bahuśaḥ. Cf. various renderings of bahuśas, Apte, PSED, p. 698a. The word may also be rendered in this context as 'copiously', 'extensively'.

abhyāsāhita. Cf. abhyāsamārga, 'path of repeated meditational practice', Conze, MDPL, p. 67. I have rendered it as "repeated practice," with the adjective 'meditational' in parentheses.

gotra. On gotra, see BHSD, p. 216a. On the three gotras of Śrāvaka, Pratyekabuddha, and Buddha, see AKB VI.23, p. 348; notes to folio 246, supra. Cf. niyatagotraka, AVSN, p. 246.

bodhayogāt. Here 'bodha' is used in the sense of wisdom (prajñā). On various meanings of bodha, see PSED, p. 704b.

manmatha. Cf. Apte, PSED, p. 743c, which renders it 'cupid, the god of love'; passion, etc.

eradication. The word is °apakāri° The variant "°apahāri°" would have been better, but one of the meanings of apa+ kṛ is 'to remove'. Cf. PSED, p. 94c.

niḥśreyas and abhyudaya. On these terms, see PSED, p. 566c and p. 133b.

Folio 312

mahodaya. See under mahā, PSED, p. 749a.

jitendriya. 'Indriya' is also translated 'faculty', as well as 'organ of sense'. Rhys Davids remarks (PED, p. 121b) that it is often wrongly interpreted as 'organ'. But see DPL, p. 159a; PSED, p. 248b.

śloka. Monier-Williams states that a śloka is "a stanza (especially) a particular kind of common epic metre (also called anuṣṭubh) consisting of 4 pādas or quarter verses of 8 syllables each," SED, p. 1104c. The total syllables in a śloka are 32, and thus the total syllables in the Nibandhana are 44,000 (1375 ˘ 32).

Terms and Variants

Nibandhana. For the names of various types of commentaries in the Buddhist tradition including nibandhana, see E. Obermiller (tr.), History of Buddhism (Chos-ḥbyung) by Bu-ston (Heidelberg, 1931), Pt. I, p. 58. See also AVSN, p. 71, n. 1.

parahitaiṣī. It is significant that the copyist wishes for the welfare of (all) 'other' (para) beings, like a Bodhisattva working for others, never seeking personal liberation till other beings have been liberated. Cf. WE, pp. 74–75, 252. See also BDSL, pp.17–18.

Corrections to the Text of the Arthaviniścaya-sūtra

(ed. N. H. Samtani)

Page	Line	Incorrect	Correct
11	7	त्रायस्त्रिंशाः	त्रयस्त्रिंशाः
17	5–6	एकोतीभावाद- वितर्कविचारं	एकोतीभावाद- वितर्कमविचारं
25	14	परिपूरिताति	परिपूरितानि
31	11	लोकिक्कीं	लौकिक्कीं
42	9	प्राहाणाद्	प्रहाणाद्
44	21	विमोच्यन्मे	विमोचयन्मे
45	12	धर्मेऽवेत्य प्रसादेन	धर्मेऽवेत्यप्रसादेन
47	3	प्रतिपन्नका	प्रतिपन्नकाः
47	4	सङ्के अनागामिनाः	सङ्के अनागामिनः
47	4	अर्हत्व	अर्हत्त्व
47	6	समाधिसम्पन्नः	समाधिसम्पन्नः प्रज्ञासम्पन्नः
47	7	विमुक्तिज्ञानदर्शसम्पन्नः	विमुक्तिज्ञानदर्शनसम्पन्नः
47	10	अकल्मषाणि	अकल्माषाणि
47	11	सुमाप्तानि	सुसमाप्तानि
48	4	अस्थानं चास्थानतः	अस्थानं चास्थानतः, इदं तथागतस्य प्रथमं बलम्।
50	6	पुनर्मायिन्तरायिका	पुनर्मयान्तरायिका

Corrections

Page	Line	Incorrect	Correct
54	8–9	सूक्ष्मछविता	सूक्ष्मच्छविता
55	1	[रु]रोर्णललाटता	[रु]रोर्णाललाटता
64	10	आयतनपाणि[रु]	आयतपाणि[रु]

Bibliography

The letters a, b, and c after page numbers in dictionary references indicate columns on the page. Cy. = commentary

Entries with Abbreviations

A = Aṭṭhakathā

Abhis. Ā = Abhisamayālaṅkāra-Āloka of Haribhadra published along with Aṣṭasāhasrikā Prajñāpāramitā, ed. P.L. Vaidya (Darbhanga, 1960).

Adv. = Abhidharmadīpa with Vibhāṣāprabhā-vṛtti, ed. P.S. Jaini (Patna, 1959).

AI = Asokan Inscriptions, ed. Radhagovinda Basak (Calcutta, 1959).

AK = Abhidharmakośa, edited with Bhāṣya by Pradhan. See AKB.

AKB = Abhidharmakośa-bhāṣya of Vasubandhu, ed. P. Pradhan (Patna, 1967).

AKB(E) = Abhidharmakośabhāṣyam, French trans. by Louis de La Vallée Poussin, English trans. by Leo M. Pruden (Berkeley, 1988–90), 4 vols.

AKV (Dwa) = Abhidharmakośa and Bhāṣya with Sphuṭārthā Commentary (Vyākhyā) of Yaśomitra, ed. Swami Dwarikadas Shastri (Varanasi, 1970).

AKV (Wog.) Sphuṭārthā Abhidharmakośa-vyākhyā of Yaśomitra, ed. by Unrai Wogihara in Roman characters (Tokyo, 1932–36).

AN = Aṅguttaranikāya, ed. R. Morris et. al. (PTS, London, 1885–1910) 6 vols.

AP = Abhidhamma Philosophy or the Psycho-ethical philosophy of early Buddhism by Bhikkhu J. Kashyap, Vol. I (Nalanda, 1959).

ASM = Abhidharmasamuccaya of Asaṅga, ed. P. Pradhan (Santiniketan, 1950).

AV = Ālayavijñāna (On the Origin and Early Development of a Central Concept of Yogācāra Philosophy) by Lambert Schmithausen (Tokyo, 1987), Pts I & II.

AVS = Arthaviniścaya-sūtra and its Commentary (Nibandhana), ed. N.H. Samtani (Patna, 1971).

AVSN = Arthaviniścayasūtra-Nibandhana. See AVS.

BA = The Book of Analysis (Trans. of Vibhaṅga), tr. by P. A. Thittila (PTS, London, 1969).

BD = Buddhist Dictionary (Manual of Buddhist Terms and Doctrines) by Nyanatiloka (Kandy, 1980).

BDSL = Bodhisattva Doctrine in Buddhist Sanskrit Literature by Har Dayal (London, 1932).

BHSD = Buddhist Hybrid Sanskrit Dictionary by Franklin Edgerton (New Haven, 1953).

BI = Buddhist Insight (Essays by Alex Wayman), ed. George Elder (Delhi, 1984).

BLT = Buddhism and Lamaism of Tibet by L.A. Waddell (New Delhi, 1979).

BMPE = A Buddhist Manual of Psychological Ethics (trans. of Dhammasaṅgaṇi) by C.A.F. Rhys Davids (London, 1900).

Bodhic. = Budhicaryāvatāra, ed. by P.L. Vaidya (Darbhanga, 1960).

Buddha C. = Buddha-carita of Aśvaghoṣa by E.H. Johnston (Calcutta, 1936). Reference to cantos and verses.

CP = Compendium of Philosophy by S.Z. Aung and C.A.F. Rhys Davids (PTS, London, 1910).

CPD = Critical Pali Dictionary, begun by V. Trenckner, ed. by Dines Andersen and others (Copenhagen, 1924–continuing).

Dharma S. = Dharmasaṅgraha, ed. by Kenji Kasawara, ed. by F. Max Muller, H. Wenzel (Oxford, 1885). Reference to articles.

Dhp = Dhammapada, ed. J. Kashyap (Nalanda, 1959) Reference to verses.

Dhs = Dhammasaṅgaṇi, ed. P.V. Bapat and R.D. Vadekar (Poona, 1940). Reference to articles.

DN = Dīghanikāya, ed. T. W. Rhys Davids and J.E. Carpenter (PTS, London, 1890–1911).

DNA = Dīghanikāya-aṭṭhakathā (Sumaṅgala-vilāsinī), ed. T. W. Rhys Davids, J.E. Carpenter, W. Stede (PTS, London, 1886–1992).

DOB = Dialogues of the Buddha (trans. of the Dīghanikāya) by T.W. Rhys Davids and C.A.F. Rhys Davids (Sacred Books of the Buddhists, London, 1899–1910), 3 vols.

DPL = Dictionary of the Pali Language by R.C. Childers (Kyoto, 1976).

DPPN = Dictionary of Pali Proper Names by G.P. Malalasekera (PTS, London, 1960), 2 vols.

EBM = Early Buddhist Mythology by J.R. Haldar (New Delhi, 1977).

EBTK = Early Buddhist Theory of Knowledge by K.N. Jayatilleke (London, 1963)

EMB = Early Monastic Buddhism by N. Dutt (Calcutta, 1960).

Ency. of Bud. = Encyclopaedia of Buddhism ed. G.P. Malalasekera (Colombo, 1961–continuing).

GV = Gaṇḍavyūha, ed. D.T. Suzuki and H. Idzumi (Kyoto, 1934–36).

IHQ = Indian Historical Quarterly.

IIJ = Indo-Iranian Journal.

JRAS = Journal of Royal Asiatic Society, London.

KV = Kathāvatthu, ed. A.C. Taylor (London, PTS, 1894–97). References to chapters and kathās.

LOB = The Life of Buddha as Legend and History by E.J. Thomas (London, 1969).

LSPW = The Large Sutra on Perfect Wisdom (with the divisions of the Abhisamayālaṅkāra), tr. by Edward Conze (Delhi, 1979).

LV = Lalitavistara, ed. S. Lefmann (Halle, 1902–1908).

LVP-AK = L'Abhidharma-kośa de Vasubandhu, tr. Louis de La Vallée Poussin [Abhidharmakośa and Bhāṣya] (Paris, 1923–31).

MBM = Mahāyāna Buddhist Meditation, ed. Minoru Kiyota (Delhi, 1991).

MBP = A Manual of Buddhist Philosophy by W.M. McGovern (London, 1923).

MDPL = Materials for a Dictionary of the Prajñāpāramitā Literature by Edward Conze (Tokyo, 1973).

ME = Meditation on Emptiness by Jeffrey Hopkins (London, 1983).

Mhvg = Mahāvagga in the Vinayapiṭaka, ed. H. Oldenberg (PTS, London, 1979).

Mhvs = Mahāvaṁsa, ed. W. Geiger (London, 1908). References to chapters and verses.

MLS = The Middle Length Sayings (Trans. of Majjhimanikāya), tr. by I.B. Horner (PTS, London, 1967–70), 3 vols.

MMK = Mūlamadhyamakakārikās, avec la Prasannapadā Commentaire de Candrakīrti (St. Petersburg, 1903–13 (Reprint Delhi, 1992).

MN = Majjhimanikāya, ed. V. Trenckner (PTS, London, 1888–1925), 4 vols.

MNA = Majjhimanikāya-aṭṭhakathā (Papañcasūdanī), ed. J. H. Woods, D. Kosambi, I.B. Horner (PTS, London, 1923–38), 5 vols.

MP = Milindapañha, ed. V. Trenckner (PTS, London, 1880).

MSA = Mahayānasūtrālaṅkāra, ed. S. Levi (Paris, 1907–11).

MV = Mahāvastu, ed. E. Senart (Paris, 1882–1897).

MVS = Madhyāntavibhāga-śāstra, ed. R.C. Pandeya (Delhi, 1971).

MVY = Mahāvyutpatti, ed. Sasaki (Kyoto, 1916). Reference to numbered entries.

NE = Nyingma Edition of the Tibetan Buddhist Canon, ed. Tarthang Tulku (Berkeley, 1981).

Nib. = Nibandhana = Commentary on the Arthaviniścayasūtra (See AVSN).

PED = Pali Text Society's Pali-English Dictionary, ed. T.W. Rhys Davids and W. Stede (London, 1959).

PP = Path of Purification (Tr. of Visuddhimagga) by Bhikkhu Nyanamoli (Colombo, 1964). References to chapters and articles.

PSED = Practical Sanskrit-English Dictionary by V.S. Apte (Delhi, 1989).

Psm. = Paṭisambhidāmagga, ed. C. Taylor (PTS, London, 1905–1907).

PTS = Pali Text Society, London.

Pts. of Contr. = Points of Controversy (tr. of Kathāvatthu) by S.Z. Aung and C.F.A. Rhys Davids (PTS, London, 1960).

RGV = Ratnagotravibhāga, Mahāyānottaratantraśāstra, ed. E.H. Johnston (Patna, 1950).

SBE = Sacred Books of East (Series).

SBT = Systems of Buddhist Thought by Yamakami Sogen (Calcutta, 1912).

SDEBP = The Samadhi of the Direct Encounter with the Buddhas of the Present by Paul Harrison (Tokyo, 1990).

SED = A Sanskrit-English Dictionary by Sir Monier Monier-Williams (Oxford, 1956).

Śikṣ = Śikṣāsamuccaya, ed. C. Bendall (Hague, 1957).

SN = Saṁyuttanikāya, ed. Leon Feer (London, 1884–1904).

SP = Saddharmapuṇḍarīka-sūtra, ed. H. Kern and B. Nanjio (St. Petersburg, 1908–12).

Toh. = A Complete Catalogue of the Tibetan Buddhist Canons, ed. by Hakuji Ui (Tokyo, 1934).

Vbh. = Vibhaṅga, ed. C.A.F. Rhys Davids (PTS, London, 1904).

Vbh.A. = Vibhaṅga-Aṭṭhakathā, ed. Buddhadatta Thera (London, 1923).

Vin. or Vinaya = Vinayapiṭaka, ed. H. Oldenberg (London, 1879–83).

Vism = Visuddhimagga (Devanāgarī), ed. Dharmananda Kosambi (Bombay, 1940). See also Roman edition by H.C. Warren, revised by Dharmanand Kosambi, Harvard Oriental Series, Vol. 41 (Delhi Reprint, 1989). References to chapters and articles.

WE = Ways of Enlightenment: Buddhist Studies at Nyingma Institute (Berkeley, 1993).

Wog. = U. Wogihara's edition of AKV (see AKV[Wog.]).)

YB = Yogācārabhūmi of Ācārya Asaṅga, Pt. I ed. Vidushekhara Bhattacharya (Calcutta, 1957).

Entries without Abbreviation

Andersen, Dines and Smith, Helmer (eds.), Suttanipāta (PTS, London, 1913). Reference to verses.

Bailey, D.R.S. (ed.), The Śatapañcāśatka of Mātṛceṭa (Cambridge, 1951).

Bapat, P.V., "Four Auspicious Things of Buddhists," Indian Historical Research Institute, Silver Jubilee Commemoration Volume (1953).

Bapat, P.V. and Gokhale, V.V., Vinayasūtra with Guṇaprabha's Vṛtti (Commentary) Chap. I (Patna, 1982).

Bays, G. (tr.), Voice of the Buddha: The Beauty of Compassion (tr. of Lalitavistara Sūtra) (Berkeley, 1983).

Bendall, C.C. and Rouse, W.H.D., Śikṣāsamuccaya: A Compendium of Buddhist Doctrine (Delhi, 1971).

Buddhadasa Bhikkhu, Ānāpānasati (Mindfulness of Breathing): The Sixteen Steps to Awakening (Bangkok, 1976).

Burlingame, E.W., Buddhist Legends (Harvard University Press, 1921), 3 vols.

Chatterjee, A.K., Yogācāra Idealism (Delhi, 1987).

Conze, Edward, Buddhist Thought In India (London, 1962)

Cowell, E.B. and R.A. Neil (ed.), Divyāvadāna (Cambridge, 1886).

Cox, Collett, Disputed Dharmas: Early Buddhist Theories on Existence (Tokyo, 1995).

Davids, Rhys, C.A.F. (ed.), Vibhaṅga (PTS, London, 1904).

Davidson, R.M., "Āśrayaparāvṛtti and Mahāyanābhidharma," in N.H. Samtani and H.S. Prasad (ed.), Amalā Prajñā: Aspects of Buddhist Studies (Prof. P.V. Bapat Felicitation Volume) (Delhi, 1989).

Dhammakaya Foundation, Buddhism into the Year 2000 (International Conference Proceedings) (Bangkok, 1994).

Dutt, Nalinaksha (ed.), Bodhisattvabhūmi (Patna, 1966).

Fausboll, V. (tr.), Suttanipāta (Collection of Discourses), SBE (Delhi, Reprint, 1973), Vol X. References to verses.

Ferrari, Alfonsa, Arthaviniścaya (Testo e Versione, Atti Della Reale Accademia D'Italia. Memorie Della Classe Di Scienze Morali e Storiche (Serie Settima, Vol. IV, Fasc. 13) (Rome, 1944).

Gethin, R.M.L., The Buddhist Path to Awakening: A Study of Bodhipakkhiyā Dhammā (Leiden, 1992).

Getty, Alice, Gods of Northern Buddhism (Delhi, 1978).

Grimm, George, The Doctrine of Buddha: The Religion of Reason and Meditation (Delhi, 1982).

Grunwedel, A., Buddhist Art in India (London, 1901).

Guenther, H.V. and Kawamura, L. (trs.) Mind in Buddhist Psychology (Berkeley, 1975).

Guru, D.K., A Manual of Sanskrit Grammar (Bombay, 1938).

Gyatso, Tenzin (His Holiness the XIV Dalai Lama), The Opening of the Wisdom Eye (Adyar, 1977).

Hardy, E. (ed.), Nettippakaraṇa (London, 1961).

Hartmann, Jens-Uwe (ed. and tr.), Varṇārhavarṇastotra des Mātṛceṭa (Göttingen, 1987).

Hastings, J., Encyclopedia of Religion and Ethics (Edinburgh, 1908–28).

Hirakawa, Akira, et. al., Index to the Abhidharmakośabhāṣya (P. Pradhan, ed.) (Tokyo, 1973).

Horner, I.B., The Early Buddhist Theory of Man Perfected: A Study of the Arahan (London, 1936).

Horner, I.B., The Book of the Discipline, Vol. IV (London, 1962).

Horner, I.B., Milinda's Questions (London, 1969), 2 vols.

Jaini, P.S., Milindaṭikā (PTS, London, 1961).

Jaini, P.S., "Vaibhāṣika Theory of Words and Meanings," Bulletin of the School of Oriental and African Studies, Vol. XXII, Pt. 1 (1959).

Jones, J.J. (tr.), The Mahāvastu (London, 1973–78), 3 vols.

Kern, H. (tr.), The Saddharmapuṇḍarīka or the Lotus of the True Law (SBE Vol. XXI) (Oxford, 1884).

Khantipalo, Dhammapada (English tr. in verse) (Bangkok, 1977).

Kloppenberg, Ria, The Paccekabuddha: A Buddhist Ascetic (Leiden, 1974).

Kosambi, Dharmanand (ed.), Abhidhammatthasaṅgaha of Anuruddha (Sarnath, 1941).

Law, B.C., Designation of Human Types (tr. of Puggalapaññatti) (London, 1979).

Law, B. C., History of Pali Literature (Varanasi, 1974), 2 vols.

Lindtner, Chr., Nāgārjuniana: Studies in the Writings and Philosophy of Nāgārjuna (Copenhagen, 1982).

Mejor, Marek, Vasubandhu's Abhidharmakośa and the Commentaries Preserved in the Tanjur (Stuttgart, 1991).

Morris, R. (ed.), Puggalapaññatti (PTS, London, 1883).

Muller, Max F. (tr.), Dhammapada (SBE Vol, X, Pt. 1) (Delhi, Reprint 1973).

Nanamoli, Bhikkhu, The Guide (tr. of Nettippakaraṇa) (London, 1977).

Norman, H.C. Dhammapada-aṭṭhakathā (Commentary) (PTS, London, 1906), Vol. I.

Norman, K.R., Elders' Verses (Tr. of Theragāthā) (PTS, Oxford, 1990), Vol. I.

Obermiller, E. (tr.), History of Buddhism in India and Tibet Pt. I (Chos-ḥbyung) by Bu-ston (Heidelberg, 1931).

Obermiller, E., The Sublime Science of the Great Vehicle to Salvation: Being A Manual of Buddhist Monism (Acta Orientalia IX, 1931), repr. with Introduction by H.S. Prasad together with Skt. text of Ratnagotravibhaga (see RGV, above) under the title Uttaratantra of Maitreya (Delhi, 1991).

Oldenberg, H. (ed.), Theragāthā (PTS, London, 1883).

Pandeya, R.C., Buddhist Studies in India (Delhi, 1975).

Potter, Karl H., et. al., eds. Encyclopedia of Indian Philosophies, Vol. VII (Abhidharma Buddhism to 150 A.D.) (Delhi, 1996).

Rao Hanumantha, B.S.L., Religion in Andhra (Tripurasundari, 1973).

Ray, Reginald, Buddhist Saints in India: A Study in Buddhist Values and Orientations (Oxford, 1994).

Rewatadhamma, Abhidhammatthasaṅgaha Vibhāvinīṭīkā (Varanasi, 1965).

Rockhill, W.W., Life of Buddha (Varanasi, 1972).

Rockhill, W.W., Udānavarga (A Collection of Verses from the Buddhist Canon, compiled by Dharmatrāta) (Delhi, 1982).

Sakuma, H.S., Die Āśrayaparivṛtti-Theorie in der Yogācārabhūmi (Stuttgart, 1990) 2 vols. .

Samtani, N.H., "A Study of Aspects of Rāga," in R.K. Sharma (ed.), Researches in Indian and Buddhist Philosophy (Essays in Honor of Professor Alex Wayman) (Delhi, 1993).

Samtani, N.H., "On Some Buddhist Terms Beginning with Brahma," BHARATI (V.S. Agrawala Volume), Journal of Banaras Hindu University (Varanasi, 1971).

Samtani, N.H. and Prasad, H. (eds.), Amalā Prajñā: Aspects of Buddhist Studies (Professor P.V. Bapat Felicitation Volume) (Delhi, 1989).

Sangharakshita, A Survey of Buddhism (London, 1987).

Sangharakshita, The Three Jewels (London, 1967).

Shastri Shanti, Bhikshu (ed.), Pañcaskandha-prakaraṇa of Vasubandhu (Kelaniya, 1969).

Silva, L.D., Dīghanikāya-aṭṭhakathā-ṭikā (London, PTS, 1970).

Sparham, Gareth (tr.), The Tibetan Dhammapada (New Delhi, 1983).

Speyer, J. (ed.), Avadānaśataka (St. Petersburg, 1906–1909).

Stcherbatsky, T., The Conception of Buddhist Nirvāṇa (Leningrad, 1927).

Suzuki, D. T., Studies in the Laṅkāvatāra-sūtra (Boulder, 1981).

Suzuki, D.T., Outlines of Mahayana Buddhism (New York, 1967).

Thera, Nyanaponika, The Heart of Buddhist Meditation (A Handbook of Mental Training based on the Buddha's Way of Mindfulness) (London, 1969).

Thera, Piyadassi, Buddha's Ancient Path (London, 1964).

Tin, Daw Mya (tr.), Dhammapada: Verses and Stories (Reprinted with Introduction, several indices, and variant readings by N.H. Samtani) (Sarnath, 1990).

Tin, Pe Maung (tr.), Expositor (tr. of Aṭṭhasālinī) (PTS, London, 1920).

Tin, Pe Maung (tr.), The Path of Purity (Being a Translation of Buddhaghosa's Visuddhimagga) (London, 1971).

Thurman, R.A.F., Tsongkhapa's Speech of Gold in the Essence of True Eloquence (Princeton, 1984).

Tripathi, Chandrabhal, Funfundzwanzig Sūtras des Nidānasaṁyukta (Sanskrittexte aus den Turfanfunden) (Berlin, 1962).

Tulku, Lama Doboom (ed.), Buddhist Translations: Problems and Perspectives (New Delhi, 1995).

Vadekar, R. D. (ed.), Milindapañho (Bombay, 1940).

Vaidya, P.L., Mahāyāna-sūtra-Saṅgraha (Darbhanga, 1961) Vol. I.

Vipassana Research Institute, Mahāsatipaṭṭhāna-Sutta (Igatpuri, 1993).

Walpola Rahula, Le Compendium de la Super-Doctrine (Philosophie) (Abhidharmasamuccaya d'Asaṅga) (Paris, 1971).

Wayman, Alex and Hideko, Lion's Roar of Queen Śrīmālā (New York, 1974).

Winternitz, Maurice, History of Indian Literature (Delhi, 1977) Vol. I & II.

Woodward, F.L. (tr.), The Book of Gradual Sayings (Aṅguttara Nikāya) (London, 1982) Vol. II.

Woodward, F.L. (tr.), The Book of Kindred Sayings, (Saṁyutta Nikāya) (London and Oxford, 1956, 1990) Vols. IV–V.

Yamashita, Koichi, Pātañjala Yoga Philosophy with Reference to Buddhism (Calcutta, 1994).

Zaher, Leah (ed.), Meditative States in Tibetan Buddhism: The Concentrations and Formless Absorptions (London, 1983).

Zhechen Gyaltsab, Path of Heroes: Birth of Enlightenment (Berkeley, 1995).

Sanskrit-English Glossary

Entries are given in Sanskrit alphabetical order. Only principal page references are given; consult the index for additional references. Some Sanskrit terms in the glossary are not found in the translation, but have been provided on the basis of the original text.

Abbreviations: cm. = commented; def. = defined; ety. = etymology; en. = enumerated; exp. = explanation, explained; ot. = translations found in other published works; n. = note; x° = term note.

A

Akliṣṭa = free from defilement, 113

Adṛṣṭatattva = one who has not seen the truth, 58

Adharma = evil state, 113

Adhigama = attainment, 48; realization, 198

Adhicittaśikṣā = precepts concerning mind, 52

Adhiprajñāśikśā = precepts concerning wisdom, 52

Adhimukti = disposition, 191

Adhivacana = appellation, 85

Adhiśīlaśikṣā = precepts on morality, 52; training in morality, 185

Adhyātma = inner, 141°

Adhyātmasamprasāda = inward tranquility, 122°

Anabhisamskāra = lack of effort, 152; effortless, 194

Anavadya = blameless, 76

Anāgāmī = non-returner, 141, 182

Anābhoga = not inclined toward, 123°; mind not directed toward anything, 127°

Anāsrava = pure (ot. undefiled, cankerless)

Aniyatavedanīya karma = action of unfixed nature, 111

Anivṛta = undefiled, 80

Anukampaka = compassionate one, 220

Anuttara = transcendental, 180

Anudarśana = contemplation, 145

Anupaśyī = one who contemplates, 146° (ot. one who observes)

Anubandha = continuum, 191°

Anuloma = direct order

Anuvyañjana = minor mark (eighty, of the Buddha), en. 41ff.; cm. (last mark only), 218

Anuśaya = latent defilement, 118, 183 (ot. latent bias)

Anuśāsana = instruction, 177, 220

Anusandhi = logical connection, 45°, 47

Anusmṛti = recollection, 193; remembering well, 34

Antarāya = impediment, 77; obstruction, 198

Apakṣāla = fault, 124

Apavarga = beatitude, 177

Apavāda = denunciation, 46

Apratipatti = non-comprehension, 47

Apratisaṅkhyānirodha = cessation without wisdom, 66°

Apramāṇa(s) = immeasurables, boundless states, 49, 123

Apramoṣa = non-forgetfulness, 155

Abhijñā = intuition, 136°; higher knowledge, 152°

Abhinirvṛtti = rebirth, 102 (ot. reproduction)

Abhiniveśa = strong attachment, 102°

Abhiṣvaṅga = attachment, 91

Abhisamaya = realization, 108°, 174

Abhisandhi = intention, 92° (ot. purpose)

Abhisambodha = enlightenment, 159°; comprehension, 197°

Ayoniśo manaskāra = improper attention, 69°, 189° (ot. not systematic attention, disorderly attention)

Araṇa = without defilement, 51

Arati = discontent, 132°

Artha = category, subject matter, 55°; topic, 47; reality, 179°; object, 180

Arthaviniścaya = Compendium of Categories, investigation into dharmas, 46, 53°, 54°

Arhat = perfect one, 174 (ot. holy one)
Avakrānti = descent into womb, 102
Avabodha = knowledge, 118 (ot. understanding)
Avarabhāgīya = (belonging to) lower, 182
Avavāda = admonition, 220
Avijñapti = non-communicated state, 165°
Avijñapti rūpa = unmanifested form, 56°
Avidyā = ignorance, exp. 7, cm. 72 (ot. nescience)
Avetyaprasāda = faith based on comprehension, 173°, cm. 174
Avyākṛta = neutral, 80; indeterminate, 60
Avyāhata-jñāna = unobstructed (ot. unhindered) knowledge, 192
Aśubha = repulsiveness, 132 (ot. loathsome)
Aśaikṣa = one who no longer needs training, 112n.; adept, 180
Asaṁskṛta = unconditioned, 189
Asapatnam = free from jealousy, 131
Asamprajanya = lack of clearness, 157
Ahaṁkāra = idea of self, 66 (ot. I-making, self-conceit)
Ahita = harm, 195
Ahetuvāda = theory of non-causation, 190n.

Ā

Ākālika = timeless, 33, cm. 178
Ākiñcanyātana = state of nothingness, 15, 127
Ātāpi = ardent, 21, cm. 145
Ātmagraha = falsely taking aggregate of consciousness to be the 'self', 58
Ātmābhāva = personality, 70; individuality, 101; obtaining one's own individual being, 102
Ātmavādins = those who maintain the theory (of existence) of self, 65
Ātmavādopādāna = clinging to belief in the existence of self, 94n.
Ātmā = self, 58
Ādhyātmika = personal, 65
Ānāpāna = breathing in and breathing out, cm.169; ~smṛti = mindfulness of breathing in and breathing out, 169
Āniñjakarma = action without karmic consequence, 190n.
Āniñjya = imperturbable, 80n.
Ābhiprāyika = intentional, 70
Āyatana = sense fields (twelve), en. 6, cm. 65ff.

Ārāma = park, 49

Ārūpya-dhatu = formless realm, 127

Ārūpya-samāpatti = formless attainment, 126ff.

Āryakānta = dear to Noble Ones, 185, 219

Āryasatya = Noble Truth, 13, 107 cm.

Ālambana = object, 62; base, 72

Āvaraṇa = (lit.) covering, hindrance, 146; obstruction, 112

Āveṇika (dharma) = special dharmas, 48n.

Āvenika Buddha-dharma(s) = special dharmas of the Buddha, 37, cm. 203ff.

Āśaya = intention, 166, 195; mental disposition, 71

Āśraya = basis of personal existence, 64°; personality, 166

Āśvāsa-praśvāsa = breathing in and breathing out, 79

Āsrava = outflows, 49, 56, def. 114, 194° (ot. cankers, intoxicants)

Āryāṣṭāṅga-mārga = Noble Eightfold Path, 26ff., cm. 165ff.

Āveṇika = special, unmixed, cm. 203°

I

Indriya = faculty, (twenty-two), en. 14, cm.115ff.; (five) en. 4, exp. 24, cm.154 (ot. controlling faculty)

U

Udghaṭitajña = who understand through brief explanation, 209

Uddeśa = list (of topics), 4, 40, 45°, 107 (ot. outline, program)

Upakleśa = secondary defilement, sub-defilement, 46°, 150n.

Upadeśa = exposition, 180 (ot. sermon, teaching)

Upadhi = attachment, 113

Upapatti = coming into existence, 102

Upaśleṣa = adherence, 131° (ot. contagious, contagion)

Upādāna = kleśa = defilement, clinging, 58, ety. 93

Upādāna-skandha = aggregate of clinging 3, cm. 58

Upāya = means, 147

Upāyāsa = despair, 70°

Upekṣā = equanimity, 132, 133°

Ṛ

ṛddhi = psychic power, cm. 152°

ṛddhipāda = basis of psychic power, 23, 151ff.

E

Ekotībhāva = absorbed in a single object (of mind), 122°

AI

Aihipaśyika = come and see (the Dharma) 179°

AU

Auddhatya = excitement, 146 (ot. flurry)

K

Karuṇā = compassion, 16, exp. 132
Kalyāṇa = virtuous, 3, 155 (ot. auspicious, good)
Kalyāṇamitra = spiritual guide, 169° (ot. spiritual friend, virtuous advisor)
Kāmabhava = realm of sense desires, exp. 10, cm. 96, 100
Kāmarāga = attachment to sense desire, 132; sensual lust, 140
Kāya = body, collection, 146; class, 82 (ot. group)
Kāya-viveka = bodily detachment, 220
Kāya-vyapakṛṣta = withdrawn in physical person, 139°
Kudṛṣṭi = wrong view, 186°
Kuśala = wholesome, 76, 216 (ot. skillful, good)
Kuśalamūla = roots of merit, 177
Kuśalamūla karma = roots of wholesome actions, 216
Kṛpā = compassion. See mahākṛpā
Kevalam = sole (course not found among outsiders), 52
Kaukṛtya = remorse, 146 (ot. restlessness, worry)
Kausīdya = indolence, 157
Kleśopakleśa = major and secondary defilements, 182
Kṣema = security, 76
Kṣobha = disturbance, 122 (ot. agitation)

G

Gati =destiny, 92 (ot. place, rebirth)

C

Citta = consciousness, 112; mind, 191
Cittakarmaṇyatā = lightness of mind, 122
Cittaviveka = mental detachment, 220
Cittasantati = mind continuum, 91, 93

Cittaikāgratā = concentration of mind, 153
Cintana = reflection, 121
Cintā = reflection, 146
Cetanā = volition, 8, 78n., 152
Caitasika = mental state, 92°
Caitta = mental factor, 57, 192

CH

Chanda = desire, 149°; zeal, 152

J

Janma = birth, 102
Jarā = decay, exp. 12, cm. 104 (ot. old age, aging)
Jñānadarśana = knowledge and wisdom, cm. 142
Jñānasampadā = achievement of knowledge, 175

T

Tattva = truth
Tathatā, tathātva = suchness of phenomena, 179°
Tathāgata = (epithet of) Buddha, 33, 175°
Tṛṣṇā = craving, 91 (ot. thirst)
Triśaraṇa = triple refuge, 77

D

Darśana = vision, 104, 112, 142°; insight, 93, 94
Darśana-bhāvanā-heya = abandoned by insight and meditation, 77
Darśana-mārga = path of vision, 112, 181
Duḥkha = suffering (Noble Truth) exp. 13, cm. 107ff.
Duḥkha-duḥkhatā = suffering as suffering, 109
Dṛṣṭa-dharma = (in) this very life, 116, cm. 140
Dṛṣṭa-satya = one who has realized the truth, 149
Deśanā-dharma = Dharma that is taught, 201
Daurmanasya = mental pain, 124 (ot. sadness, grief)
Dravya = entity, 191
Dveṣa = ill will, 79 (ot. hatred)

DH

Dhandha = sluggish, 136

Dharma = Sūtra in the form of discourse, 51 (many other meanings)

Dharma-dhātu = element of object of mind, 63°, 66°

Dharma-paryāya = Dharma discourse, 53°

Dharmapravicaya = investigation into dharmas, 46°, 159°, 193

Dharmānudharma-pratipanna = on (the path of) dharma in all its aspects, 181°

Dhātu = element, 5, 60°, 191; realm, 92

Dhyāna = meditation, 121° (ot. absorption, meditative absorption, contemplation, musing)

Dhyānāntara = intermediate dhyāna, 118°, 119

N

Nandīrāga = pleasure and lust, 110

Narottama = best among men (Buddha's epithet), 214

Nānātvasaṁjñā = perception of multiplicity, 204

Nāma = name (formless), cm. 85

Niḥśreyas = final beatitude, 221°

Niḥsaraṇa = escape, 75; release, 127

Nikāyasabhāgatā = sameness of being, 106

Nidāna = origin, 109 (ot. cause, introduction)

Nibandhana = commentary, 220°

Nimitta = sign, 59

Nirukti = language, 201° (ot. etymology)

Nirupadhi = absence of any clinging or attachment, 113

Nirodha = cessation, 71, 108, cm. 112, 153 (ot. destruction, extinction)

Nirodha-samāpatti = attainment of cessation, 171°

Nirjvara = free from fever (of latent defilements), 33, cm. 178

Nirdeśa = exposition, 145, 170

Nirmala = immaculate, 76

Niryāṇa(1) = 'going forth' 160; complete release, 179

Niryāṇa(2) = way out (of saṁsāra), 196, 198°

Nirvacana = explanation, 102°

Nirvāṇa = Cessation of suffering (duḥka-nirodha). No translation can be wholly adequate. The term is exp. 113 and cm. 112–13, 180

Nirvṛtti = birth, coming out of the mother's womb, 102°

Nirvedhabhāgīya = pertaining to penetration, 112n.

Nivṛtti = withdrawal, 71; cessation, 76–77
Nairyāṇikatā = going forth, 180°
Naiṣkramya = renunciation, 50
Nyāya = ultimate truth, 51; nirvāṇa, 180 (ot. right path)
Nyāyapratipanna = progressing towards nirvāṇa, 180

P

Paramārthajñāna = knowledge of ultimately real categories, 201
Pariccheda = distinguishing (of signs), 59
Paribheda = disintegration, 104
Paryavadāta = pure, 52
Paryavasthāna = outburst of defilement, 93°
Paryāya = synonym, 72, 77
Pāpa = evil, 149
Pāpaka = sinful, 155
Puṇyajñāna-sambhāra = equipment of merit and knowledge, 212
Pudgala = individual, 159°
Puruṣapudgala = individuals, 182°
Pṛthagjanatā = being a worldling (bound to the things of this world), 176
Pragraha = exertion, 171
Prajñā = wisdom, exp. 2,. exp. 156; insight, 139
Praṇidhāna = vow, 186° (ot. earnest resolve)
Pratigha = hatred, 93 (ot. counteract, cure)
Pratighasaṁsparśa = encounter, contact, 89
Pratighasaṁjñā = perception of resistance, 127°
Pratipakṣa = antidote, 121, 185
Pratipati = comprehension, 47; practice, 220n.
Pratipatti dharma = Dharma to be practiced, 201°
Pratipad = course, 17, 136, ety. 192; path, 114, 192
Pratibandha = fetter, 171°
Pratibhāna = ready exposition, 201° (ot. eloquence)
Pratiloma = reverse order, 71
Prativedha = deep understanding, 71°
Pratisaṁkhyānirodha = cessation through wisdom, 66°
Pratisaṁkhyāna-bala = power of careful consideration, 185°
Pratisandhi = conception, 84

Pratisaṁvid = special knowledge, 201°

Pratītyasamutpāda = Conditioned co-production, exp. 6ff., cm. 66ff. (ot. dependent origination, conditioned origination, dependent arising)

Pratyakṣavṛtti = experienced (lit., seen) directly, 204°

Pratyaya = condition, 81; means, 185 (ot. cause, relation)

Pratyekabuddha = Buddha by himself, 159°

Pradhānāni = (plural of pradhāna) efforts, 149

Pravṛtti = activity of life, 77; constant activity, 91; worldly activity, 68

Praśama = quietude, 171

Prasaṅga= occasion, 91

Prasāda (1) faith, serenity of mind, 155°

Prasāda (2) sensitiveness, 63°

Prasrabdhi (vl. praśrabdhi) = tranquility, 76, 122, 152, 170°; rapture, 25, cm. 160 (ot. repose, calmness)

Prahāṇa = abandonment, 198

Prahāṇasampad = achievement of abandonment, 175

Prātimokṣa = code of moral conduct, 219n.

Prīti = rapture, 121

B

Bala = Power (five), en. 25, cm. 157; (ten) of Tathāgata exp. 34, cm. 188ff.

Bāhuśrutya = vast (learning), 48

Bodhi = enlightenment, 150° (ot. awakening)

Bodhipakṣya dharmas = factors that are an aid to gaining bodhi (ot. helpful to awakening; wings to awakening)

Bodhyaṅga = constituent of enlightenment, 159

Brahmacarya = highest path, cm. 52° (ot. highest spiritual life)

Brahmasvara = sublime voice, 214

Brahmībhūta = being at the highest stage, 52

Brāhmavihāra(s) = sublime state(s), 15, 130°

BH

Bhagavān = Blessed One, 47; Lord, 50

Bhava = becoming, process of coming to be, 96°, cm. 100 (ot. existence)

Bhāvanā = meditation, 75, 93, 147, 170

Bhāvāgrika = last stage of worldly existence (in ārūpyadhātu), 182

Bhāvanābala = power of meditation, 185°

Bhāvanāmārga = path of meditation, 112

Bhāvāgrika = last stage of worldly existence (in ārūpyadhātu), 182

Bhujiṣya = leading to freedom, 185°

Bhūmi = stage, 92

M

Mati = thought, 170

Manaskāra = thought, 150

Manmatha-śāsana = tamer (of embodiment) of passionate desires (Cupid), 221°

Mahākṛpā = great compassion, 210°, 220

Mahāpuruṣa = Great Personage, 37, cm. 210

Mahābhūta = great (primary) elements, 86

Mārga = path 108 (ot. way)

Māhātmya = glory, 46 (ot. majesty)

Mīmāṁsā = investigation, 153 (ot. exploration)

Muditā = sympathetic joy, 16

Maitrī = loving kindness 130 (ot. friendliness)

Moha = infatuation (ot. delusion)

Y

Yathābhūtam = truly, 108 (ot. in reality)

Yukti = reasoning, 80; rational basis, 117 (ot. appropriate argument)

Yoniśo manasikāra (in verbal formation) = paying proper attention, 189 (ot. systematic attention)

R

Rasarasāgratā = exquisite sense of taste, 214n.

Rāga = lust, 94°; attachment, 110; passion, 153 (ot. greed)

L

Lakṣaṇa(s) = mark(s), 209

Laya = sluggishness, 149°, 150

Lākṣaṇika = definitive, 70

Laukīkavītarāga = worldlings free from lust, 194°

V

Vacana = scriptures, 60

Vastu = entity, 146, 153; objective entity, 69; thing, 191

Vāsanā = infusion, 69; perfuming impression, 192 (ot. residue, trace)

Vikṣepa = distraction, 157

Vicāra = investigation, 79°; sustained thought, 121° (ot. discursive thought)

Vicikitsā = doubt, 116

Vijña = wise, 179

Vijñāna = consciousness, 5, 6, cm. 60

Vijñānakāya = class of consciousness, 123

Vijñānasthiti(s) = abode(s) of consciousness, 111°

Vitarka = initial application of mind, 79°; initial thought, 121° (ot. applied thought)

Vidyācaraṇa-sampanna = endowed with knowledge and right conduct, 33, cm. 175

Viniścyajñāna = knowledge through discernment, 189

Vineya = trainee, 53

Vipakṣa = opponent, 193; opposite states, 77 (ot. hostile)

Vipañcitajña = who comprehend through detailed explanation, 209°

Vipariṇāma = change, 109 (ot. transformation)

Vipariṇāmaduḥkhatā = suffering produced by change, 109n.

Viparyāsa = perversion, 145n. (ot. perverted view)

Vipaśyanā = insight, 136 (ot. inward vision, wisdom)

Vipāka = result of karma, 155, 191 (ot. fruition)

Viprayukta (dharma) = unassociated (category), 85; (saṁskāra) = unassociated karma formations, 57°

Vibhaṅga = analysis, classification, 82°

Virāga = removal of attachment, 112 (ot. dispassion, detachment)

Vivikta = to be detached, 127°; aloof, 121°

Viveka = aloofness, 121°; detachment, 127°, cm., ety. 153

Viśārada = self-confident, 197°

Viśuddhi = purity, immaculateness, 193

Viṣamahetuvāda = mistaken causal theory, 190

Visaṁyoga = disjunction, 192°

Vihiṁsā = cruelty, 132° (ot. violence, hurting)

Vītarāga = free from attachment, 116n.; free from lust, 194°

Vīrya = energy, cm. 117

Vṛtti = commentary, cm. 47

Vedanā = feeling, 56, 116n. (ot. sensation)

Vaiśāradya = fearlessness, self-confidence, 197°

Vyavasarga = renunciation, cm., ety. 153

Vyavasthāna = exact distinction, 193°

Vyāpāda = malice, 132

Vyutthita = arising from meditation (samādhi), 186

Vyupaśama = quietude, 112; quiescence, 121

Vrata = religious observance, 94 (ot. rite, vow)

Ś

Śakti = power, 189

Śamatha = calm, 136; mental calm, 150

Śastā = teacher, 177, cm. 220

Śīla = moral conduct, moral virtues, 185, 186; morality, 94; virtuous conduct, 183

Śūnyatā = emptiness, 193 (ot. void)

Śūnyatā-samādhi = oncentration on emptiness, 193

Śaikṣa = to be trained, 180° (ot. trainee)

Śrāmaṇya = entry into religious life, 180° (ot. life of recluse, religious life)

Śrāmaṇya-phala = fruit of religious life, 177

Śrāvaka = disciple (lit., 'hearer') (of the Buddha), 159°, 220°

Śrūtasampanna = endowed with learning, 183

S

Saṁvara = pure restraint, 186

Saṁvedanā = experiencing, 170° (ot. being aware of)

Saṁsāra = world of transmigration, 155°; ety. what imparts movement, 70 (ot. world)

Saṁskāra = karma formations, 57°, 60 (ot. habitual tendencies)

Saṁskāra-duḥkhatī = suffering born of conditioned things, 109

Saṁskāropekṣā = equanimity of conditioned states, 123

Saṁskṛta = conditioned, 189 (ot. composite, compounded)

Sakṛdāgāmi = Once-returner, 181

Saṁkṣiptaruci = penchant for brevity, 209°

Saṁkleśa = defilement, 193

Saṁkliṣṭa = soiled, 60

Saṅgha = Assembly, cm. 183 (ot. Order, Community)

Saṁjñā = perception, cm. 57

Satkāyadṛṣṭi = belief in the permanent existence of individuality, 186°

Sattva = being, 59

Saddharma = true Dharma, 220

Santati, see citta-santati

Santāna = lineage, 52; continuous consciousness, 64°, 73n; continuity, 102,103; stream of personality 136, 185; continuity of stream, 180

Samavāya = togetherness, 68; meeting, 89

Samādhi = concentration, 18ff., 153 (ot. contemplation, meditation)

Samādhi-bhāvanā = cultivation of concentration, exp.18ff., cm.139ff.

Samāpatti = meditation, 121°; meditative attainment, 112, 113; higher meditation, 127°

Samāpanna = meditating person, yogi, 56, 165° (ot. entered into meditation)

Samāropa = superimposition, 46° (ot. imputation)

Samāhita = collected 76; concentrated, 121n., 204

Samudaya = arising, 109

Sampad = accomplishment, 198

Samprajanya = clear awareness, 123°

Sampratyaya = conviction, 174

Samprasāda = tranquility, 122°

Sambhāra = equipment, 77

Sammoha = intense delusion, 8; confusion, 70 (ot. infatuation)

Samyakprahāṇa = right effort, 148°

Samyaksambuddha = Fully Awakened One, 108; Rightly and Fully Awakened One, cm. 174°; Perfectly Awakened One, 159

Sarvajñatā = omniscience, 190

Savitarka, savicara = with initial and sustained thought, 121°

Sāndṛṣṭika = realized in this very life, 178°

Sāmantaka = border (dhyāna), 171°

Sāvadya = blameworthy, 76

Sāsrava = full of outflows, 76°; impure, 109°

Siṁhanāda = lion's roar (used in connection with Buddha), 197

Sukha = joy, 121°, 122n.; happiness, 170°

Sukhavihāra = living happily, 116

Supratipanna = well established in practice, 180°

Sūtra (1) = aphorism, 47°

Sūtra (2) = discourse on Dharma (by Buddha), 3, 54°

Sūtraśarīra = framework of Sutra, exp. 45

Skandha = aggregate, 5, 56, cm. 60, 106

Sthāna = possible, 189°

Smṛti = mindfulness, 14, cm. 155

Smṛtyupasthāna = foundation of mindfulness, exp. 21, cm. 145ff.

Srota āpatti = attaining the stream, 32, 173n.

Srota āpanna = stream winner, cm. 181n.

Svabhāva = innate nature, 79

Svasantati = one's own stream of consciousness, 146

Svasāmānya = unique and general (characteristics), cm. 147

H

Hetu = cause, 108, 190 (ot. reason, motive)

English-Sanskrit Glossary

This glossary is intended as an aid for readers who would like to know the Sanskrit for terms used in the translation. Only principal page references are given; consult the index for additional references.

Abbreviations: cm. = commented; def. = defined; ety. = etymology; en. = enumerated; exp. = explanation, explained; n. = note; x° = term note; vl = variant reading.

Abandonment = prahāṇa, 198

Abode of consciousness = vijñānasthiti, 110

Absolute and infallible knowledge = asaṅgāpratihata-jñāna, cm. 204

Absorbed in single object = ekotībhāva, 122

Abusive appellation = sañcodana, 203

Action without karmic consequence = āniñja karma, 190n.

Activity of life = pravṛtti, 77

Adept = aśaikṣa, 180, 183. An Arhat is called aśaikṣa because he requires no further training.

Admonition = avavāda, 220

Aggregates (five) = skandha(s), 4, en. 5, cm. 56ff.

Aggregates of clinging (five) = upādāna skandhas, 4, en. 5, cm. 58ff.

Aloofness = viveka, 121°

Antidote = pratipakṣa, 121, 185

Application of energy = vīryaprayoga, 149

Ardent = ātāpi, cm. 145

Arising from meditation = vyutthita, 186

Assembly = Saṅgha, gaṇa, cm. 183
Attachment = abhiṣvaṅga, 91; rāga, 110; upadhi, 113
Attainment of cessation = nirodha-samāpatti, 171°
Avoidance of unwholesome thoughts = akuśala-vitarka-vivarjana, 220

B

Bases of psychic power (four) = ṛddhipāda(s), exp. 23, cm. 152ff.
Basis of personality = āśraya, 64°
Beatitude = apavarga, 177
Becoming, process of coming to be = bhava, 96°, cm. 100
Belief in permanent existence of individuality = satkāyadṛṣṭi, 186°
Believers in existence of self = ātmavādins, 65
Belonging to self = ātmīya, 58
Best among men (adj. of Buddha) = narottama, 214
Bestowing fearlessness = abhayadāna, 213
Beyond logical reasoning (dharma) =atarkyatvāt, 179° (and endnote)
Blameless = anavadya, 76
Blessed One = Bhagavān, 48, ety. exp. 49, 174
Breathing in and out = ānāpāna, cm. 169
Buddha by himself = Pratyekabuddha, 159°

C

Calm = śamatha, 136, 150
Capable = bhavya, 176
Category = artha, 55
Cause = hetu, 108, 190
Cessation = nirodha, 71, 112; nivṛtti, 76–77
Class of consciousness = vijñānakāya, 123
Classification = vibhaṅga, 82°
Clear awareness = samprajanya, 123°
Clinging = upādāna, 5; kleśa, cm. 58
Clinging to the belief in existence of self = ātmavadopādāna 94n.
Collected, see concentrated
Commentary = vṛtti, 47; nibandhana, 220°
Compassion = karuṇā, 16, exp. 132; kṛpā with prefix
mahā (great), 210°, 220
Compassionate One = anukampaka, 220

Compendium of categories = Arthaviniścaya (Sūtra), 4, 53, 54°
Complete release = niryāṇa, 179
Comprehension = abhisambodha, 197°; pratipatti, 47
Concentrated = samāhita, 121n., 204; collected = samāhita, 76
Concentration = samādhi, exp. 32, 123°, 138, 153, 155; ekāgratā, 153
Concentration of investigation = mīmāṁsā samādhi, 153°
Conception (in womb) = pratisandhi, 84
Condition = pratyaya, 81
Conditioned = saṁskṛta, 189
Conditioned coproduction = pratītyasamutpāda, 4, 6ff., cm. 66ff.
Confusion = sammoha, 70
Consciousness = citta 112, 192; vijñāna, 5, 57
Consequent action = pṛṣṭha-karmapatha, 198n.
Constituent of enlightenment =bodhyaṅga, en., cm. 25, 159ff.
Constituent of attaining the stream = srota āpattyaṅga, 25ff., 173°ff.
Contemplation = anudarśana, 145
Contemplator (one who contemplates) = anupaśyī, 146
Continuity of consciousness = santāna, 64°
Councils of Dharma = dharma-saṅgīti, 40, 208°
Course (of meditation) = pratipad, 17ff., cm. 136ff.
Craving = tṛṣṇā, 6, 91ff., 92n.
Cruelty = vihiṁsā, 132°
Cultivation of concentration = samādhi-bhāvanā, 138ff.

D

Deep understanding = prativedha, 71°
Defilement (latent) = anuśaya, 118, 183
Defilement = kleśa, 69; saṁkleśa, 193
Definitive = lākṣaṇika, 70
Deliverance of mind = cetovimukti, exp. 194
Delusion = sammoha, 102
Denunciation = apavāda, 46
Descent into womb = avakrānti, 102
Desire = chanda, 149°; prārthayate, 110°
Destiny = gati, 92
Detachment = viveka, 127°

Dharma discourse = dharmaparyāya, 3, 53°
Dharma to be practiced = pratipatti-dharma, 201°
Dharmas acting as aid to enlightenment = bodhipakṣya dharmas, 75°
Direct experience = pratyakṣavṛtti, 204°
Direct order = anuloma, 71
Discernment = viniścaya, 156°
Disciple = śrāvaka (lit. hearer), 159°, 180°; śisya, 199
Discontent = arati 132°
Discourse on Dharma = deśanā (dharma), 51, 201; dharmaparyāya, 53°; Sūtra, 54°
Disintegration = paribheda, 104
Disjunction = visaṁyoga, 192°
Dispassion = virāga, 23, cm. 153
Disposition = adhimukti, 191°
Distinguishing (of signs) = pariccheda, 59
Distraction = vikṣepa, 157
Distress = daurmanasya, 116°; vyasana, 133
Disturbance = kṣobha, 122

E

Effort = pradhānāni (plural), (singular, pradhāna), 149 (vl. prahāṇa)
Element = dhātu, 5, 60°, 191
Eloquence, see ready exposition
Encounter = pratigha, 89 (see also resistance)
Endowed with knowledge and right conduct = vidyācaraṇa-sampanna, 175°
Enlightenment = bodhi, 159°; abhisambodha, 159°
Enthusiastic determination = abhyutsāha, 155°
Entity = dravya, 110, 191; vastu, 146, 153
Equipment (as an aid to enlightenment) = sambhāra, 77
Established norm = siddhānta, 121
Evenly luminous (mind) = samaprabhāsa (citta), 20, 143n.
Evil = pāpa, 149
Evil state = adharma, 113
Excitement = auddhatya, 146
Exertion = pragraha, 171
Experiencing directly, see direct experience

Explanation = nirvacana, 102°

Exposition = nirdeśa, 45°, 170; upadeśa, 180°

Extremely hateful (person) = tīvra-dveṣa, cm. 17, 136

Extremely infatuated (person) = tīvra-moha, 17, cm. 136

Extremely lustful (person) = tīvra-raga, 17, cm. 136, cm. 200

F

Faculty/faculties (twenty-two and five) = indriya(s),14,24, cm.115ff., cm. 155

Faculty of knowing what is unknown = anājñātam ānjñāsyāmīndriya, 14, cm. 116

Faculty of mind = mana indriya, 14, 115

Faculty of one whose knowledge has been perfected = ājñātāvīndriya, cm. 116

Faculty of perfect knowledge = ājñendriya, 14, cm. 116

Faith = prasada, 155°; śraddhā, 149

Faith based on comprehension = avetyaprasāda, 173°

Fault = apakṣāla, 124

Fearlessness = vaiśāradya, 197°

Feeling = vedanā, 56, exp. 10, cm. 89ff.; anubhava, 79

Fetter = pratibandha, 171

Final attainment = samudāgama, 195°

Firmly maintains = pratijānīte = 197°

Fitting and unhindered expression = yuktamuktābhilāpitā, 201°

Forest haunt(s) = araṇyāyatana , 219

Formless (meditative) attainment = ārūpya samāpatti(s), 15, cm. 126ff.

Formless (skandhas) = nāma, 85

Foundation of mindfulness = smṛtyupasthāna, 144ff.

Framework of a Sūtra = sūtra-śarīra, exp. 45–47

Free from error = aviparīta, 178°

Fruit of reclusive life = śrāmaṇya-phala, 177

Future = anutpanna, 150°

G

Going forth = niryāṇa, 160; nairyāṇikatā, 180°

Great (primary) elements = mahābhūta, 86

Great Personage = mahāpuruṣa, 37, exp. 210

Grounds of self-confidence = vaiśāradya(s) (four), exp. 35ff. 196ff., 197°

H

Hatred = pratigha, 93

Heavenly eye = divya-cakṣu, exp. 193

Hell = naraka, ety. 96n.; niraya, 29

Higher knowledge = abhijñā, 152°

Higher meditation = samāpatti, 15, 127°

Hindrance = āvaraṇa (lit., covering), 146

I

Immeasurable = apramāṇa, 123

Immaculateness of mind = cetaso nairmalyaṁ, 194

Immediate succeeding meditation = ānantarya samādhi, 137°

Immorality = dauśīlya, 186

Impediment = antarāya, 198

Imperturbable = āniñjya, 80n.

Improper attention = ayoniśo manaskāra, 69°, 189°

In accord with Dharma = saha dharmeṇa, 35, 196°

Inauthentic intention = kṛtrimāśaya, 40, 208

Individual = pudgala, 159°; individuals = puruṣa-pudgala(s), 182

Individual body = satkāya, cm. 192°

Individuality = ātmabhāva, 101

Indolence = kausīdya, 157

Inestimable merit = apramāṇapuṇya, 40, 207°

Infatuation = moha, 79

Infusion = vāsanā, 69

Initial application of mind = vitarka, 79°

Initial thought = vitarka, 14, 121°, 124

Innate nature = svabhāva, 79

Inner = adhyātma, 141°

Insight = vipaśyana, 136; darśana, 93, 94

Instruction = anuśāsana, 177, 220

Intention = abhisandhi, 92°

Intermediate dhyāna = dhyānāntara, 118°, 119

Intuition = abhijñā, 136°

Investigation into dharmas = dharma-pravicaya, 25, 46°, 159° (meaning of AVS)

Inward tranquility = adhyātma-samprasāda (of citta), 122°
Isolated = vivicyate, 153

K

Karma formations = saṁskāra, 57°, 59
Knowledge = avabodha, 118°; bodha, 198°; jñāna, 49, 142, 254°
Knowledge and vision = jñānadarśana, 142
Knowledge of specific nature of karma = karma-svakajñāna, 195°

L

Lack of effort = anabhisaṁskāra, 152°
Loss of mindfulness = muṣitasmṛtitā, 204°
Lightness of mind = cittakarmaṇyatā, 122
Lion's roar (of Buddha) = siṁhanāda, 35, 36
List of topics = uddeśa, 4, 40, 45°, 107
Living happily = sukhavihāra, 116°
Lofty = mahadgata, 131°
Logical connection = anusandhi, 45°, 47
Lord = Bhagavān, 50°
Loss of awareness = muṣitasmṛti, 157
Loving kindness = maitrī, 130
Lust = rāga, 94°

M

Major and secondary defilements = kleśopakleśa, 203
Makes a vow = cittam praṇidadhāti, 150°
Malice = vyāpāda, 132
Mark(s) = lakṣaṇa, 209
Mark of Great Personage = Mahāpuruṣalakṣaṇa, 205ff., 210°
Means = pratyaya, 185
Meditating person = samāpanna, yogi, 56, 165°
Meditation = dhyāna, ety. exp. 121°; bhāvanā, 75, 93, 120ff.
Meditative attainment = samāpatti, 112–13, 121°, 127°
Mental calm, see calm
Mental disposition = āśaya, 166°; adhimukti, 191
Mental pain = daurmanasya, 14, 116°, 124
Mental power = bala, 157n.

Mental state/factor = cetasika, 92°; caitta, 57, 192
Meritorious action = puṇya, 216°
Mind = citta, 22, 64, 147n,; manas, 14, 115; manodhātu, 4, 63
Mind absorbed in a single object = cetasa ekotībhāva, 14, 122°
Mind continuum = cittasantati, 91, 93
Mindfulness of breathing in and breathing out = ānāpānasmṛti, 169ff.
Minor mark (of the Buddha) = anuvyañjana, 41, 217ff.
Miraculous power = adhiṣṭhāna, 211°
Mistaken causal theory = viṣamahetuvāda, 190
Moral conduct = śīla, 185;
Moral practices dear to Noble Ones = āryakānta śīla, 219
Morality = śīla, 94
Most perfect (Dharma) = paripūrṇa, 3, cm. 52

N

Neutral (indeterminate) = avyākṛta, 80
Noble Eightfold Path = āryāṣṭāṇga mārga, 26, 161ff.
Noble One = Ārya, ety. 123
Noble Truth = āryasatya, cm. 13, 107ff.
Noble wisdom = yaprajñā, 194
Non-communicated state = avijñapti, 165°
Non-forgetfulness = apramoṣa, 155°
Not being overpowered = anavamṛdyatā, 199°
Not inclined or directed towards = anābhoga, 123°, 127°

O

Object = ālambana, 62; artha, 180
Obstruction = āvaraṇa 112
Occasion = prasaṅga, 91
Old age, see decay
On the path of Dharma in all aspects = dharmānudharma-pratipanna, 181°
One comprehending through detailed explanation = vipañcitajña, 209°
One who wishes for the welfare of (all) other beings = parahitaiṣī, 221°
Origin = nidāna, 109
Outburst of defilement = paryavasthāna, 93°
Outflows = āsrava, 56, 194°
Outline = uddeśa, 45°

P

Passion = rāga, 79, cm. 153°

Path = mārga, pratipad, 114°, 192

Path of meditation = bhāvanā-mārga, 112, 181

Penetration = prativedha, 139; anupraveśa, 201°

Perception = saṁjñā, cm. 59, cm. 85

Perception of multiplicity = nānātvasaṁjñā, 204°

Perception of resistance = pratighasaṁjñā, 127°

Perfuming impression = vāsanā, 192°

Person having penchant for brevity = saṁkṣiptaruci, 209°

Person in meditation = samāpanna, 165°

Personality = ātmabhavā, 166°

Personality (or frame) = ātmabhavā, 70, 166

Perversion = viparyāsa, 145n.

Perverted mind = viparyasta-citta, 146

Pleasure and lust = nandīrāga, 110

Possible and impossible = sthāna and asthāna, 189°

Power of careful consideration = pratisaṁkhyāna-bala, 185°

Power of mindfulness = smṛtibala, 159n.

Powers (five) = bala(s) (pañca), 157 ff; (ten = daśa), 188ff.

Practice = pratipatti, 220n.

Practice free from delusion = asammohakriyā, 172

Practicing according to Dharma = anudharmacārī, 181°

Precepts concerning mind = adhicittaśikṣā, 52

Precepts concerning morality = adhiśīlaśikṣā, 52

Precepts concerning wisdom = adhiprajñāśikṣā, 52

Present = pratyutpanna, 150

Process of coming to be, see becoming

Progress toward nirvāṇa = nyāyapratipanna, 180°

Proper attention = yoniśo manaskāra; see also improper attention

Psychic power = ṛddhi, exp. 152

Pure = anāsrava, 52

Q

Quietude = vyupaśama, cm. 112; praśama, 171

R

Radiates = sphurati, 143°

Rapture = prīti, 121°

Rational basis = yukti, 117

Ready exposition = pratibhāna, 201°

Realization = abhisamaya, 108°, 174; adhigama, 198

Realized in this very life = sāndṛṣṭika, 178°

Reality = artha, 179°; = yathābhūta, 155n.

Realm = dhātu, 92

Reasoning = yukti, 80

Religious life (i.e., life of a recluse) = śrāmaṇya, 180°

Remorse = kaukṛtya, 146°

Renunciation = naiṣkramya, 50; vyavasarga, 153

Repeated (meditational) practice = abhyāsāhita, 221°

Repulsiveness = aśubha, 132°

Resistance = pratigha, 127°; see also encounter

Restraint = saṁvara, 186n.

Reverse order = pratiloma, 71

Right effort = cm. samyakprahāṇa, cm. 148 ff.; vl. samyakpradhāna, 149°

Right instruction = yathārthānuśāsana, 177°

Right mindfulness = samyaksmṛti, 164 n.

Right thought = samyaksaṁkalpa, 26, 161°

Rightly acts = samyag vidhatte, 195

Rightly and fully Awakened One = samyaksambuddha, 33, cm. 174°

Roots of merit = kuśalamūla, 177

Roots of wholesome (actions) = kuśalamūla, 216

S

Scriptures = vacana, 60

Seclusion = viveka, exp. 141

Secluded uninhabited and sheltered place = śūnyāgāra, 219

Secondary (or sub-) defilement = upakleśa 46°, 150n., 182

Self = ātmā, 58

Self-confidence = vaiśāradya, 197°

Self-confident = viśārada, 197°

Sensation, see feeling

Sense fields (twelve) = āyatana(s), en. 6, cm. 65ff.

Sensual lust = kāmarāga, 140°

Serentiy = prasāda, 155°

Sharp wisdom = tīkṣṇa prajñā, 136°

Sign = nimitta, 59

Sinful = pāpaka, 155

Sluggishness = laya, 149°

Special (extraordinary) = āveṇika, 48 n., 203°

Special dharmas of the Buddha = āveṇika buddha dharma(s), 202ff., 203°

Special knowledge = pratisaṁvid, 200ff., 201°

Spiritual guide = kalyāṇamitra, 169°

Stage = bhūmi, 92

State of nothingness = ākiñcanyātana, 15, cm. 127

State of worlding = pṛthagjanatā, 176

Stream of personality = santāna, 136°

Stumbling blocks = antarāyakara (dharmas), 198°

Sublime state = brāhmavihāra, 15, 130°

Suchness of phenomena = tathatā, tathātva, 179°

Suffering = duḥkha, exp. 13, cm. 107ff.

Suffering produced by change = vipariṇāma-duḥkhatā, 109n.

Super knowledge = abhijñā, 194

Superimposition = samāropa, 46°

Sustained thought = vicāra, 14, 121°, 124

Sympathetic joy = muditā, 16, 132, 171°

T

Tamer of passionate desire (Cupid) = manmathaśāsana, 221°

Teacher (in reference to Buddha) = śāsta, 33, cm. 77, cm. 220; guru (in ref. to teacher of our Commentator), 45, 209, 214°

Theory of non-causation = ahetuvāda, 190n.

Thing = vastu, 191

Thought = manaskāra, 150; saṁkalpa, 26; vitarka, 125

Timeless (dharma) = ākālika (dharma), 48, cm. 178°

Trainee = śaikṣa, 180; vineya, 53

Training = śikṣā, 175°

Tranquility = prasrabdhi, 76, 122, 170°

Transcendental = anuttara, 180
Transcendental faculty = lokottara indriya (five = pañca), 17ff., cm. 136
Triple refuge = triśaraṇa, 77
True Dharma = saddharma, 220
Truly knows = yathābhūtaṁ prajānāti, 30, 169
Ultimate real categories, knowledge of = parmārthajñāna, 201
Ultimate truth = nyāya, 51; nirvāṇa, 180
Unique and general characteristics = sva-sāmānya (lakṣaṇa), 147
Unmanifested form = avijñapti rūpa, 56°
Unobstructed knowledge = avyāhata-jñāna, 193
Unshakable knowledge = avaivartya-jñāna, 36, 200
Virtuous = kalyāṇa, 155
Virtuous conduct = śīla, 183
Vision = darśana 104, 112, 142
Volition = cetanā, 8, 78n., 152
Vow = praṇidhāna, 186°
Way out = niryāṇa, 198°
Well established in practice = supratipanna, 180°
Wisdom = prajñā, 155, 157
Wishes = prārthayate, 110°
Withdrawal = nirvṛtti, 71
Withdrawn in physical person = kāya-vyapkṛṣṭa, 139°
Worldling free from lust = laukika-vītarāga, 194°
Worldly activity = pravṛtti, 68
Worthy of obeisance (epithet of Saṅgha) = añjalikaraṇīya, cm. 184
Wrong view = kudṛṣṭi, 186°
Zealously = satkṛtya, 210°

Sanskrit-Tibetan Term List
Tibetan-Sanskrit Term List

These lists of some of the key terms in the text were prepared originally by Dharma Publishing staff, then reviewed at the Central Institute of Higher Tibetan Studies under the direction of Professor Ngawang Samten, who consulted the Tibetan edition of the Arthaviniścaya Sūtra. The Sanskrit-Tibetan list follows the order of the Sanskrit alphabet; the Tibetan-Sanskrit list follows the order of the Tibetan alphabet.

Sanskrit-Tibetan

Akliṣṭa = nyon mongs can min

Adharma = chos ma yin pa

Adhigama = rtogs pa, 'thob pa

Adhimukti = mos pa, 'dod pa

Adhivacana = tshig bla dags

Adhyātma = nang gi bdag

Adhyātmasamprasāda = nang gi bdag rab tu dang ba

Anavadya = kha na ma tho ba med pa

Anābhoga = rtsol pa med pa

Anāsrava = zag med, dri med

Anivṛta = ma bsgribs pa

Anuttara = bla na med pa

Anuvyañjana = dpe byad bzang po

Anuśaya = phra rgyas

Anuśāsana = rjes su bstan pa

Antarāya = bar chad

Apakṣāla = skyon

Apramāṇa = tshad med pa

Abhinirvṛtti = mngon par 'grub pa

Abhisamaya = mngon par rtogs pa

Abhiṣvaṅga = chags pa

Abhisandhi = dgongs pa, bsam pa

Araṇa = nyon mongs med pa

Arati = mi dga' ba, mi bde ba

Artha = don

Arhat = dgra bcom pa

Avijñapti = rnam par rig byed ma yin pa

Avetyaprasāda = shes nas dad pa

Sanskrit-Tibetan Word List

Aśaikṣa = mi slob pa

Asaṁskṛta = 'dus ma byas

Ākiñcanyātana = ci yang med pa'i skye mched

Ātmā = bdag

Ātmagraha = bdag tu 'dzin pa

Āniñjya = mi g.yo ba

Ābhiprāyika = dgongs pa can

Āyatana = skye mched

Ārūpya-dhatu = gzugs med pa'i khams

Ārūpya-samāpatti = gzugs med pa'i snyoms par 'jug pa

Āryasatya = 'phags pa'i bden pa

Ālambana = dmigs pa

Āvaraṇa = sgrib pa

Āveṇika = ma 'dres

Āśaya = bsam pa

Āsrava =zag pa

Āryāṣṭāṅga-mārga = 'phags pa'i lam yan lag brgyad

I

Indriya = dbang po

U

Upakleśa = nye ba'i nyon mongs pa

Upadeśa = bstan pa

Upādāna = nye bar len pa

Upāya = thabs

Upekṣā = btang snyoms

Ṛ

ṛddhi = rdzu 'phrul

ṛddhipāda = rdzu 'phrul gyi rkang pa

AU

Auddhatya = rgod pa

K

Karuṇā = snying rje

Kalyāṇamitra = dge ba bshes gnyen

Kāmarāga = 'dod pa, 'dod chags

Kudṛṣṭi = lta ngan

Kuśala = dge ba

G

Gati = 'gro ba

C

Citta = sems

Cintā = bsam pa

Cetanā = sems pa

Caitta = sems las byung ba

CH

Chanda = 'dun pa

J

Janma = skye ba

Jarā = rga ba

Jñāna = ye shes

T

Tathāgata = de bzhin gshegs pa

Tṛṣṇā = sred pa

D

Darśana = mthong ba

Darśana-marga = mthong lam

Duḥkha = sdug bsngal

Dravya = rdzas

Dveṣa = zhe sdang

DH

Dharma = chos

Dharma-dhātu = chos kyi khams

Dharma-paryāya = chos kyi rnam grangs

Dharma pravicaya = chos rnams rab tu rnam par 'byed pa

Dhātu = khams

Dhyāna = bsam gtan

N

Nāma = ming

Nimitta = mtshan ma

Nirodha = 'gog pa

Nirodha-samāpatti = 'gog pa'i snyoms par 'jug pa

Nirdeśa = bstan pa

Nirmala = dri med

Nirvāṇa = mya ngan las 'das pa

Nivṛtti = ldog pa, log pa

Naiṣkramya = nges par 'byung ba

Nyāya = rig pa

P

Pariccheda = yongs su chad pa

Paribheda = 'joms par byed pa, yongs su 'jig pa

Paryavadāta = yongs su byang ba

Pāpa = sdig pa

Puṇyajnāna-sambhāra = bsod nams dang ye shes kyi tshogs

Pudgala = gang zag

Puruṣapudgala = skyes bu, mi gang zag

Pṛṭhagjanatā = so so'i skye bo

Prajñā = shes rab

Praṇidhāna = smon lam

Pratigha = khong khro

Pratipakṣa = gnyen po

Pratipad = lam

Pratibandha = gegs byed

Pratītyasamutpāda = rten cing 'brel bar 'byung ba

Pratyaya = rkyen

Pratyekabuddha = rang sangs rgyas

Prasāda = rab tu dang ba

Prasrabdhi = shin tu sbyangs pa

Prahāṇa = spangs pa

Prātimokṣa = so sor thar pa

Prīti = dga' ba

B

Bala = stobs

Bodhi = byang chub

Bodhipakṣya dharmas = byang chub kyi phyogs dang mthun pa'i chos

Bodhyaṅga = byang chub kyi yan lag

Brahmacarya = tshangs par spyod pa

Brahmavihāra = tshangs pa'i gnas

BH

Bhagavān = bcom ldan 'das

Bhava = srid pa

Bhāvanā = bsgom pa, sgom pa

Bhūmi = sa

M

Mati = blo gros

Manaskāra = yid la byed pa

Mahākṛpā = thugs rje chen po

Mahāpuruṣa = skyes bu chen po

Mahābhūta = 'byung ba chen po

Mārga = lam

Mīmāṁsā = dpyod pa

Muditā = dga' ba

Maitrī = byams pa

Moha = gti mug

Y

Yathābhūtam = yang dag pa ji lta ba bzhin du

Yukti = rigs pa

R

Rāga = 'dod chags

L

Lakṣaṇa = mtshan nyid

V

Vacana = gsung

Vastu = dngos po

Vāsanā = bag chags

Vikṣepa = rnam par g.yengs pa

Vicāra = dpyod pa

Vicikitsā = the tshom

Vijñāna = rnam par shes pa

Vitarka = rnam par rtog pa

Vineya = gdul bya, 'dul bya

Viparyāsa = phyin ci log pa

Vipaśyanā = lhag mthong

Vibhaṅga = rnam par dbye ba

Virāga = 'dod chags dang bral ba

Viveka = dben pa

Viśuddhi = rnam par dag pa

Vihiṁsā = rnam par 'tshe ba

Vītarāga = 'dod chags dang bral ba

Vīrya = brston 'grus

Vedanā = tshor ba

Vaiśāradya = mi 'jigs pa

Vyāpāda = gnod sems

Vrata = brtul zhugs

Ś

Śakti = mthu

Śamatha = zhi gnas

Śīla = tshul khrims

Śūnyatā = stong pa nyid

Śaikṣa = slob pa

Śrāmaṇya = dge sbyong gi tshul

Śravaka = nyan thos

S

Saṁvara = sdom pa

Saṁsāra = 'khor ba

Saṁskāra = 'du byed

Saṁskāra-duḥkhatā = 'du byed kyi sdug bsngal

Saṁskṛta = 'dus byas

Saṁkleśa = kun nas nyon mongs

Saṅgha = dge 'dun

Saṁjñā = 'du shes

Sattva = sems can

Saddharma = dam chos

Santāna = rgyun, rgyud

Samādhi = ting nge 'dzin

Samādhi-bhāvanā = ting nge 'dzin sgom pa

Samāpatti = snyoms 'jug

Samāhita = mnyam par bzhag pa

Samudaya = kun 'byung ba

Samprajanya = shes bzhin

Sampratyaya = yid ches

Sambhāra = tshogs

Sammoha = kun tu rmongs pa

Samyaksambuddha = rdzogs pa'i sangs rgyas

Sarvajñatā = kun mkhyen, thams cad mkhyen pa

Sāvadya = kha na ma tho ba dang bcas pa

Sāsrava = zag pa dang bcas pa

Siṁhanāda = seng ge'i sgra

Sukha = bde ba

Sūtra = mdo

Skandha = phung po

Sthāna = gnas, 'jog pa

Sparśa = reg pa

Smṛti = dran pa

Smṛtyupasthāna = dran pa nye bar gzhag pa

Svabhāva = rang bzhin

H

Hetu = rgyu

Tibetan-Sanskrit

Ka

Kun mkhyen = sarvajñatā

Kun tu rmongs pa = sammoha

Kun nas nyon mongs = saṁkleśa

Kun 'byung ba = samudaya

rKyen = pratyaya

sKye ba = janma

sKyes pa = puruṣa

sKyes bu = puruṣa-pudgala,

sKyes bu chen po = mahāpuruṣa

sKye mched = āyatana

sKyon = apakṣāla

Kha

Kha na ma tho ba bcas pa = sāvadya

Kha na ma tho ba med pa = anavadya

Khams = dhātu

Khong khro = pratigha

'Khor ba = saṁsāra

Ga

Gang zag = pudgala

Gegs byed = pratibanda

dGa' ba = prīti, muditā

dGe ba = kuśala

dGe 'dun = saṅgha

dGe sbyong gi tshul = śrāmaṇya

dGe legs = kuśala

dGongs pa = abhisandhi

dGongs pa can = ābhiprāyika

dGra bcom pa = Arhat

'Gog pa = nirodha

'Gog pa'i snyoms par 'jug pa = nirodha-samāpatti

'Gro ba = gati

rGa ba = jarā

rGod pa = auddhatya

rGyu = hetu

rGyud = santāna

rGyun = santāna

sGom pa = bhāvanā

sGrib pa = āvaraṇa

bsGom pa = bhāvanā

Nga

Nges par 'byung ba =naiṣkramya

dNgos po = vastu

mNgon par 'grub pa = abhinirvṛtti

mNgon par rtogs pa =Abhisamaya

Ca

Ci yang med pa'i skye mched = ākiñcanyātana

bCom ldan 'das = Bhagavān

Cha

Chags pa = abhiṣvaṅga

Chos = dharma, Dharma

Chos kyi khams = dharma-dhātu

Chos kyi rnam grangs = dharma-paryāya

Chos rnams rab tu rnam par 'byed pa = dharma pravicaya

Chos ma yin pa = adharma

Ja

'Jog pa = sthāna

'Joms par byed pa = paribheda

rJes su bstan pa = Anuśāsana

Nya

Nyan thos = Śrāvaka

Nye ba'i nyon mongs pa = upakleśa

Nye bar len pa = upādāna

Nyon mongs can min = akliṣṭa

Nyon mongs med pa = araṇa

gNyen po = pratipakṣa

mNyam par bzhag pa = samāhita

sNyoms 'jug = samāpatti

sNying rje = Karuṇā

Ta

Ting nge 'dzin = samādhi

Ting nge 'dzin sgom pa = samādhi bhāvanā

gTi mug = moha

btang snyoms = upekṣā

rTen cing 'brel bar 'byung ba = pratītyasamutpāda

rTogs pa = adhigama

lTa ngan = kudṛṣṭi

sTong pa nyid = śūnyatā

sTobs = bala

brTul zhugs = vrata

bsTan pa = nirdeśa

Tha

Thabs = upāya

Thams cad mkhyen pa = sarvajñatā

Thugs rje chen po = mahākṛpā

The tshom = vicikitsā

mThu = śakti

mThong ba = darśana

mThong lam = darśana-mārga

'Thob pa = adhigama

Da

Dam chos = saddharma

De bzhin gshegs pa = Tathāgata

Don = artha

Dran pa = smṛti

Dran pa nye bar gzhag pa = smṛtyupasthāna

Dri med = anāsrava, nirmala

gDul bya = vineya

bDag = ātmā

bDag tu 'dzin pa = ātmagraha

bDe ba = sukha

mDo = Sūtra

'Dun pa = chanda
'Dul bya = vineya
'Dus byas = saṁskṛta
'Du byed = saṁskāra
'Du byed kyi sdug bsngal = saṁskāra-duḥkhatā
'Du shes = saṁjñā
'dus ma byas = asaṁskṛta
'Dod chags = kāmarāga
'Dod chags dang bral ba = virāga, vītarāga
'Dod pa = adhimukti
lDog pa = nivṛtti
sDig pa = pāpa
sDug bsngal = duḥkha
sDom pa = saṁvara

Na
Nang gi bdag= adhyātma
Nang gi bdag rab tu dang ba = Adhyātmasamprasāda
gNas = sthāna
gNod sems = vyāpāda
rNam par rtog pa = vitarka
rNam par dag pa = viśuddhi
rNam par dbye bar bya ba = vibhaṅga
rNam par 'tshe ba = vihiṁsā
rNam par g.yengs pa = vikṣepa
rNam par rig byed ma yin pa = avijñapti
rNam par shes pa = Vijñāna

Pa
dPe byad bzang po = anuvyañjana
dPyad par bya = mīmāṁsā
dPyod pa = vicāra
sPangs pa = prahāṇa

Pha
Phung po = skandha
Phyin ci log pa = viparyāsa
Phra rgyas = anuśaya
'Phags pa'i bden pa = āryasatya
'Phags pa'i lam yan lag brgyad = āryāṣṭāṅga-mārga

Ba
Bag chags = vāsanā
Bar chad = antarāya
Bla na med pa = anuttara
Byang chub = bodhi
Byang chub kyi phyogs dang mthun pa'i chos = bodhipakṣya dharmas
Byang chub kyi yan lag = bodhyaṅga
Byams pa = maitrī
Blo gros = mati
dBang = indriya
dBen pa = viveka
'Byung ba che = mahābhūta

Ma
Ma bsgribs pa = anivṛta
Ma 'dres = āveṇika
Mi dga' ba = arati
Mi 'jigs pa = vaiśāradya
Mi bde ba = arati
Mi g.yo ba = āniñjya
Mi slob pa = aśaikṣa
Ming = nāma
Mos pa = adhimukti
Mya ngan las 'das pa = nirvāṇa
dMigs pa, dmigs yul = ālambana

sMon lam = praṇidhāna

Tsa

rtsol pa med pa = anābhoga

brTson 'grus = vīrya

Tsha

Tshad med pa = apramāṇa

Tshig bla dags = Adhivacana

Tshangs par spyod pa = brahmacarya

Tshangs pa'i gnas, tshad med = brahmavihāra

Tshad med = apramāṇa (brahmavihāra)

Tshul = nyāya

Tshul khrims = śīla

Tshogs = sambhāra

Tshor ba = vedanā

mTshan ma = nimitta

mTshan nyid = lakṣaṇa

Dza

rDzas = dravya

rDzu 'phrul = ṛddhi

rDzu 'phrul gyi rkang pa = ṛddhipāda

rDzogs pa'i sangs rgyas = samyaksambuddha

Zha

Zhi gnas = śamatha

Zhe sdang = dveṣa

Za

zag med = anāsrava

zag pa = āsrava

Zag pa dang bcas pa = sāsrava

gZugs med pa'i khams = ārūpya-dhātu

Ya

Yang dag pa bzhin du = yathābhūtam

Ye shes = jñāna

Yid ches = sampratyaya

Yid la byed pa = manaskāra

yongs su chad pa = pariccheda

yongs su 'jig pa = paribheda

Yongs su byang ba = paryavadāta

Ra

Rang bzhin = svabhāva

Rang sangs rgyas = Pratyekabuddha

Rab tu dang ba = prasāda

Rigs pa = yukti

Reg pa = sparśa

La

Lam = mārga, pratipad

Lugs = nyāya

Len pa *see* nye bar len pa

Log pa = nivṛtti

Sha

Shin tu sbyangs pa = prasrabdhi

Shes nas dad pa = avetyaprasāda

Shes bzhin = samprajanya

Shes rab = prajñā

bShes gnyen = kalyāṇamitra

Sa

Sa = bhūmi

Seng ge sgra = siṁhanāda

Sems = citta, āśaya

Sems can = sattva

Sems pa = cetanā

Sems las byung ba = caitta, caitsika

So so'i skye bo = pṛṭhagjanatā

So sor thar pa = prātimokṣa

Srid pa = bhava

Sred pa = tṛṣṇā

Slob pa = śaikṣa

gSungs pa = vacana

bSam gtan = dhyāna

bSam pa = abhisandhi, āśaya,

bSod nams dang ye shes kyi tshogs = puṇyajñāna-sambhara

INDEX

cm. = commented; en. = enumerated; ety. = etymology given; exp. = explained, explanation; n. = note; x° = term note. References to notes and term notes on the Sūtra refer only to the Sūtra as embodied in the commentary.

171; first as signifying living happily in this very life, 141n.; for gaining special wisdom, 143; fourth, 21; fourth, free from eight faults (apakṣālas) of, 143n.; indications of dhyāna restraint (saṁvar), 219; intermediate, 98n., 136°; painful course in, exp. 136; pure and undefiled state, 141; see also concentration, meditation, samādhi

Dhyānāntara meditation, 118°

Disappearance = absence of conditioned and non-conditioned states, exp. in third Noble Truth, 113

Disciple, enlightenment of, 159

Disciples (Śrāvakas), well gone but not fully gone, exp. 176; led to hear by others, ety., exp. 220

Discontent, 132

Disease and physician, simile of, re Noble Truths, 108

Disgust for the body, 140n.

Disjunction (from all defilements), 192°

Dispassion (virāga), def. 172, exp. 153; contemplation of, 32

Dispositions (adhimukti) of beings, cm. 191

Distraction, freedom from, 155

Disturbed mind, listeners with, 209

Diverse dispositions of beings, knowledge of Buddha, cm. 191

Divine eye and higher knowledge, 142

Divine eye of Tathāgata, 195

Door to immortality, 181n.

Doubt, associated with action, 73; removal of by clear awareness, 146

Doubting existence of good and bad actions, 74

Doubts (eight) to be abandoned by insight, 94n.

Dṛṣṭadharma, exp. 141

Dull wisdom (manda-prajñā), 136°

Dwelling alone, 139°

Earth element, exp. 9, 86, 111

Earthen storehouse, 140

Eastern Park (Pūrvārāma), 3, cm. 49

Effort (vyāyāma), 152; in formless attainments, 136; lack of (anabhisaṁskāra), 152°; required in anāgamya and intermediate dhyānas, 136

Eightfold Path, Noble (āryāaṣṭāṅga mārga), exp. 26ff., cm. 165ff.; see also path

Eighty minor marks of Buddha, cm. 41ff., not commented, 218n.

Elements (dhātu), eighteen, 5; cm. 62ff.; bhūta and bhautika, 85°; see also dhātu

Embryonic stages of consciousness (six), en. 86

Emptiness, as general characteristic of objects of all foundations of mindfulness, 147n.

Encounter contact (pratigha saṁsparśa), 89

Energy (vīrya), def. 155; activating, 22; as constituent of enlightenment, 25; constant practice of,

Faculty (indriya) , ety. exp. 115; having authority over apprehending its own object, 115; of faith, 24, 117°; of knowing what is unknown, cm. 116; of one whose knowledge has been perfected, cm. 116; of pain, cm. 116; of perfect knowledge, 116; of pleasure in dhyāna, 117; of vitality, 116; of wisdom, 24, 155°; see also faculties (five); faculties (twenty-two)

Faith (prasada) in Buddha, exp. 33, cm. 174, def., 155°; in Sangha (gāthā quoted), 184n.; (śraddhā), faculty of, 14; exp. 24; = serenity of mind, 117°; as karma formations involving effort, 152; as wholesome thought, 149; based on comprehension, exp. 173; four kinds as to object, sequence of exp. 187; in Buddha, on arising from meditation, 174; in Buddha, Dharma, and Sangha, 173; in Dharma, based on comprehension, exp. 33, cm. 178ff.; in moral conduct as purifying the mind, 187n.; in moral precepts (śīla), dear to Noble Ones, 173; in moral precepts, on seeing the Four Truths, 186; in Sangha based on comprehension, exp. 33, cm. 180ff.; having authority over equipment for purification, 116; *see also* serenity of mind

Falsehood, 26, def. 27; (unconventional) exp. 162n.; abstinence from, 26

False knowledge, 73

False view, 73

Family, loving kindness to, 133

Fasting as leading to path of heaven, delusion of, 94

Faults (eight) = apakṣālas, en. 124°

Faults (doṣas) (five), en. 152

Fearlessness of Tathāgata, 197°; see also self-confidence

Feeling(s) (vedanā), 6; aggregate of, exp. 59; = experience, 85; and perception as activities of mind, 171; as pain, 90; born of contact of eye, 90; desire arises through it, 14; neutral, exp. 90; not absent in any meditative state, 124; pleasurable, exp. 90; six classes, 10; specific intention of the Blessed One regarding, 90; three kinds, exp. 79, 89; six classes of, 89; unique characteristic of, exp. 147

Felicity, whole body of four elements filled and pervaded with (in dhyāna), 141

Female faculty, 14, cm. 116

Final beatitude, 221°

Fire element, exp. 9, 111

Firm undertaking of Tathāgata in former times to constantly perform wholesome deeds, 210

Flesh, sale of, 29

Food, solid and liquid, gift of, 211°

Forest, haunts, meditation in, 43; monk, going to, 20

Forgetfulness, 75

Form (rūpa), exp. 9, 59; disappearance of gross, 127

Formless attainments (ārūpya samāpattis) (four), 4, 15, exp., cm. 126ff.; (three), 136

Formless, realm, and faculties, 116; coming to be in (ārūpyabhava), exp. 11, 101; skandha, 85

Kleśa, see defilement

Knowability, obstacle of, 204°

Knower of world (lokavid), epithet of Buddha, exp. 176

Knowing without delusion (in mindfulness of breathing), 172

Knowledge (jñāna), and powers of Tathāgata), 142°; and right conduct together signifying Noble Eightfold Path, 175; and right conduct (vidyācaraṇa); and right view, 175; and self-confidence, 199; and vision, 183, 204, cm. 142; and wisdom, 175; as eye and feet, 172; as three trainings, 175; of all that is knowable, 176; purified, leading to morality and meditation, 175; signifying right view, 183; see also knowledge of Buddha; unobstructed knowledge

Knowledge of Buddha, of cessation as well as non-origin, 118; of destruction of defilements, 194, 195; of dharmas, cm. 201; of diverse dispositions of beings, cm. 191; of faculties, 195; of former existences of beings, 193; of innate nature of things, 191; of possible and impossible, 195; of powerful attachment and discord of beings felt toward one another, 191; of result of karma, 191; see also knowledge

Knowledges, order of, concerning one's own accomplishment and that of others, 199n.

Kumbhopama Sūtra, 80

Kuśala (wholesome), ety. exp. 76

Lack of clear consciousness, 75

Lack of faith, 157

Lamentation (parideva), 6; exp. 70

Language, as meaning linguistic expression, 201; special knowledge of, 36–37; cm. 201

Languages of devas, etc., 201

Latent defilement(s) (anuśaya), 75°, 118; and Arhats, 141; relinquishment of, 113; see also defilement

Lay people, wrong livelihood of, 29

Letters bored in wood by an insect (popular saying), 221n.

Liberation through Sāṁkhya, Yoga and Jñāna paths, delusion of, 94

Life and vital heat, loss of (in death), 106

Life faculty, def. 103; cessation of, exp. 106; laying down the aggregates of = death, 106

Life force, change in, 105n.

Light, perception of, 142; pure and radiant, 20

Limbs of Buddha, without impurity or perspiration, 213

Linking of consciousness in the next birth, 83

Lion's roar of Tathāgata, 35;

List (of topics), 40; (uddeśa), 4, 45, 209°

Listeners (to Sūtra) whose minds were disturbed due to improper attention, 209°

Living beings, sale of as wrong livelihood, 29

Living happily in this very life, 19, 116

Observing the movement of breathing in and breathing out, 170

Obstructed and unobstructed knowledge, cm. 204

Obstruction in karma, 195

Obstructive dharmas, perfect comprehension of, 198; avoiding, 199

Old age, cm. 12; cm. 104ff.; see also decay

Om Namo Buddhāya, 45°

Omniscience (of Tathāgata), 190

Once-returner (sakṛdāgāmi), 33, 181

One direction (spread of maitrī), cm. 131

One whose knowledge has been perfected, 118n.

One-pointedness of mind, 125, 153, 156; as both hostile and favorable constituent in dhyānas, 125n.

Opposite forces, abandoning in concentration, 138

Order of faculties, exp. 155

Order of four foundations of mindfulness, exp. 147

Organic sense faculties, destruction of in death, 106

Other masters' explanations, of mindfulness of breathing, 172; of states of abandonment, 113

Our teacher (i.e., Commentator's teacher), 150°

Outbursts (of defilements), 93°

Outer world, ignorance of, 73

Outflows (āsravas), 114, 194°; see also defilements

Outsiders (those who do not follow the Buddha's path), exp. 176°

Padma (cold hell), 11, exp. 97

Pain, bodily and mental, 116

Painful feeling, exp. 90

Pair of fish, auspicious mark above the inner surface of the fingers of Buddha, 218n.

Pairs (four) of individuals in Saṅgha, 182

Paranirmitavaśavartin (devas), 11, exp. 98

Parittābhā (gods) 11, exp. 98

Parittaśubhā (devas), 11, exp. 99

Passions, freedom from, as exp. of Dharma, 33

Path (Noble Eightfold), 26ff., exp., ety. 114, cm. 165ff.

Path (pratipad), and Four Truths, 118; as meaning Noble Path, 198; leading to all destinies, cm. 192, 178; leading to cessation of suffering, 13, 114; leading to deliverance, cm. 198°; of abandonment, 137; of Bodhisattva and Pratyekabuddha, 178°; of meditation, 139, 160, 181; of practice, 219°; of vision, 112, 181; to heaven and beatitude, 177; see also mārga

Perception (samjñā), aggregate of, 5, exp., 59; and feeling, activities of mind, 171; as boil and dart, 100n.; elimination of, 127; = grasping of characteristics, 85; non-attention to in formless meditation, 127; of daylight in samādhi bhāvanā, exp. 143; of daylight in meditation, 20; of

Practices conducive to deliverance, ignorance of, 75

Practicing, concentration and removal of sluggishness, 149; in accord with Dharma (anudharmacārī), 181°

Praising persons worthy of praise, by the Buddha (in past lives), 215

Prakaraṇas, 100n.

Prasāda (palace), ety. 49

Praśākhā, embryonic stage, 86

Pratāpana (hot hell), 11, exp. 97

Prātimokṣa, training in, 219n.; characteristic of restraint, 219

Pratītyasamutpāda, see conditioned co-production

Pratyekabuddha, as ṛṣi, 220; (associated with) deeds performed in the past, 133; enlightenment of, 159; path of, 178°; super knowledge of world systems, 194

Preliminary path (of dhyāna), 136

Present (pratyatupanna), as easily understood, 150

Preta (ghosts), exp. ety. 97

Preventing people from doing harm by the Tathāgata, 195

Pride, crushing of, 33

Primary material elements as undefiled and neutral, 80

Process, of becoming, 103; of coming to be (bhava) 6; of wisdom directed toward the object of mindfulness, 169

Proper and improper attention for extinction of defilements, 189°

Proper insight, 139

Protecting wholesome thoughts, 23

Psychic power(s) (ṛddhi), born of energy, 23; born of zeal, 23; four bases of, 23, exp. 152; having nature of samādhi, 153; having the characteristics of zeal, 152

Pudgala, ety. 182

Puṇyaprasavā (devas), 11; exp. 99

Pure (anāsrava) faculties, exp. 117–18

Pure, consciousness (grasping characteristics of), 127; meditation, 121; morality, 219; penetration, 139; restraint of ever-changing mind, 186

Purification, by equanimity and mindfulness, 117; of equanimity and mindfulness as hostile constituents in fourth dhyāna, 125; of knowledge leads to purification of morality and meditation, 175

Purity = immaculateness, 193

Pūrvārama, see Eastern Park

Quietude, 75, exp. 112–13, 171

Radiant light, 20

Raft, parable of, in exp. of Dharma, 113°

Rāhulabhadra (Ācārya), 51

Rain of Dharma, 53

Rapture (in meditation), 30; and joy, 14, 121°, 141; body and mind benefited by, 160; born of concentration, 20; constituent of enlightenment, 25, cm. 160; = mental

kalaviṅka (bird), cm. 214; fills the world systems, 214n.

Volition (cetanā), mental karmic formation, 8

Vrata (religious observance), exp. 99°

Washing away of accumulated blemishes by living beings through meditative practices: wish of Commentator for, 221°

Water element, exp. 9, 66, 111

Weapons, sale of, 29

Wearing (special) dress and ornaments as religious observance, 94°

Webbed hands and feet (mark of Great Personage), 38, cm. 211

Welcome, to bid by raising open hands, 29

Well established in mindfulness, 155°

Well-grasped instruction, exp. 142

Well-placed feet, one of 32 marks of Great Personage, 38, cm. 210

Well-shaped and wide forehead of Buddha (minor mark), 42

Well-cultivated mind, 15–16, cm. 131

Wheel, auspicious sign, on the hands and feet of the Buddha, 42, 218n.; mark on soles of feet, 38; beautiful and perfect, 210

Wholesome, deeds practiced by Tathāgata in former lives, 210; mind, one-pointedness of, 121; thoughts, arising of, 147; thoughts, faith and the like, 149; way of action of body, speech, and mind, exp. 26–27

Wisdom (prajña), 145, 219, def., 117; acquisition of, cm. 143; associated with foundations of mindfulness, 147; consummation of, 143; faculty of, 14, exp. 24; having the characteristic of understanding the truth, 183; having the nature of discernment of dharmas, 156; nature of, 169n.

Withdrawal (nirvṛtti) from saṁsāra, exp. in pratītya-samutpāda, 71

Withdrawing mentally, in cultivation of concentration, 140

Woman, monk's passion for, 29

Women and men, mutually infatuated, 60

World, of different elements, 34; of harm, 81; of transmigration, 155

World systems, Tathāgata's capacity to see innumerable, 194

Worldlings free from lust (laukika vītarāga), 194°

Worldly, cm. 155; path, 116; prosperity, 221°

Wound, giving joy when sprinkled with water, simile of, 109

Wreckage (in old age), cm. 105

Wrinkles, cm. 104

Wrong livelihood, exp. 29

Wrong path, preventing others from taking by Tathāgata, 199

Wrong view, exp. 28; exp. as belief in existence of individuality (satkāyadṛṣṭi), 186; clinging to or esteeming (dṛṣṭiparāmarśa), 94n.

Wrongful conduct, abstinence from, 26; seeking sexual pleasures, exp. 27

Yāmā (devas), 11; ety. 98°

Yoga (as mārga), 94n.

Yogi (meditator), 122°, 187; bodily and mentally aloof, 169; fond of learning and reflection, 169; practicing mindfulness of breathing, 169

Zeal, applying great, 15–17; concentration caused by, 112; predominance of, 152; psychic power born of, 23A

Tibetan Translation Series

Sūtra

Dhammapada: Sayings of the Buddha
The Fortunate Aeon: The Bhadrakalpika Sūtra
Voice of the Buddha: The Lalitavistara Sūtra
Wisdom of Buddha: The Saṁdhinirmocana Sūtra
Gathering the Meanings: The Arthaviniścaya Sūtra and its Commentary Nibandhana

Śāstra

Master of Wisdom: Six Texts by Nāgārjuna
Joy for the World: Candragomin's Lokananda
Elegant Sayings, by Nāgārjuna and Sakya Pandita
Buddha's Lions: Abhayadatta's Lives of the Eighty-Four Siddhas
Invitation to Enlightenment: Letters by Mātṛceṭa and Candragomin
Leaves of the Heaven Tree, based on Kṣemendra's Avadanas
The Marvelous Companion: Āryaśura's Jātakamāla
Golden Zephyr: Nāgārjuna's Letter to a Friend

Works by Tibetan Masters

Calm and Clear: Teachings of Lama Mipham
Legend of the Great Stupa: Teachings of Padmasambhava
The Life and Liberation of Padmasambhava
Mother of Knowledge: Life of Yeshe Tshogyal
Kindly Bent to Ease Us, Parts I-III, by Longchenpa
Mind in Buddhist Psychology, by Yeshe Gyaltsen
Path of Heroes, by Zhechen Gyaltsab

Dr. N.H. Samtani took his undergraduate degree in Sanskrit at Bombay University. He obtained his M.A. at the Pali Research Institute of Nalanda under the celebrated Buddhist scholar Bhikkhu J. Kashyap. He completed his Ph.D. at the University of Delhi under the eminent scholars Professors P.V. Bapat and V.V. Gokhale. His doctoral thesis, a critical edition of the texts translated here together with exhaustive notes and commentary, was published in 1971 by the K.P. Jayaswal Research Institute, Patna.

From 1960–84 Professor Samtani taught Pali and Buddhist Sanskrit texts at Banaras Hindu University and guided research in textual studies. During his tenure he served as Chair of the Department of Pali and Buddhist Studies. He has been a visiting professor at distinguished universities in the United States, Canada, and Thailand. Among his many other positions, he served as Deputy Director of the Bhikkhu J. Kashyap Institute of Buddhist and Asian Studies and headed a project at the Central Institute of Higher Tibetan Studies, Sarnath. He also served as Honorary Editor at the Vipassana Research Institute, Igatpuri. Most recently he served as Visiting Professor and Honorary Director of the Centre for Mahayana Buddhist Studies at Nagarjuna University, Andhra Pradesh (1994–96 and 1999–2001).

In 2002, the President of India awarded Professor Samtani the President's Certificate of Honour for his scholarly contributions in the fields of Pali studies. He has edited three volumes and published more than fifty articles in research journals and books. Presently he lives with his wife in Sugata Kutir, Varanasi, Uttar Pradesh, not far from Sarnath, the location where the Buddha first turned the Wheel of the Dharma.